国际结算
（双语版）

王瑛 主编
杨碧琴 张玉荣 副主编

十二五高等院校应用型特色规划教材

清华大学出版社
北京

内容简介

国际结算是研究不同国家当事人之间因各种往来而发生的债权债务经由银行来办理清算的一门实用学科。该课程旨在使学生了解和掌握从事涉外经济以及金融工作所必需的国际间债权债务结算知识。本书根据国际贸易与结算相关最新惯例、规则，借鉴国外原版教材，立足于教学内容本土化，是一本能够反映当前国际结算领域发展前沿和满足本科教学实际需要的《国际结算》课程双语教材。

本书通过对国际结算的基本理论、基本操作和国际惯例的讲解，使学生对国际结算知识有系统全面的了解和认识，并能较熟练地进行各种实际业务操作。本书以银行为中心的结算体系为主线，以国际结算的主要研究对象（国际结算的主要工具、方法、相关单据及具体的单据业务）为内容，同时增加了CDCS考试介绍与复习指导。

本书适用于高等院校金融学、国际经济与贸易及其他经管类专业的专业课教学，也可作为涉外企事业单位相关工作从业人员的继续教育参考用书。

本书封面贴有清华大学出版社防伪标签，无标签者不得销售。
版权所有，侵权必究。举报：010-62782989，beiqinquan@tup.tsinghua.edu.cn。

图书在版编目(CIP)数据

国际结算：双语版：汉、英/王瑛主编．--北京：清华大学出版社，2016（2024.2重印）
十二五高等院校应用型特色规划教材
ISBN 978-7-302-43969-1

Ⅰ．①国⋯ Ⅱ．①王⋯ Ⅲ．①国际结算－高等学校－教材－汉、英 Ⅳ．①F830.73

中国版本图书馆 CIP 数据核字(2016)第 117596 号

责任编辑：彭 欣
封面设计：汉风唐韵
责任校对：王荣静
责任印制：杨 艳

出版发行：清华大学出版社
网　　址：https://www.tup.com.cn，https://www.wqxuetang.com
地　　址：北京清华大学学研大厦 A 座　　邮　编：100084
社 总 机：010-83470000　　邮　购：010-62786544
投稿与读者服务：010-62776969，c-service@tup.tsinghua.edu.cn
质量反馈：010-62772015，zhiliang@tup.tsinghua.edu.cn

印 装 者：北京鑫海金澳胶印有限公司
经　　销：全国新华书店
开　　本：185mm×260mm　　印　张：19.5　　字　数：445 千字
版　　次：2016 年 7 月第 1 版　　印　次：2024 年 2 月第 6 次印刷
定　　价：49.00 元

产品编号：065671-02

前　言

当今世界经济全球化向各领域全方位渗透，国际贸易顺势迅速发展。与此同时，国际市场发生了根本性变化，国际贸易竞争空前激烈，竞争手段层出不穷。中国充分利用经济全球化发展契机，创造出了"后来居上"的贸易奇迹。

国际贸易发展离不开国际金融的支持，经济全球化进程必然要求金融的全球化。中国对外贸易的迅猛发展，催生了大量国际金融需求，国际贸易结算是其中最重要的基础性金融需求之一。国际贸易结算涉及结算方式、结算工具的选择和运用、结算货币的组合、风险的承担与转移等问题，需要我国对外贸易从业人员在各个环节慎重行事。这就要求我国对外贸易相关领域人士掌握国际贸易结算的理论知识和实务技能，从而使我国进出口商、银行、金融担保机构等行为主体的经济利益最大化。

2009 年，中国政府开始积极推动跨境贸易人民币结算工作，并以此作为人民币国际化的突破口和重中之重。2015 年 12 月，国际货币基金组织（IMF）正式批准人民币加入特别提款权（SDR）货币篮子，人民币国际化又迈出关键一步。人民币国际地位的显著提升为我国进出口商和贸易伙伴提供了新的结算货币选项，同时也为重构国际结算格局和秩序提出了新问题，各方均需调整经济决策以便更好地适应新形势。因此，我们适时编写了本教材，以满足高等院校《国际结算》课程教学及国际贸易结算从业人员实践工作的需要。

本教材在编写过程中着重突出以下特点。

一、科学性、通用性强。本教材结合国际经济与贸易、金融学、国际商务、商务英语等专业的课程设置要求，根据高等教育针对本科生的培养目标进行编写，能够满足相关专业不同层次高等院校的教学需要，同时也可供研究人员或国际结算从业人员参考使用。

二、实用性强。国际结算是一门理论与实务相结合的课程，尤其强调理论在实际业务中的应用。因此，本教材突出应用，引入大量经典实例，并附有各种票据和单据的样例，在每一章的末尾，还配有题型丰富的课后思考题和练习题，帮助读者巩固和检验所学知识，提高学以致用的实战能力。

三、"双语"有机融合。传统双语教材一般全篇辅以汉语和英语双语表述，不仅给读者以累赘、重复之感，而且给"原汁原味"的英文内容画蛇添足。本教材力求突破传统双语教材的缺点，主要内容以英文表述，目的是提高学生的专业英语水平；对于关键术语和学生理解较为困难的内容附加中文解释、中文案例和知识延伸材料，帮助学生加深对重点、难点内容的理解。我们希望通过这种编写方式，可以真正实现"双语"的有机融合，既有利于"教"，也有利于"学"。

四、与跟单信用证专家资格认证考试（CDCS）接轨。本教材在附录部分新增了

CDCS考试的介绍和备考辅导习题。CDCS考试由国际商会(ICC)授权,英国注册银行家协会(CIB)和国际金融服务协会(IFSA)合作共同推出,是一个证明跟单信用证人员理论能力及实际业务操作能力的专业认证考试,其含金量受到国际社会的广泛认可。

本教材共分为8章,涵盖国际结算票据、国际贸易结算方式、国际贸易结算所涉单据及审核、非贸易结算等内容。该课程可用36个学时进行教学,具体学时分配参考如下:

章 目	教 学 内 容	课 时 安 排
Chapter 1	Introduction	4
Chapter 2	Instruments of International Settlement	6
Chapter 3	Payment method Ⅰ: Remittance	2
Chapter 4	Payment method Ⅱ: Collection	4
Chapter 5	Payment method Ⅲ: L/C	10
Chapter 6	Other Methods of International Settlement	4
Chapter 7	Documents Used in international Settlement	4
Chapter 8	Non-trade Settlement	2

在教材编写和出版过程中,清华大学出版社给予了许多指导和帮助,尤其是责任编辑彭欣老师默默付出了很多,在此表示诚挚的谢意!北方民族大学经济学院、海南师范大学经管学院的领导和师生,以及银行国际结算部门和一些外贸企业的从业人员也对本教材的编写和出版给予了支持和帮助,在此一并表示感谢。

本教材作为宁夏回族自治区"十三五"重点建设专业支持下的教改成果,凝聚了三位编者的心血,也体现了她们对所从事专业的热爱,但由于编写时间和人员水平有限,本教材难免存在错误和疏漏之处,恳请广大读者提出宝贵意见,以便我们今后加以修订和完善。

编　者

Preface

During the past decades, we have seen the globalization of markets a dramatic fall in trade barriers, and a huge growth in the international trade. Companies of all sizes are seeking to take advantage of the opportunities in this new world economy.

International trade, however, adds an additional layer of risk for buyers and sellers familiar only with doing business in their home markets. Foreign exchange risk, currency regulations, political unrest, economic fluctuation, or social upheaval involved in the cross-boarder transaction, questions of payment, and different business customs may all contribute to the uncertainty. Ultimately, sellers want to get paid and buyers want to get what they pay for. It is very important to choose the right payment method which may be the key to a transaction's feasibility and profitability.

This course, named International Settlement, is designed to help both buyers and sellers learn about international payment options, like remittance, collection, Letter of Credit, etc.

This book consists of eight chapters, which as a whole incorporates theory and practice to develop students' actual operation capability. It covers topics such as instruments of international settlement, methods of settlement in international trade, documents used in international settlement, and so on.

Hope everybody gains!

Key Issues in International Settlement

There are several common issues that affect what the payment method will be beneficiary to be used in an international transaction. Each participant in the transaction should consider these issues, though they will differently affect each other and to a variant degree. It is also important for you to consider the following issues before you study this course. Therefore, careful thinking of these issues can make you know better about what international settlement will solve.

I. Who will Bear the Credit Risks?

In almost all business transactions the buyer would prefer to obtain easy, extended, and inexpensive (preferably free) credit terms. Credit gives buyer the opportunity to resell the goods before having to pay for them. In many instances, the buyer will have a market for goods but not possess sufficient working capital to make an outright purchase and payment prior to their resale. Credit makes many such transactions possible.

At the same time, the seller has a different set of priorities. Having paid for product development, raw materials, component parts, labor, and other overhead, the seller needs to get his investment back. The seller may not know the buyer or may not trust that the buyer is financially stable enough to make payment at a future date. International transactions would not be so stable, secure, transparent, or reliable as domestic transactions and many things can happen during the days between sale and payment. Anyhow, the seller would always prefer to be paid immediately, either at(on) delivery or even prior to delivery.

In a word, each party prefers that the counterpart bear the credit risks.

→ **BUYER/IMPORTER vs. SELLER/EXPORTER: different parties have different wants on credit-risks bearing**

BUYER/IMPORTER: prefers that the seller bear the credit risk and wants to make certain that he could receive the goods once he has paid.

SELLER/EXPORTER: prefers that the buyer bear the credit risk and wants to make certain that he could receive payment for goods shipped.

II. Who will Finance the Transaction?

In an international transaction it may take from several weeks to several months for merchandise to find its way from the seller's warehouse to the buyer's control. Goods should be ready to be sold abroad, trucked or sent by rail to the shipment port, cleared for export, shipped to destination port, possibly even transshipped from another port, warehoused awaiting customs clearance for import, inspected, sent overland and finally inventoried at the buyer's warehouse. The seller has already made a substantial investment in manufacturing the product and doesn't feel that he should bear the brunt of financing costs.

At the same time, the buyer well knows that it may take one or two months before he even sees the goods in his warehouse, another one or even more months before he sells the goods, and another one or several months before he gets paid from his customers. Why should he pay for the goods or pay for the financing of goods he doesn't even see in his warehouse?

Although both parties wish that the counterparty would finance the transaction and pay for the financing costs, the reality is that both parties typically need to compromise somewhat in order to make the transaction successful.

→ **BUYER/IMPORTER vs. SELLER/EXPORTER: different parties have different wishes on finance**

BUYER/IMPORTER: needs funds for payment before resale of goods, and prefers that the seller finance the transaction.

SELLER/EXPORTER: needs funds for production before payment received, and prefers that the buyer finance the transaction.

III. In What Currency will Payment be Made?

The currency (or currency group) selected for payment in a contract has a significant effect upon the ultimate return of the transaction for either the buyer or the seller. If the specified currency appreciates during the contract-made date and the payment date, it is a hardship for the buyer. If it depreciates, it is a benefit to her.

In most instances, the specified currency of the transaction will be a "hard currency", such as the US dollar (USD), the Swiss franc (CHF) or the Japanese yen (JPY). Table 1-1 shows some currencies commonly used in international transactions. In some instances, however, it will be impossible to conclude a transaction in anything other than a local, less stable currency. In these instances, it may be necessary to "hedge" the foreign exchange risks.

表 1-1 常用国家或地区的货币名称和符号代码(部分)

国家或地区名称	货币名称	货币符号	国家或地区名称	货币名称	货币符号
中国	人民币	RMB	印度	卢比	INR
欧盟①	欧元	EUR	加拿大	加拿大元	CAD
英国	英镑	GBP	新西兰	新西兰元	NZD
瑞士	瑞士法郎	CHF	新加坡	新加坡元	SGD
美国	美元	USD	马来西亚	林吉特	MYP
日本	日元	JPY	越南	越南盾	VND
中国香港	港元	HKD	泰国	泰铢	THB
韩国	韩元	KRW	巴基斯坦	卢比	PKP
澳大利亚	澳大利亚元	AUD	科威特	第纳尔	KWD
俄罗斯	卢布	SUR	蒙古	图格里克	MNT

→ **BUYER/IMPORTER vs. SELLER/EXPORTER: different parties have different wants on currency for payment**

BUYER/IMPORTER: wants typically to make payment in her home currency or in a currency that is expected to depreciate in the near future.

SELLER/EXPORTER: wants typically to receive payment in own currency, a hard currency, or in a currency that is expected to appreciate in the near future.

Ⅳ. Who Will Bear the Transportation Costs and Risks?

Who pays for transportation and who assumes the risk if the traded goods are damaged or lost in shipment are also the key issues in international transactions. This is especially true in transactions involving high-value or perishable goods and unusual destinations. Both the cost and risk increase as goods are shipped to remote locations or transsshipped or handled over and over again.

The seller probably feels that his quoted price is excellent and that it is the buyer's business to get the goods to the buyer's home market.

The buyer, on the other hand, doesn't agree that the seller's quoted price only covering costs and duties within the place of origin, and believes the price quoted by the seller should also cover the landed cost in his own market.

Even if the buyer agrees to handle insurance coverage, the seller may have "insurable interest" in the goods if the goods are transported on the way, especially if they have not yet been paid for. Timeliness may also be an issue of risk-taking as some goods are time-

---

① 欧洲联盟(European Union),简称欧盟,由欧洲共同体(European Communities,又称欧洲共同市场)发展而来。截至 2015 年 6 月,欧盟共有 28 个成员,按英文名称排序依次为:奥地利、比利时、保加利亚、塞浦路斯、克罗地亚、捷克共和国、丹麦、爱沙尼亚、芬兰、法国、德国、希腊、匈牙利、爱尔兰、意大利、拉脱维亚、立陶宛、卢森堡、马耳他、荷兰、波兰、葡萄牙、罗马尼亚、斯洛伐克、斯洛文尼亚、西班牙、瑞典和英国。

sensitive.

→ BUYER/IMPORTER vs. SELLER/EXPORTER: different parties have different wants on transport costs and risks bearing

BUYER/IMPORTER: wants (typically) the seller to bear the transportation and the related insurance costs and to have the goods delivered to a local, home-country delivery point where ownership is assumed.

SELLER/EXPORTER: wants (typically) the buyer to bear the transportation and the related insurance costs and to deliver the goods and transfer ownership at his own warehouse or at a local port.

The Learning Objectives of this Book

Since international trade settlement plays the most important role in international settlement activities, this book lays emphasis on international trade settlement.

This book is meant to offer a reference for students study international trade, finance and practitioners working on international trade. The purposes of this book are:

(1) Providing information on fundamental principles and theories which are closely associated with the international settlement;

(2) Offering the basic experience and skills on how to deal with the safe exchange between the proceeds and goods in the international trade;

(3) Helping readers to be familiar with well-known customs and practice on international settlement.

目录

Chapter 1　Introduction ·· 1

1.1　Basic Concepts and Contents of International Settlement ················ 1
　　1.1.1　Basic Concepts of International Settlement ·········· 1
　　1.1.2　Types of International Settlement ·········· 4
　　1.1.3　Basic Contents of International Settlement ·········· 6
1.2　Evolution of International Settlement ·········· 13
　　1.2.1　From Cash Settlement to Non-cash Settlement ·········· 13
　　1.2.2　From Direct Payment to Payment Effected through a Financial Intermediary ·········· 13
　　1.2.3　From Payments under Simple Price Terms to Payments under More Complex Price Terms ·········· 14
　　1.2.4　New Tendency: Settlement through the Internet ·········· 14
1.3　The International Chamber of Commerce (ICC) ·········· 14
1.4　International Payment Systems ·········· 16
　　1.4.1　Brief Introduction ·········· 16
　　1.4.2　International Clearing Systems ·········· 17

Chapter 2　Instruments of International Settlement ·········· 25

2.1　An Overview of Negotiable Instruments ·········· 25
　　2.1.1　Characteristics of a Negotiable Instrument ·········· 26
　　2.1.2　Functions of Negotiable Instruments ·········· 27
2.2　Bill of Exchange(汇票) ·········· 28
　　2.2.1　Definition of a Bill of Exchange ·········· 28
　　2.2.2　Essentials to a Bill of Exchange ·········· 29
　　2.2.3　Parties to a Bill of Exchange ·········· 33
　　2.2.4　Acts of Bills of Exchange ·········· 37
　　2.2.5　Classification of Bill of Exchange ·········· 49
　　2.2.6　Advantages of a Bill of Exchange ·········· 54
2.3　Promissory Note(本票) ·········· 54
　　2.3.1　Definition of a Promissory Note ·········· 54

  2.3.2 Characteristics of a Promissory Note ······ 55
  2.3.3 Essentials to a Promissory Note ······ 55
  2.3.4 Classification of Promissory Note ······ 56
  2.3.5 Parties to a Promissory Note ······ 58
  2.3.6 Difference between a Promissory Note and a Bill of Exchange ······ 58
2.4 Cheque(支票) ······ 59
  2.4.1 Definition of a Cheque ······ 59
  2.4.2 Essentials to a Cheque ······ 60
  2.4.3 Features of a Cheque ······ 61
  2.4.4 Parties to a Cheque ······ 61
  2.4.5 Classification of Cheque ······ 61
  2.4.6 Difference between a Cheque and a Bill of Exchange ······ 62

Chapter 3 Payment Method Ⅰ: Remittance ······ 67

3.1 Outline of Remittance ······ 67
 3.1.1 Definition of Remittance ······ 67
  3.1.2 Parties to a Remittance ······ 68
  3.1.3 Types of Remittance ······ 69
3.2 Procedure for Remittance ······ 72
  3.2.1 Procedure for T/T ······ 72
  3.2.2 Procedure for M/T ······ 72
  3.3.3 Procedure for D/D ······ 73
  3.3.4 Reimbursement Methods ······ 73
  3.3.5 Cancellation of the Remittance ······ 74
3.3 Comparison of the T/T, M/T and D/D ······ 75
3.4 Advantages and Disadvantages of Remittance ······ 76
  3.4.1 Advantages of Remittance ······ 76
  3.4.2 Disadvantages of Remittance ······ 76
3.5 Function of Remittance in International Trade ······ 77
  3.5.1 Open Account ······ 77
  3.5.2 Consignment ······ 78
  3.5.3 Payment in Advance ······ 78

Chapter 4 Payment Method Ⅱ: Collection ······ 85

4.1 An Overview of Collection ······ 85
  4.1.1 Definition of Collection ······ 85
  4.1.2 The Nature and Application of a Collection ······ 86
  4.1.2 Parties to Collection ······ 88

    4.1.3 Types of Collection …… 90
 4.2 Documentary Collection Practice …… 95
    4.2.1 Procedure of Documentary Collection …… 95
    4.2.2 Collection Application Form and Order …… 97
    4.2.3 Uniform Rules for Collection …… 99
 4.3 Risk Protection and Financing under Collection …… 101
    4.3.1 Risks Involved …… 101
    4.3.2 Notes, Tips, and Cautions …… 103
    4.3.3 Financing under the Collection …… 105

Chapter 5 Payment Method III: L/C …… 109

 5.1 An Overview of L/C …… 109
    5.1.1 Definition of L/C …… 110
    5.1.2 Characteristics of L/C …… 112
    5.1.3 International Rules and Customs for L/C …… 114
    5.1.4 Contents and Form of L/C …… 114
    5.1.5 Parties Involved in an L/C …… 118
 5.2 Types of L/C …… 125
    5.2.1 According to whether Accompanied by Commercial Documents …… 125
    5.2.2 According to whether Confirmed by Another Bank …… 126
    5.2.3 According to the Mode of Availability …… 127
    5.2.4 Straight L/C …… 131
    5.2.5 Anticipatory L/C …… 131
    5.2.6 Transferable L/C …… 132
    5.2.7 Back-to-Back L/C …… 133
    5.2.8 Revolving L/C …… 135
    5.2.9 Reciprocal L/C …… 136
    5.2.10 Traveler's L/C …… 137
 5.3 Procedures of Documentary L/C …… 138
    5.3.1 Issuance …… 139
    5.3.2 Amendment …… 143
    5.3.3 Utilization and Settlement …… 145
 5.4 Risks under L/C and Protection …… 151
 5.5 Financing under L/C …… 153
    5.5.1 Financing Provided to the Exporter …… 153
    5.5.2 Financing Provided to the Importer …… 155
 5.6 Introduction to UCP600 …… 157

Chapter 6 Other Methods of International Settlement 186

6.1 Bank's Letter of Guarantee(L/G) 186
    6.1.1 Definition of L/G 187
    6.1.2 Parties to An L/G 187
    6.1.3 Types of L/G 188
    6.1.4 Procedure of L/G 191
    6.1.5 Contents of L/G 192
    6.1.6 Differences between L/G and L/C 193

6.2 Standby L/C 195
    6.2.1 Definition of Standby L/C 195
    6.2.2 Characteristics and Types of Standby L/C 196
    6.2.3 Differences between Standby L/C and L/C 197
    6.2.4 Differences between Standby L/C and L/G 198

6.3 International Factoring 198
    6.3.1 Definition of International Factoring 199
    6.3.2 Parties to International Factoring 200
    6.3.3 Types of International Factoring 201
    6.3.4 Procedures of International Factoring 202
    6.3.5 Application of International Factoring 203
    6.3.6 Advantages of International Factoring 204
    6.3.7 Compassion between International Factoring and Traditional Payment Method 205

6.4 Forfaiting 206
    6.4.1 Definition of Forfaiting 206
    6.4.2 Characteristics of Forfaiting 207
    6.4.3 Parties to Forfaiting 207
    6.4.4 Procedure of Forfaiting 208
    6.4.5 Advantages and Disadvantages of Forfaiting 209
    6.4.6 Difference between Factoring and Forfaiting 209

Chapter 7 Documents Used in International Settlement 214

7.1 Documents 214
7.2 Invoice 219
    7.2.1 Commercial Invoice 219
    7.2.2 Other Invoice 222
7.3 Transport Documents 224
    7.3.1 Marine Bill of Lading 224

- 7.3.2 Sea Waybill ⋯⋯ 230
- 7.3.3 Airway Bill ⋯⋯ 230
- 7.3.4 Railway Bill ⋯⋯ 231
- 7.4 Insurance Documents ⋯⋯ 232
  - 7.4.1 Insurance Policy ⋯⋯ 232
  - 7.4.2 Insurance Certificate ⋯⋯ 234
- 7.5 Other Documents ⋯⋯ 235
  - 7.5.1 Packing List ⋯⋯ 235
  - 7.5.2 Certificate of Origin ⋯⋯ 236
  - 7.5.3 Inspection Certificate ⋯⋯ 240
  - 7.5.4 Export License ⋯⋯ 242
- 7.6 Documents Examination and Disposal of Discrepancies ⋯⋯ 242
  - 7.6.1 Documents Examination ⋯⋯ 243
  - 7.6.2 Documents Checklists ⋯⋯ 243
  - 7.6.3 Disposal of Discrepancies ⋯⋯ 247

Chapter 8 Non-trade Settlement ⋯⋯ 254

- 8.1 Non-trade Settlement ⋯⋯ 254
- 8.2 Overseas Chinese Remittance ⋯⋯ 255
- 8.3 Traveler's Cheque ⋯⋯ 256
  - 8.3.1 Definition of Traveler's Cheque ⋯⋯ 256
  - 8.3.2 Parties to a Traveler's Cheque ⋯⋯ 257
  - 8.3.3 Procedures of Traveler's Cheque Transaction ⋯⋯ 257
  - 8.3.4 Advantages of the Traveler's Cheque ⋯⋯ 258
- 8.4 Credit Card ⋯⋯ 259
  - 8.4.1 Definition of Credit Card ⋯⋯ 260
  - 8.4.2 Parties to a Credit Card ⋯⋯ 260
  - 8.4.3 Procedure of Credit Card ⋯⋯ 260
  - 8.4.4 Function of Credit Card ⋯⋯ 262

附录 Ⅰ CDCS 考试 ⋯⋯ 266

跟单信用证专家(Certified Documentary Credit Specialist,CDCS)考试 ⋯⋯ 266
模拟题 ⋯⋯ 267

附录 Ⅱ UCP600 中文版 ⋯⋯ 277

参考文献 ⋯⋯ 292

Chapter 1

Introduction

According to China's Customs statistics, China import and export trade volume is 26.43 trillion RMB in 2014. China has become the world's largest exporter and the second largest importer. How do we settle the huge amount of import and export with other countries? This chapter mainly introduces the concept and content of international settlement, evolution of international settlements, basis and conditions of international settlement, and the international settlement system.

★ Learning Objectives

(1) To enable the readers to understand the concepts and contents of international settlement.

(2) To enable the readers to understand international trade payment methods.

(3) To help the readers to know the ICC and her function.

(4) To help the readers to know the international clearing systems.

1.1 Basic Concepts and Contents of International Settlement

1.1.1 Basic Concepts of International Settlement

● **Definition of International Settlement**

International settlement refers to the financial activities conducted among different countries in which payments are effected or funds are transferred from one country to another in order to settle accounts, debts or claims emerged in the course of political, economic or cultural contacts among them. In short, International settlement is the money transfer via banks to settle accounts, debts and claims among different countries.

国际结算是指国际间由于政治、经济、文化等方面的交往或联系而发生的以货币表示的债权债务清偿行为或资金转移行为。简而言之，国际结算是不同国家通过银行结算账户清偿债权债务关系的一种资金转移行为。

虽然国际结算和国内结算都是当事人通过银行办理的货币收付行为，但两者存在明显区别，具体表现为：

（1）国际结算当事人面临的不确定性更大、风险更高。由于当事人之间距离远，文化及商业传统差异大，所处政治、法律和经济环境不同，国际结算对于债权人（卖方、出口商）和债务人（买方、进口商）而言具有更大的不确定性和更高的风险。

（2）货币的活动范围不同。国内结算中货币只需在一国范围内即可完成转移过程，国际结算中货币收付活动则是跨国进行的。

（3）使用的货币不同。国内结算使用本国货币，国际结算涉及货币币种选择问题。

（4）遵循的法律不同。国内结算遵循同一法律，国际结算遵循国际惯例或根据当事双方事先协定。

- **Supervision Mechanism of Performance**

In the traditional society, within a relatively small business circle, deals are made between acquaintances. Following moral standard enables the businessmen to do business with more people and earn more money.

In modern business living, the business circle may extend to the whole world, "*acquaintance*" and "*reputation*" won't motivate people to fulfill the obligation. It's not very difficult for a party to catch chance to maximize his benefit, which leads him to take the risks. Under such circumstances, although happened breach might be compensated by law, it could be time-consuming or cannot make ends meet. In a word, the possible cost may be too high.

If there is a third party, who possesses a good reputation, familiar with both parties mentioned above, or even capable of threatening the party who is on the cards to default, takes the role of witness, supervisor and the guarantor to both sides, it must be a strong drive for the two parties to fulfill the agreement. In practice, the most qualified third party is commercial banks.

The relationship between enterprises and banks is something like "*acquaintance*" in traditional society; they maintain their long-term relationship by credit, thus entering into a credit chain[①]. In this credit chain, parties concerned are likely to achieve a triple-win if they cooperate well enough.

- **Roles of Commercial bank in the International Settlement**

（1）Facilitating funds transfer. In current international business environment, through worldwide network, banks could easily separately transfer money between parties.

（2）Promoting conclusion of international trade. As an intermediary with good reputations, banks act as counterparts of both sides (the importer and the exporter), and are capable of supervising both sides, so as to promote the business to succeed.

（3）Extending loans for international trade. Banks could facilitate finance for both the importer and the exporter.

---

① 一方（进口商）和他的银行（A银行）之间的信用链可以通过全球银行网络连接到另一方（出口商）和他的银行（B银行）。进口商和出口商之间通过银行的间接信用链远比他们之间的直接信用链坚固。

(4) Helping foreign trade company to manage foreign exchange exposures. Banks could reduce, or even eliminate foreign exchange exposure by purchasing hedging products for themselves and for enterprises, such as foreign exchange forward, futures and options.

 1-1

我国银行国际结算业务发展现状及风险管理研究

依据1985年"七五"计划,各专业银行业务经营范围允许交叉,国内银行相继推出了国际贸易结算业务。与此同时,一些外资或侨资银行也加入国际结算阵营,中国银行"一统天下"的时代彻底结束。金融脱媒现象的普遍发生,使得银行在资金供需双方间的中介作用越来越小。

1. 国际结算产品种类

从各个银行官方网站可以查询到其国际结算的所有产品。目前,国际结算主要集中在信用证、汇付、托收等传统的结算方式,新型的结算方式并不多见,而且主要集中在部分银行。中国银行、建设银行两家银行国际业务发展较为成熟,产品种类较多。而工商银行和农业银行起步晚,业务发展缓慢。

2. 国际结算总量

加入世贸组织以后,我国国际贸易结构不断优化,贸易总额不断攀升,越来越多的商业银行开始重视国际结算业务,中国银行国际结算业务2013年稳步上升,始终位于领先地位。集团全年完成国际结算业务量为3.42万亿美元,比2012年增长23.02%,位列全国第一,国际结算占全部佣金收入的17%。2011—2013年,工商银行国际结算业务量的涨幅最大,两年涨幅高达118%。四大银行的国际结算量差距也相对明显,2013年,中国银行的业务量是农业银行的4.38倍,占四大银行国际结算业务总量的44.8%,工商银行占30.5%(见图1-1)。

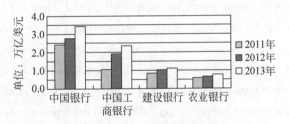

图1-1 四大国有银行国际结算总量(2011—2013年)

3. 国际结算手续费收入

我国各商业银行2012年及2013年国际结算与清算的手续费收入如图1-2所示,全年收入增长率处于10%左右的水平,同时,招商银行、中信银行、民生银行等小型商业银行的国际结算收入远远落后于四大国有商业银行。

(资料来源:张新荣.我国银行国际结算业务发展现状及风险管理研究[J].对外经贸,2014,(7))

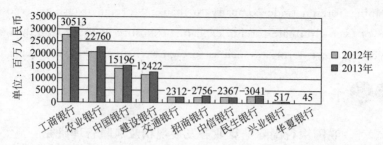

图 1-2　2012 年、2013 年我国各商业银行国际结算与清算手续费收入
（数据说明：工商银行数据包括现金管理手续费收入，兴业银行数据为支付结算手续费收入）

1.1.2　Types of International Settlement

Most international settlements originate from international trade, and they are money transfers as a result of international clearing. To be specific, international settlements may arise from five types of international transactions, and accordingly be divided into five types as follows.

（1）International goods-trade settlement, arising from commercial payments. International goods-trade settlement refers to the payment involved in visible trade (the import and export of commodities). Importers in one country make payment to exporters in another country for the traded goods, and exporters receive payment from the overseas buyers.

（2）International service-trade settlement, arising from payments for service trade such as technology or latent transfer, licensing, copyright selling, consultation, etc. Services rendered by individuals or enterprises in one country to those in another country must be paid, say, insurance premium, freight, postage, cable charges, commission.

（3）Payments for financial transaction and capital flow. International financial transaction covers foreign exchange market transactions, government supported export credits, syndicated loans, international bond issues, etc. Following the trend of globalization, capital flow in and out either among developed countries, among developing countries, or among developed and developing countries by FDI, issuing stocks, etc.

（4）Payments between governments. The government of one country may make payment to that of another country for political, military or economic reasons, such as giving aids and grants, providing disaster relief, etc.

（5）Others. Other modes of international settlements include overseas remittances, educational expenses, and inheritances.

According to the nature of transaction activities, the first two types would together be referred to international trade settlement, and the others to international non-trade settlement.

根据国际收支平衡表掌握国际结算的分类

中国国际收支平衡表(BPM6)

项 目	类 别
1. 经常账户	
1.A 货物和服务	
1.A.a 货物	国际贸易结算
1.A.b 服务	国际非贸易结算
1.A.b.1 加工服务	
1.A.b.2 维护和维修服务	
1.A.b.3 运输	
1.A.b.4 旅行	
1.A.b.5 建设	
1.A.b.6 保险和养老金服务	
1.A.b.7 金融服务	
1.A.b.8 知识产权使用费	
1.A.b.9 电信、计算机和信息服务	
1.A.b.10 其他商业服务	
1.A.b.11 个人、文化和娱乐服务	
1.A.b.12 别处未提及的政府服务	
1.B 初次收入	国际非贸易结算
1.B.1 雇员报酬	
1.B.2 投资收益	
1.B.3 其他初次收入	
1.C 二次收入	国际非贸易结算
2. 资本和金融账户	国际非贸易结算
2.1 资本账户	
2.2 金融账户	
2.2.1 非储备性质的金融账户	
2.2.1.1 直接投资	
2.2.1.2 证券投资	
2.2.1.3 金融衍生工具	
2.2.1.4 其他投资	
2.2.2 储备资产	
2.2.2.1 货币黄金	
2.2.2.2 特别提款权	
2.2.2.3 在国际货币基金组织的储备头寸	
2.2.2.4 外汇储备	

1.1.3　Basic Contents of International Settlement

International settlement centers on payment methods covering contract items of sales amount, currency used and how to make or collect payments for each individual transaction. Thus, international settlement is also called payment terms or payment methods in a contract in international trade. As traders are located in different countries, payments in modern international settlement are made via banks against various financial instruments and/or different commercial documents. So financial instruments, payment methods, commercial documents and the settlement system via commercial banks are the four important and closely related contents in international settlement.

(1) **Financial instruments**(金融票据)

Nowadays, International settlement is mainly bank non-cash settlement, and the main tool is financial instruments. Financial instruments mainly refer to bills of exchange, promissory notes and cheque. They are also known as negotiable instruments. In general terms, these instruments are the orders given to the bank by one trader who asks the bank to make/collect payments to/from the other trader. When such orders are performed by the bank, funds are successfully transferred from the buyer to the seller.

(2) **Payment methods**(支付方式)

The trading parties determine not only "when", "where" and "how" to move the goods—the delivery of the goods, but also "when", "where" and "how" to move the money—the payment for the goods. At this stage it is difficult to make a clear-cut differentiation between the "when", the "where" and the "how", because they are all influenced by complex factors. These factors include the business relationship between the seller and the buyer, the nature of the merchandise, industry norms, the distance between the buyer and the seller, the market expectation on exchange volatility, political situation and economic stability in trade-concerned countries.

It's widely known that payments to settle international transactions are either on commercial credit or bank credit. Several usual methods of payment are described briefly here, on which detailed discussions will be made in the following chapters.

※ **Payment in Advance**(预付货款)

Payment in advance is also called advance payment which means that the buyer should pay the seller prior to shipment of the goods ordered or provision of services. While this method of payment is expensive and contains certain degree of risks, which provides the seller with the most security but leaves the buyer at great risk that the seller will not comply with all the terms of the contract, so that it is not uncommon when the manufacturing process or services delivered are specialized and capital intensive. Due to the high degree of risk, the buyer should always consider whether any alternatives are available before agreeing to cash in advance terms. In such circumstances the parties may agree to do the business by partial payment in advance or by progress payment(分期付款).

Moreover, there are some issues that should be considered in using advance payment. The credit standing of the exporter must be exceedingly good; the economic and political conditions in the exporter's country should be stable enough; the importer should have sufficient balance sheet liquidity or be confident of obtaining working capital by way of import financing; the importer should have the knowledge that the exchange control authorities in her country will permit advance payment to be made.

Generally, the reasons for adopting this method may be summarized as follows: (1) the seller may be unwilling to ship goods to the country of the buyer for reasons of country risks; (2) the buyer may wish to encourage the seller into a long-term trade relationship; (3) the seller may not have finance to buy and/or prepare the goods for shipment; (4) the buyer feels comfortable with her relationship with the seller and with credit and country risk.

预付货款是指买方(进口商)先将货款的全部或者一部分通过银行汇交卖方(出口商),卖方收到货款后,根据买卖双方事先约定好的合同规定,在一定时间内或立即将货物发运给出口商。

※ **Open Account(O/A,赊销)**

Open account business, also called sale on credit, means that the buyer agrees to pay for goods ordered within a designated time after their shipment. Open account provides for payment at some stated specific future date and without the buyer issuing any negotiable instrument evidencing her legal commitment. That is, in an open account trade arrangement, the goods are shipped to a buyer without guarantee of payment so that open account provides the buyer with the greatest security and flexibility, but leaves the seller at greatest risk that the buyer will not comply with the terms of the contract and pay as promised. Generally, open account terms are utilized only when goods are shipped to a foreign branch or subsidiary of a multinational company or when there is a high degree of trust between the seller and the buyer, and the seller has significant faith in the buyer's ability and willingness to pay. If the transaction is with an unknown buyer, the seller is advised to find a different payment method.

The essential features of open account business are: (1) the credit standing of the importer must be very good; (2) the exporter is confident that the government of the importer's country will not impose regulations deferring or blocking the transfer of funds; (3) the exporter has sufficient liquidity to extend any necessary credit to the importer or has access to export financing; and (4) it is simple to administer and involves few banking fees or other costs.

Open account trading is most commonly used in situations where the two companies concerned know each other well and have a long-established trading relationship. Sales, for example, between sellers and buyers in countries in Western Europe and the USA are often conducted on this basis. In some cases sellers also use the procedure as a way to secure contracts with parties in a number of developing countries where Documentary Credit terms have applied in the past.

赊销是以信用为基础的销售方式。卖方与买方签订购货协议后,卖方同意买方在付款之前取走货物,而买方按照协议在规定日期以付款或分期付款的形式付清货款。

※ **Remittance**(汇付)

Remittance refers to the transfer of funds from one party to another among different countries. That is, a bank (the remitting bank), at the request of its customer (the remitter), transfers a certain sum of money to its overseas branch or correspondent bank (the paying bank) and instructs them to pay to a named person or corporation (the payee or beneficiary) who is domiciled in the country.

汇付是指资金从一国的一方转移到另一国的一方,即银行(汇出行)在客户的要求下(汇款人),将一定数额的资金转移到海外分行或代理行(付款银行),指示他们支付给指定人或公司(收款人或受益人)的一种支付行为。

※ **Documentary Collection**(跟单托收)

A documentary collection is an order by the seller to his bank, which involved in the transaction do not guarantee payment but act only as an intermediary, to collect payment from the buyer in exchange for the transfer of documents that enable the holder to take possession of the goods.

Collection is excellent for buyers who wish to purchase goods without risking prepayment and without having to go through the more cumbersome letter of credit procedures, while the seller would bear risks.

An essential feature of collection is that although it is safer than open account for the seller, there is the possibility that the buyer or the banker refuses to honor the bill of exchange and takes up the shipping documents, especially at a time when the market is falling. On this occasion, the seller may not receive his payment although he is still the owner of the goods. Therefore, from the seller's standpoint, documentary collection falls somewhere in between a letter of credit and open account in its desirability. This kind of payment method is generally utilized when the buyer and seller have an established and ongoing business relationship, and when the transaction does not require the additional protection and expense of a documentary credit.

跟单托收是指金融单据附带着商业票据的托收,即卖方把金融票据连同商业票据委托银行立即或在未来某个时间点代为收款。

※ **Letter of Credit**(L/C,信用证)

A letter of credit is a bank's promise to pay a seller on behalf of the buyer so long as the seller complies with precisely defined terms and conditions specified in the credit, which provides the most satisfactory method of settling international transactions. Its primary function is relying on the bank's undertaking to pay, thereby enabling the seller or the exporter to receive payment as soon as possible after the shipment of his goods and also enabling the buyer or the importer to arrange with her bank for the financing of the payment. Therefore, Letter of credit is the most common form of international payment because they provide a high degree of protection for both the buyer and the seller.

Documentary credits constitute the main subject matter of this book, and their features and operation are accordingly described in detail in other chapters. The documentary credit structure provides the seller with an independent bank undertaking of payment. The buyer, on the other hand, knows that payment will not be made unless the seller presents documentary evidence covering the goods and his shipment.

信用证是开证行应开证申请人(卖方)的要求并按其指示,向受益人(买方)开具的载有一定金额、在一定期限内凭符合规定的单据付款的书面保证文件。

※ **Banker's Letter of Guarantee**(L/G,银行保函)

In international trade, the buyer wants to be certain that the seller is in a position to honor her commitment as offered or contracted. The former therefore makes it a condition that appropriate security is provided. On the other hand, the seller must find a way to be assured of receiving payment if no special security is provided for the payment such as in open account business and documentary collections. Such security may be obtained through banks in the form of a guarantee. A banker's letter of guarantee is used as an instrument for securing performance or payment especially in international business.

A bank guarantee is a written promise issued by a bank at the request of its customer, undertaking to make payment to the beneficiary within the limits of a stated sum of money in the event of default by the principal. It may also be defined as the irrevocable obligation of a bank to pay a sum of money in the event of non-performance of a contract by the principal.

银行保函是指银行或其他金融机构作为担保人,根据委托人的申请,以第三者的身份保证委托人如未对受益人履行某项契约的义务时,向受益人有条件地支付一定金额的经济赔偿的书面担保。简言之,银行保函就是银行向受益人开立的保证文件。

※ **Stand-by Letter of Credit**(备用信用证)

Stand-by Letter of Credit, like a commercial letter of credit, is a promise by the issuer to honor the beneficiary-presentation of the document or documents specified in the letter of credit.

备用信用证,又称商业票据信用证、担保信用证,是指开证行根据开证申请人的请求对受益人开立的承诺承担某项义务的银行保证书。开证行保证在开证申请人未能履行其义务时,受益人只要凭备用信用证的规定并提交开证人违约证明,即可取得开证行的偿付。

※ **International Factoring**(国际保理)

International Factoring is a complete financial package that combines credit protection, accounts receivable bookkeeping, and collection services. When an exporter and an importer enter into an international transaction contract in which O/A or D/A has been agreed upon, the exporter and an international factor can establish an agreement, under which the factor purchases the exporter's accounts receivable, normally without recourse, and assumes the responsibility for the importer's financial ability to pay.

国际保理业务,即国际保付代理业务,是一项流行于欧美的金融服务,是继汇付、托收、信用证之后出现的新型国际结算方式。国际保理是在托收、赊账等情况下,保理商(factor)向出口商提供的一项包括对买方资信调查、百分之百的风险担保、催收应收账款、财务管理及融通资金等金融服务在内的综合性金融服务。简言之,它是一种出口商以商业信用方式出售商品,装运后将发票等收账凭据转让给保理商,从而从保理商处获得资金融通的业务。

※ **Forfaiting**(福费廷)

Forfaiting, also called bill buy-up or bill buy-out, is a kind of trade financing that bank, as the buyer-up, purchase without recourse from the exporter the accepted usance draft so as to provide finance to the exporter.

福费廷也称包买票据或买断票据,是指银行(或包买人)对国际贸易延期付款方式中出口商持有的远期承兑汇票或本票进行无追索权的贴现(即买断)。

福费廷是英文 forfaiting 的音译,意为放弃。在福费廷业务中,这种放弃包括两方面:一是出口商卖断票据,放弃了对所出售票据的一切权利;二是银行(包买人)买断票据,也必须放弃对出口商所贴现款项的追索权,由此可能承担票据拒付的风险。

(3) **Commercial documents**(商业票据)

In international settlement, documents play a decisive role. The involved banks regard goods receipts as the premise of international trade settlement and mediation, or otherwise they have to put considerable human, material and financial resources to participate into every link of monitoring trades.

Commercial documents refer to the documents which are issued by sellers, buyers or other traders, for facilitating trade and payment. The major commercial documents include commercial invoice, packing list, bill of lading, insurance policy, inspection certificate and certificate of origin, etc.

In the process of international trade settlements, the relevant parties are dealing with documents, not goods. Banks will generally pay against documents; exporters will only receive payment by handling over the required documents. The documents called for by a payment method will differ somewhat according to the nature of the transaction, the goods and the countries of exporters and importers.

信用证支付方式对商业票据有着严格的要求,因为信用证方式是纯单据业务(pure documentary transaction)。银行处理信用证业务时,只凭单据,不问货物,只审查受益人所提交的单据是否与信用证条款要求相符,以决定其是否履行付款责任。在信用证业务中,只要受益人提交符合信用证条款的单据,开证行就应承担付款责任,进口商也应接受单据并向开证行付款赎单。如果进口商付款后发现货物有缺陷,可凭单据向有关责任方提出损害赔偿要求,与银行无关。

需要特别注意,银行要求信用证与单据"表面严格相符"(the doctrine of strict compliance)。"严格相符的原则"不仅要求"单证相符",还要求"单单相符"。银行依据严格相符原则付款既是义务,也是权利。如果单据与信用证的指示不符,银行应该拒付,否则将自担风险。

(4) Settlement system via commercial banks(商业银行清算系统)

The fulfillment of international settlement relies on the fund transfers between the seller and the buyer through their respective accounts. Yet, fund transfers are processed and settled through certain clearing systems. International banking is completed through the cooperation of commercial banks all over the world. The challenge today is to move money as fast as possible, offer financial services at the lowest cost and provide most information to the clients. In recent years, payment services have been the keystone of international correspondent banking competition and cooperation. The so-called correspondent bank may be defined as a bank having direct connection, or friendly service relations with another bank. Even for large international banks, say Bank of China, the establishment of correspondent relationship is still very important because they cannot do any business without the cooperation of local banks.

Correspondent Bank could provide the following services: (1) collecting cheques, bill of exchange, and other credit instruments; (2) making loan or investments as an agent for their customer banks; (3) making credit investigations on firms borrowing in the open market; (4) providing banks with foreign exchange facilities, including commercial and traveler's cheques; and (5) providing banks with funds/loans needed.

A current account may be opened between banks with the establishment of a correspondent banking relationship. Any bank, before opening an account in its correspondent bank, should be aware of the detailed conditions of this connection, such as amount of initial deposit, minimum credit balance for covering the cost of services provided, interest rate of the account, overbill of exchange permission, and how often the statement of account would be sent.

To select a good correspondent bank is very important. The following factors shall be taken into account: (1) reputation of the bank; (2) size of the bank; (3) location of the bank; (4) services offered by the bank; (5) fundamental policies and strength of the bank; (6) physical features and personnel; and (7) momentum of early start, etc.

When establishing a correspondent banking relationship, two banks concerned will exchange information on the services they can perform or services in which they can cooperate with each other. Usually "A" Bank and "B" Bank shall be supplied with the control documents when they are establishing an agency banking relationship. The control documents include: (1) lists of specimen of authorized signatures[①]; (2) telegraphic test keys[②]; (3) terms and conditions; and (4) SWIFT authentic key[③].

中国商业银行清算系统

在经济全球化高速发展的今天,每个国家的银行体系中都包含一个或数个现代化的支付清算系统,以快捷、有效、安全地清偿经济活动所产生的债权和债务。我国人民币业务主要有以下三个清算系统。

1. 中国现代化支付系统(CNAPS)

中国现代化支付系统是中国人民银行按照我国支付清算需要,并利用现代计算机技术和通信网络自主开发建设的,能够高效、安全处理各银行办理的异地、同城各种支付业务及其资金清算和货币市场交易的资金清算的应用系统。它是各银行和货币市场的公共支付清算平台,是人民银行发挥其金融服务职能的重要核心支持系统。

2. 大额实时支付系统(HVPS)

大额实时支付系统(简称大额支付系统)采用逐笔实时方式处理支付业务,全额清算资金。建设大额实时支付系统的目的,就是为了给各银行和广大企业单位及金融市场提供快速、高效、安全、可靠的支付清算服务,防范支付风险。它对中央银行更加灵活、有效地实施货币政策和实施货币市场交易的及时清算具有重要作用。该系统可以处理同城和异地、商业银行跨行之间和行内的各种大额贷记及紧急的小额贷记支付业务,处理人民银行系统的各种贷记支付业务,处理债券交易的即时转账业务。

3. 小额批量支付系统(BEPS)

小额批量支付系统(简称小额支付系统)是中国现代化支付系统的主要业务子系统和组成部分。它主要处理同城和异地纸凭证截留的借记支付业务和小额贷记支付业务,支付指令批量发送,轧差净额清算资金,旨在为社会提供低成本、大业务量的支付清算服务。小额支付系统实行7×24小时连续运行,能支撑多种支付工具的使用,满足社会多样化的支付清算需求,成为银行业金融机构跨行支付清算和业务创新的安全高效的平台。

---

① The authorized signatures are used for authentication of the messages, letters, remittances, letters of credit, etc., addressed by the bank to its correspondent bank. A bank's signature book contains facsimiles of signatures of authorized officers. A bank bill of exchange will not be paid if it bears no authorized signatures. When signatures thereon, such as letters of credit are found out of their previous shapes compared with the specimen in authorized signature book, they have to be confirmed by tested telex.

② The telegraphic test keys are code arrangements that enable the banks to receive cables from other banks to verify that the cables/telexes are authentic in the absence of written signatures. These codes are strictly confidential. In compliance with the request in "A" Bank, "B" Bank is enclosing under sealed cover a table of his serial and rotation numbers to be used in conjunction of telex/cable messages from "B" to "A". It is important to destroy the testing documents and confirm that fact by returning letter duly signed as soon as "A" receives the canceling letter.

③ This is an electronic "key" that is used between SWIFT member banks for authenticating all messages to be transmitted through SWIFT.

1.2 Evolution of International Settlement

1.2.1 From Cash Settlement to Non-cash Settlement

Before the sixth century B. C. , goods were exchanged between traders in different countries on a barter basis. A barter system puts the trading parties at great inconvenience. Then, a medium of exchange was created in the form of coins at the beginning of the fifth century B. C. , thereby ending the barter transactions. These coins were measured and exchanged by weight and fineness among trading countries for settling international payments. Since then, international payments have been effected by shipping precious metals taking the form of coins, bars or bullions to or from the trading countries. This direct transfer of precious metals started cash settlement era.

However, the shipment of gold or silver across national boundaries was not only expensive but also risky. Freight charges were high, the risks of being lost, stolen or robbed was omnipresent, and what is more, the speed of transferring funds depended on the speed of transportation facilities, which often slowed the turnover of funds. From the thirteenth century A. D. , bills of exchange were created and gradually took the place of coins in international payments. With the establishment of foreign exchange banks at the end of the eighteenth century, international payments could be settled by way of transferring funds through the accounts opened in those banks. From then on, the non-cash settlement era began. Nowadays non-cash settlements are universally adopted all over the world. There is no denying the fact that the establishment of foreign exchange markets does play a critical role in creating and developing non-cash settlements, for foreign exchange banks are allowed to buy and sell foreign exchange freely in these markets so as to meet the needs of international banking business.

1.2.2 From Direct Payment to Payment Effected through a Financial Intermediary

As mentioned above, initially, international trade payments were made by the buyers directly to the sellers by means of precious metal shipments. As foreign exchange banks were set up over time in different regions over the world, the payment channel has changed, especially after a new means of payment, namely the bill of exchange, had been widely used in international payments and settlements. The commercial banks acted as the intermediaries effecting international payments by the buyers to the sellers. With the worldwide banking network and modern banking technicality, banks can not only provide easy and quick transfer of funds needed for conducting international trade but also furnish their customers with valuable economic and credit information. Nowadays they have become the center of international settlement.

1.2.3 From Payments under Simple Price Terms to Payments under More Complex Price Terms

In the past, international trade payments were settled on very simple price terms, such as cash on delivery, cash on shipment, cash with order, cash before shipment, etc. In modern international trade, a more comprehensive and exact set of terms has been developed. As indicated in INCOTERMS 2010 (International Rules for the Interpretation of Trade Terms) ICC Publication, the price terms available for use are multifarious and more complicated than before.

1.2.4 New Tendency: Settlement through the Internet

As an international business with a long history, international trade payment has been adjusting its best trade-off point between ensuring performance and lowering transaction costs in the wake of change of the global economy and development of science and technology. Relative stability of international economic and financial system after the Second World War, and the globalization of world economy make international trade settlement develop more and more towards lowering its transaction costs. In the 1960s, western countries started to try and promote the use of EDI technology[①] in international trade, i. e., non-paper trade, which greatly facilitates the development and efficiency of international trade settlement. With the development of computer technology, business is done and payments and settlements are effected through all kinds of payment systems, making it quicker, safer and more convenient for both the buyer and the seller. Nowadays, the Internet has been developing very fast and people are trying to make payment on line more and more.

1.3 The International Chamber of Commerce (ICC)

The ICC is an international organization that promotes international trade and investment. It was founded in 1919 and the headquarter is located in Paris.

---

① EDI refers to the Electronic Data Interchange, a combination of modern computer and data network technology, which is mainly used in automatically transmission of standardized commercial forms between various computer systems of organizations. Standard documents recognized in this system, such as order, contract, invoice, delivery order, customs clearance, license of import and export, etc. are to be transformed into digital structure, then can be identified and handled by computer. And such data can be interchanged through digital network between computer systems of different countries, so that business information is to be handles automatically.

The ICC publishes some documents such as the "INCOTERMS","Uniform Rule for Collections (URC)" and "Uniform Customs and Practice for Documentary Credits (UCP)" for the international businesses to observe so that international trade may proceed more smoothly and efficiently. The publications issued by the ICC are used as guidelines and rules. It is suggested that the publications, though with no force of law, should be given substantial weight by a court in accordance with the merits of the particular decision. Besides, the ICC provides some other services to the exporters, including the ICC International Court of Arbitration. In November 1994, China Chamber of International Commerce was authorized to be one of the ICC members.

The ICC Commission on Banking Technique and Practice draws its members from countries in which the ICC is represented by a National Committee. It usually meets twice a year. The purposes of ICC Banking Commission are listed as follows: (1) to organize meetings for bankers from quite a lot of countries worldwide in order to discuss common problems; (2) to keep in touch with special international organizations and pass on the ideas and opinions of bankers to those organizations such as: UNCTAD (United Nations Conference on Trade and Development, about the problems of fraud in documentary L/C transactions), UNECE (United Nations Economic Commission for Europe), UNCITRAL (United Nations Commission on International Trade Law, about the matters like documentary L/C, collections, bank guarantees and rules for electronic funds transfers); and (3) to give definitions about, to make harmonious environment for international business and simplify the practices and relevant special terms used in international banking.

国际商会简介

国际商会(ICC)于1919年在美国发起,1920年正式成立,总部设在法国巴黎。ICC的基本目的是为开放的世界经济服务,坚信国际商业交流将带来更大的繁荣和国家之间的和平。它是最具影响力的世界性民间商业组织之一,只要提及国际贸易惯例,就不可避免地要谈及国际商会。ICC是联合国重要对话伙伴,并与世界贸易组织、欧盟、经合组织等国际组织保持着密切联系。目前,ICC的会员已扩展到全球150多个国家和地区。中国国际商会于1994年代表中国加入国际商会,国际商会中国国家委员会(ICC China)秘书局设在中国国际商会。

国际商会的组织机构包括:理事会,执行局,财政委员会,会长、副会长和秘书长,所属各专业委员会和会员,会员大会,此外还设有国家特派员。国际商会现下属24个专业委员会及工作机构,分别是:关税和贸易总协定经济咨询委员会,国际贸易政策委员会,多国企业和国际投资委员会,国际商业惯例委员会,计算机、电报和信息政策委员会,银行技术和惯例委员会,知识和工业产权委员会,环境委员会,能源委员会,海运委员会,空运委员会,税务委员会,有关竞争法律和实务委员会,保险委员会,销售、广告和批售委员会,国际仲裁委员会,国际商会国际局,国际商会仲裁院,国际商合国际商业法律和实务学会,东西方委员会,国际商会/中国国际商会合作委员会,国际商会国际海事局,国际商会海事合作中心和国际商会反假冒情报局。

国际商会的主要职能有四个:(1)在国际范围内代表商业界,特别是对联合国和政府专门机构充当商业发言人;(2)促进建立在自由和公正竞争基础上的世界贸易和投资;(3)协调统一贸易惯例,并为进出口商制定贸易术语和各种指南;(4)为商业提供实际服务。

1.4 International Payment Systems

1.4.1 Brief Introduction

"Payment" is the transmission of an instruction to transfer funds that results from a transaction in the economy, and "settlement" is the final and unconditional transfer of the value specified in a payment instruction. Thus, if a customer pays a department store bill by cheque, "payment" occurs when the cheque is placed in the hands of the department store, and "settlement" occurs when the cheque clears and the department store's bank account is credited. If the customer pays the bill with cash, payment and settlement are simultaneous. Each nation has its own national currency, and also its own payment and settlement system.

Payment system is also called clearing system, refers to the process that banks draw a sum of money from the payer's account and deposit it to the payee's. Payment system is from intermediary institutions to provide payment and settlement services and realize the transfer payment instructions and fund settlement of professional and technical means to form, to realize creditor's rights debt repayment and transfer of a financial arrangement.

A payment system is the means whereby funds are transferred from the payer's bank account to the payee's one. It includes: (1) policies and procedures, including rules for crediting and debiting balances; (2) a medium for storing and transmitting payment information; and (3) financial intermediaries for organizing information flow, carrying out value transfer instructions, and generally administering payment activities.

There are four types of funds transfer (coin and currency, cheque, wire, and automated clearing house). These are designated as primary payment systems because each one alone is sufficient to transfer value from one party to another. There are also different types of secondary payment systems that convey payment information but ultimately require one of the primary payment systems to transfer funds.

A bank usually has a lot of overseas relational banks, with which it opens account and entrusts business. In vostro accounts of a bank, some banks have receivables, and the others have payables. In an agreed interval, such bank should pay all banks with new receivables and demand payment from all banks with net payables. And other banks should also act in this way, which, with no doubt, is time-and-energy-consuming. In today's banking, banks have close ties with each other, normally open accounts with the same clearing instruction, and keep certain sum of funds.

国际结算和国际清算的联系与区别

结算主要是指债权人和债务人通过银行清算债权债务关系。清算是指银行之间通过清算网络来结算债权债务关系。由于银行之间的债权债务关系主要是由结算引起的,因此,结算是清算的前提和基础,清算是结算的继续和完成。

国际结算与国际清算是紧密联系、不可分割的。国际结算是国际间清偿债权和债务的货币收付行为,是以货币收付来清偿国与国之间因经济文化交流、政策性事务性的交流所产生的债权债务。国际结算的目的是以有效的方式和手段来实现国际间以货币表现的债权债务的清偿。国际清算是指两个或两个以上缔约国之间的债权债务,通过互相抵偿的方法,以进行国际结算的一种方式。一般是根据清算协定,把双方的债权和债务都记入清算账户,定期进行结算,使收支达成平衡。由两国缔约者,称为"双边清算";由三国(或更多国)缔约者,称为"三边"或"多边清算"。

1.4.2 International Clearing Systems

In the past, most of debits and credits to be cleared were in the form of paper instruments, which were cleared manually, taking several days, or even weeks, accordingly slowing down turnover of banks and exposing them to higher foreign exchange risks. Along with the ever-changing business environment and rapidly developing information technology, fund transfers between banks are mainly done through electronic systems. Funds debited will be transferred and settled from the sending participant's (say, remitting bank's) account to the recipient's (e.g. the paying bank's) account, in real-time, almost without time interruption, and without manual operation. And the recipient bank can use the funds transferred to its account immediately. The whole clearing jobs could be done on one-day-interval.

Ever improved E-commerce technology is promoting international settlement to develop itself towards a non-paper, automatically handled transaction. Nowadays, five vital electronic fund transfer systems have been widely used, i.e., SWIFT, CHIPS, CHAPS, TARGET and Fed Wire.

● **SWIFT**(环球银行金融电讯协会)

SWIFT, standing for the Society for Worldwide International Financial Telecommunication, born in 1973 at the center of Brussels and supported only by 239 banks in 15 countries at its beginning, has over 7000 financial institutions in 192 countries or areas based in the Netherlands, Hong Kong of China, the United Kingdom, and the United States. It provides worldwide assistance in more than 10 languages 24 hours a day and 7 days a week. It started the mission of creating a shared worldwide data processing and communication link and a common language for international financial transactions.

The SWIFT network has grown considerably from its birth on. SWIFT has been in continuous operations since May 1977, four years after its foundation. It carried 1.2 billion messages in 2000, i. e., 330000 average daily transactions, and the average daily value of payment messages is estimated to be above USD 5 trillion. Its membership now consists of over 8000 international financial institutions (including branches) in 206 economies all around the world. SWIFT is a step forward to improve the cooperation among international correspondent banks. The network covers most of Western Europe, North America, parts of South America and the Far East. In 1983, Bank of China became the member of the SWIFT, and soon afterwards hundreds of Chinese banks and their branches became its members.

SWIFT provides messaging services to banks, broker-dealers and investment managers, as well as to market infrastructures (here means clearing and settling house) in cover transfer, international trade payments, treasury, securities, foreign exchange transactions, and so on. It has many benefits and applies not only to SWIFT members but to their correspondent banks and customers. The system enables member banks to transmit between their own international payments, statements and other transactions associated with international banking. The use of the network is more convenient and reliable than past methods of communication (mail, telex and cable), and enables the banks to offer better services to their customers.

SWIFT is an international communication network connecting the world major banks together, helping its members from different countries to easily get in touch with each other. The banks use computer systems to speed up the transfer of international payments and other financial business. Financial messages will be passed on, stored, with test keys added automatically. Once the test keys verified, the messages will be categorized and handled automatically, too. This switching system operates 24 hours, 7 days a week and can achieve same-day transfer. It has demonstrated to the world its high speed and accuracy. The principal function of SWIFT is to provide its member banks with access to the system for the settlement of international money transfers. However, SWIFT itself is not a system allowing member banks to settle payments among them; settlements among banks still require an international clearing house such as CHIPS.

To safely and efficiently transfer customers' messages and settle the funds, SWIFT introduces a series of standard formats for a variety of financial messages. For example,

MT100 is a set of customer transfer messages used for fund transfer instruction in which at least one of the end-parties is a non-financial institution. MT400 is used to advise the payment to a collection, and MT700 is used to issue a documentary credit indicating the terms and conditions of a Documentary Credit. Message Test Standards have been designed and users are able to transmit all types of customer and bank transfers such as confirmation of foreign exchange deals, statements, collection and documentary credit messages.

SWIFT operates in the following way: SWIFT messages are transmitted among countries via central, interconnected operating centers located in Brussels, Amsterdam, and Culpeper of Virginia. These operating centers are in turn connected by international data-transmission lines to regional processors in most member countries. Banks in an individual country use the available national communication facilities to send messages to the regional processor. Technically, a member bank in SWIFT has computer "hookups" in the systems that permit banks to relay funds to one another simultaneously.

In order to ensure error-free identification of parties in automated systems, SWIFT developed the Bank Identifier Code (BIC), which identifies precisely the financial institution involved in financial transactions. The BIC is made of eight or eleven consecutive alphanumeric characters without any spaces or other characters, with the first four-character code being called the Bank Code. It is unique to each financial institution and can only be made up of letters. The 5th and 6th code are country codes identifying the country in which the financial institution is located, which are followed by the last two location codes, maybe alphabetical or numeral, providing geographical distinction within a country, e.g. cities, states, provinces and time zones. Only a SWIFT BIC can appear in the header of a SWIFT message as Sender or Receiver.

 1-4

SWIFT 银行识别代码

SWIFT 银行识别代码(Bank Identifier Code, BIC)是由电脑可以自动判读的八位或十一位英文字母或阿拉伯数字组成,用于在 SWIFT 电文中明确区分金融交易中相关的不同金融机构。每家申请加入 SWIFT 组织的银行都必须事先按照 SWIFT 组织的统一原则,制定出本行的 SWIFT 地址代码,经 SWIFT 组织批准后正式生效。BIC 由十一位数字或字母组成,这些数字或字母又可以拆分为银行代码、国家代码、地区代码和分行代码四部分。

(1) 银行代码:由四位英文字母组成,每家银行只有一个银行代码,并由其自主决定,通常是该行的行名字头缩写,适用于该行所有的分支机构。

(2) 国家代码:由两位英文字母组成,用以区分用户所在的国家和地理区域。

(3) 地区代码:由 0、1 以外的两位数字或两位字母组成,用以区分位于所在国家的地理位置,如时区、省、州、城市等。

(4) 分行代码：由三位字母或数字组成，用来区分一个国家里某一分行、组织或部门。如果银行的 BIC 只有八位而无分行代码时，其初始值订为"×××"。

以中国银行北京分行为例，其银行识别代码为 BKCHCNBJ300。其含义为：BKCH（银行代码）、CN（国家代码）、BJ（地区代码）、300（分行代码）。

● **CHIPS**（清算所同业支付系统）

CHIPS stands for the Clearing House Inter-bank Payment System. It was developed in 1971 by the New York Clearing House Association for transfer of international dollar payments. Operated real-time, it is a final payment system for business-to-business transactions, linking about 140 depository institutions, called also settling banks, which have offices or affiliates in New York City. Over $600 billion is passed through CHIPS every day. This represents about 90% of all international inter-bank dollar-denominated transactions. Most dollar-based international transactions flow through New York correspondent banks that clear transactions through CHIPS.

CHIPS works as a netting system. This means that only information, and not funds, is transferred during a specified period. At the end of the period (for CHIPS the period is one business day) only the net amount is actually transferred from one party to an other. If Bank A should send $10000000 in transfers to Bank B and Bank B should sends $8000000 in transfers to Bank A on the same business day, only the net amount of $2000000 is actually transferred from Band A to Bank B at the end of the day.

The core of CHIPS is the Universal Identifier Database (UID), in which all corporate customers of the member's bank has its own UIN, a unique identifier telling the CHIPS what private account and bank information to use for processing payments. It allows straight-through processing without manual lookups or costly delays.

On each business day, starting at 7 o'clock, CHIPS begins to receive the participant's instructions, verifying UIN, matching and sending them to the receivers concerned. Immediately following the closing of the CHIPS network at 16：30 (Eastern Standard Time), the CHIPS computer produces a settlement report showing the net debit or credit position of each participant. Then until 17：45, the settling participants (non-settling participant is netted against the position of its correspondent settling participant) with net debit positions have to transfer their debit amounts through FED WIRE, operated by the Federal Reserve and used for domestic money transfers, to the CHIPS settlement account on the books of the New York Fed. The CHIPS then transfers those funds via FED WIRE, out of the settlement account to those settling participants with net credit positions. The process is usually completed by 18：00.

● **CHAPS**（英镑清算系统）

CHAPS stands for the Clearing House Automated Payment System. It is an electronic transfer system for sending same-day payments among banks. CHAPS offer its member banks and their participants an efficient, risk-free, reliable same-day payment mechanism.

Every CHAPS payment is unconditional, irrevocable and guaranteed. CHAPS is available nationwide in Britain and is operated by a number of settlement banks who communicate directly through computers.

CHAPS was developed in 1984. Now it is one of the largest real-time gross settlement systems in the world, second only to FED WIRE in the USA. Since January 4th, 1999, the CHAPS clearing company has operated two separate clearings, CHAPS Sterling and CHAPS Euro. There are 21 member banks currently participating in the Euro and/or Sterling clearing, such as Bank of England, Deutsche Bank, Dresdner Bank, Barclays Bank, Citibank, Standard Chartered Bank. The CHAPS Company is managed by a board of directors drawn from its member banks, led by a Company Chairman and the CHAPS Company Manager.

CHAPS is operating in the following way: Each bank sends instructions of the payments to the other ones through a so-called "gateway". It uses common software and there is no central executive on computer. Once the messages have been accepted in the system as being authentic, they cannot be revoked. This allows same-day transfer throughout the clearing system. Larger companies may be able to link their own technology into the system and operate payments and receipts electronically. Small companies can instruct their banks to make these payments in the usual way—by telephone call. CHAPS makes it possible that the expensive telegraphic transfer no longer needs to be used. Meanwhile, treasurers of companies are able to monitor their cash positions more easily.

- **TARGET**（泛欧实时全额自动清算系统）

TARGET stands for the Trans-European Automated Real-time Gross Settlement Express Transfer system, and it is the real-time gross settlement system for Euro, commencing operation on January 4th, 1999.

TARGET consists of 15 national Real-time Gross Settlement (RTGS) systems and the ECB Payment Mechanism (EPM) that are interlinked so as to provide a uniform platform for the processing of cross-border payments, which accounts for approximately 40% of the total payments value involving two interlinked RTGS systems and 20% in terms of volume of all TARGET payments (both cross-border and domestic payments).

There are more than 5000 RTGS participants in TARGET and almost all EU Credit Institutions are accessible via TARGET, including those countries which have not adopted Euro as their currency (Non-Euro area countries). TARGET has already become one of the largest payment systems in the world. Usually, payment instruction takes at most several minutes, even within several seconds, to be debited with the sending bank's account.

- **FED WIRE**（联邦资金转账系统）

FED WIRE stands for the Federal Reserve Wire Transfer System. It is a fund transfer system operated nationwide in the USA by the Federal Reserve System. This fund-transfer network handles transfers from one financial institution to another with an account balance held with the Fed. The transfer of reserve account balances is used for the buying and selling of the Fed funds, and credit transfers on behalf of bank customers.

Fund transfer operation under FED WIRE is as follows: (1) In making a FED WIRE transfer, a payer gives instructions to a bank in which the payer has an available balance; (2) The paying bank passes instructions on to the Fed to move funds from the bank's reserve balance account to another bank's in which the payee has an account; (3) Though initially generated by voice, paper instructions, or electronic data, the actual transfer of funds is merely a bookkeeping entry at the Fed. The Fed credits the reserve account of the payee's bank and debits the reserve account of the payer's bank; (4) Wires also provide a confirmation number to the payer so that the transaction can be traced; (5) When a bank receives an incoming wire, the receiving firm is given notification that funds have been received. This is also an important feature for many types of transactions. No other mechanism provides confirmation help and notification to the parties in a payment transaction.

However, FED WIRE does not permit much additional information to be carried along with the wire information. It is not uncommon for a firm to receive a wire payment and to be in the dark concerning the purpose of the payment.

- **Limitations of these International Clearing Systems**

Each clearing system introduced previously has its own contributions as well as limitations. CHIPS and CHAPS are connected with their own central bank respectively, easily clearing the net position for its settling members, yet limiting the number of participating members on the basis of qualification or location and by operating only in the local business time. Transferring Euro only in the EU member states, including Euro-zone countries and non-Euro-zone countries, limits the worldwide use of TARGET. Working in different currencies, in more than 10 languages, 24 hours a day and 7 days a week, SWIFT is the most popular international payment system in the world, even though it cannot yet make the ultimate net debit or credit settlement at present.

★ Key Words

International Settlement 国际结算　　financial instruments 金融票据
payment methods 支付方式　　commercial documents 商业票据
settlement system via commercial banks 商业银行清算系统
FEDWIRE 联邦资金转账系统　　CHIPS 清算所同业支付系统
CHAPS 银行自动收付系统　　TARGET 泛欧实时全额自动清算系统
SWIFT 全球银行金融电讯协会

★ Exercise

一、单项选择题（Exclusive Choice Question）

1. 国际结算制度的核心是（   ）。
   A. 信用制度   B. 银行制度
   C. 贸易制度   D. 外汇管理制度
2. 现代国际结算使用的主要工具是（   ）。
   A. 票据   B. 现金   C. 信用证   D. 汇票
3. 商品进出口款项的结算属于（   ）。
   A. 双边结算   B. 多边结算
   C. 贸易结算   D. 非贸易结算
4. 传统的国际贸易和结算中的信用主要是（   ）两类。
   A. 系统信用和银行信用   B. 系统信用和司法信用
   C. 商业信用和司法信用   D. 商业信用和银行信用
5. 以下哪一个不是建立代理行关系的步骤（   ）。
   A. 考察了解对方银行的资信   B. 签订代理协议并互换控制文件
   C. 双方银行确认控制文件   D. 了解对方银行的习惯做法
6. Which of the following is the USD payment and settlement system（   ）.
   A. CHAPS   B. CHIPS
   C. TARGET   D. BOJ-NET
7. At present, the biggest amount of currency in the global international settlement is（   ）.
   A. JPY   B. EUR
   C. USD   D. GBP
8. In the case of other conditions unchanged, which of the following currency settlement should the importer choose（   ）?
   A. have down trend of currency
   B. have up trend of currency
   C. the value of currency is fixed
   D. currency fluctuates up and down significantly

二、判断题（True or False）

1. The international settlement caused by the international tourism and international insurance caused is international trade settlement.（   ）
2. All the international settlement methods have directly or indirectly ways to provide financing.（   ）
3. Cargo documents is the precondition for the bank as international trade settlement and mediation. Otherwise, the bank will take considerable human, material and financial resources to participate in every link of monitoring trades.（   ）

4. 以银行为中心的现代电子转账划拨支付体系是国际间资金得以安全有效结算的基础设施。（　　）

5. 国际性的商业银行在国际结算中发挥了"两个中心"的职能，它们既是国际结算的中心，又是国际信贷的中心。（　　）

6. 美国某企业有一笔 90 天期的日元应付货款，若预测日元兑美元将升值，为了减少外汇风险损失，该企业应尽可能推迟结汇。（　　）

Chapter 2

Instruments of International Settlement

Chinese company A received an order valued 10 million from the United States, with six months usance L/C settlement. This L/C requires company A issuing an usance draft, the drawer is itself, the drawee is Citibank, and New York ticket terms indicate the L/C No. and the issuing date of the blank draft endorsed. How to issue such a draft so as to meet the requirements of the L/C? To answer this question, we should at first learn what negotiable instruments are for international settlement. In this chapter, we will learn three important negotiable instruments: bills of exchange, promissory notes and cheques.

★ Learning Objectives

(1) To enable the readers to understand the five main characteristics of negotiable instruments.

(2) To enable the readers to understand the functions of negotiable instruments.

(3) To enable the readers to understand what a bill of exchange is, what the necessary items are, how many parties to it, what the acts are of a bill, how many types of bills are, and what the advantages are to use a bill.

(4) To enable the readers to understand what a promissory note is, what the necessary items are, how many parties, what the acts of a note are, and how many types of notes are.

(5) To enable the readers to understand what a cheque is, what the necessary items are, how many parties to it, what the acts of a note are, and how many types of cheques are.

(6) To enable the readers to understand the differences and similarities of a bill of exchange, a promissory note and a cheque.

2.1 An Overview of Negotiable Instruments

In a broad sense, a negotiable instrument refers to any commercial title ownership. In a narrow sense, a negotiable instrument is a written document that contains an unconditional promise or order made by the drawer to pay a fixed amount of money to the bearer at a definite time or during a definite period. This chapter will focus on negotiable instruments in the narrow sense.

As we know, it is owing to the creation and use of various documents that banks are capable of taking part in international trade payment. Among the documents, negotiable instrument is a kind of certificate in writing which aims at obtaining a certain amount of proceeds. It clearly records the currency to circulate among participants, facilitating the transfer of credits and acting as payment and credit tools in merchandise exchange, to some extent.

2.1.1 Characteristics of a Negotiable Instrument

Negotiation means that the title can be transferred merely by delivering the certificate of title or by endorsement on the certificate completed by delivery.

Negotiable instruments, also named financial document or instrument, are payment tools as well as credit tools for domestic and international transactions, which can substitute for cash to a certain extent, but are more convenient than cash. Strictly speaking, a negotiable instrument is an unconditional order or promise to pay an amount of money that is easily transferable from one person to another. Generally speaking, a negotiable instrument has five main characteristics, i. e., right to be paid, non causative nature, requisite in form, negotiability and recoursement, among which negotiability is the most important one.

通常来说，票据有五个主要特征，包括：设权性、无因性、要式性、流通性和可追索性，其中流通性是最重要的特征之一。票据的设权性是指持票人的票据权利随票据的设立而产生，离开了票据就不能证明其票据权利；票据的无因性是指票据一旦做成，票据上的权利即与其原因关系相分离，成为独立的票据债权债务关系，不再受先前的原因关系存在与否的影响；票据的要式性是指票据的形式必须符合法律规定，票据上的记载项目必须齐全且符合规定；票据的流通性是指在法定的合理时限内，票据经过背书、交付等可以将票据权利转让给后手，手续简便但效力明确；票据的可追索性是指票据的付款人或承兑人如果对合格票据拒绝承兑或拒绝付款，正当持票人为维护其票据权利，有权通过法定程序向所有票据债务人起诉、追索，要求得到票据权利。

Negotiability is the legal feature which some business instruments have of transferring title of goods to the receiver of them irrespective of the title of the giver, providing that receiver takes the instruments in good faith and for value, which means:

- The transferee in good faith and for value can acquire a better title than that held by all his prior parties. For instance, a transfer, say person A, who acquired the instrument by fraud has only an empty title to it, but *a bona fide* transferee, say person B, for value from that person A, acquires a perfect title. What's important in practice is that a holder in due course like person B acquires an absolute right to payment of the full amount of the negotiable instrument and can enforce this right against all parties to the instrument if the instrument is not paid by the drawee.

The right of a person as a holder in due course is particularly vital to a bank involved in international business. A holder in due course (HDC) is a holder who, by meeting certain acquisition requirements, takes the instrument *free* of most of the defenses and claims that could be asserted against the transferor. Stated another way, an HDC can normally acquire a higher level of immunity than can an ordinary holder in regard to defenses against payment on the instrument or ownership claims to the instrument by other parties.

Imagine that a bank paid a certain sum of money for obtaining a bill of exchange and became a *bona fide* transferee. If the importer refused to pay the money under the contract out of a number of reasons, the bank should be reimbursed at least by the drawer, i. e., exporter, so that benefits of the bank would be protected.

- The holder needs not give notice of the transfer to his/her prior parties, especial to original debtor, to obtain a full title, so that the negotiable instrument can be effected only by delivery or endorsement with a simple signature, and be negotiated as many times as possible before the maturity date.
- The holder can sue in his or her own name. A transferee or holder who takes an instrument in good faith can sue on the basis of a breach of warranty as soon as he or she has reason to know of the breach, in his or her own name, instead of the first hand or any others.

2.1.2 Functions of Negotiable Instruments

- **Acting as payment instruments.** Most of international trades are settled by means of non-cash, in which payment tools are necessary, and negotiable instruments are good tools to meet this requirement.
- **Acting as credit instruments.** One party involved in a transaction may ask the counterpart for providing credit as the promise to fulfill the contract beforehand.
- **Acting as circulating instruments.** Negotiable instruments can be transferred by endorsement, along with the rights associated, functioning as a circulating tool and being generally accepted.
- **Acting as financing instruments.** If one person or corporate was trapped in cash chain crisis, holding some negotiable instruments, then he could transfer the possession of these instruments to another, to get financed successfully against cash chain crisis.

 2-1

Even though negotiable instruments have important functions in international transactions, which promote them to substitute currency's role to some extent, these instruments themselves are not currency. The main differences between instruments and currency are: (1) instruments rely on private credit of issuer, acceptor or endorser without mandatory circulation of legal currency; (2) the creditor has to accept when the debtor repays with the legal currency, but he has title to refuse accepting the instrument as repayment if he does not agree; and (3) instrument can be restricted by time, limitation, and invalidity. Instrument can play the roles of payment and credit, but they will no longer have those currency functions following their termination.

提示:票据虽然在一定程度上可以代替现金,但票据本身并不是货币。票据与货币的主要区别在于:(1)票据依靠出票人的私人信用不能像法定货币一样强制流通;(2)债权人不得不接受债务人偿还的法定货币,但是如果债权人不愿意,他可以拒绝接受票据作为偿付;(3)票据可以通过时间、限制条款和效力进行限制。票据可以充当支付和信用的角色,它们终止后将不再具有那些货币功能。

2.2　Bill of Exchange(汇票)

2.2.1　Definition of a Bill of Exchange

Generally, sellers of goods, in practice, almost never stand upon their rights to demand cash. Instead, they readily take certain substitutes, such as bills of exchange. Bills of exchange, a key form of negotiable instruments, enjoy a wide range of uses in commercial, financial and banking transactions. More often than not, bills of exchange are traditionally used in international trade where they offer written evidence of the financial obligations underlying trade transactions. Furthermore, bills of exchange have grown into a very flexible instrument in the areas of finance and banking.

- A bill of exchange, also called a draft or a bill, is an unconditional order in writing addressed by one party (drawer) to another (drawee), signed by the party giving it, requiring the party to whom it is addressed to pay on demand, or at a fixed or determinable future time, a certain sum in money to, or to the order of, a specified party or to bearer.
- In simple words, a bill of exchange is actually a piece of paper with words and sum of money on it, which is used to transfer money from one person to another instead of the actual money itself. Chart 2.1 is the typical bills of exchange:

汇票是最重要的一种票据,它最能反映票据的性质、特征和规律,最集中地体现票据所具有的信用、支付和融资等各种经济功能,从而成为票据的典型代表。我国《票据法》第19条对汇票的定义:汇票是出票人签发的,委托付款人在见票时或者在指定日期无条件支付确定的金额给收款人或者持票人的票据。英国票据法对汇票的定义为:汇票是由一人签发给另一人的无条件书面命令,要求受票人见票时或于未来某一规定的或可以确定的时间,将一定金额的款项支付给某一特定的人或其指定人,或持票人。

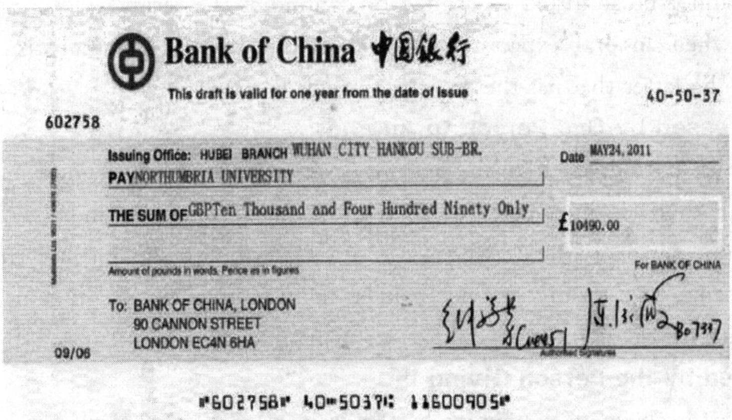

Chart 2.1

2.2.2 Essentials to a Bill of Exchange

According to the nature and importance, the essentials to a bill of exchange can be classified as: absolutely necessary items, relatively necessary items, and items at will.

In conformity with the Bills of Exchange Act 1882 of the United Kingdom and the Uniform Law on Bills of Exchange and Promissory Notes 1930 of Geneva, a bill of exchange must fulfill the following requirements:

1. Absolutely Necessary Items

● **It must contain the words "Bill of Exchange" or "Bill of exchange"**

The purpose of indicating these words on a bill of exchange is to distinguish a bill from other kinds of credit instruments such as promissory note or cheque. It is not definitely required in the Bills of Exchange Act of the United Kingdom, but in practice, indicating the above-mentioned word can be of great convenience to the relevant parties.

● **An Unconditional Order**

"Unconditional order" means the order which should be carried out without any conditions. If the payment instruction is subject to any condition, it is not a bill of exchange. Please compare the following examples:

※ "Pay to the order of the Bank of China the sum of thirty-five thousand US dollars." Bill of exchange with such order is valid.

※ "Pay to the order of the Bank of China the sum of thirty-five thousand US dollars when the ship 'Dongfang' reaches the port of New York." Bill of exchange with such order is an invalid because the "when" clause makes the bill a conditional one.

● **In Writing**

The bill of exchange must be written by hand, or typewritten or printed. Oral expressions cannot be admitted to change or contradict the terms of a bill of exchange. This means when an oral expression concerning the bill is different from the bill in writing, it is the latter that has the priority.

- **Addressed by One Person to Another**

A bill must be addressed by one person to another so that there must be one person as drawer and another person as drawee. In the case that the drawer and the drawee on the bill are the same person or the drawee is a fictitious person, the holder may treat it either as a bill of exchange or a promissory note. It is likely to have one or joint drawees, but no drawees in alternative or in succession.

- **Signed by the Person Giving It**

If a bill of exchange is not signed by the drawer, it is not valid. It is necessary for the drawer to sign himself. He can authorize somebody else to write his signature. For a company bill, if an individual is signing for his company, these words "For", "On behalf of", "For and on behalf of" and "Per pro" should prefix the name of the company, followed by the person's name and his designation. For example:

For ABC CO. , London

(*Signature*)

John Smith , Manager

- **A Certain Sum in Money**

"A certain sum in money" specifies that the consideration in bills of exchange must be legal tender (legal currency) and must be a definite sum even though the amount may be payable with interest, by stated installments or according to an indicated rate of exchange. The sum should be expressed in words and in figures explicitly. If the amount expressed in figure is not the same as that in words, it is the amount denoted in words that is treated as the amount payable.

※ **Payable at a fixed amount**

If a bill is "Payable at USD three hundred only", it is a valid bill of exchange. If a bill is "Payable at about USD three hundred", it is an invalid bill of exchange.

※ **Payable with interest**

The interest rate should be specified in order to make the amount payable a certain one. If a bill is "payable at USD three hundred with an interest", it is an invalid bill of exchange. If a bill is "payable at USD three hundred plus interest at 5% p.a. (from the date hereof to the date of payment)", it is a valid bill of exchange. In practice, interest will be calculated with the issuing date as the date of commencement and the date of payment as the final date.

※ **Payable by installments**

The installment must be clearly stated; otherwise the bill will be invalid. For example, a bill written with "pay to the order of Shanghai Export and Import Co. the sum of two thousand US dollars by installments" is an invalid bill of exchange, while a bill written with "at one month after date pay to the order of Shanghai Export and Import Co. the sum of two thousand US dollars by ten equal consecutive monthly installments" is a valid one.

※ **Payable according to an indicated rate of exchange**

The rate of exchange must be indicated if the amount is payable in another equivalent currency. For example, a bill written with "pay to the order of Shanghai Export and Import Co. the sum of two thousand US dollars converted into CNY" is not valid because the relevant parties do not know that the amount to be converted is against which day's rate, while a bill written with "pay to the order of Shanghai Export and Import Co. the sum of two thousand US dollars converted into CNY equivalent at current rate in Shanghai" is a valid one.

- **In Money**

The bill of exchange should be made payable only in money other than in other kinds of physical goods or intangible services. For example, a bill written with "pay to the order of Bob the sum of USD three hundred and give him some books" is not acceptable.

- **Payable to or to the Order of a Specific Person or to Bearer**

A bill of exchange must specify who is entitled to the money which the drawer authorizes to be paid. That is to say, a bill of exchange must be payable to a person or his order or to the bearer. Therefore, three types of bill can be classified: restrictive order bill, demonstrative order bill and bearer order bill. Different types of order will decide the negotiability of a bill and the way of negotiation. Another thing that should be noted here is that the word "order" in "types of order" differs from the "order" in "unconditional order". The former refers to the status of the payee, whereas the "order" in "unconditional order" means that the payment instruction should be made as a payment order rather than a payment request.

※ **Restrictive order**（限制性抬头）

A restrictive order bill is a bill payable to a specified person only or to a specified person, not negotiable/transferable. When the bill contains words such as "only" and "not transferable" to prohibit transfer, it is a restrictive order bill and not transferable. For example: a bill with "pay to Liming only" or "pay to Liming not transferable", means that the money should be paid to Liming, and Liming can not transfer the bill to another person. This kind of bill does not have a wide application in international trade because it lacks negotiability.

※ **Demonstrative order/indicative order**（指示性抬头）

A demonstrative order/indicative order bill of exchange is a bill payable to a specified person or some other person designated by him, without further words prohibiting transfer. For example: a bill with "pay to the order of Liming" or "pay to Liming or order", is negotiable and it can be transferred by the payee, through endorsement and delivery. The negotiability is made safe by endorsement and it has been widely applied in international trade.

※ **Bearer order**(持票人或来人抬头)

"To bearer" means that the money should be paid to the person who is in possession of the bill. That is to say, any person holding a bearer order bill of exchange will become the owner of the bill. For example, a bill with "pay to bearer" is to the order of the bearer, also negotiable, and can be transferred by the bearer through mere delivery and no endorsement is required. It enjoys full negotiability but it is not safe for the absence of endorsement.

- **Date and Place of Issue**

The date of issue refers to the date when the bill is drawn. It performs two functions: one is to make certain that the date of presentation or the date of acceptance is not before the date of issue; the other is to compute the maturity date if the time bill is payable after date of issue.

Although not a requisite, it is recommended that, considering the rules or laws concerning bills of exchange may vary from country to country, the place of issue should be indicated in the bill. When a discrepancy arises concerning the validity of a bill, the validity is normally judged in conformity with the laws of the places of issue.

2. Relatively Necessary Items

- **Tenor**

Tenor means the time to effect payment and it is indicated in the definition of the bill of exchange as "on demand or at a fixed or determinable future time". Tenor is often expressed as the due date or maturity date. A bill must be payable on demand or at a fixed or determinable future time.

- **The Date and the Place of Payment**

Payment will normally be effected in the city where the drawee resides. If a bill does not bear the date of payment, payment should be made the moment the bill is sighted and presented. Besides, some other things like the interest and the rate of interest, the reason of issuing, number of the bill and so on may be included in the bill of exchange.

3. Items at Will

- **Pay this first/second bill**(second/first of the same date and tenor being unpaid)

Bills of exchange usually are made out in duplicate which represent one liability only. If one of them is paid, the other becomes null and void, such wording can be seen in the first copy of bill in duplicate as "second of the same tenor and date unpaid", and in the second copy could be "first of the same tenor and date unpaid". With these wordings, double payments under one set of bills of exchange will be avoided.

我国《票据法》关于汇票必要记载事项的规定

汇票是一种要式文件,应当具备必要的形式和内容。我国《票据法》第 22 条规定,汇票必须记载下列事项:(1)表明"汇票"的字样;(2)无条件支付的委托;(3)确定的金额;(4)付款人名称;(5)收款人名称;(6)出票日期;(7)出票人签章。汇票上未记载前款规定事项之一的,汇票无效。

我国《票据法》第 23 条规定:"汇票上记载付款日期、付款地、出票地等事项的,应当清楚、明确。汇票上未记载付款日期的,为见票即付。汇票上未记载付款地的,付款人的营业场所、住所或者经常居住地为付款地。汇票上未记载出票地的,出票人的营业场所、住所或者经常居住地为出票地。"同时,我国《票据法》第 23 条规定:"汇票上可以记载本法规定事项以外的其他出票事项,但是该记载事项不具有汇票上的效力。"

由此可以看出,我国《票据法》规定的汇票七个必要记载事项均为绝对必要记载事项,缺少任何一个事项均会导致票据无效。付款日期、付款地、出票地等事项则为相对必要记载事项,也称法定记载事项,是指法律规定这些事项应当记载,若不记载,票据仍有效,未记载事项按法律规定行事。

2.2.3 Parties to a Bill of Exchange

Basically, there are three key parties to a bill of exchange: (1) the Drawer; (2) the Drawee; and (3) the Payee. Besides, there might be other parties: (4) the Acceptor; (5) the Endorser; (6) the Endorsee; (7) the Holder; (8) the Discounter; and (9) the Guarantor.

Attention should be paid to the fact that parties ranging from No. (4) to No. (9) may sometimes double for each other or represent one of those in 2 or 3 of the three key parties. Now we'll discuss these parties in detail.

- **The Drawer**(出票人)

The drawer is the person who draws a bill and is normally the exporter or her banker in international trade. She is the first party of the bill. It is the drawer who orders the drawee to pay the sum of money specified. The drawer has to sign the bill and by doing so, she becomes liable immediately upon it. She undertakes that the bill will be paid. If it is not paid, she undertakes that she will compensate the holder or endorser who has to pay it.

- **The Drawee**(付款人)

The drawee is the person who is to pay the money and is usually the importer or the appointed banker under a letter of credit in international trade. In other words, she is the party to whom the bill of exchange is addressed. The drawee is the party who will effect payments to the payee. In this sense, she can also be called the payer and she is another debtor to the bill. However, when the bill is presented to her, the drawee can make a choice whether to honor it (agree to make acceptance or payment) or not (refuse to make acceptance or payment), because she can not prevent any party from drawing a bill of exchange on her to whom she owes no debt. This means that before the drawee agrees to honor the bill of exchange, she is not yet a debtor to the bill, and if she agrees, she acknowledges her indebtedness to the bill and in the case of a time bill, she becomes an acceptor.

- **The Payee**（收款人）

The payee is the party who is to be paid the money on the due date, which may be, and often is, the same person as the drawer and he is usually the exporter himself or his appointed banker in international trade or he may be the bearer of the bill. The payee is the first creditor to the bill and the first legal owner of the instrument. He can either claim payment against the bill or transfer (negotiate) the bill of exchange to another party. If the bill is transferred, he is called the original holder/transferor because the bill is taken away from him while the transferee, the person who takes the bill, becomes the new holder.

Normally, the payee is the drawer. In a bill of exchange, you will find pay me or pay us. We must be familiar with the following expression because it is often used to describe the three immediate parties of a bill of exchange.

The bill is drawn by A on B payable to C. Here, the drawer is A, the drawee is B and the Payee is C. If the drawer and the payee are the same person, the bill may read as: "the bill is drawn by us on ourselves payable to you."

- **The Acceptor**（承兑人）

The acceptor is a special drawee. If the drawee accepts the bill by writing her name or the word "Accepted" together with her name and the date on the bill, she now becomes the acceptor. Her acceptance makes the acceptor assume primary liability to the bill of exchange. As a result, the drawee holds secondary liability to the bill of exchange as mentioned above.

- **The Endorser**（背书人）

The endorser is the party who signs his/her name on the back of a bill for the purpose of negotiation. Being the first holder, the payee will be the first endorser. When the payee becomes the endorser, he transforms himself from a creditor to a debtor because he obligates himself that he will be liable to the endorsee and his/her subsequent parties. If the bill is dishonored, he must compensate the holder of the bill or any subsequent endorser who is obliged to pay it. In the process of negotiation, we will have the first endorser, the second endorser, the third endorser and so forth and the list can go on and on.

- **The Endorsee**(被背书人)

The endorsee is just the party to whom a bill is endorsed by the endorser. He/she becomes the new holder to the bill and is the creditor to the bill. An endorsee occurs in a "special endorsement", where the bill is endorsed to named payee. An endorsee can also become an endorser if he/she wishes to transfer the bill to another party by signing his/her name on its back. And by doing so, he/she transforms himself/herself into a debtor. If the process of negotiation creates a sequence of endorsers, similarly, it will also bring about a series of endorsees. For example, if a bill has been transferred from A to B to C and C is the holder, from the stand point of C, A and B will be his prior parties. If C continues to transfer the bill to D and D to E, then D and E will be called his/her subsequent parties.

- **The Holder**(持票人)

The holder is a party who is in possession of the bill. A holder can be the payee or the endorsee. The payee will always be the original holder and a holder is a creditor to the bill. A person holding a forged bill or one who has gotten a bill payable to the order of another in an illegal way is not a holder, but a wrongful possessor. Only the legal possessor can become the holder. The perfect title to a bill of exchange will be accrued to the holder in due course.

※ **The Holder for value**(付对价持票人)

Value refers to anything which is sufficient to support a simple contract and may be given in the form of goods, services or money. A holder for value is the holder of a bill for which value has been given either by himself/herself or by the prior parties. In the former case, we usually refer to the payee. In the latter case, according to *Bills of Exchange Act*, a holder for value usually refers to the holder when the value is given by the prior parties rather than by himself/herself. For instance, if a bill is drawn by A on B payable to C and accepted by B; C endorses the bill and gives it to D as a gift. Although D gives no value for the bill by himself/herself, he/she is qualified as a holder for value for the reason that the value has already been given by C, his/her prior party. In other words, the rights of a holder for value can not be superior to his/her direct prior party.

※ **The Holder in due course**(正当持票人)

A holder in due course can also be referred to as *bona fide* holder. According to *Bills of Exchange Act*, a holder in due course is the person who is in possession of an instrument, that is: (1) complete and regular on its face[①]; (2) taken before maturity; (3) taken in good faith and for value; and (4) taken without notice of its previous dishonor and without notice of any infirmity in the instrument or defect in the title of the person negotiating it.

---

① A complete and regular bill is the one that contains all the essentials required.

Which person is the holder for value and which party is the holder in due course?

If an instrument has been drawn by A on B payable to C, accepted by B and then delivered to C. Later on, C endorses the instrument and gives it to D as a gift but then D loses it in the street where it is found by E who transfers it for value to F who again endorses it and gives it to G as a gift. C is the payee or the original holder so he can only be the holder for value but not the holder in due course. D obtains the bill as a gift and not for value, he is not a holder in due course but he is qualified as the holder for value because the value has been given and transferred to him by his prior party C. E is a wrongful possessor and cannot be qualified as a holder. F has taken the bill for value and he can establish himself as a holder in due course as long as he takes the instrument in good faith. This means that the defective title of the instrument on the part of E may not prevent F from becoming a holder in due course. G gives no value for the bill and can not be the holder in due course but he can be the holder for value because the value has been given by his prior party F. The full benefits of negotiability do not pass to a holder for value; these benefits are passed on only if the holder for value is also qualified as a holder in due course. When an instrument is dishonored, a holder in due course obtains perfect title to the bill and can claim payment from all parties liable on the instrument and prior parties have no defense to a claim for payment by a holder in due course.

 2-2

正当持票人制度

根据各国票据法及相关法律规定，持票人须是票据权利人，即只有持票人才能行使票据权利。但并不是所有的持票人都能不受票据债务人的任何抗辩理由而享有真正的票据权利。《英国票据法》将持票人分成三类：持票人、对价持票人和正当持票人。只有正当持票人的票据权利不受前手权利瑕疵和对人抗辩的影响，他可以向所有对票据负有义务的当事人主张付款。正当持票人是善意地取得完整、正规的票据并对前手的任何所有权瑕疵毫不知情的人。《美国统一商法典》将持票人分为正当持票人和非正当持票人两类，其正当持票人的概念与英国票据法中基本相同。日内瓦票据法体系并没有正当持票人概念，它是通过抗辩制度和善意取得制度以达到对不同持票人加以相应保护或权利限制的效果。

我国《票据法》没有使用正当持票人的概念，只使用了持票人的概念。但从我国《票据法》第10条第2款、第12条、第13条的规定来看，能够受到我国票据法保护的持票人必须已经支付对价，没有欺诈、胁迫、恶意、重大过失，对曾经发生的抗辩事由不知情。我国应在《票据法》中进一步突现正当持票人的内涵，明确其地位，使此概念清晰化，以更好地保证权利人的利益，维护和促进票据的流通和信用，保障交易安全。

（资料来源：姜琳琳.浅析普通法系的正当持票人制度[J].法制与社会，2008年第9期.）

- **The Discounter**(贴现人)

The term "discounter", not often used, normally refers to the discount house or the bank that discounts bills of exchange on the customers' behalf. By the nature of the arrangement, a discounter is usually a holder for value who is a holder giving value for a bill.

- **The Guarantor**(保证人)

The guarantor is another third party who guarantees the acceptance and the payment of a bill of exchange. The guaranteed can be the drawer, endorser, acceptor or acceptor for honor. The obligations of the guarantor are the same as those of the guaranteed.

2.2.4 Acts of Bills of Exchange

The acts of a bill of exchange refer to the legal acts carried out to bear the obligations to a bill of exchange. Usually, there are three stages for a sight bill of exchange: to draw, to present and to pay. A usance bill of exchange, however, involves more stages like acceptance or some other possible stages.

- **To Issue/ To Draw**(出票)

To issue/draw is the beginning of a bill of exchange. It comprises two acts to be performed by the drawer. One is to draw a bill and sign it; the other is to deliver it to the payee. Thus, the liability of the bill is established and the payee becomes the creditor to the bill.

出票是汇票的起始，它由出票人的两个行为组成：一是开立汇票和签名，二是把汇票转移给收款人。

When issuing a bill, the drawer must draw it correctly and completely, making sure it contains all the essentials stipulated. The drawer must sign the bill as well. A bill without a signature or with a false signature is not valid. A bill can be made in the name of a person, a company or by some other person under his authority. A bill made in this way engages the drawer under the primary liability to it. A bill is not a "voucher of payment" but some "money in credit", which means that the payee's right to the bill will entirely depend on the creditworthiness of the drawer.

Delivery means the transfer of possession from one person to another. Only writing a bill without delivering is invalid. Delivery is an essential act. It is stated in *Bill of Exchange Act* that whatever acts such as issuing, endorsement or acceptance without delivering would be invalid acts. After being drawn and delivered to the payee, the bill becomes irrevocable and in the meantime the drawer engages to the payee and related holders that the bill should be paid or accepted. If it is dishonored by the drawee, the holder has the right of recourse against the drawer who is primarily liable thereon.

Delivery can be divided into two kinds: actual delivery and constructive delivery. Actual delivery means the hand-over of a bill. Constructive delivery, in contrast, means the bill is not physically handed over, but the physical control is transferred through some overt action in respect of it.

- **Endorsement**(背书)

Endorsement means that the holder of a bill transfers the bill by signing his/her name on the back of the bill or together with the name of the transferee (endorsee), which is an act of negotiation. The signature indicates the holder's intention to transfer his/her rights in the bill of exchange. To be valid, an endorsement must satisfy the following criteria: (1) it must be written on the back of the bill; (2) it must be of the entire bill and not part; and (3) if there are two or more payees, all of them must endorse the bill before it is transferred unless one of them has the authority to make endorsement on behalf of all the others.

背书是指汇票的持票人通过在汇票背面签名的方式或共同签名给被背书人来转让汇票。签名表明持有人转让其汇票权利的意图。一份有效背书必须满足以下条件：(1)必须写在汇票背面；(2)必须是完整的汇票而不是一部分；(3)如果有两个或两个以上受款人，他们都必须在汇票转让之前背书，除非其中一人有权作出背书代表所有其他人。

It should also be noted that if an endorsement has the name of the payee or endorsee wrongly named or mis-spelt, or even forged, such things would be disregarded since such a bill can be treated as a bearer bill and a bearer bill can be negotiated and transferred by delivery without any endorsement.

Endorsement is applicable only to negotiable bills of exchange and the negotiability of a bill is determined by the status of its payee, or, in other words, by the bill's type of order. If a bill is of bearer order, no endorsement is required and mere delivery is sufficient to transfer the title of the bill. Endorsement is also not applicable to a restrictive order bill, because this kind of bill has no negotiability and transfer is prohibited.

To an endorsee, all the endorsers and drawers are his/her prior parties. On the other hand, to the endorser and drawer, all the parties to whom he/she transfers the bill are his/her subsequent parties. The prior parties are liable to the subsequent parties for the payment or acceptance of the bill.

Generally speaking, there are four kinds of endorsement:

※ **Special endorsement**(特别背书)

A special endorsement is also called an endorsement in full which specifies an endorsee to whom or to whose order the bill is to be paid, in addition to the signature of an endorser. Thus, if a bill is endorsed "Pay to C" or "Pay to the order of C" above the endorser's signature, no one would expect C can transfer the draft or receive its payment.

For example:

    Pay to the order of E Co., New York (*the endorsee*)
    For ABC Co., New York (*the endorser*)
    Signature (*of the endorser*)

A bill so endorsed remains a demonstrative order bill. It can be further transferred by endorsement and delivery. A series consecutive special endorsements show a clear chain of endorsers. The special endorsement not only shows a chain of endorsers but also gives the holder full right of recourse against the entire prior endorses.

※ **Blank endorsement**(空白背书)

A blank endorsement means that the endorser transfers the bill by signing his/her name without writing the name of the endorsee. In other words, the endorsement normally consists of the signature of the endorser only. It is also referred to as a general endorsement.

For example:

    For ABC Co. , New York   (*the endorser*)
    Signature   (*of the endorser*)

When a blank endorsement is made on a bill, it will transform the original bill from demonstrative order to bearer order. If the bill is to be further transferred, mere delivery is required. On the other hand, a blank endorsement can be transformed to a special endorsement by adding above the endorser's signature such words "pay to" or "pay to the order" of the transferee or some other person.

A holder's legal title to the bill should be proved by consecutive endorsements. Even if the last endorsement is made in blank, he/she is still a legal holder. When a blank endorsement is followed by another blank one, the subsequent party will be deemed as the endorsee of the prior endorsement. Therefore, a series of blank endorsements can also be made consecutive.

※ **Restrictive endorsement**(限制性背书)

Restrictive endorsement is the endorsement prohibiting further transfer of the bill, i. e. the transferee can not transfer his/her right to payment. Restrictive endorsement will transform the demonstrative order to a restrictive order. The transferee can only claim payment against the bill and no further transfer is allowed.

For example:

    Pay to E Bank only…   (*the endorsee*)
    For ABC Co. , New York… (*the endorser*)
    Signature   (*of the endorser*)

Or

    Pay to E Bank not negotiable… (*the endorsee*)
    For ABC Co. , New York… (*the endorser*)
    Signature   (*of the endorser*)

Or

    Pay to E Bank not transferable… (*the endorsee*)
    For ABC Co. , New York… (*the endorser*)
    Signature   (*of the endorser*)

※ **Conditional endorsement**(附条件背书)

A conditional endorsement adding some words that create a specified term or condition to be met before the special endorsee is entitled to receive payment, and the endorser is liable only if the specified term or condition is fulfilled. Two points should be noticed, so far as conditional endorsements, which should not be confused with "unconditional order" stated in the definition of a bill, are concerned. Firstly, a bill of exchange should be made an unconditional order at the time of issuing. But an endorsement can be made conditional. The conditional endorsement does not affect the bill as an unconditional order to pay and it has no binding on the drawer and drawee. Secondly, when he/she agrees to honor the bill, he/she can choose to either honor it under the fulfillment of a certain condition or disregard the condition. In fact, conditional endorsement refers to a conditional delivery, which means that the bill will be delivered to the endorsee only when he/she fulfills the conditions. Conditionally endorsed bill can be further transferred.

附条件的背书有效吗？

A公司与B公司签订购销合同，约定A出售三批原料给B公司，货款由B通过汇票一次性支付。B在交付第二批货后，交给A一张银行汇票，却在背书栏上写着：须在交完货后才付款。请问B公司开具的这张附有交货条件的背书有效吗？

由案例我们可以看出：汇票是出票人签发的，委托付款人在见票时或者在指定日期无条件支付确定的金额给收款人或者持票人的票据。汇票分为银行汇票和商业汇票。因此，汇票的一个重要特征就是无条件支付的委托。汇票应记载付款日期、付款地、出票地等事项，未记载付款日期的，视为见票即付。背书是指在票据背面或者粘单上记载有关事项并签章的票据行为。依据我国《票据法》第24条规定："汇票可以记载本法规定事项以外的其他出票事项，但是该记载事项不具有汇票上的效力。"第33条规定："背书不得附有条件，背书附有条件的，所附条件不具有汇票上的效力。将汇票金额一部分转让的背书或者将汇票金额分别转让给两人以上的背书无效。"《日内瓦汇票和本票统一法公约》也规定，背书必须是无条件的，如附加条件，则条件视同无记载。在英国也否定附加条件的效力，付款人不受条件约束，无论条件是否成就，付款人向被背书人所作付款有效。

B公司给A公司的汇票，如果没有明确注明付款日期，而在背书上记载"须在交完货后才付款"，这样的背书对持有该汇票的A公司和付款银行没有约束力，A公司可持汇票支取货款。如果汇票上明确记载付款日期，则应按规定日期支取。

● **Presentation**(提示)

The act of submitting bill to the payer for acceptance or payment is called presentation. As bill is a kind of choice in action, the holder has to show the bill to the payer so as to prove his/her right to payment. There are two types of presentation, presentation for acceptance and presentation for payment. Presentation for acceptance means that the holder of a usance bill of exchange requires the payer to accept the bill by signing her name on the bill or even writing "Accepted" and the date on the face of it. Presentation for payment means that the holder presents a bill to the payer (or the acceptor of a usance bill of exchange) and requires her (or the acceptor of a usance bill of exchange) to effect payment.

A sight bill of exchange only needs presentation once: presentation for payment, while a usance bill needs twice: the first for acceptance, and the second for payment.

Presentation must be made within the reasonable time. According to *Bills of Exchange Act* 1882, the sight bill should be presented for payment and the usance bill should be presented for acceptance at a reasonable time on a business day before it is overdue. According to *Uniform Law for Bills of Exchange and Promissory Notes* signed at Geneva of 1930, the reasonable time for acceptance is within one year after it is issued, and presentation for payment should be made either on the due date or within two business days after the due date.

Presentation must also be made at the proper place specified on the bill. If no place is specified, the bill should be presented at the drawee or the acceptor's business office. If no business office is specified, the bill should be presented at the drawee or the acceptor's residence.

As most drawees on a bill will be banks, there are three channels for presentation: (1) to do it over the counter of the paying bank; (2) to exchange the bill through a clearing house; and (3) to dispatch the bill to the paying bank for acceptance or payment.

If the bill is duly presented and dishonored by the drawee, the holder will obtain an immediate right of recourse against all the prior parties till the drawer. Should the holder present the bill after the due day, he/she would lose the right of recourse against them, which means the drawee and all the other prior parties are discharged of their liability on the bill.

It is excused that the presentation for payment is delayed owing to circumstances beyond the control of the holder and cannot be attributed to default, misconduct or negligence on his/her part. For example, when the presentation is by post, a postal strike would be a valid cause for delay. Of course, if any of the liable parties waive the need for presentation, the delayed presentation or non-presentation is excused.

提示是指持票人向付款人出示票据,要求其履行票据义务的行为。票据是一种权利凭证,要实现权利,票据持有人必须向付款人提示票据,以便要求实现票据权利。按提示内容的不同,提示分为承兑提示和付款提示。远期汇票向付款人提示要求承兑;即期汇票或已承兑的远期汇票向付款人或承兑人提示要求付款。即期汇票只需一次提示,把承兑和付款一次完成。远期汇票需两次提示,承兑和付款先后完成,其中:(1)承兑提示是持票人在票据到期前向付款人出示票据,要求其承兑或承诺到期付款的行为。承兑提示只是针对远期票据主要是汇票而言的,即期汇票、本票、支票不必作承兑提示;(2)付款提示是指持票人在即期或远期票据到期日向付款人出示票据要求其付款的行为。汇票、本票、支票均需作付款提示。

● **Acceptance**(承兑)

Acceptance acted by the drawee who promises to make payment at the bill maturity. The drawee has no liability on the bill until she signs the bill in such a way as to signify acceptance of liability to pay the money stated in the bill. A valid acceptance requires two acts: one is for the drawee to write the word "Accepted" on the face of a bill and sign below. The mere signature of the drawee, without additional words, is sufficient. The other is for the drawee to return the accepted bill to the payee. In practice, the return of the accepted bill can be replaced by the drawee's issuing of an acceptance notice to the payee. In case of a usance bill after sight, the accepting date is deemed to be the sight date from which the maturity date can be worked out. After acceptance, the drawee will then credit the amount payable to the payee's account at maturity.

承兑是指远期汇票的付款人在汇票上签名,同意按出票人指示到期付款的行为。付款人承兑汇票后即成为承兑人。承兑人的签名表明其承诺付款责任,承兑人不得以出票人的签字是伪造的、背书人无行为能力等理由否认承兑的效力。承兑包括两个动作:第一,写明"已承兑"字样并签名,仅有受票人的签名也有效;第二,将已承兑汇票交付持票人。完成上述两个动作后,承兑就是有效和不可撤销的。

Acceptance can be classified into general acceptance and qualified acceptance. A general acceptance is the one by which the drawee confirms the order given by the drawer without any qualification. While a qualified acceptance is the one by which the drawee accepts the bill with conditions, which means that he/she revises the terms on the original bill. Qualified acceptance could be subdivided into four types as follows.

※ **Conditional acceptance**

The payment to be made by the acceptor depends on the fulfillments of some conditions, for example, acceptance with words "Accepted, June 20 2007, payable after receiving the bill of lading".

※ **Partial acceptance**

The acceptor will pay only part of the amount stated thereon. For example, acceptance with words "Accepted, June 20 2007, payable on amount of $ 300 million only", while the whole amount stated thereon is $ 500 million.

※ **Local acceptance**

The payment will be made only at a particular place specified by the acceptor, for example, acceptance with words "Accepted, June 20 2007, payable at Bank of China and there only".

※ **Time acceptance**

The payment will be changed in comparison with the tenor stated in the original bill. It could be deferred or moved to an earlier date, for example, acceptance with words "Accepted, June 20 2007, payable at 6 months after date".

However, the bill holder is entitled to refuse such qualified acceptance, because a valid acceptance requires: (1) the word "Accepted" must be followed by the drawee's signature without additional word(s); (2) it must not be expressed that the drawee will carry out his/her promise by any other means than the payment of money. The bill can be considered as being dishonored if the holder refuses additional restrictions. The holder will lose his right of recourse when he is not authorized to take qualified acceptance by the issuer and all endorsers beforehand and afterwards. In other words, the obligations of all prior parties are cancelled.

The drawee is allowed to have reasonable time to deliberate whether or not to accept the bill. According to *Bills of Exchange Act* 1882, acceptance is generally to be made at a reasonable hour on a business day subsequent to the presentation of the bill before it is overdue. According to *Uniform Law for Bills of Exchange and Promissory Notes* at Geneva of 1930, acceptance should be made within the first or the second presentation. When the drawee has made his/her acceptance, he/she is known as the acceptor instead of the drawee and becomes primarily liable to the bill. When this happens, the drawer will be secondarily liable to the bill. Only after the bill is accepted by the payer and handed back to the person who presents it for acceptance can an acceptance be considered as being complete.

● **Payment**(付款)

The ultimate purpose for a bill of exchange is to get paid. "Payment" means that the payer pays the amount stipulated in the bill to its holder. In the case of a sight bill, the payer must make payment when the bill is presented to him. In the case of a usance bill, the payer must make payment when it is presented to him/her on the maturity date of the bill. When the holder of the bill has got the payment, he/she must sign his/her name on the bill to indicate that payment has been made in his/her favor and hand the bill back to the payer for his/her file.

付款是指在即期票据或到期的远期票据的持票人向付款人出示票据时,付款人支付票款的行为。付款是票据流通过程的终结,是票据债权债务的最后清偿。在付款时,付款人必须做到以下几点:(1)付款应该由受票人、承兑人完成,而不是出票人或背书人;(2)付款应该是在汇票到期后完成,不能提前进行支付;(3)如果汇票被转移给持票人,银行需要核查背书或至少在支付前鉴定背书的连贯性;(4)付款应该是善意的,即不知道持票人权利的瑕疵。

Only when payment is made in due course will a bill be discharged. The so-called payment in due course includes the following: (1) payment should be made by or on behalf of the drawee or the acceptor and not by the drawer or any endorser[①]; (2) payment should be made on or after the maturity date of the bill and can not be made in advance; (3) payment should be made to the holder and if the bill has been transferred, the bank will check the endorsements or at least the sequence of the endorsement before making payment; and (4) payment should be made in good faith, without knowing that the holder's title thereto is defective. In a word, payment in due course means payment made at or after the maturity of the bill to the holder thereof in good faith and without notice that his/her title to the bill is defective. When the payment is made in due course, it is the final payment and the bill is discharged. That is to say, the drawee's or the acceptor's liability to the bill ends and so does the liabilities of other debtors to the bill such as the drawer and the endorsers, if any.

● **Negotiation and Discount**(议付和贴现)

Negotiation is an process of the act which a bank purchases a bill from its holder at a price less than the face value[②]. The amount of interest charged by a bank on a negotiation is calculated according to the length of time that the bank is going to buy the bill, which is the period between the date of negotiation and the date when the bank gets the proceeds. This period includes the time in getting the exchange begin to become effective. In addition, the bank will deduct the postal charges and stamp duty, if any, plus a commission.

"Discount" means the purchasing of a usance bill of exchange at a discount. Discounting a bill of exchange is to sell a usance bill of exchange that has already been accepted by the drawee but not yet fallen due to a financial institution at a price less than its face value. The process of discounting a bill is called negotiation.

议付是指银行以比票面价值低的折扣从持有者手中购入汇票。银行的议付收益根据银行购入汇票的时间长短来计算,另外银行将扣除邮政费用和印花税及可能有的佣金。

贴现意味着以折扣的方式买入远期汇票,是指远期汇票承兑后尚未到期,由银行或贴现公司从票面金额中扣减按照一定贴现率计算的贴现息后,将净款付给持票人,从而贴息买入票据的行为。

When a bank negotiates a bill, it in fact buys it and then sends it for collection in its own right. When a bank negotiates a bill drawn on a foreign country, it runs the exchange rate risk. After a bank negotiates a bill, it becomes the "holder in due course" of the bill, which means the bank is now the party who takes the bill in good faith for value, and who has the right to claim payment on his/her own behalf, and to sue on the bill when it is dishonored.

---

① The payment made by the drawer or any endorser is not a final payment because he may claim payment from the drawee or the acceptor.

② The interest from the date when the bill is transferred to the maturity date of the bill is deducted before the face value of the bill is paid.

- **Honor and Dishonor**(付款和拒付)

"Honor" refers to the process in which the drawee effects payment or acceptance when a bill is presented to him/her for payment or for acceptance. In contrary, if the drawee refuses to effect payment or acceptance when a bill is presented to him/her for payment or acceptance, the act is called dishonor.

A bill is dishonored more often for non-payment than for non-acceptance. A bill is considered to be dishonored for non-payment when: (1) a drawee is not able or refuses to pay the bill of exchange when it is presented; or (2) the bill remains overdue and unpaid when the presentation is excused, for example, when the drawee is a non-existent person. Besides, a bill is considered to be dishonored when: (1) the drawee refuses to accept it; (2) when the drawee cannot be traced or when the drawee avoids the presentation on purpose, or (3) when acceptance is excused.

付款是指当汇票被提示支付或承兑时受票人付款或承兑的行为。如果付款人拒绝付款或承兑,这种行为被称为拒付。拒付中不付款比不承兑更经常发生。拒付分为以下情形:(1)付款人在汇票被提示时拒绝支付;(2)虽未明确拒付,但在规定时效内未作承兑或付款,比如,受票人不存在。另外,以下情形也被认为拒付:(1)受票人拒绝承兑;(2)受票人避而不见;(3)承兑被当作借口。

When a bill is addressed to more than one drawee, the bill must be presented to all of them for acceptance. In case that a bill was accepted not by all of them, it should be regarded as being dishonored. But when the drawees of a bill are partners or one of them has authority to accept the bill for the rest, the bill can be presented to one of them or the one who has the authority to accept it.

When a bill is dishonored either by non-acceptance or non-payment, the right of recourse will be accrued to the holder at once, which means that the holder may exercise his/her right of recourse against his/her prior endorsers and drawer for payment.

- **Notice of Dishonor**(拒付通知)

Notice of dishonor is an advising act taken by the holder to all endorsers about the dishonor. The notice may be given in writing or in words. The purpose of giving such notice is to inform the drawer and prior endorsers the default of acceptance or payment so that they may get ready to honor the payment. According to the *Bills of Exchange Act* 1882, when a bill of exchange has been dishonored by non-acceptance or by non-payment, a notice of dishonor must be given to the drawer and each endorser; otherwise the holder shall be discharged of the right of recourse against the drawer and all the endorsers. For a holder in due course, however, his/her recourse claim shall not be prejudiced by such an omission. According to the *Geneva's Uniform Law* 1930, the holder's right of recourse shall remain unless the drawer and/or the endorsers do suffer loss due to his/her omission of giving the notice when the holder must compensate for the loss.

拒付通知是持票人将遭到拒付的事实以书面形式通知前手。进行拒付通知的目的是通知出票人和前手承兑或付款的问题以使他们准备付款。根据1882年英国《票据法》,当汇票被拒绝承兑或付款后,必须给出票人和每一个背书人拒付通知,否则持票人不能向其行使追索权。根据1930年《日内瓦统一票据法》,持票人的追索权将会保留,除非出票人和/或背书人由于他的通知疏忽遭受损失,在这种情况下,持票人必须赔偿损失。

Two methods are generally applied to deliver the notice of dishonor to the prior parties and the drawer. One method is that the notice of dishonor must be given on the next business day after the dishonor of the bill of exchange by the holder to his/her direct prior party (parties) who shall do so in quick succession till the notice is given to the drawer. Any party failing to do it shall remain liable to the holder and lose his/her own right of recourse against all his/her prior endorsers and the drawer. For a holder in due course, however, his/her recourse claim shall not be prejudiced by such an omission. It could be shown in Figure 2.1 below.

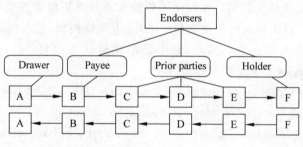

Figure 2.1

The other method is that the holder gives the notice of dishonor to each endorser and the drawer separately in order to retain their liability thereon. In this case, there is no need for each subsequent party to inform his/her direct prior party. Take the above-mentioned as an example. F, the holder, will give notice to prior parties E, D, C, and the payee B till the drawer A. In practice, the first method is preferred as the holder may have no knowledge of every prior party and he/she can be fairly certain that each prior party will pass on the notice.

If the drawer or the endorser states besides his/her name on the bill such wordings as "Notice of dishonor excused", it means that in the event the bill is dishonored, the holder can claim compensation from the drawer or the endorser without giving a notice of dishonor.

如果出票人或背书人在汇票其名字处注有"拒付通知原谅"字样,这意味当汇票拒付后,持票人可以不必进行拒付通知而要求赔偿。

● **Protest**(拒绝证书)

"Protest" is a special term here. It refers to the legal consequence of dishonoring a bill, whether by non-payment or by non-acceptance. Protest is a formal legal procedure, which goes some way towards protecting the payee's rights but which does not guarantee that he can surely get payment. However, it is very important to make every effort to protest in order that recourse is not lost to the liable party.

拒绝证书是由拒付地点的法定公证机构或其他有权出具证书的机构出具的证明拒付事实的书面文件。拒绝证书是一个正式的法律程序,在一定程度上保护卖方权利,但不保证进口商一定付款。

After a bill is dishonored and a notice of dishonor is given, the holder may hand the bill again to a notary party who will present it again to the drawee so as to obtain a legal proof of the act of dishonor. If it is dishonored again, the notary then will draw a protest[①] and return it to the holder together with the bill, against which the holder may exercise his/her right of recourse against the prior parties.

According to the *British Bills of Exchange Act*, foreign bills should be protested whereas inland bill need not. If a foreign bill is not so protested, the holder will lose his/her right of recourse against the prior parties.

Charges for protest paid to the notary public should be for the account of drawer. In order to save this expenditure, the drawer may add wordings "protest waived" or "please do not protest if dishonored", so that he will not be responsible for the protest fee. Charges should be for the account of holder when he/she has made protest on the bill of exchange with indication of protest waived.

● **Recourse and Without Recourse**(追索权和无追索权)

"Recourse" refers to the right of a holder of a bill to demand payment from a prior party who may be the drawer or endorser of the instrument who is primarily liable (normally the acceptor) for failing to pay. In other words, right of recourse means that the holder has the right to claim compensation from the drawer and the endorsers when the bill has been dishonored. The compensation should include the amount payable on the bill with interest, the fees for giving the notice of dishonor and protest and other incurred expenses.

追索是持票人在票据被拒付时,对背书人、出票人及其他债务人行使请求偿还的行为。追索权意味着汇票持有人当被拒付时有权要求出票人和背书人的赔偿。赔偿应该包括:汇票金额及利息、拒付通知及拒付证书的费用及其他产生的费用。

The holder may exercise his/her right of recourse only when he/she has completed the following procedures: (1) presenting the bill to the drawee for acceptance or payment but it is dishonored by non-acceptance or non-payment; (2) giving notice of dishonor to his/her prior party in one business day following the day of dishonor; and (3) making a protest for non-acceptance or non-payment in one business day following the day of dishonor.

---

① A protest is an official certificate that evidences the dishonor and states why it is made.

The recourse claim should be enforced within the legal limit of time, which differs among countries. According to the *British Bills of Exchange Act* it is 6 years; according to the *Geneva Uniform Laws* it is 1 year.

Generally speaking, the holder gives notice to the immediate endorser who in turn gives notice of dishonor to his/her immediate endorser and so on. When more prior parties are involved, the notice is passed up through the chain of endorsers to the last party: the drawer. For the safety sake, the holder should pass the notice of dishonor to all the prior parties in case that the holder should lose recourse if the notice is not passed on.

If any party in the chain fails to pass on the notice of dishonor, it remains liable to the holders, but has no right of recourse against the drawer and his/her prior endorsers unless his/her failure to pass on the notice is caused by circumstances beyond his/her control. Here is a flow of recourse to illustrate it further (see Figure 2.2).

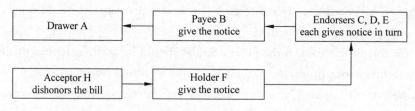

Figure 2.2

If any party in the chain writes "without recourse" on the bill of exchange when it is transferred to him/her, he/she is discharged from the liability and the party concerned has no right of recourse against him/her.

NOTE: All of the legal acts explained above apply to all negotiable instruments, i.e., bill of exchange, promissory note and cheque with some exceptions which will be stated in related section hereunder.

 2-4

汇票遭拒付的法律纠纷

某医药公司 A 于 2009 年 9 月 16 日开立票面金额为 500 万元的银行承兑汇票,期限 6 个月,承兑人为×银行、收款人为某天然气公司 B,后该汇票经 8 次背书至某化工公司 C。2010 年 2 月 20 日,最后持票人 C 向×银行委托收款,×银行在审票时,发现该票第一粘单处通过透光检验有其他印章痕迹,粘单撕毁前法定代表人或授权代理人签章与撕毁后该处签章明显不一致,×银行以此为由退票。收到×银行退票后,C 及该票据其他背书人逐级向其前手追索,直至追索至第五手背书人药品批发公司 D,2010 年 12 月 D 向其前手支付了票据款项。2011 年 4 月 5 日,D 将出票人 A 及×银行告向人民法院,请求法院判决×银行及 A 向其支付 500 万元,并承担延期支付的利息及本案诉讼费。

案例分析:药品批发公司所持有的汇票确实存在瑕疵,×银行对此拒绝付款,合法合规,但 C 提供了各前手出具的证明,该证据足以证明涉案票据及其基础关系的真实性,×银行案例应当向其支付票据款项 500 万元,但×银行作为承兑人,依照法律规定及行业惯例对涉案票据进行审查,并在票据存在瑕疵的情况下,依法依规予以拒付,并不存在过错。综上,二审法院判决如下:(1)×银行向药品批发公司 D 支付票据金额 500 万元;(2)撤销一审法院关于×银行向 D 支付利息的判决;(3)本案一审二审受理费由 D 承担。

由上述案例可知:(1)慎重处理每张瑕疵票据,决定解付时尤甚。我国法律明确规定承兑人有责任审查票据是否存在伪造变造等情形。若承兑人未能识别出伪造、变造的票据而错误付款的,应当承担相关责任。因此在该审查要求下,仅从形式上判断认定背书是否连续显然是不够的。(2)虽然二审法院认为×银行拒绝付款合法合规,但该种判决结果对于该类型瑕疵票据的处理并不完全具有示范作用,即该种判决并不代表对于粘单撕毁的票据进行拒付今后均会得到法院支持。

(资料来源:王良艳.票据遭拒付的法律纠纷[J].法制与社会,2013 年第 9 期.)

2.2.5 Classification of Bill of Exchange

● **According to whether Commercial Documents are Attached thereto**

※ **Clean bill of exchange**(光票)

A clean bill of exchange is the one that is not accompanied by any commercial documents, especially not accompanied by the shipping documents. The drawer of a clean bill of exchange may be a business, an individual, or a bank. The payee may be a business, an individual, or a bank.

Such a bill may be drawn for many purposes, among which are the collection of an open account, the sale of stocks and bonds, payment for services, and other transactions that arise in international trade but for which no shipping documents exist or the shipping documents have for some reason been sent separately to the buyer. Only when the importer is considered to be trustworthy or "open account" is in use can a clean bill of exchange be used. Generally speaking, clean bills of exchange are not often used.

※ **Documentary bill of exchange**(跟单汇票)

A documentary bill of exchange is a bill accompanied by commercial documents like the invoice, B/L, and insurance policy that are needed to complete the export transaction. When a documentary bill is presented to the drawee for payment or for acceptance, the drawee will not effect the payment or acceptance unless the shipping documents are also presented to her.

A documentary bill of exchange is welcomed by both the importer and the exporter in that both have more security. Therefore, in international trade, a documentary bill of exchange is most often used in international settlement.

康茂工艺制品公司陷入"空头光票"陷阱案例

2002年10月中旬，中国康茂公司从网上收到一封来自尼日利亚一家公司的邮件，这家公司的英文名称为 umeer Ventures Nigeria Company（以下简称K公司）。K公司声称在康茂公司的网站上看到康茂公司的产品，对此很感兴趣，并且说这样的棉布包袋在非洲有很大的市场，想试订一批样品，看到产品的质量和工艺后再下订单。两公司随即用电子邮件和电话进行联络。

不久，康茂公司收到K公司寄来的价值6500英镑的光票一张，在随附的信函中说明，康茂公司应尽快按照此金额生产样品并分两次空运到拉各斯；并解释之所以这样做，是为了赶上那里即将举行的两次交易会。

康茂公司一拿到光票就委托中国银行驻马店分行国际营业部验证真伪，经过鉴定证实了该光票的真实性。确认后，康茂公司委托中行办理托收解付手续。一个月后，接中行通知光票退回，因为K公司所在英国的银行账户上没有存款，无法进行结算，建议通知康茂公司通过其他方式索款。但这时公司两票货早已发出，如果K公司已经把货提走，康茂公司将毫无办法，钱货两空。

由上述案例可知：出口企业在国际贸易中要学会保护自己，始终提高警惕，不要因为金额小就忽视任何一笔交易或急于拓展市场而过分迁就客户，要利用好外汇指定银行等机构信息广泛、相对准确的特点，多方了解客户，防止因不了解客户导致被骗。另外，根据国际贸易惯例和经验，建议出口企业在选择支付手段时应优先考虑跟单信用证或出口保理。

（资料来源：单书珩.出口企业警惕："空头光票"陷阱[J].中国外汇管理，2003年第9期.）

- **According to the Tenor**

  ※ **Sight bill of exchange**（即期汇票）

A sight bill is a bill which is payable on demand, or at sight, or on presentation, and in which no time for payment is expressed. It means that the drawee will be required to pay at once when she sees the bill or when the bill is presented to her for payment, so the date of presentment is the due date to effect payment. If no time of payment is stated in a bill, it will be treated as a sight bill of exchange. A sight bill of exchange is also called a demand bill, and which is usually expressed in the following ways:

-On demand pay…

-On presentation pay…

-At sight pay…

A sight bill of exchange is used when the exporter wants to sell goods to the importer for immediate payment. In some countries it is customary for the drawee to delay payment of a sight bill of exchange until the merchandise arrives. For this reason the exporter should always have an understanding with the customer.

※ Usance bill of exchange(远期汇票)

A usance bill of exchange is the bill that specifies payment a certain number of days after sight, which can also be called time bill or term bill. The date on which the drawee/acceptor sights the bill is considered as the date on which the bill is accepted. The acceptor adds the date to his/her acceptance. In this way the date of payments is fixed. The date on which payment should be effected is called maturity date of the bill. A usance bill of exchange is usually expressed in the following ways:

① **Payable at a fixed time after sight**(见票后定期付款)

The sight here refers to the accepting date. Accepting a bill or acceptance can be understood as a formal promise from the drawee to pay when the bill falls due and the promise is given when the drawee sees the bill. For this type of bill, acceptance is a must for the purpose of determining the actual due date. For example, "Pay 30 days after sight..." means 30 days after the accepting date is the due date to effect payment.

② **Payable at a fixed time after date**(出票后定期付款)

The date here refers to the issuing date of the bill. For example, "Pay 60 days after date..." means that the due date will be 60 days after the issuing date. Although accepting is not needed to calculate the due date for this type of bill, acceptance is recommended for the purpose of making certain of the obligations of the drawee to the bill.

③ **Payable at a fixed future date**(定日付款)

In practice, a bill is usually made at a fixed time after the B/L date. For example, "pay 3 months after the B/L date..." is a valid bill because the B/L date is a determinable future date. Another bill "pay 1 month after the death of B..." is also a normal bill because though the time of happening may be uncertain, the event is sure to happen. However, a bill which is payable on arrival of goods at a specified port or on a person's marriage can not be a valid one. In these cases, at the time when the bill is drawn, no one can tell whether the event is going to take place, so the bill will be regarded as conditional instructions. For example, "Pay 30 days after the ship 'Dongfang' reaches the port of London" is unacceptable as bill of exchange.

How to calculate the due date?

If a bill is payable at a fixed time after sight, after date or after the happening of a specific event, the time of payment is calculated by counting in the date of payment but counting out the accepting date, the issuing date or the date of happening of the specified event. After calculation, if the date of payment falls on a non-business day, the bill shall be payable on the succeeding business day.

If a bill is payable at a fixed time from a fixed date, then this fixed date should be counted in.

> If a bill is payable at X months after sight/date/stated date, the word "month" here means a calendar month and the date of payment should fall on the corresponding date of the month due.

- **According to the Drawer**

  ※ **Commercial bill of exchange**(商业汇票)

  A commercial bill of exchange refers to a bill issued by one trader on another or on a bank. It is also called trade bill. In international payments, the drawer of a commercial bill of exchange is normally the exporter, who draws a bill for the purpose of getting payment for the goods he sells. A commercial bill of exchange is usually accompanied by shipping documents.

  ※ **Banker's bill of exchange**(银行汇票)

  A Banker's bill of exchange is a bill drawn by a bank on another bank, it is also called bank bill of exchange. In other words, a banker's bill of exchange is an order to pay a sum of money (a bill of exchange) drawn payable to order (if drawn to bearer, it is not a valid bank bill of exchange) by a bank as drawer on the same bank as drawee. In international payments, after a bank bill of exchange is issued, it is normally given to the remitter (usually the importer) for him/her to send to the bank nominated by the exporter. Usually, the bill of exchange is sent together with a letter or a copy of the invoice if the payment is concerned with a consignment of goods. On the other hand, the bank drawing the bill of exchange must send a notification of payment to the overseas paying bank so that the latter can cheque the bill of exchange presented to it. Occasionally, the bill of exchange may be sent to the beneficiary on behalf of the customer.

- **According to the Acceptor**

  ※ **Commercial acceptance bill of exchange**(商业承兑汇票)

  A commercial acceptance bill of exchange is a usance bill of exchange accepted by a business or individual.

  ※ **Banker's acceptance bill of exchange**(银行承兑汇票)

  A banker's acceptance bill of exchange is a usance bill of exchange accepted by a bank. This kind of bill is more preferable and negotiable than the commercial acceptance bill of exchange and more acceptable in the discount market.

- **Accommodation[①](Finance) Bill of Exchange**(通融汇票)

  An accommodation bill of exchange is a bill to which a party has given its acceptance for the accommodation of the drawer. In other words, an accommodation bill is a bill of exchange that is signed by someone (the accommodation party) who promises to pay it to

---

① The word "accommodation" here is a special term, which means facilitating funds.

help another person to raise money.

An accommodation bill is used for straight borrowing/financing transactions in which there are no related transactions such as imports or exports. It is different from the normal bill in that the "value" is not to be given by the drawer to the acceptor. In contrast, the drawer of a normal bill is supposed to get payment.

The aim of an accommodation bill of exchange is normally to give help to someone who is not himself totally credit worthy. In other words, the accommodation party lends his/her name (by accepting the bill of exchange) to somebody else (the drawer of an accommodation bill of exchange) for the latter to raise money. The drawer of an accommodation bill of exchange is accommodated by the accommodation party. The drawer is liable to provide the funds to pay the bill of exchange when it matures.

The Accommodation bill of exchange is widely used by corporations to borrow money for fixed short periods. The drawer of an accommodation bill of exchange is authorized by the drawee (usually a bank) to draw the bill of exchange and then the drawee accepts the bill of exchange, which indicates that the drawee starts to undertake to pay the bill of exchange on the due date. The drawer of an accommodation bill of exchange is the borrower, the principal debtor.

 2-6

警惕"光票"贴现汇票的潜在风险

"光票"贴现汇票就是没有真实贸易背景,为融资而开出和贴现的银行承兑汇票。当中小企业融资难而银行依赖信贷主业收益低时,银行承兑汇票的承兑与贴现,就会受到市场追捧,也会得到金融管理层的大力支持。以2001年中国工商银行上海票据中心建立为标志,银行承兑汇票的贴现量,逐年翻番,利率从高到低,先行参与贴现的少数银行因此获得超额利润,现在则全国各家银行低价争利,异地上门服务。这种票据一开就是千万元甚至上亿元,还未出笼就被贴现市场上的中介热传,四处寻找出价最低的贴现银行。在包头、大连、烟台、株洲、湛江、太原和江浙地区,这样的票据层出不穷。

开出银行承兑汇票,现行的银行政策是,企业必须缴付30%以上的保证金;银行的通常标准是50%。也就是说,企业开出1亿元的"光票",相当于由银行创造了5000万元的基础货币。巨量货币创造出来做什么用了?用于生产和贸易肯定是有的,但不少是用在了资本市场和房地产上。据有关研究机构的报告称,目前企业贷款的80%没有按照规定进入实业投资或贸易领域;招商银行的一份报告说该行近50%的贷款规模用于票据贴现。

"光票"贴现,其罪主要有三:一是肢解贴现流程,形成资金分流,可构成贪污罪、行贿罪等;二是制作假单证,是为造假罪;三是促成资金流动性过剩,可谓扰乱经济金融秩序罪。钱潮滚滚,中央银行稳定货币的政策受到巨大挑战。

(资料来源:张从文.流动性过剩大溃口[J].中国市场,2007年第5期.)

2.2.6 Advantages of a Bill of Exchange

In international trade, negotiable instruments have always been used. The bill of exchange has been oiling the wheels of international trade for centuries. The main advantages of a bill of exchange are concluded as follows.

- Representing written evidence of a debt, the due date of which is fixed. As evidence of a debt, the bill of exchange can be used in a court of law in an effort to get payment.
- Facilitating the level of business activity and promoting transactions by providing a freely negotiable document acceptable to anyone. With an accepted bill of exchange, the exporter is guaranteed with more security, because the importer is legally bound to pay.
- Making the exporter capable of keeping his goods under control by using his banks until the time of payment (D/P) or of acceptance (D/A).
- Exerting vital functions in documentary credits which constitute an important element in international trade. In common, a bill of exchange plays a key part in documentary collection which is also a principle method of payment in international trade.
- Bearing a very high degree of confidence that originates from its negotiable status.
- *The Uniform Rules of Customs and Practice* (UCR) issued by ICC makes the bill of exchange ready to be accepted as an integral part of international trade, and trade organizations and banks all over the world are ready to accept a bill of exchange.
- Being drawn for periods to meet the trade terms that have been agreed on by the exporter and the importer. A bill of exchange is used as a means of providing the buyer a period of credit (time in which to pay).

2.3 Promissory Note(本票)

2.3.1 Definition of a Promissory Note

As defined in the *Bills of Exchange Act* 1882 *of the United Kingdom*, promissory note is an unconditional promise in writing made by one person (the maker) to another (the payee or the holder), signed by the drawer, engaging to pay on demand or at a fixed or determinable future time a sum certain in money, to or to the order of a specified person or to the bearer. See Chart 2.2:

```
┌─────────────────────────────────────────────────────────────────┐
│                        PROMISSORY  NOTE                         │
│  No. × × ×                                         New York,    │
│  March 15,2015                                                  │
│  USD 50000                                                      │
│     On demand we promise to pay to the order of Henry Co. ,the sum of USD fifty thousand only. │
│                                                    For A Company│
└─────────────────────────────────────────────────────────────────┘
```

Chart 2.2

本票是出票人向收款人签发的,保证即期或定期或在将来某一确定日期,对收款人或其指定人或持票来人支付一定金额的无条件支付承诺。我国现行《票据法》只承认银行本票,出票人资格由中国人民银行审定。

2.3.2　Characteristics of a Promissory Note

- A promissory note is an unconditional promise to pay.
- There are only two basic parties to a promissory note, i. e. , the maker and the payee. The maker corresponds to the drawer as well as the drawee of a bill of exchange. The maker can be more than one person and they are jointly and separately responsible for the payment of the promissory note.
- There is no need to accept a promissory note if it is payable at a fixed or determinable future time, because in all cases the maker is the primarily liable party.
- Promissory notes can be made only by bankers in countries like China, but sometimes commercial firms are also allowed to be the maker in countries like the US and France. Promissory notes made by bankers are called cashier' cheque or cashier's order. They are all sight notes. And in international trade, most promissory notes are drawn by bankers that are not negotiable. Moreover, a promissory note is sometimes used in international trade especially when the settlement is made by remittance.
- Promissory notes other than those issued by bankers are not very widely used in modern commercial transactions. Bearer promissory notes payable on demand and issued by bankers are equivalent to bank notes of large denomination, which may cause inflation. As a result, they are prohibited by the government in many countries.

2.3.3　Essentials to a Promissory Note

According to the relevant law in China, a promissory note usually should include the following items: (1) the word "promissory note"; (2) unconditional promise to pay the amount of money; (3) status of the payee; (4) maker's signature; (5) the date of making the promissory note; (6) tenor of the payment; (7) places of payment and issuing[①].

In conformity with the *Uniform Law on Bills of Exchange and Promissory Notes* 1930 *of Geneva*, a promissory note requires: (1) the words "Promissory Note"; (2) an unconditional promise to pay; (3) payee or his order; (4) maker's signature; (5) date and place of issue; (6) period of payment; (7) a certain sum of money; and (8) place of payment.

2.3.4 Classification of Promissory Note

- **According to the Tenor**

※ **Sight promissory note(即期本票)**

Sight promissory note is a promissory note that is payable when the promissory note is sighted. In the event that no tenor is indicated on the note, the note is deemed to be a sight one. Banker's notes are usually made on demand.

※ **Term promissory note(远期本票)**

Term promissory note is a promissory note that is payable at a fixed or determinable future time.

- **According to the Maker**

※ **Commercial promissory note(商业本票)**

Commercial promissory note is a promissory note whose maker is a firm or a trader. By issuing a commercial promissory note, the firm can raise funds from the public. However, because of its low creditworthiness, commercial promissory note is acceptable only when it is guaranteed by the firm's or trader's bank. For this reason, a commercial promissory note is generally replaced by a letter of guarantee.

※ **Banker's promissory note(银行本票)**

Banker's promissory note is a promissory note whose maker is a bank. A banker's promissory note made by a bank payable to a specified person can be deemed as cash. A sight banker's promissory note payable to bearer is a "legal tender" which is part of the currency realm and an uncontrolled issue of banker's sight bearer order notes by commercial banks will certainly disturb a country's monetary system. Therefore, commercial banks can only issue notes payable to a specified person. Banker's sight bearer order notes are put under special statutory basis and can be issued by the central bank or the authorized banks only.

NOTE: A commercial promissory note can be a sight promissory note or a term promissory note; whereas a banker's promissory note is always a sight one.

---

① If a promissory note does not indicate the places of payment and issuing, the business quarter of the maker of the promissory note is taken as the place of making payment and issuing.

● **International Money Order**(国际小额本票)

Usually denominated in US dollars with the maximum amount USD 2500, international money order is issued by clearing banks in New York for the payee's convenience when he is traveling outside the U. S. It can also be used to settle payments in international trade when the amount is small. International money order is favorable to the maker because the clearing bank can take hold of the capital from the time of purchasing the note by the payee to the time that it is exchanged for collection.

● **Treasury Bill**(国库券)

Treasury bill is also referred to the government bond with the maker to be the Ministry of Finance. In Britain, it is a short-dated government security. Treasury bills bear no formal interest, but are promises to pay in 91 days' time. It is issued at a discount on their redemption price.

2-7

我国设立商业本票的时机成熟了吗？

商业本票，又称一般本票或者商业期票，是企业为筹措短期资金，由企业以自己的信用担保发行的一种本票，它与银行本票相对而言。欧美及我国的台湾地区都认可商业本票和银行本票的合法效力，但我国《票据法》第73条第2款规定："本法所称本票，是指银行本票。"可见我国只承认银行本票，不承认其他任何企业签发的商业本票。

在我国计划经济时期，银行与一般企业的性质不同，法律地位也不同，承认银行信用，限制甚至禁止商业信用，均是由我国当时信用体系不完善的特殊背景所决定的。时至今日，我国的市场信用体系已逐步建立，很多企业特别是一些大型企业的信用日趋提高。况且，与2004年《票据法》同年公布的《中国人民银行法》、《商业银行法》已经明确规定："我国的银行，除了中国人民银行以外，都是商业银行，其性质均是企业法人。"也就是说，在市场经济的运作中，商业银行和非金融企业已具有同等的法律地位。而《票据法》仍然排斥商业信用，这种制度设计能否对我国市场经济的发展起到促进作用，值得商榷。市场经济立法应当体现"身份平等"的精神，"身份平等"才是真正的契约精神，我国票据市场经营主体应实现"从身份到契约"转变。

与真实票据(主要是商业汇票)相比，商业本票没有真实的交易背景，代表了纯粹融资性的债权债务关系。在当今发达国家金融体系内，商业票据市场已成为货币市场的重要组成部分。随着经济社会的发展和融资模式的多元化，融资性票据具有一定的市场需求。虽然我国在法律上对融资性票据进行了限制，但十几年来，我国企业还是积累了可资利用的经验。特别是2004年中央银行颁布了《证券公司短期融资券管理办法》，证券公司短期融资券实质上就是专用于大型企业的融资性商业本票。证券融资券的成功发行，也为商业本票制度的建立打下了坚实的基础。深圳九家企业1996年首发商业本票,中集集团曾于1996年、1997年通过国际市场分别发行5000万美元和7000万美元的一年期无担保商业票据;中化国际也于2000年11月在美国发行了25亿美元的商业票据,目前,中化已连续8年在美国成功发行商业票据。另外,部分企业在证券市场上发行的期限在1年和1年以内的短期融资券和部分金融机构发行的短期金融债券也具备了融资性票据的特征这充分说明融资性的商业本票在我国有生存的空间。

根据当前经济、金融发展的需要,在规范管理的前提下,选择票据业务管理组织经验、制度建设经验较强,物质和技术条件准备比较充分,市场经济和信用程度较高,票据专营机构有一定发展的地区,试点商业本票业务,为我国商业票据业务和票据市场的发展探索新的途径,是完全可行的。

(资料来源:王际航.对我国商业本票制度的法学探析[J].河北青年管理干部学院学报,2009年第2期.)

2.3.5 Parties to a Promissory Note

- **The Maker/The Issuer**(制票人/出票人)

The maker of a promissory note is the principal debtor who engages to pay the promissory note within the tenor. The maker is just the payer of the note, and he/she must realize that in whose favor he is making the promise.

- **The Payee**(收款人)

The payee is the party to be paid the money on the due date. He/She is the first creditor to the promissory note and the first legal owner of the instrument. If the promissory note is transferred, he/she is called the original holder/transferor.

- **The Endorser**(背书人)

A promissory note can be endorsed in the same way as a bill of exchange or cheque, which we will introduce next. The endorser is liable to pay the promissory note or compensate the holder (or any subsequent endorser) for non-payment provided that the necessary proceedings in dishonor have been taken.

2.3.6 Difference between a Promissory Note and a Bill of Exchange

Although a promissory note has much in common with a bill of exchange, there are differences between the two, which lies in:

- A promissory note is a promise to pay, whereas a bill of exchange is an order to pay. The maker of a promissory note is the person who draws an instrument on himself/herself. That means the payment will be made by the maker himself/herself. So the maker of a note will make a "promise" to the payee that he/she will make payment at maturity, rather than an "order" to himself/herself to make such a payment. The maker is primarily liable on a promissory note. However, a bill of exchange is an order to pay. The order is given by the drawer to the drawee. The drawer is primarily liable to a sight bill or a usance bill before acceptance and the acceptor assumes the primary liability only after the bill is accepted by him/her.

- There are only two immediate parties to a promissory note, namely, the maker and the payee, whereas there are three basic parties to a bill of exchange, namely, the drawer, the drawee, and the payee. The maker and the payee cannot be the same person for a promissory note, whereas a bill of exchange allows the drawer and the payee to be the same person.

- Unlike a bill of exchange, when a promissory note is dishonored, it is not necessary to protest it so as to retain the liability of the maker and endorser.

- A promissory note is never accepted because the maker of a promissory note is the payer of it while a usance bill of exchange should be accepted. So the maker of a promissory note is totally liable on the note while the drawer of a bill of exchange is liable on the bill before it is accepted and the acceptor is primarily liable on the bill after it is accepted.

- If a bill of exchange is drawn on more than one person and it is accepted in the usual way, the acceptors are always held to be "jointly" liable. But a promissory note with more than one maker carries "joint" or "joint and several" liability, whichever is set out in the promissory note.

- A promissory note is a solo note when issued, whereas a bill of exchange is usually in a duplicate set when issued. When one set of a bill is accepted or paid, the other becomes void automatically.

2.4 Cheque(支票)

2.4.1 Definition of a Cheque

A cheque is an unconditional order signed by the drawer who entrusts the bank or other financial organizations to pay a certain sum in money to the payee or the bearer of it. In other words, A cheque is a bill of exchange drawn on a banker and payable on demand, which is a special piece of paper used to transfer money from one person to another instead of using the actual money itself.

支票由出票人签发，委托办理支票存款业务的银行或其他金融机构在见票时无条件支付确定的金额给收款人或持票人。支票都是即期的。各国法律禁止签发空头支票，为了避免出票人开出空头支票，保证支票提示时付款，支票的收款人或持票人可要求银行对支票"保付"(certified to pay)。保付是由付款银行在支票上加盖"保付"戳记，以表明在支票提示时一定付款。支票一经保付，付款责任即由银行承担。

The drawer writes the cheque which is usually a pre-printed form provided by his/her bank and gives the cheque to the payee who either cashes it or pays it into his/her own account. Chart 2.3 is the sample of cheque.

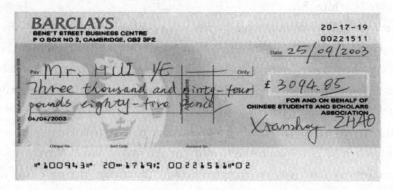

Chart 2.3

One of the key legal acts on a cheque is still issuing. Besides, there are also acts of endorsement, payment, dishonor, notice of dishonor and recourse, etc. under a cheque, but without acceptance because a cheque is payable at sight.

Dishonoring a cheque would also happen somewhat despite of bank being the payer. This, however, will not hurt the credit reputation of banks because they are never the debtor of cheque (except for confirmed cheque). Dishonor normally arises out of the wrongful acts of issuing, endorsing or something else. The probable reasons of dishonor could be: (1) signature not in consistent with the agreed one; (2) insufficient funds; (3) amount in words and in figures not consistent; (4) lack of amounts in words; (5) out of date or stale; (6) lack of payee's endorsement; and (7) incorrect issuing.

2.4.2 Essentials to a Cheque

In conformity with the *Uniform Law on Bills of Exchange and Promissory Notes* 1930 *of Geneva*, a cheque requires: (1) the word "Cheque"; (2) unconditional pay order in writing; (3) the name and address of the paying bank; (4) drawer's signature; (5) place and date of issue; (6) the words "at sight"; (7) A certain sum of money; and (8) payee or his/her order.

NOTE: A cheque's date of issue is critical, used as the basis of calculating its validity. A cheque should be presented within its validity; otherwise it is null and void. It, however, does not mean that the payment obligation to the drawer is cancelled. Period of validity set by the *Geneva Uniform Laws* is 8 days from the issuing date within a nation, 20 days within a continent, and 70 days beyond a continent; the period set by the British Act is not clearly defined, but within a reasonable time. *Laws of People's Republic of China on Negotiable Instruments* specifies: "the cheque holder should present for payment within 10 days from the issuing date."

2.4.3　Features of a Cheque

- A cheque must be unconditional.
- A cheque must be drawn on a bank.
- A certain sum in money must be written on a cheque, which should be signed by the drawer, both in words and figures.
- The date of a cheque is not essential in that it can be antedated, post-dated or dated on a non-business day.
- The payee may be bearer, a specified person or his/her order.

2.4.4　Parties to a Cheque

● **The drawer**(出票人)

The drawer is the person making out the cheque. He/she should be a depositor keeping an account current in the paying bank. When he/she draws a cheque, it is his/her responsibility to make sure that there is enough balance in his/her account to cover the cheque amount. Otherwise, the cheque will be dishonored.

● **The drawee**(受票人)

The drawee is the banker with which the drawer maintains an account, and on whom the cheque is drawn and to whom the order to pay is given.

● **The collecting bank**(代收行)

The payee's bank is the bank which collects/obtains payment for its customer from the paying bank, namely the drawer's bank. When a customer cashes a personal cheque at his/her own bank, the bank is both the paying bank and collecting bank.

2.4.5　Classification of Cheque

● **Uncrossed Cheque**(未划线支票)

An uncrossed cheque does not have to be paid through a bank account, and payment can be made over the counter, i.e. in cash.

● **Crossed Cheque**(划线支票)

A crossed cheque is the one on the face of which two parallel lines are printed. A crossed cheque cannot be cashed; money is transmitted only through the banks, which implicates that a crossing is in effect an instruction by the drawer or holder to the paying bank, to pay the fund to bank only instead of over the counter of the paying bank. A cheque can be crossed by the drawer, the payee or the collecting bank. Usually there are two ways of crossing:

※ **General crossings**(普通划线)

A general crossing is the usual type of crossing. A general crossing consists of two parallel transverse, or more common, bevel lines across the face of cheque without indicating the name of collecting bank. The effect of a general crossing is to make the cheque payable only through another banker which must be deposited into a bank account for clearing.

※ **Special crossings and "not negotiable" crossing**(特别划线和"不可流通"划线)

A special crossing consists of the name of a particular bank and often a particular branch, which is entitled to present the cheque for payment.

The difference between the general crossings and the special crossings is that a specially crossed cheque must be lodged in an account with the bank stipulated in the special crossings and not with any bank, while a generally crossed cheque is lodged in an account with any bank.

When "Not Negotiable" is added to the special crossings, this ensures that no one can obtain a good title unless he/she is the actual and true owner. So this form of crossings gives excellent protection to the drawer, because if a cheque is marked with "Not transferable", whether it is accompanied by crossings or not, it is valid only between the drawer and the payee. In other words, it cannot be transferred by the payee to anybody else.

- **Certified Cheque**(保付支票)

A certified cheque is certified by the drawee bank. Once a cheque is certified by the drawee bank, all other obligors on the cheque will be discharged of the liability of the payment.

- **Traveler's Cheque**(旅行支票)

A traveler's cheque can be either considered as a promissory note or a cheque. It is a promissory note because it is drawn by the issuing bank upon itself payable to a traveler. However, a customer who wishes to obtain a traveler's cheque should first make payment equivalent to the face value to its issuer. Then as a payee, the customer can cash the cheque or make use of it to pay for the commodities he/she bought or services he/she enjoyed abroad. To the customer, purchasing a traveler's cheque is similar to depositing money into the issuing bank, while to cash is like to withdraw the money from the issuing bank or his/her agents. So it can also be called a cheque. Similar to the international money order, the major advantage for the traveler's cheque is the easiness to carry and the safety to use because they are replaceable. Here is a sample of traveler's cheque(see Chart 2.4):

2.4.6 Difference between a Cheque and a Bill of Exchange

- A bill of exchange may be drawn upon any person, whereas a cheque must be drawn upon a banker.
- Unless a bill is payable on demand, it is usually accepted, whereupon the acceptor is the primarily liable party. A cheque need not be accepted for it is payable only on

初签栏　　　　　支票号码　　　转让栏　　　复签栏　　　日期栏

Chart 2.4

demand and the drawer is the party primarily liable.

- A bill must be presented for payment when due, or else the drawer will be discharged. Whereas a cheque must be presented for payment within a reasonable or certain period, such as 30 days according to the regulations of the country concerned. The drawer of a cheque is not discharged even though it has not been presented for payment within the stipulated time unless the delay in presentation incurs losses to the drawer.

 2-8

上海京元国际物流诉上海富岭隐天国际货运代理公司支票追索权纠纷案

2011年5月,富岭因与美通公司有业务关系,向美通公司出具了一张上海银行支票作为担保,支票上盖有富岭公司的财务专用章、法定代表人印鉴和付款账号,其余均为空白;支票复印件(含存根联)由徐×签收。

2013年10月23日,富岭公司办理了上述支票银行账户的撤销手续。2013年12月12日,京元公司持票向银行提示付款。当时,支票正面记载:出票日期2013年12月12日,收款人上海中翱国际货物运输代理有限公司,金额为人民币45385元,用途为运费,密码一栏空白;支票背面记载:中翱公司背书给京元公司,背书人签章处盖有中翱公司财务专用章和徐×个人印鉴。次日,上海银行以"已销户"为由退票。

本案例所涉支票在向银行提示付款时记载完整,属有效票据。支票未记载密码不影响效力。京元公司以背书方式合法取得支票,有权行使票据追索权,富岭公司不能以账户撤销为由拒绝承担票据责任。二审判决:富岭公司应于判决生效后10日内支付京元公司支票款45385元及相应利息(以45385元为本金,按中国人民银行规定的企业同期流动资金贷款利率,从2013年12月13日计算至实际清偿日);二审诉讼费用均由富岭公司负担。

(资料来源:范德鸿.支票账户撤销不能免除出票人的票据责任[J].上海政法学院学报,2015年第1期.)

★ Key Words

Bill of exchange(汇票)　　　　　　　Unconditional order(无条件支付命令)
The holder in due course(正当持票人)　To Issue/ To Draw(出票)
Endorsement(背书)　　　　　　　　Presentation(提示)
Acceptance(承兑)　　　　　　　　　Payment(付款)
Negotiation and Discount(议付和贴现)　Honor and Dishonor(付款和拒付)
Notice of Dishonor(拒付通知)　　　　Protest(拒绝证书)
Recourse(追索权)　　　　　　　　　Clean bill of exchange(光票)
Documentary bill of exchange(跟单汇票)　Sight bill of exchange(即期汇票)
Usance bill of exchange(远期汇票)　　Commercial bill of exchange(商业汇票)
Banker's bill of exchange(银行汇票)　Accommodation Bill of Exchange(通融汇票)
Promissory Note(本票)　　　　　　　Sight promissory note(即期本票)
Term promissory note(远期本票)　　　Commercial promissory note(商业本票)
Banker's promissory note(银行本票)　International Money Order(国际小额本票)
Treasury Bill(国库券)　　　　　　　Cheque(支票)
Uncrossed Cheque(未划线支票)　　　　Crossed Cheque(划线支票)
Certified cheque(保付支票)　　　　　Traveler's Cheque(旅行支票)

★ Exercise

一、单项选择(Exclusive Choice Question)

1. A bank issues a draft and makes another bank as the drawee, and the character of this draft is (　　).

　　A. commercial draft　　　　　　　B. bank's draft
　　C. commercial acceptance draft　　D. bank's acceptance draft

2. Contrast to the means of payment, a traveler's cheque is (　　) in the character.

　　A. promissory note　　　　　　　B. bill of exchange
　　C. cheque　　　　　　　　　　　D. letter of credit

3. Which of the following is not the basic party of draft. (　　)

　　A. drawer　　B. drawee　　C. payee　　D. endorser

4. 在汇票背书转让过程中,只有(　　)。

　　A. 背书人具有向付款人要求付款的权利
　　B. 持票人具有向付款人要求付款的权利
　　C. 出票人具有向付款人要求付款的权利
　　D. 承兑人具有向付款人要求付款的权利

5. 票据的作成,形式上需要记载的必要项目必须齐全,各个必要项目又必须符合票据法律规定,方可使票据产生法律效力。这是票据的(　　)性质。

　　A. 要式性　　B. 设权性　　C. 提示性　　D. 流通转让性

6. 汇票的付款期限的下述记载方式中,( )必须由付款人承兑后才能确定具体的付款日期。
    A. at sight   B. at ×× days after sight
    C. at ×× days after date   D. at ×× days after shipment

7. 以下哪一个不是汇票与本票的区别( )。
    A. 前者的主债务人会因为承兑人发生变化,后者的主债务人不会发生变化
    B. 前者可能会开一式两份,后者只有一份
    C. 前者使用过程中需要承兑,后者则不需要承兑
    D. 前者是无条件支付承诺,后者则要求他人付款

8. 以下哪个不属于旅行支票的特点( )。
    A. 面额固定   B. 不能挂失   C. 兑取方便   D. 携带安全

二、多选题(Multiple Choice Question)

1. 下列哪些属于汇票绝对必要记载的项目( )。
    A. 出票地   B. 付款时间   C. 付款人名称   D. 出票人签字

2. 汇款头寸的偿付表现为( )。
    A. 汇款双方银行有往来账户时,可直接通过账户收付
    B. 汇款双方银行在同一代理行开有往来账户,可通过代理行转账
    C. 汇款双方国家如订立支付协定,则通过清算账户办理
    D. 汇款双方银行通过各自的代理行办理

3. 汇款业务采用"中心汇票"的优点在于( )。
    A. 中心汇票的流通性较强   B. 银行可占用客户资金
    C. 汇票可代替现金流通   D. 不占用汇出行的资金

4. 票据的基本关系人有( )。
    A. 出票人   B. 背书人   C. 被背书人   D. 付款人

5. 汇票与本票的区别在于( )。
    A. 前者是无条件支付承诺,后者则要求他人付款
    B. 前者可能会开一式两份,后者只有一份
    C. 前者使用过程中需要承兑,后者则不需要承兑
    D. 前者的主债务人会因为承兑人发生变化,后者的主债务人不会发生变化

6. 国际货款收付在采用非现金结算时的支付工具是( )。
    A. 货币   B. 支票   C. 汇票   D. 本票

7. 一张汇票,可以是一张( )。
    A. 即期汇票   B. 跟单汇票
    C. 商业汇票   D. 银行承兑汇票

8. 远期汇票付款期限的规定方法有( )。
    A. 见票即付   B. 见票后若干天付
    C. 出票后若干天付   D. 提单日后若干天付

三、判断题（True or False）

1. 如果票据受让人是以善意并付对价获得票据，其权利不受前手权利缺陷的影响。（   ）

2. 汇票是出票人的支付承诺。（   ）

3. 汇票上金额须用文字大写和数字小写分别表明。如果大小写金额不符，则以小写为准。（   ）

4. 票据贴现，其他条件相等时，贴现率越高，收款人所得的净值就越大。（   ）

5. 本票是出票人的支付命令。（   ）

6. 支票可以有即期和远期之分。（   ）

7. 划线支票是只能够提取现金的支票。（   ）

8. 支票的主债务人始终是出票人。（   ）

四、实务操作题（Practice）

1. 国际出口公司（International Exporting Co.）出口价值1000000美元的机器设备和零部件给环球进口公司（Global Importing Co.），合同编号为No.1256。国际出口公司于2013年12月20日开出汇票，汇票编号为No.SN2358，要求环球进口公司在见票后30天付款给中国银行上海分行（Bank of China, Shanghai Branch）。环球进口公司于2014年1月10日承兑了该汇票，请按上述条件填写下列汇票。

BILL OF EXCHANGE

No._____ Exchange for _____, Shanghai, _____

At _____ sight of this First of Exchange(_____)

pay to the order _____

the sum of _____

To: _____

_____

2. 美国纽约A公司进口德国柏林B公司价值20000欧元的零部件，合同编号：HX1234，本票编号：BT2389。A公司于2014年5月5日开出商业本票，承诺见票后付款给德国B公司，请按上述条件填写下列本票。

_____

No._____   New York, _____

_____ 20000

On demand We promise to pay to the order of _____, the sum of _____

For A Company

New York

_____

Chapter 3

Payment Method Ⅰ: Remittance

A Brazil's company A wants to buy $500000 goods from Chinese company B in an emergency. The two companies agree to use remittance to pay. Which kind of remittance company B should choose? Do you know the characteristics and process of three kinds of remittance? This chapter mainly introduces the definition, parties and procedures of remittance, the advantages and disadvantages of using remittance in practice, and the function of remittance in international trade.

★ Learning Objectives

(1) To enable the readers to understand the concepts of remittance and reverse remittance, master the basic parties to remittance.

(2) To enable the readers to know the three types of remittance, i.e., T/T, M/T and D/D, their basic procedures, advantages and disadvantages.

(3) To enable the readers to master the reimbursement of remittance by different account.

(4) To enable the readers to know the definition of remittance cancellation and its specific operation.

(5) To enable the readers to find out the application of remittance in international trade.

3.1 Outline of Remittance

3.1.1 Definition of Remittance

Based on the movement direction of the instruments in relation to that of the funds flow, payment methods can be classified into two types: remittance and reverse remittance. Remittance indicates that the funds flow in the same direction as the credit instruments transmitted; the funds and the instruments must move from the debtor to the creditor, and the typical payment method is remittance. Reverse remittance indicates that the funds flow in the opposite direction of the credit instruments transmitted; the creditor draws instruments entrusting a bank to claim reimbursement from foreign debtor, and the typical payment methods are collection and letter of credit. Chart 3.1 and Chart 3.2

illustrate what remittance and reverse remittance are.

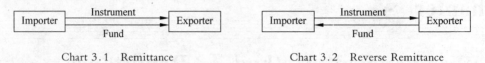

Chart 3.1　Remittance　　　　　　　Chart 3.2　Reverse Remittance

Remittance refers to the transfer of funds from one party to another among different countries through banks. At the request of its customer, a bank transfers a certain sum of money to its overseas branches or correspondent banks and instructs them to pay a named person or corporation in that country. Hence, Remittance is also one of banking customer service, in which the payer will actively transfer fund to the payee to settle the debt.

根据结算工具传送方向和资金流向是否相同,结算方式可分为两类:顺汇和逆汇。顺汇是指结算工具的流向与资金的流向一致,典型的顺汇结算方式是汇款。逆汇是结算工具的流向与货款的流向相反,典型的逆汇结算方式是托收和信用证。

汇款又称汇付,是银行(汇出行)应汇款人的要求,以一定的方式将款项通过国外联行或代理行(汇入行)交付收款人的结算方式。因此,汇款也是一种银行的客户服务,付款人将资金转移给收款人以结清债务。

Remittance is one of the customer services offered by a bank and it is used for both commercial and non-commercial settlements. When two people live in the same country, this type of remittance is called domestic remittance, while the remittance will be a foreign banking business if the two people live in different countries, which will be the focus in this chapter.

International remittance happens when a customer (payer) asks her bank to send a sum of money to a beneficiary abroad by one of the transfer methods at her option. The beneficiary can be paid at the designated bank, either the remitting bank's overseas branch or its correspondent. That is to say, when remittance is adopted in international trade, the buyer on her own initiative remits money to the seller through a bank in accordance with the terms and time stipulated in the contract.

Remittance is based on the trader's credit. That is, banks only transfer the funds at the request of the remitter and they assume no payment undertaking to the beneficiary.

The operations conducted by the remitting bank are called the outward remittance and those carried out by the paying bank are called the inward remittance. That is to say, when the home bank is acting as the remitting bank, the remittance handled by it is called an outward remittance; when the home bank is acting as the paying bank, the remittance handled by it is called an inward remittance.

3.1.2　Parties to a Remittance

● **Remitter**(汇款人)

The remitter is the person who requires the bank to remit funds to a beneficiary in a foreign country. In international trade, he/she is often the buyer or the importer. The remitter is also the payer.

● **Remitting Bank**(汇出行)

Remitting bank is the bank transferring funds at the request of a remitter to its correspondent or its branch in another country and instructing the latter to pay a certain amount of money to the payee or the beneficiary. Normally, the remitting bank will usually be located in the same city as that of the remitter and is often the importer's bank in international trade.

● **Paying Bank**(汇入行)

A paying bank is the bank entrusted by the remitting bank to pay a certain sum of money to the payee or the beneficiary named in the remittance advice. The paying bank is usually located in the same city as that of the exporter and is often the exporter's bank in international trade.

● **Beneficiary or Payee**(受益人或收款人)

The beneficiary or payee is the person who is addressed to receive the funds by remittance. He is the seller or exporter in international trade.

3.1.3 Types of Remittance

Based on the manner by which the payment instruction is transmitted from the remitting bank to the paying bank, there are three basic types of remittance: Telegraphic Transfer (T/T), Mail Transfer (M/T) and remittance by banker's demand bill of exchange (D/D). In practice, the type of remittance is determined by the client herself when she fills in the remittance application form at a bank. Chart 3.3 shows the three types of remittance and their characteristics, respectively.

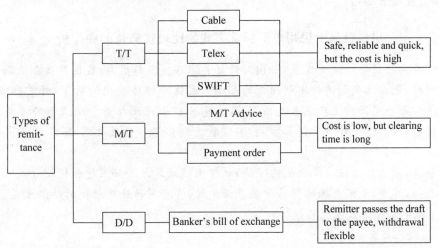

Chart 3.3　The Three Types of Remittance

● T/T(电汇)

By telegraphic transfer, the payment instruction given by the remitting bank to the paying bank will be transmitted by telecommunication, such as cable, telex or computer system, say SWIFT. It is therefore quicker, but more expensive than mail transfer. It is often used when the remittance amount is large and the funds transfer is subject to a time limit. The key point is that the paying bank must authenticate whether the instruction is given really by the remitting bank indicated in the telecommunications, for the funds should eventually be reimbursed by this remitting bank to the paying bank. In the history of international banking, there were numerous cases of cheating money by fake instruction in the name of a remitting bank. The method of authenticating the remitting bank is to check its test key (remittance by SWIFT should be authenticated by SWIFT authentic key). After receiving the instruction from the remitting bank, the paying bank will, firstly, check the test key according to the pre-determined rule. The paying bank would refuse to inform the payee if the test key is incorrect.

The main messages in a remittance by T/T are as follows: (1) test key of the remitting bank; (2) name and address of the remitter; (3) name and address of the payee; (4) currency and amount of funds; and (5) reimbursement of remittance cover.

电汇汇款是汇款人委托银行以电报、电传或SWIFT等电讯手段发出付款通知书给收款人所在地的汇入行,委托它解付一定金额给指定收款人的汇款方式。电汇速度快但比票汇成本高,所以常用于大额和紧急资金的转移。电汇的关键点是付款银行必须验证给定的指令是否真是汇款银行的指示,因为资金要从汇出行解付给汇入行。电汇的主要信息如下:(1)汇出行的密押;(2)汇款人的姓名和地址;(3)收款人的姓名和地址;(4)资金的币种和金额;(5)汇款的偿付。

 3-1

出口贸易中采用电汇结算方式的比较优势及问题探析

随着外向型经济的快速发展,我国对外贸易依存度不断提高,我国外贸企业融入世界经济的同时,也由此受到国外不利因素的影响。在国际经济危机影响下,外需严重缩水,加之危机传导引发国内生产成本大幅上升,我国出口企业面临着前所未有的考验。在国内外危机当头时刻,一种合理结算方式,不仅能达到良好的收益效果,还能节省出口成本和费用。

近年来,随着信用证结算比例的下降,非信用证结算方式如汇付和托收方式的使用比例趋于升高,其中,电汇是国际贸易中最灵活方便,资金周转速度最快的结汇方式。

一、电汇结算方式的比较优势

1. 风险比较优势

电汇结算方式作为一种商业信用,其风险跟实际使用情况有关。如果是前T/T,则对出口商极其有利,出口商是先拿到货款再出运货物;如果采用后T/T,则对出口商极其不利。就目前所使用的电汇业务来看,主要是前T/T和凭提单付款相结合。出口商先要求对方通过电汇支付一部分货款,剩余的款项在货物装船后,凭提单影印件付款。出口公司一般以货物的生产成本作为预付款的比例,因此,即使货物出运后剩余货款没有追回,也不会损失太大。

2. 费用比较优势

电汇结算方式下,两地银行都不需要处理单据,相应的费用就比较低,这是出口商愿意采用电汇结算方式的重要原因。

3. 程序和时间比较优势

电汇结算方式手续简便,速度快,一般3个工作日内可以到账,能为进出口商节约时间,降低汇率变动风险。

(翁旭青.出口贸易中采用电汇结算方式的比较优势及问题探析[J].商业经济,2012年第10期.)

- M/T(信汇)

In M/T, the payment instruction can take the form of Mail Transfer Advice or Mail Transfer Payment Order or Debit Advice, which means that the remitting bank, at the request of the remitter, transfers the funds by means of sending/posting a payment instruction to the paying bank, asking the latter to pay a certain sum of money to the payee. Post service is typically used to transfer the payment instructions. It is exactly the same as a telegraphic transfer, except that instruction from the remitting bank to the paying bank is transmitted by airmail instead of by a cable. Pay attention to that a payment instruction is an authenticated order in writing addressed by the remitting bank to the paying bank. Owing to the mail time being much longer than that of telecommunication, the M/T is not broadly used in international trade.

信汇是汇出行应汇款人的申请,将信汇委托书或支付委托书邮寄给汇入行,授权其解付一定金额给收款人的一种汇款方式。信汇业务的程序与电汇程序基本相同,所不同的是指令从汇出行发送给汇入行是通过航空信函的方式而不是电报。信汇的优点是费用较为低廉,但收款人收到的时间较晚。由于信汇的时间比电汇长、操作手续多,在国际贸易中已极少使用。

- D/D(票汇)

In D/D, the payment instruction is written down directly on the surface of the banker's bill of exchange, which is a negotiable instrument drawn by the remitting bank on its overseas correspondent bank, ordering the latter to pay on demand the stated amount to the holder of the bill of exchange. It is often used when the client wants to control the fund-transfer. After being issued, the banker's bill of exchange should be handed over to the remitter, who may dispatch or even bring it to the beneficiary abroad. Upon receipt of the bill of exchange, the payee can either present it for payment at the counter of the drawee bank or collect it though his account bank.

票汇是汇出行应汇款人申请,代汇款人开立以其分行或代理行为解付行的银行即期汇票,并交还汇款人,由汇款人自寄或自带给国外收款人,由收款人到汇入行凭票取款的汇款方式。由于存在丢失和损毁的风险,实际业务中,票汇的使用不是很多。

3.2 Procedure for Remittance

3.2.1 Procedure for T/T

If a payer wants to send a payment more quickly, he may do so by requesting a telegraphic transfer which will be sent by telex or cable. The remitter and the beneficiary have signed a contract which stipulates that money is to be paid through T/T.

The whole procedure virtually is done by entries over banking accounts, where the remitting bank (buyer's bank) debits his account and credits the account of the correspondent bank. On receipt of the payment instructions, the latter (the paying bank) passes a reciprocal entry over its account with the remitting bank and pays the money over to the exporter. Chart 3.4 shows the procedures of T/T. 1) The buyer (remitter) and the seller (payee) signed the sales contract, stipulating T/T as the payment method. 2) The remitter fills an application for remittance in T/T, and submits the application form, the proceeds and other relative charges to the remitting bank. 3) Upon receipt of the application form, the proceeds and other relative charges, the remitting bank offers the remitter a receipt; 4) the remitting bank sends a payment order by cable/telex/SWIFT to the paying bank. 5) After receiving the payment order from the remitting bank, the paying bank notifies the payee of the payment. 6) The payee gets payment from the paying bank. 7) The paying bank sends a debit advice to the remitting bank indicating the released payment.

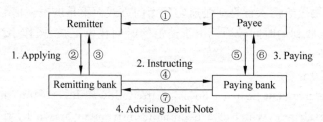

Chart 3.4　Procedures of T/T

3.2.2 Procedure for M/T

Procedure of M/T is almost the same as the T/T, except that the truthfulness of the instruction received should be authenticated by means of authorized signature pre-agreed instead of test key. The procedures of M/T are the same as those of T/T, see Chart 3.4.

3.3.3 Procedure for D/D

A banker's bill of exchange is a cheque issued by a bank upon another bank. This bill of exchange is normally a sight bill of exchange. The remitter (importer) obtains a banker's bill of exchange from the issuing bank and sends it to the beneficiary. Chart 3.5 shows the procedures of D/D.

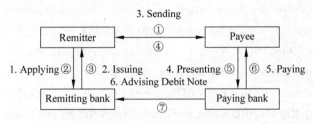

Chart 3.5　Procedures of D/D

Chart 3.5 shows the procedures of D/D. 1) The buyer (remitter) and the seller (payee) signed the sales contract, stipulating D/D as the payment method. 2) The remitter fills an application for remittance in D/D, and submits the application form, the proceeds and other relative charges to the remitting bank. 3) Upon receipt of the application form, the proceeds and other relative charges, the remitting bank draws a demand draft and delivers it to the remitter. 4) the remitting bank sends the draft to the payee. 5) The payee presents the draft to the paying bank for payment. 6) The paying bank checks the authenticity of the draft from the payee, debits the remitting bank's account, and then effects payment. 7) The paying bank sends a debit advice to the remitting bank indicating the released payment.

3.3.4 Reimbursement Methods

Under each remittance, the remitting bank has to instruct the paying bank clearly how to handle the "remittance cover". Methods of reimbursement are specified in the telegraphic text under a T/T, or in the payment order under an M/T, or on the face of bank bill of exchange under a D/D. There are varieties of reimbursement methods:

● **Crediting *Nostro* Account of the Paying Bank**(汇出行主动贷记汇入行账户)

If the paying bank opens a current account with the remitting bank, the reimbursement instructions should be written as: "In cover, we have credited the sum to your account with us."

● **Debiting Remitting Bank's *Nostro* Account**(汇出行授权汇入行借记)

If the paying bank maintains the remitting bank's account, the reimbursement may be instructed as: "Please debit the sum to our account with you." or "You are authorized to debit the sum to our account with you." After effecting payment, the paying bank debits the sum to the account of the remitting bank with them.

● **Instructing a Reimbursing Bank to Effect Payment by Debiting the Remitting Bank's *Nostro* Account**(指示偿付行借记汇出行账户)

If the remitting bank does not open an account with the paying bank, the former may instruct its correspondent with which it maintains an account, to debit this account and credit the paying bank's account if the paying bank has an account with that correspondent, too, or to pay the amount to another bank with which the paying bank maintains an account. The reimbursement clause is thus written: "In cover, we have authorized Bank of China, New York to debit our account and credit your account with the above sum." or "In cover, we have instructed Bank of China, New York to pay the proceeds to your account with Standard Chartered Bank, New York."

● **Instructing the Paying Bank to Claim Reimbursement from Another Branch of the same bank or another bank with which the remitting bank opens an account**(指示付款行从汇出行开立账户的相同的另一个分支行或其他银行索款)

The instructions are written as: "In cover, please reimburse yourselves to the debiting of our account with Bank of China, New York." or "In cover, please claim on Bank of China, New York."

● **According to the Payments Agreement between two Countries**(依据两国之间的清算协议)

In case there is a payment agreement signed by two countries concerned the reimbursement. Instructions must abide by the terms in that agreement. The instructions are thus: "In cover, you are authorized to debit our Central Bank's clearing account with your Central Bank." or "In cover, we have requested our Central Bank to credit the sum to the clearing account of your Central Bank with them."

3.2.5 Cancellation of the Remittance

● **Cancellation of T/T or M/T**(电汇或信汇的退汇)

Telegraphic transfer or mail transfer can be cancelled before the payment is made. It is usually done at the request of the remitter or the payee who refuses to receive the payment. Whenever the paying bank receives an advice from the remitting bank to cancel the latter's payment order, it will do accordingly. Once the payment has been made, the remittance cannot be cancelled. The remitter himself may contact the payee to claim back the remittance payment.

● **Cancellation of D/D**(票汇的退汇)

If the remitter requests the remitting bank to cancel a bank bill of exchange already issued by reason of its being lost or stolen, the latter is generally reluctant to do so because the remitting bank assumes the responsibility of guaranteeing the bill of exchange's payment once it is issued. However, if the paying bank confirms that the original one has not yet been paid, the remitting bank may issue a duplicate of bill of exchange against a letter of indemnity from the remitter.

3.3 Comparison of the T/T, M/T and D/D

A customer can request his banker to transfer the funds by any method. However, in addition to the differences mentioned above, the remitter should also understand that the costs, the speed and the reliability of the different methods of remittance could be significantly varied.

A telegraphic transfer is the most expensive, but its speed could save substantial interest payment if the transferred funds are large. It is one of the most reliable forms of money transfer because it will depend on the inter-bank transfer system rather than the mailing system of the post office. As a result, traders always use this form of transmission if they are to settle the payment by remittance.

A mail transfer by the banker instead of the customer is a little safer and is not very expensive, but the speed of the transfer is slow and the mailed M/T payment order could be delayed, destroyed or even stolen. Such delay involves additional interest payment to be made by the remitter to the beneficiary.

A bank bill of exchange sent by the customer himself is the least expensive, but is the slowest form of transmission and the customer should also bear the risk of theft, destruction or loss of the bill of exchange in transit by airmail.

Table 3.1 shows a comparison of T/T, M/T and D/D.

Table 3.1 Comparison of T/T, M/T and D/D

Method \ Items	T/T	M/T	D/D
Transfer methods	Cable/Telex/SWIFT	Airmail	Mail or carried by remitter
Transfer time	Fastest	Slow	Slowest
Authentication	Test key of SWIFT; Authentication key	Authorized signature	Authorized signature
Security	Quite safe	Reliable, but payment order may be lost in post	Demand draft may be lost or delayed
Charge	High	Low	Lowest

无论采用电汇、信汇还是票汇，其所使用的结算工具的传送方向与资金的流动方向都相同，均属顺汇。但这三种汇付方式在交款速度、安全性、费用等方面各有利弊。一般而言，电汇最受卖方欢迎，也是目前实际国际业务中主要采用的汇付方式。

3.4 Advantages and Disadvantages of Remittance

3.4.1 Advantages of Remittance

T/T is the fastest way to transfer funds. It involves bank-to-bank instructions with banks responsible for making payments, so it is quite safe, especially when a large amount is transferred.

M/T involves bank-to-bank instructions with banks responsible for making payments, so it is rather reliable.

Demand bill of exchange can be used for paying small amounts. Demand bill of exchange is a negotiable instrument, which can be transferred from one person to another by endorsement, so that it is more convenient in use for payment. In time of war, one can transfer funds out of the enemy country by means of the demand bill of exchange in virtue of its negotiability.

3.4.2 Disadvantages of Remittance

T/T is more expensive as compared with M/T or D/D, but if the amount transferred is large, the interest cost which should be otherwise incurred due to time delay can be saved. The beneficiary must await notification from the bank concerned.

As the mail transfer exclusively depends on international airmail service, its transmission is slower than that of T/T and cannot serve the purpose of quick payment, and it is possible for the mail transfer order to be delayed or lost in the post, thus causing difficulty for its payment. Unlike the remittance by demand bill of exchange, the beneficiary must await notification from the bank concerned.

As a remitter himself/herself is responsible for mailing the demand bill of exchange, its transmission is slower than that of T/T and cannot serve the purpose of quick payment. It is possible for a demand bill of exchange to be lost, stolen or destroyed. The remitting bank is generally reluctant to stop payment on a bill of exchange issued by itself because this would mean an act of dishonor on its part which will have an unfavorable effect on its credit-worthiness. Moreover, to stop payment on lost bill of exchange is time consuming.

NOTE: The advantages and disadvantages of the three methods of fund transfer have to be balanced when transferring funds. Generally speaking, M/T is less used than T/T and D/D nowadays, except for small amount remittances made by individuals for family maintenance, cash gift, etc. T/T is favorable to the seller because he can get money at an early date, speed up the turnover of funds, increase the income of interests and avoid the risk of fluctuation in the exchange rate. However, the buyer has to pay more cable expenses and bank charges. Therefore, if T/T is not definitely stipulated in the sale contract, the buyer makes payment only by M/T. Sometimes the amount of payment is comparatively large, the money market fluctuates greatly and the currency of settlement being used is likely to devaluate. In these cases, T/T is preferable, but it should be definitely stipulated in the contract.

3.5 Function of Remittance in International Trade

As a frequently used payment method in international trade, remittance has its own advantages and disadvantages compared with other payment methods such as collection and letter of credit. When importer and exporter are credible and reliable partners, remittance is definitely an effective method of payment. Remittance has found a wide application in international commercial settlement in the form of open account, consignment and payment in advance.

3.5.1 Open Account

Open account is also called payment after arrival of goods, and it is just the opposite of payment in advance. Open account means that the seller will make the delivery of goods or the provision of services before the buyer makes payment. Although the time of payment is agreed to be made on a predetermined future date, the seller is in fact selling on credit without any safeguards about the performance of the buyer. This method of payment is in the buyer's favor and she can make payment only when the goods or services are received or inspected.

赊销也称为先发货后付款,意味着卖方在买方付款之前先交付货物或提供服务。虽然双方约定一个预先确定的未来日期为付款日,但是卖方没有任何保障措施,这种方式对买方有利。

Under open account, the payment is at the time specified in the contract. On due date, it is up to the customer to arrange payment, it is a good idea to arrange with each customer to remit her payment by T/T to the seller's bank. Typical arrangements are: "Open account, 90 days from arrival of the goods"; "Open account, 90 days from invoice date"; or "Open account, cash within 30 days, 1% discount".

Open account is unfavorable to the seller on the following grounds: (1) the seller bears the risk of non-payment; (2) the seller releases the title to the goods without having assurance of payment; (3) the seller's own capital is tied up until he receives the payment; and (4) there is possibility that political events will impose regulations which defer or block the movements of funds to seller.

This method of payment is used where there is complete trust between the seller and the buyer. The seller should make sure that: (1) the buyer's financial standing must be good enough to support the whole performing procedure including producing, shipping, customs clearing and so on; (2) the buyer will effect payment at the agreed date; and (3) the buyer's country will not impose regulations deferring or blocking the funds transfer. Moreover, the seller should require that the open account be taken under a bank guarantee so as to minimize his risks.

Open account is used under the following conditions: (1) the market is in the buyer's market with conditions favoring the importer. In order to be competitive, the exporter has to offer this favorable term to the importer; (2) there is a long-standing or regular business relationship between the importer and the exporter, or (3) when a multi-national company ships the goods to its foreign branches or subsidiaries.

3.5.2 Consignment

Under a consignment, the exporter ships the goods to the importer and retains the title to the goods until the payment is made by the importer. The exporter is called the consignor and the importer is called the consignee. Similar to open account, the method is in favor of the importer who will make payment only when the goods are sold to a third party.

寄售是由出口商先将货物运至国外,委托国外商人在当地市场代为销售,货物售出后,被委托人将货款扣除佣金后通过银行汇交出口商。

This method is disadvantageous to the exporter on the following grounds: (1) exporter bears the risks of non-payment though he retains the title to himself; (2) there is the possibility that political events will impose regulations which will defer or block the movement of funds to him; and (3) his capital is tied up until the goods are sold to a third party. Thus, similar to open account, the exporter should require that the consignment be used under a bank guarantee.

Consignment is used under the following conditions: (1) the exporter wants to make a trial sale for a new product in order to get to know the market conditions for his subsequent sales; (2) the exporter wants to maintain large inventories in a local market in order to compete with local competitors; (3) the goods are unsalable ones; or (4) the exporter wants to dispose of exhibits after a sales promotion.

3.5.3 Payment in Advance

Payment in advance refers to that the buyer places the funds at the disposal of the seller prior to the delivery of goods or the provision of services and it is just the opposite of open account. Obviously, this method is favorable to the exporter while putting the importer at a great risk of non-delivery. In fact, importers are seldom prepared to make full payment in advance of the shipment of goods. It is more common to find that they are prepared to pay in advance only a certain percentage of the value of the goods, that is, the so-called down payment.

预付货款是买方先将货款的全部或者一部分通过银行汇交卖方,卖方收到货款后,根据买卖双方事先签订的合约,在一定时间内或立即将货物运交进口商的结算方式。这种方法对出口商有利,对进口商不利。

Generally, there are some disadvantages to the buyer when payment in advance is used for a transaction between the buyer and the seller. The buyer bears the risk of non-delivery.

Taking into the consideration of the greatest risks under payment in advance, the buyer has to consider the following key points: (1) the credit standing of the seller must be exceedingly good, and the buyer trusts that the seller will deliver the goods in due time; (2) the political and economic environment in the seller's country should be stable enough so that the government will not prohibit exportation of the goods contracted after payment has been effected; (3) the buyer should have sufficient balance sheet liquidity or she is confident of obtaining capital to support him paying in advance.

Payment in advance places the burden for financing the transaction entirely on the buyer. Actually, this method of payment is the worst thing for the buyer to do unless she does not have other choice. However, the buyer may change her situation by combining payment in advance with bank guarantee or standby credit so as to minimize her risks.

On the other hand, there are three advantages to the seller. Firstly, the seller can immediately use the fund to run the operation. Secondly, this method of payment helps the seller under the circumstance of funds shortage. Thirdly, when payment in advance is used, the seller has no financial risk. That is to say, this method of payment is the safest for the seller to fulfill his obligation under a specific transaction.

Payment in advance is used for the following situations: (1) when demand for commodities is greater than supply in market, the importer has to offer favorable terms to the exporter to secure the goods; (2) when the manufacturing process or services delivered are specialized or capital intensive, the importer may agree to finance the exporter by partial payment in advance and partial progress payment; (3) the exporter may insist on settling the payment in advance when the buyer's credit standing is doubtful or when there is an unstable political and economic environment in the buyer's country which is beyond the seller's control and will result in the delay in receipt of funds.

NOTE: No matter it is a payment in advance, open account or consignment, it is a business of remittance in the eyes of the handling banks. As pointed out above, remittance is made on trader's credit; the trader will suffer a loss as a result of the other party's non-performance, either in the form of non-payment or in the form of non-delivery.

注意:不管是预付货款、赊销或寄售,都是通过银行来进行商业汇款。汇款基于商业信用,交易商因为另一方的不付款或不发货会遭受损失。

延伸阅读 3-2

预付货款的出口收汇风险防范

（一）慎重选择贸易伙伴，做好对贸易伙伴的资信调查工作

一般情况下，预付货款中的进口商对出口商的资信会进行周密的调查，在确信预付货款中出口商能按时出运合同规定的货物时才能选择使用。但事实上，预付货款中的出口商对进口商的资信也必须进行周密的调查，只有在确信进口商的预付货款到账后才能交货或交单，因为预付货款并不等于货款已到账。

（二）明确规定合同中预付条款，最好选择我国银行的海外分支机构作为汇出行

由于各个银行的规模、实力和信誉不同，也不排除进口商与汇出行相互勾结，因此最好选择我国银行的海外分支机构作为汇出行，随时了解进口商的动态，以保证安全收汇。

（三）把握收到汇款收据、汇款凭证、取款通知书不等于收到货款信汇

在信汇、电汇业务中，出口商切莫一收到汇入行的取款通知书，便马上装货、制单并向进口商交单，而后才凭取款通知书向汇入行取款，此时汇款可能早已被汇款人撤销而收不到货款。因为在电汇、信汇情况下，只要汇入行还未将款项交付给收款人，只要汇入行收到汇出行的撤销通知便会立即止付。即使是收款人已凭取款通知书前来取款，只要尚未解付，汇入行也不能把款项交付收款人，这样就会导致出口商钱货两空，所以收到取款通知书并不是收到货款。

（四）保持清醒的头脑：支票到手不是货款到手，支票到账也不能算货款收妥

支票付款中即使是出口商已经收到支票，也必须明白支票到手也不等于货款到手，支票到账也不能算货款收妥。其原因是：（1）支票可能被出票人止付而成为废票。在国际贸易实践中，即使是信用度比较高的银行支票，如果进口商希望止付支票项下的货款，向出票银行声称支票丢失，银行也会停止付款。（2）虽然某些国家的法律规定签发空头支票（没有存款或存款不足）要负法律责任，出票人在支票付款提示期内也不得撤销已开出的支票，但支票付款后一般都有退单期，在退单期内，出票人可以用种种理由随时要求付款银行追回已付的款项，只有在付款后一定的退票期内未见退票，这笔货款才算收妥，此时才能寄提单或交付货物。

（五）切记银行汇票到手并不意味着货款一定能收到

企业收到外商交来的汇票或复印件时，应立即提交银行细心谨慎地审核其真实性，以免上当受骗。在票汇业务中，一些不法进口商利用伪造的、过期的、无法兑现的票据"随订单付现"（CASH WITH ORDER，简称 C.W.O.），或者通过一些规模较小、资信较差银行开来汇票，待收到货运单据并提货后通知汇入行止付。

（六）选择妥当运输方式

不同的运输方式，其运输单据的性质是不一样的。货物的运输应采用海运方式，因为只有海运提单代表货物的所有权，这是出口商在收汇时唯一能约束进口商的方面。

总之，预付货款下无论运用汇票、本票和支票中的哪种支付工具，也无论运用信汇、电

汇和票汇哪一种支付方式,出口商不能凭汇款收据、汇款凭证、取款通知书票据而必须坚持收到货款后才能发货或移交代表货物所有权的凭证,只有这样才能安全收汇,避免钱货两空。

(资料来源:徐龙伟,涂丽亚.从票汇撤销谈预付货款下出口收汇风险防范[J].对外经贸实务,2011年第1期.)

★ Key Words

Remittance(汇付/顺汇)　　　　　　　Reverse remittance(逆汇)
Remitter(汇款人)　　　　　　　　　Remitting Bank(汇出行)
Paying Bank(汇入行)　　　　　　　Beneficiary or Payee(受益人或收款人)
T/T(电汇)　　　　　　　　　　　　M/T(信汇)
D/D(票汇)　　　　　　　　　　　　Applying(申请)
Issuing(开立)　　　　　　　　　　Instructing(指示)
Sending(发送)　　　　　　　　　　Presenting(提示)
Paying(支付)　　　　　　　　　　　Advising(通知)
Reimbursement methods(汇款的偿付方法)
Cancellation of the remittance(汇款的退汇)

★ Exercise

一、单项选择(Exclusive Choice Question)

1. In the business of T/T,(　　) must be listed in the cable or telex in order to verify the authenticity of message.
　A. test key　　　　　　　　　　　B. signature of the authorized
　C. bank's agreement　　　　　　　D. cable confirmation

2. Which the following belongs to remittance payment?(　　)
　A. bank guarantee　　　　　　　　B. remittance
　C. letter of credit　　　　　　　　D. collection

3. Which of the following settlement way is good for exporter?(　　)
　A. payment in advance　　　　　　B. open account
　C. deferred payment　　　　　　　D. consignment

4. A bank in London entrusts a foreign correspondent bank to pay the payee, reimbursement of remittance cover as follows(　　).
　A. debit the correspondent bank account actively
　B. credit the correspondent bank account actively
　C. debit the correspondent bank account with authorization
　D. credit the correspondent bank account with authorization

5. If a importer asks his bank to make a telegraphic transfer to an exporter abroad, he should(　　).

A. pay the home currency equivalent of the sum in foreign currency

B. pay the bank's commission

C. get a permission from the authorities

D. pay the bank in foreign currency

6. 适宜采用电汇结算的业务,一般是（   ）。

    A. 零星的、小额货款   B. 付款时间紧急的大额货款

    C. 贸易从属费用   D. 不紧急的款项

7. 银行办理业务时通常无法占用客户资金的汇款方式（   ）。

    A. 电汇   B. 票汇   C. 信汇   D. 以上都是

8. 目前最受卖方欢迎的汇付方式为（   ）。

    A. 托收   B. 电汇   C. 信汇   D. 票汇

9. 信汇的特点不包括：（   ）。

    A. 费用低廉   B. 速度较慢

    C. 资金可能被银行短期占用   D. 取款灵活

10. 汇款人在委托汇出行办理汇款时要出具（   ），它是汇款人与汇出行之间的契约。

    A. 汇票通知书   B. 支付委托书   C. 汇款申请书   D. 电报证实书

二、多选题（Multiple Choice Question）

1. 电汇的特点包括：（   ）。

    A. 顺汇结算   B. 速度最快   C. 费用高   D. 安全可靠

2. 关于顺汇的描述正确的是（   ）。

    A. 债务人主动向债权人付款

    B. 资金流向结算工具的传递方向相同

    C. 包括汇款和托收两种形式

    D. 不仅有商业信用也有银行信用

3. 为什么预付货款对出口商有利（   ）。

    A. 货物未发出,已收到一笔货款,等同于得到无息贷款

    B. 收款后再发货,降低了货物出售的风险,如果进口商毁约,出口商可没收预付款

    C. 出口商可以充分利用预收货款,甚至可在收到货款后,再购货发出

    D. 货物到手前付出货款,会造成进口商资金周转困难及利息损失

4. 关于顺汇的描述正确的是（   ）。

    A. 债务人主动向债权人付款

    B. 资金流向结算工具的传递方向相同

    C. 包括汇款各托收两种形式

    D. 不仅有商业信用也有银行信用

5. 进口商如何防范预付货款风险（   ）。

    A. 收款人取款时,要出具个人书面担保或银行保函

B. 收款人取款时,保证提供全套货运单据

C. 凭借进口商与出口商之间的信誉

D. 向出口商提出对进口商品折价支付,作为抵补预付货款造成的资金利息损失

6. 汇款当事人之间具有委托与被委托关系的有(　　)。

A. 汇款人与收款人　　　　　　　B. 汇款人与汇出行

C. 汇出行与解付行　　　　　　　D. 汇入行与收款人

三、判断题(True or False)

1. 通常票汇方式下收款人收妥资金的时间比使用电汇方式要短。(　　)

2. 使用电汇时资金到账速度快,但是费用比信汇高。(　　)

3. 汇款结算都是通过银行来传递资金的,所以是以银行信用为基础的结算方式。(　　)

4. 未开设清算账户的两家银行之间发生汇款业务时,至少需要通过一家碰头行才能结清头寸。(　　)

5. 预付货款可以保证进口商得到所需的货款。(　　)

6. 信汇委托书可以通过背书而流通转让。(　　)

7. 对进口商而言,售定比预付货款的风险要小。(　　)

8. 使用票汇时,银行即期汇款一经交付,通常不能主动止付;但若遗失或被偷盗,则可办理挂失止付。(　　)

四、实务操作题(Practice)

请根据信息填写相关电文

Remitting bank：Bank of China, Tianjin

Paying bank：Bank of China, Luxemburg

Date of cable：9 June

Test：2563

Ref No.：208TT219

Amount：USD1,660.00

Payee：Marie Clauda Dumont, Luxemburg,

Account No. 0-1647295/550 with Banque International du Luxemburg

Message：Payroll

Remitter：Crystal Palace Hotel, Tianjin

Cover：Debit our H.O. account

FROM：＿＿＿＿＿＿＿＿＿＿＿＿＿

TO：＿＿＿＿＿＿＿＿＿＿＿＿＿

DATE：＿＿＿＿＿＿＿＿＿＿＿＿＿

TEST ＿＿＿＿＿＿ OUR REF ＿＿＿＿＿＿ NO ANY CHARGES FOR US

PAY：＿＿＿＿＿＿＿＿＿＿＿＿＿

TO：＿＿＿＿＿＿＿＿＿＿＿＿＿

FOR CREDITING ACCOUNT NO. _____
OF _____
MESSAGE _____
ORDER _____
COVER _____

Chapter 4

Payment Method II: Collection

China Importing and Exporting Company exports equipment to Company A in the United States. It commissions the Beijing branch, Bank of China to handle collection, making the payment condition D/P at sight. Can you issue this documentary draft? Can you draw a flow chart of collection? Collection is another way quite popular in international trade settlement, which is handled by banks in charge of presenting documents to the buyer and releasing them to the buyer by his acceptance of bill of exchange or payment for goods, and then the buyer can claim the goods from the shipping company with a title document got from the bank. This chapter mainly introduces the definition, parties and procedures of collection in the international trade.

★ Learning Objectives

(1) To enable the readers to know the definition and basic parties to collection.

(2) To enable the readers to understand the procedures of documentary collection and different terms of releasing documents.

(3) To enable the readers to be familiar with widely used international customs and practices like UCR522.

(4) To enable the readers to understand the financing function of collection to the seller or the buyer.

4.1 An Overview of Collection

4.1.1 Definition of Collection

Collection is a kind of payment system, in which creditors submit financial documents or commercial documents or both for obtaining proceeds to the remitting bank and ask it to entrust his relational bank (collecting bank) to make the documents available to the payer.

From the standpoint of banking, collection, as defined in "Uniform Rules for Collections" i. e. URC522 set by ICC, means the handling by banks of documents in accordance with instructions received, in order to: (1) obtain payment and/or acceptance; (2) deliver commercial documents against payment and/or against acceptance; and

(3) deliver documents① on other terms and conditions.

托收是指由债权人提交金融单据或商业单据给托收行,并由托收行委托它的相关银行(代收行)向付款人收取款项的结算方式。国际商会第 522 号出版物《托收统一规则》对托收的正式定义是,托收意指银行按照从出口商那里收到的指示办理:(1)获得金融单据的付款及/或承兑,或者(2)凭付款及/或承兑交出单据,或者(3)以其他条款和条件交出单据。

Under a collection, banks act as only a collecting agent to assist the exporter in obtaining payment or acceptance of his bill of exchange before the release of documents to the importer. Banks are required to release documents only if specified conditions are met by the importer. They will act in good faith and exercise reasonable care to verify that the documents submitted appear to be as listed in the collection application, but are not responsible for: (1) verifying the quality and quantity of the merchandise being shipped against documents in that banks deal in documents alone, ensuring only that documents specified in the collection application are provided to them by the exporter for presentation to the importer and banks have no further obligation to examine the documents submitted; (2) guaranteeing payment in the event of non-payment or non-acceptance of the bill of exchange.

For the seller and the buyer, a collection falls between a documentary credit and open account in its desirability and security, and can be seen as a compromise between open account and advance payment, for the buyer cannot take possession of the goods without either making payment or accepting a bill of exchange and the seller can also demonstrate that he has already fulfilled his obligations under the contract to dispatching the goods on time by presenting the proper documents through banks to the buyer, thus diminishing the possibility of non-delivery under the cash in advance terms. Besides, the procedure of a collection is easier than a documentary L/c and the bank charges are lower, for although the seller prepares and presents documents to the banks in much the same way as for a documentary L/c, the banks involved in a collection have no obligation to pay upon presentation of documents by the seller as they should in a documentary L/c business.

4.1.2 The Nature and Application of a Collection

From the above definition of a collection, we can see that banks involved in a collection business serve as intermediaries authorized by the seller to collect payment from

---

① Documents here refer to financial documents and/or commercial documents. Financial documents include bills of exchange, promissory notes and checks for obtaining the payment of money from the buyer. The commercial documents reflect that the seller has already fulfilled his obligations under the contract, which include bill of loading, commercial invoice, insurance policy and so forth, or any other documents whatsoever, not being financial documents. 单据这里意指金融单据及/或商业单据。金融单据包括用于获得买方货币付款的汇票、本票和支票。商业单据反映卖方已履行了合同义务,包括海运提单、商业发票、保单或不是金融单据的其他任何单据。

the buyer by a bill of exchange drawn by the seller on the buyer in exchange for the transfer of documents that enable the holder to take the possession of the goods. Therefore, collection is still based on commercial credit instead of bank credit, i.e., whether the exporter can get paid or not fully depends on the credit of the buyer. Although the banks involved in collection, they do not act as surety of payment but rather only as a collector of funds under a transaction and provide a channel to transfer funds between the buyer and the seller, thus earning a commission fee for their services, who do not guarantee payment or assume any credit risk.

As mentioned in Chapter 3, collection is a type of reverse remittance used to settle claims and debts from the perspective of international exchange, i.e., the exporter draws a bill of exchange as the settlement instrument and presents it to the buyer through the banks for payment, while the actual flow of funds is still from the buyer to the seller.

Collections are welcome by the exporter when he is reluctant to supply the goods on an open account basis but does not need the security under a documentary credit. In a collection, the seller cannot be sure at the time of dispatch of the goods that the buyer will actually pay the sum owed. Therefore, this kind of settlement is basically appreciated in the following cases: (1) the seller has no doubt about the buyer's willingness and ability to pay for maintaining the long-lasting business relationship between them; (2) the political and legal environment in the importing country is considered to be stable; (3) the importing country has placed no restrictions on imports (e.g. exchange controls) or has issued all the necessary authorizations; and (4) the shipped goods are easily remarkable.

Since collection is based on the commercial credit, besides the considerations mentioned above, the exporter should also set up alternative procedures for resale, reshipment or warehousing of the goods in the event of non-payment by the buyer when the goods have already arrived in the importing country.

 4-1

托收结算方式的适用

在以下几种情况中,恰当使用托收结算方式能增强出口商在国际市场中的竞争力。

1. 如果卖方所售货物处于滞销状态或市场竞争激烈,卖方除了采取降低价格的手段外,还可以采用托收结算方式,减轻进口商的资金负担,甚至为进口商提供资金融通,从而有利于促进交易的达成。

2. 对于实力和资信状况良好的买家,卖方可以接受托收结算方式。托收属于商业信用,卖方能否顺利收汇完全取决于买方的诚信和支付能力,因此买方拥有强大的经营实力和良好的资信状况是托收方式下卖方顺利收汇的有力保证。

3. 风险偏好较高的出口企业也可适当使用托收结算方式。风险与收益是并存的,如果企业的出口战略是迅速占领某国外市场,只要公司或专业机构风险评估通过,即可使用托收结算方式。

4. 对于数额不大的货款卖方也可使用托收方式进行结算。例如出口货款的尾数、样品费、佣金、代垫费用、其他贸易小额费用、进口索赔款及非贸易等事项的收款，即使最后买方拒付，也不会造成出口商损失惨重。

5. 如果可以投保出口信用险，企业可以适度使用托收方式。投保了出口信用险，出口企业就可将收汇风险转嫁给保险公司，即使出现买方拒付的情况，出口商也可以向保险公司提出理赔，得到货款。

4.1.2　Parties to Collection

- **The Principal/Drawer**（委托人）

The principal is generally the seller/exporter under a sales contract who entrusts his bank to collect the selling proceeds from the buyer through its correspondent bank abroad. It is also the principal's obligation to prepare the collection documents and submit them to his bank with a collection application for payment from the buyer. Since the relationship between the principal and the drawee is bound by the sales contract between them, the collection application should be clearly and unambiguously stated according to the sales contract. The principal should, therefore, take great care in preparing the collection application so that it could give complete and clear instructions.

- **The Remitting Bank**（托收行）

The remitting bank is the bank entrusted by the principal to handle a collection and is usually the exporter's own bank. The remitting bank receives documents from the seller for forwarding to the buyer's bank along with instructions for payment. The relationship between the principal and the remitting bank is bound by the collection application, based on which the remitting bank serves as an agent for the principal to collect the proceeds of sale.

If the remitting bank elects to handle a collection, it has to examine carefully the collection application and the accompanied documents given by the principal and act upon the instructions given by the principal and in accordance with the rules stipulated in the URC522. If the remitting bank fails to obtain the money, the principal should assume the loss and the bank commission. But once the remitting bank provides financing to the principal under the collection, it will take the risks of non-payment by the buyer and the insolvency of the exporter.

Remitting bank will act in good faith and exercise reasonable care. It should be responsible for the losses caused by the remitting bank when advising the principal of the notice of dishonor with delay, such as the losses of the collecting bank who misses the documents because the remitting bank mails with a mistaken address.

- **The Collecting Bank/Presenting Bank**（代收行/提示行）

The term "collecting bank" is applied to any bank, other than the remitting bank, involved in processing the collection, which presents the documents to the buyer and collects payment from the buyer. Normally, it is a correspondent bank or a branch of the remitting bank located in the importer's country.

Under a collection, the relationship between the remitting bank and the collecting bank is an agent relationship bound by the corresponding banking agreement between them and the specific collection instruction. Under such an instruction, the collecting bank serves as an agent on behalf of the remitting bank to collect the proceeds and assumes no liability in the case of dishonor by the importer.

According to the URC522, in absence of a bank named by the principal, the remitting bank can choose to use any of its own or another bank as the collecting bank. In practice, the collecting bank is generally nominated by the principal. Because either party involved in international trade is willing to provide the information of his/her bank and account number to each other for reference, the exporter (the principal) knows more about the importer and his bank than the remitting bank, and through the bank nominated by the exporter the remitting bank can present the documents to the importer directly and hence straighten the payment route.

There may be situations where the collecting bank has no account relation with the drawee or is located in a different place. In consideration of convenience in payment and financing, the collecting bank may use another bank which maintains an account of the drawee or one of its branches located closer to the importer to present the documents to the drawee. This bank is called the presenting bank, which makes presentation of documents or provides financing to the drawee. In practice, the collecting bank and the presenting bank are usually the same.

- **The Drawee**(付款人)

The drawee (buyer/importer) is usually the buyer/importer under a sales contract who should make cash payment or accept a bill of exchange according to the terms of the collection instruction in exchange for the documents from the presenting/collecting bank. The drawee is the one on whom a bill of exchange is drawn and to whom presentation is to be made.

The drawee has the right to examine the documents to determine whether to accept them or not, and is obliged to pay or accept the bill of exchange on the basis of terms of the collection in cases when there is no fair and just reasons.

- **Principal's Representative in Case of Need**(需要时的代理)

Principal's representative in case of need refers to the representative nominated by the principal to take care of goods in the event of non-payment and/or non-acceptance by the importer. According to URC522, if the principal appointed such a representative, the collection instruction should clearly and fully indicate the powers of such case-of-need. In absence of such indication, banks will not accept any instructions from the case-of-need.

"需要时的代理"是指在托收业务中,如发生付款人拒付的情况,委托人可指定在付款地的代理人代为料理货物存仓、转售、运回等事宜。根据 URC522(国际商会《托收统一规则》),委托人如拟指定需要时的代理,必须在托收委托书上写明代理人的权限。如在委托书中对代理人的权限未做规定,代收行可以不受理代理人的任何指示。

4.1.3 Types of Collection

- **Clean Collection（光票托收）**

A clean collection means collection on financial instruments without being accompanied by commercial documents, such as commercial invoice, bill of lading, insurance policy, etc. A clean collection may represent an underlying merchandise transaction or a purely financial transaction involving no movement of merchandise and, therefore, no documents standing for it. Under a clean collection, the payment instrument can be a cheque, a promissory note, a bill of exchange, certificates of deposit issued by foreign banks, or dividend warrants drawn on foreign banks, etc.

"光票托收"是指金融单据不附带商业票据的托收,即卖方仅把金融单据委托银行见票时或在未来某个时间点代为收款。光票托收可能代表一种不涉及商品运动的潜在的商品交易(underlying merchandise)或纯粹的金融交易,所以没有随附单据商业单据,如商业发票、海运提单、保险单等。在光票托收方式下,支付工具可以是支票、本票、汇票、外资银行发行的存单或股息权证等。

In international trade, a bill of exchange drawn by the seller on the importer will be handed to a bank for collection, when shipping documents are sent by the exporter to the importer or the exporter's foreign agent directly, or when expenses have been incurred such as freight, insurance premium, commission or any other charges which the exporter paid on behalf of the importer. Therefore, it is a method of settlement similar to open account trade, except that the buyer is prompted to pay under a collection by the presentation of a bill of exchange whereas on open account terms the buyer agrees to settle at a predetermined time.

For a clean collection settlement, the exporter is, in fact, shipping on open account terms and lacks security. Furthermore, the paying bank under a clean collection has the right of recourse for the refunding of collection proceeds. The exporter also runs the risks of financial instruments deriving from fraudulence in bill of exchanges, promissory notes and cheques, instruments wrongfully obtained, default or invalid instruments, and inexperience or oversight of bank staff, etc. Therefore, clean collection is not as popular as documentary collection when used in international trade, and the amount for collection is usually not large.

The following situations are fit preferable to select clean bill of exchange collection: (1) small amount payment under trade and non-trade items; (2) foreign currency notes that cannot be converted domestically (including worn coins); and (3) collection service of securities certificates like foreign exchange cheque, promissory note, foreign bonds and deposit certificates, etc.

The procedure of clean collection is: ①The buyer (drawee) and the seller (principal) signed the sales contract, stipulating clean collection as the payment method. ② The principal fills an application for clean collection, and hands in the and documents for payment. ③After the remitting bank's verification of collection application, the remitting bank chooses the collecting bank and the optimal route for reimbursement, and sends documents and the collection order to the collecting bank within two banking days, and then urges payment to be made in time. ④On receipt of the payment from the collecting bank, the remitting bank pays the collected amount to the principal.

- **Documentary Collection**(跟单托收)

A documentary collection is an operation in which a bank collects payment on behalf of the seller (the principal) by delivering documents to the buyer. It refers to the process by which the principal submits financial documents accompanied by commercial documents or commercial documents only to remitting bank for collecting proceeds from the drawee.

Documentary collection allows the exporters to retain ownership of the goods until they receive payment or are reasonably certain that they will receive it. Compared with the clean collection, the documentary collection can be safer for the exporter by controlling the passage of title to the merchandise, such as bill of lading. Under the general rules, once the documents are passed to the bank by the exporter, the bank has an absolute right over the goods through the tire documents. The right includes the arrangements concerning the release, protection, warehousing, and shipment of the goods on behalf of the exporter.

跟单托收是卖方(委托人)在装运货物后,委托银行通过随附货运单据给买方的方式代为收款的一种结算方式。跟单托收允许出口商保留货物的所有权,直到他们收到或确信他们将收到货款。与光票托收相比,跟单托收相对更安全。出口商可以通过单据(如海运提单)控制商品所有权的转移。根据一般规则,一旦单据通过出口商交给银行,银行通过控制单据拥有货物的绝对物权。这些权利包括代表出口商安排有关货物的放行、保护、仓储和装运。

In terms of releasing documents by banks, documentary collection can be subdivided into documents against payment (D/P) and documents against acceptance (D/A).

※ **Documents against payment**(D/P)(付款交单)

In D/P terms, the collecting bank is allowed to release the documents to the drawee only upon full and immediate① cash payment. In practice, buyers prefer to postpone the takeover of the documents and payment until after the arrival of the goods. If the seller does not wish to wait for his money till then, he must include in the collection order a

---

① In international usage, "immediate" means "no later than the arrival of the goods".

clear clause stipulating "payment on first presentation of documents". This type of collection offers the greatest security to the seller. But still the buyer may refuse to pay, in which case the seller maintains tire to the shipment. The seller may decide to negotiate new terms with the buyer, locate another buyer, or have the goods returned, incurring the cost of shipping, insurance, and bank fees. D/P can also take two forms: D/P at sight and D/P at a fixed time after sight.

* **D/P at sight**(即期付款交单)

Under D/P at sight, after shipment of the goods, the exporter (seller) shall draw a sight bill of exchange and send it as well a shipping documents to his bank (remitting bank), through which and whose correspondent bank the documentary bill of exchange is presented to the importer. The importer (buyer) shall pay against the documentary bill of exchange drawn by the seller at sight. Actually, D/P at sight requires immediate payment by the importer to get hold of the documents. Sometimes no bill of exchange is required under D/P term in order to avoid the stamp duty.

* **D/P at a fixed time after sight**(远期付款交单)

D/P at a fixed time after sight, also expressed as acceptance with documents against payment, is encountered more frequently in the textbook than in practice. Under this type of collection, the bill of exchange drawn is a usance bill of exchange payable at a fixed time after sight, and the documents will not be released on acceptance but will be released only against payment at maturity. In other words, the release of documents is made against payment of a usance bill of exchange, namely when the collecting bank first presents a bill of exchange to the buyer, the buyer should make acceptance, then the accepted bill of exchange should be kept at the collecting bank together with the documents up to maturity, and when the buyer pays the bill of exchange at maturity, the collecting bank releases the documents to the buyer who then takes the possession of the shipment. This method gives the buyer time to pay for the shipment but gives the seller security that title to shipment will not be handed over until payment has been made. However, acceptance with documents against payment is handled as documents against acceptance in some Latin American countries and the Middle East Area.

According to URC522, collections should not contain bill of exchange payable at a future date with instructions that commercial documents are to be delivered against payment. If a collection contains a bill of exchange payable at a future date, the collection instruction should state whether the commercial documents are to be released to the drawee against acceptance (D/A) or against payment (D/P). In absence of such statement, commercial documents will be released only against payment and the collecting bank will not be responsible for any consequences arising out of any delay in delivery of documents.

※ ***Documents against acceptance***(D/A)(承兑交单)

In D/A terms, the collecting bank is permitted to release the documents to the buyer against acceptance of a bill of exchange promising to pay at a later date. The bill of exchange under D/A is a usance bill of exchange, which is usually drawn payable 30~180 days after sight or at a fixed future date. The accepted bill of exchange is then held by the collecting bank and presented to the buyer for payment at maturity.

Under D/A terms, the seller is extending credit to the importer by agreeing to draw a time bill of exchange and only by acceptance of the bill of exchange the buyer obtains the documents and gains the possession of the goods before payment is actually made, which is quite favorable to him. The seller's only security once the goods have been released is the acceptance obtained from the drawee. While waiting for the bill of exchange to mature, the seller bears the risk of non-payment. In D/A terms it is quite possible that the buyer may accept the bill of exchange, take possession of the goods, but then refuse to pay the bill of exchange at maturity. The seller's options are effectively reduced to trying to enforce the buyer's obligation to pay the bill of exchange through banking channels or legal action, both of which involve additional costs.

NOTE: From the perspective of the exporter, D/P is safer than D/A, and D/P at sight is safer than D/P at a fixed time after sight.

※ *Direct Collection*（直接托收）

Direct collection is an arrangement whereby the seller obtains his bank's pre-numbered direct collection letter, thus enabling him to send his documents directly to his bank's correspondent bank for collection, which will accelerate the paperwork process.

In a direct collection, the exporter forwards the documentation directly to the collecting bank and a copy of collection instruction is sent to the exporter's bank, then the collecting bank will follow the instruction as if they were received from its correspondent bank, namely the remitting bank.

Compared to the above mentioned kinds of collection, however, the principal under direct collection has to make inquiry and urge for payment by himself, which is more difficult and risky without the involvement of the remitting bank.

远期托收的方式、风险及防范

按照支付时间的不同，托收可分为即期托收和远期托收。即期托收指买方接到由卖方委托的银行所提示的金融单据（比如汇票）和/或商业单据（比如货运单据）时，立即付款，在付清货款后，领取商业单据。远期托收指买方接到由卖方委托的银行所提示的金融单据和/或商业单据时，进口商即在金融单据上承兑，并于金融单据到期日由代收银行再次向其指示后完成付款，取得商业单据。

按照金融单据是否附带商业单据，远期托收可分为远期光票托收和跟单远期托收。

远期光票托收是指金融单据不附带商业票据的远期托收，即卖方仅把金融单据委托银行在未来某个时间点代为收款。远期跟单托收是指金融单据附带着商业票据的远期托收，即卖方把金融票据连同商业票据委托银行在未来某个时间点代为收款。

按照银行交付商业单据条件的不同，跟单远期托收又可分为远期付款交单（Documents against Payment after sight，D/P after sight）和承兑交单（Documents against acceptance，D/A）。前者指卖方通过银行向买方提示金融单据和商业单据，买方在金融单据上承兑，并于金融单据到期日由银行再次向其提示时，经付款向银行取得商业单据。后者指卖方的交单以买方的承兑为条件，买方承兑汇票后，即可向银行取得商业单据，待金融单据到期日才付款。

如上所述，远期托收有远期付款交单、承兑交单和远期光票托收三种方式。这三种结算方式对卖方的风险分别为：

1. 远期付款交单。远期付款交单是所有远期托收方式中，风险最小的一种，因为银行只有在汇票到期日由买方支付货款了之后，才交付商业单据。但是，必须注意的是，由于托收属于商业信用性质而非银行信用性质，因此国际商会制定的《托收统一规则》（URC522第7条）特别指出，"托收不应含有凭付款交付商业单据的远期汇票"，意在劝阻卖方采用远期付款交单方式结算货款，否则后果自负。由此看来，虽然远期付款交单方式对卖方而言是一种最安全的远期托收方式，但由于这种方式违背了托收的性质，也得不到国际贸易惯例的支持，建议谨慎对待。如果卖方能够确保代收行在汇票到期日经由买方支付货款后才交付商业单据可采用远期付款交单，否则应该采用承兑交单方式。

2. 承兑交单。在承兑交单情况下，买方只需在汇票上履行承兑手续，即可取得商业单据，将货物取走。倘若买方到期不付款，虽然卖方有权依法对买方追索，但此时买方也多半无力偿还，或者早已宣告破产，甚至人去楼空。要防范此类风险，卖方应注意：a. 认真调查买方的资信情况、经营能力和经营作风；b. 国外代收行不能由买方指定；c. 卖方在货物装运后，直至买方付款以前，都要关心货物安全；d. 填写运输单据时一般应做指示抬头并加背书；e. 严格按合同规定装运货物、制作单据，防止被买方找到拒付借口；f. 可要求对方预付不低于货物往返运费、保险费和其他杂费的定金或预付款。

3. 远期光票托收。在光票托收中，银行只是作为卖方的受托人行事，并没有承担付款的责任，买方付不付款与银行无关，卖方向买方收取货款完全依赖买方的商业信用。因此，远期光票托收是三种远期托收方式中风险最高的一种结算方式，一般只适用于贸易的从属费用、货款尾数、佣金、样品费的结算，大额货款不宜采用此方式结算。

如果对买方资信无充分把握，卖方在采取托收方式结算货款时，可要求对方预付不低于货物往返运费、保险费和其他杂费的定金或预付款，也可采用部分货款付款交单，部分货款信用证，或由买方开立银行保证书或备用信用证担保。

4.2 Documentary Collection Practice

4.2.1 Procedure of Documentary Collection

The whole process of documentary collection, extending from the first contact between the buyer and the seller to the completion of the transaction, involves many separate steps, which focus on the exchange of documents giving title to goods for payments from the buyer.

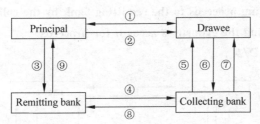

Chart 4.1 Procedure of D/P

- **Procedure of D/P**

> Stage 1: **signing a sales contract**

The exporter stipulates the terms of payment in his offer or agrees on them with the importer in the sales contract, specifying a documentary collection as the means of payment.

> Stage 2: **dispatching the goods and preparing necessary documents**

After the signing of sales contract, the exporter (principal) dispatches the goods ordered to the importer, obtains the shipping documents and usually draws a bill of exchange on the importer.

> Stage 3: **submitting documents and collection application**

The exporter assembles all the necessary documents, submits them to his bank (the remitting bank), which acts as his agent, and fills in a collection application specifying that the remitting bank shall only hand over documents to the importer upon his payment (D/P).

> Stage 4: **sending the documentation package to the collecting bank**

The remitting bank then sends the documents, together with the collection instruction, to the collecting bank.

> Stage 5: **presenting of the documents to the importer**

The collecting bank reviews the documents to make certain that they are in conformity with the collection order, then informs the importer of the arrival of the documents and notifies the importer about the terms and conditions of the collection order.

> Stage 6: **making payment or accepting the bill of exchange by the importer**

If the bill of exchange used is a sight bill of exchange, then the importer should make immediate payment to the collecting bank;

If the bill of exchange is a usance bill of exchange, the importer should first accept it upon the presentation by the collecting bank, and then makes payment when the bill of exchange is due.

➢ **Stage 7: releasing documents by the collecting bank to the importer upon his payment**

Only after the importer pays the face value of the bill of exchange plus any charges he is responsible for according to the collection order can the collecting bank then release the documents to him, who can take possession of the shipment.

➢ **Stage 8: remitting proceeds to the remitting bank by the collecting bank**

➢ **Stage 9: crediting the exporter's account for proceeds**

● **Procedure of D/A**

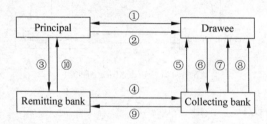

Chart 4.2　Procedure of D/A

➢ **Stage 1: signing a sales contract**

The exporter stipulates the terms of payment in his offer or agrees on them with the importer in the sales contract, specifying a documentary collection as the means of payment.

➢ **Stage 2: dispatching the goods and preparing necessary documents**

After the signing of sales contract, the exporter (principal) dispatches the goods ordered to the importer, obtains the shipping documents and usually draws a usance bill of exchange on the importer.

➢ **Stage 3: submitting documents and collection application**

The exporter assembles all the necessary documents, submits them to his bank, namely the remitting bank, and fills in a collection application specifying that the remitting bank should hand over documents to the importer only by his acceptance of the usance bill of exchange.

➢ **Stage 4: sending the documentation package to the collecting bank**

The remitting bank then sends the documents, together with the collection instructions, to the collecting bank.

➢ **Stage 5: presenting the documents to the importer**

The collecting bank reviews the documents making certain they are in conformity with the collection order, informs the importer of the arrival of the documents and notifies the importer about the terms and conditions of the collection order.

➢ **Stage 6: accepting the bill of exchange by the importer**

Since the collection is under D/A terms, the importer just writes the word "Accepted" and the date and signs across the face of the bill of exchange without making cash payment upon presentation of documents by the collecting bank.

➢ **Stage 7: releasing documents by the collecting bank**

Upon the importer's acceptance of the bill of exchange, the collecting bank releases documents to him, who can then claim the goods.

➢ **Stage 8: presenting the accepted bill of exchange by the collecting bank to the importer for payment at maturity**

➢ **Stage 9: remitting proceeds to the remitting bank by the collecting bank**

➢ **Stage 10: crediting the exporter's account for proceeds**

4.2.2 Collection Application Form and Order

● **Collection Application Form**

After dispatching the goods, the exporter is ready to request his bank to arrange for a collection. When authorizing a bank to collect the proceeds from the buyer, he should submit a collection application form, which is regarded as a contract between the principal and the remitting bank on a specific collection, together with shipping documents.

The contents of the collection application should strictly comply with the sales contract between the buyer and the seller and be clear and complete. Typically, the contents of a collection application form include: (1) details of the principal and the drawee, including full name, postal address, and the authorized signature; (2) amount and currency to be collected; (3) a list of documents and the numerical count of each document; (4) the terms of releasing documents to the drawee, such as D/P, D/A, etc.; it is also the responsibility of the party preparing the collection instruction to ensure that terms for the delivery of documents are clearly and unambiguously stated, otherwise banks will not be responsible for any consequences arising from that; (5) instructions for disposal of proceeds upon collection; (6) instructions for designating a collecting bank by the principal; if the principal names a specific collecting bank, the remitting bank is to use such bank as the collecting bank, but if the principal does not name a collecting bank the remitting bank is free to make his own choice as to the collecting bank in the country of payment; (7) other special instructions on bank charges, store and insurance of goods and whether or not to protest in the event of dishonor by the importer, and case of need; (8) the declaration of banks' disclaimers under a collection.

In practice, many bank's collection application forms no longer list all the contents above, especially the instruction on the rights and liabilities of different parties involved in a collection, and often include an indication of the collection application subject to the Uniform Rules for Collections, ICC Publication No. 522 (URC522) instead, which indirectly specifies the rights and liabilities of them in a collection process. Chart 4.3 is the sample of collection application.

托收委托书

致：中国银行广州分行
TO: BANK OF CHINA GUANGZHOU
We hand the undermentioned item for disposal in accordance with the following instructions and subject to the terms and conditions set out overleaf for

Original Collection Application
Date: 18th, May, 2003
兹送上下列文件，请按照下述指示办理，本司并同意遵照背面之条款。

[X] Please advance against the bill/documents
请予垫款
[ ] Please do not made any advance
无须垫款

[X] COLLECTION 代收
[ ] NEGOTIATION under Documentary Credit
议付信用证下单据

Please mark 请填上下列文件的份数
Number of DOCUMENTS ATTACHED

我司账号 Our A/C No. 87364-752-9251

Draft 汇票	Bill of lading 提单	Airway bill 空运单	Cargo Receipt 货物收据	Invoice 发票		Memo. 中旅社 承运单据	Cert. Of Qual/Quan. 品质/数量证明书	Cert. Of Origin 产地证明书	Ins. Pol/Cert. 保险单/证明	Packing List 装箱单	Weight List 重量单	Bene. Cert. 受益人证明书	Cable Copy 电报副本
				Comm.	Cust.								
2/2	4/4			2/2			1/1	1/1		1/1			

OTHER DOCUMENTS 其他文件

DRAWEE 付款人 Good Luck Company, Hongkong

ISSUING BANK 开证银行 | DOCUMENTARY CREDIT NO. 信用证编号

TENOR 期限 AT SIGHT DRAFT NO./DATE 票号/日期 18th, May | DRAFT AMOUNT 金额 HK$ 652, 450.00

FOR "BILLS NOT UNDER L/C" PLEASE FOLLOW INSTRUCTIONS MARKED "X" 如属非信用证下单据请按下列有 X 之条款办理

Deliver documents against PAYMENT/~~ACCEPTANCE~~ 付款/承兑交单
[ ] Acceptance/payment may be defered pending arrival of carrying vessel 货到后方承兑/交单
Collection charges outside Guangzhou for account of Drawee 外埠代收手续费付款人负担
Please collect interest at 5% p.a. from Drawee 请向付款人按年息 5% 计收利息
[X] Please waived interest/charges [ ] Do not waive interest/charges 如拒付利息/手续费可免收/~~不可免收~~ if refuse in the event of dishonour 如付款人拒绝承兑或付款
Please warehouse and insure goods for our account 请将各货物人仓投足保险，各费用由我司负责
[X] Please do not protest [ ] Protest 请不须/请做拒绝承兑/付款证书
[X] Advise dishonour by [ ] Airmail [X] Cable 若未兑付请以~~航邮~~/电报通知
[X] In case of need refer to A Trading Co., Hong Kong Who will assist you to abtain acceptance/payment but who has no authority to amend the terms of the bill 该公司会协助贵行取得承兑/付款但无权更改任何条款
[X] Designated Collecting Bank (if any): 指定托收银行 Standard Chartered Bank Ltd., Hong Kong

PAYMENT INSTRUCTIONS
请将款项收我司账号
[X] Please credit proceeds to our A/C No. 9005-2727985473
其他 [ ] Others

OTHER INSTRUCTIONS 其他指示
如有查询，请洽我司。
In case of any questions, please contact our Mr./Miss 王江 Tel No. 35678765

For: Guangdong Arts & Craft Imp. & Exp. Company

Authorized Signature(s) 负责人签字

Chart 4.3 Sample of Collection Application

- **Collection Instruction**

The collection instruction is the key document used to instruct the collecting bank on a specific collection business by the remitting bank and the handling of the transaction by the collecting bank will be governed solely by the instructions contained in the collection instruction, the contents of which should be in accordance with the collection application form.

According to URC522, documents sent for collection must be accompanied by a collection order giving the principal's complete and precise instructions. Banks are only permitted to act upon the specific instructions given by the principal in the collection order. The most important parts included in the collection instruction are instructions regarding documents and payments.

4.2.3 Uniform Rules for Collection

Although documentary collections, in one form or another, have been in use for a long time, questions arose about how to effect transactions in a practical, fair, and uniform manner. The *Uniform Rules for Collections* (URC) is the internationally recognized codification of rules unifying banking practice regarding collection operations for bill of exchanges and for documentary collections. The URC was developed by the International Chamber of Commerce (ICC) in Paris. It is revised and updated from time to time, and the valid version is 1995 Revision, ICC publication No. 522.

- **Application of URC522**

The URC522 shall apply to all collections where such rules are incorporated into the text of the collection instruction and are binding on all parties unless otherwise expressly agreed or contrary to the provisions of a national law.

- **Release of Commercial Documents**

Collections should not contain bill of exchange payable at a future date with instructions that commercial documents are to be delivered against payment. If a collection contains a bill of exchange payable at a future date, the collection instruction should state whether the commercial documents are to be released to the drawee against D/A or D/P. In absence of such statement, commercial documents will be released only against payment and the collecting bank will not be responsible for any consequences arising out of any delay in the delivery of documents. If a collection contains a bill of exchange payable at a future date and the collection instruction indicates that commercial documents are to be released against payment, documents will be released only against such payment.

- **Liabilities of Banks**

If a bank elects to handle a collection for its customer, the bank will act as an agent for its customer to collect the proceeds, and should act in good faith and exercise reasonable care upon the instructions given in the collection order. Banks will be liable for the loss caused by negligence on the part of themselves. According to URC522, Article 16, amounts collected (less charges, disbursements or expenses) must be made available without delay to the party from whom the collection instruction was received in accordance with the terms and conditions of the collection instruction.

It is the responsibility of the party preparing the collection instruction to ensure that the terms for the delivery of documents are clearly and unambiguously stated, otherwise banks will not be responsible for any consequences arising from that. If the proceeds cannot be obtained, the principal will assume the loss.

 4-3

有关托收银行谨慎注意义务的案例

委托人（出口商）×公司委托托收行 A 银行向位于 F 国的代收行 B 银行提交单据，托收方式为 D/P at sight。在向托收行 A 银行交单时，出口商×公司在其提交给托收行的托收指示中提供的进口名称和地址为"Company Y, Block NO. 2, Freedom Blvd, 9002, Country F"，并在代收行名称和地址栏位填写了从进口商处获得的下述信息：Bank B C/O Company Y, Bldg NO. 1, Street NO. 1, 9000 City E, Country F Attn：Mr. R（Bank Officer）。

A 银行寄单时，在收件人处照抄了上述代收行名称和地址栏位内容。之后由于出口商迟迟未收到货款，经查询，进口商已凭托收行 A 银行直接寄送给口商而非代收行的托收单据中的提单提货。

经分析发现，上述乌龙事件是由于委托人和托收行双方均未关注并理解进口商提供的代收行信息中的英文单词"C/O"的含义所致，加入了本不该填写在代收行地址中的内容，而造成了投递环节的张冠李戴。C/O ×××（Care of）是"由×××转交"之意。如在收件人地址缮制时加入此描述，快递公司只需把邮件交给 C/O 后面所提及的公司地址即算完成了投递。

该案例无论是从国际惯例还是法律层面分析，都是托收行在谨慎处理方面的欠缺使其面临承担相应责任的风险。URC522 第 9 条规定，银行以善意行事，并且以合理的谨慎履行职责。此案中，托收行在专业服务上有违 URC522 第 9 条规定的合理谨慎从事原则，并且托收行也不能以 URC522 第 4 条关于托收指示不正确而免责。

托收行将单据误寄进口商是由于其未理解 C/O 的含义又没与委托人做任何澄清，寄送单据时机械照搬委托人提供的地址资料。委托人在其托收指示中明确指出付款条件是 D/P at sight，即要求托收行指示代收行，凭进口商的付款方能交单给进口商；除此之外，委托人还提供了代收行的资料。因此，出口商的本意是委托托收行寄单给代收行。托收行在寄送单据时加上了 C/O 等信息，导致单据误被直接寄送给进口商，这显然有违委托人的托收指示本意。

（资料来源：徐珺.由托收案谈银行的谨慎处理原则[J].中国外汇,2014 年第 9 期）

- **Interest, Charges and Expenses**

As to the collection of interest, where the collection instruction expressly states that interest may not be waived and the drawee refuses to pay such interest, the presenting bank will not deliver documents and will not be responsible for any consequences arising out of any delay in the delivery of documents. If the collection instruction specifies that interest is to be collected and the drawee refuses to pay such interest, the presenting bank may deliver the documents against payment or acceptance or on other terms and conditions as the case may be, without collecting such interest.

- **Actions Taken in Dishonor**

A bill of exchange is dishonored when a sight bill of exchange is not paid on presentation or when a usance bill of exchange is not accepted on presentation or not paid at maturity. When an inward collection is dishonored, the collecting bank must examine the collection instruction to see whether the bill of exchange is required to be protested. Under URC522, the statement of whether protest is to be made will be clearly indicated in the collection instruction. If there is no such wording about it, the bank has no obligation to arrange protest in case of dishonor.

- **Partial Payment**

Partial payment is an important clause in the contract, in respect of clean collections, partial payments may be accepted if and to the extent to which and on the conditions on which partial payments are authorized by the law in force in the place of payment. The financial documents will be released to the drawee only when full payment thereof has been received, and in respect of documentary collections, partial payments will only be accepted if specifically authorized in the collection instruction. However, unless otherwise instructed, the presenting bank will release the documents to the drawee only after full payment has been received, and the presenting bank will not be responsible for any consequences arising out of any delay in the delivery of documents.

4.3 Risk Protection and Financing under Collection

4.3.1 Risks Involved

- **Risks for the Exporter**

Although a documentary collection makes it possible for the exporter to retain the title to the goods until the drawee either effects payment or accepts a bill of exchange compared to an open account, a documentary collection still has its demerits to the exporter, such as political risks, transfer risks, commercial risks, credit risks, uncertain date of payment, etc. Risks to the seller center around the fact that payment is not made until after the goods are shipped. The seller assumes liability for shipping, insurance, and storage while the goods are in transit and before payment is made. If the buyer does not pay the bill of exchange the seller is still responsible for these costs. If the buyer refuses payment (in D/P terms) or acceptance (in D/A terms) the seller retains ownership of the shipment. The seller may have the goods shipped back or try to sell them to another buyer. If the buyer takes no action, customs may seize the goods and auction or otherwise dispose of them. Some risks are described below:

- Non-acceptance or non-payment by the importer due to bankruptcy or insolvency of the importer, or the significant drop of market price of the merchandise may occur to the exporter. In such negative circumstances, the goods, if not taken up by the importer, may incur demurrage, warehousing, insurance and other related charges to the exporter until the importer wishes to pay for the collection or the exporter makes other arrangements to sell the goods. The goods may also have to be reshipped at the exporter's expense.
- Insurance coverage by the seller or buyer may be inadequate. If the merchandise is either damaged or lost, the importer would probably refuse to honor the collection. To avoid this problem, exporters should investigate "Contingency" or "Difference in Conditions" insurance policies and consider protecting their financial interest on all foreign shipments.
- The exporter might have to wait an indeterminate length of time to receive payment/ acceptance. This is dependent on various factors such as the method by which payment is made (terminal-based communication, SWIFT, cable, or mail) and on the availability of foreign exchange in the country of the buyer.
- The importer may not have a valid importer license which could result in the refusal to accept the goods or in a delay in payment or in acceptance of the bill of exchange. The exporter should always verify that the importer has this license (if required) before shipping on a collection basis.
- In some importing countries excising foreign exchange restrictions, the importers may fail to apply for the necessary foreign exchange in time, thus those requiting foreign exchange may have to go on a waiting list that may extend several months or even years.

● **Risks for the Importer**

A transaction based on collection terms is not entirely without risks for the importer, the main risk for buyers is that goods shipped might not conform to the goods specified, and because banks deal only in documents and not in goods, the buyer's only recourse is with the seller. Whether the goods are of the contract description entirely depends on the exporter's credit standing.

Still, in D/A term, by accepting a bill of exchange, the importer incurs two separate legal liabilities, that is, he will have another legal liability on the bill of exchange besides his liability on the sales contract. In some countries, if a bill of exchange is protested, this can ruin the reputation of a trader and may be considered an act of bankruptcy. Therefore, the consequences of non-acceptance or non-payment on the part of the importer will be worse than anything else.

4.3.2 Notes, Tips, and Cautions

- **For Sellers**
  - A seller should only agree to a collection payment if (1) the seller does not doubt the buyer's ability and willingness to pay for the goods; (2) the buyer's country is politically, economically, and legally stable; (3) there are no foreign exchange restrictions in the buyer's country, or all licenses for foreign exchange have already been obtained; and (4) the shipped goods are easily remarketable.
  - The seller should check on the buyer's creditworthiness and reputation before consenting to a documentary collection, especially D/A terms.
  - If the buyer does not get the required documents he may refuse the collection altogether, or in D/A terms he may unknowingly sign the acceptance and then find that he cannot clear the goods through customs. Although he is legally responsible for payment, he may be unable to pay because he never received the goods. Either leaves the seller in a compromised situation. So the seller should find out from the buyer what documents are required for customs clearance in the buyer's country. The seller should then assemble the documents carefully and make sure they are in the required form and endorsed or authenticated as necessary.
  - As a rule, the remitting (seller's) bank will not review the documents before forwarding them to the presenting/collecting (buyer's) bank. Review of the documentation is the primary responsibility of the buyer.

- **For Buyers**
  - A buyer should only agree to documentary collection payment terms if there is trust that the seller will ship the goods as specified in accordance with the agreement between buyer and seller.
  - The buyer should be aware of any documentation, certifications, or authorizations that may be required for customs clearance or for eventual sale of the goods in his own country, and specify all documentation required of the seller in his agreement with the seller.
  - Upon presentation by the presenting bank the buyer must carefully inspect the documents to make certain they meet all specifications for customs clearance and for eventual sale of the goods in his own country. As a special favor, the collecting bank may allow the buyer to take temporary possession of the documents for

inspection before payment. The collecting bank, however, assumes responsibility for the documents until redemption. In the above case, the buyer should immediately return the entire set of documents to the collecting bank if he is unwilling or unable to meet the agreed upon payment procedure.

- The buyer may not sample or inspect the goods before accepting and paying for the documents unless authorized to do so by the seller. The buyer may, however, specify a certificate of inspection from a reliable third party as part of the required documentation package.

- Unless bound by a separate contract, the buyer assumes no liability for goods if he refuses to take possession of the documents.

- With D/A terms, the buyer may receive the goods and resell them for profit before the time bill of exchange matures, thereby using the proceeds of the sale to pay for the goods. The buyer is responsible for payment, however, even if the goods cannot be sold.

● **For Banks**

- Documents sent for collection must be accompanied by a collection order giving the principal's complete and precise instructions. Banks are only permitted to act upon the specific instructions given by the principal in the collection order. If a remitting, collecting, or presenting bank cannot comply with the instructions in the principal's collection order, it must immediately advise the party from whom it received the order.

- Banks have the responsibility to verify that documents received with a collection order appear on their face to be as specified in the collection order, but do not have the responsibility to authenticate individual documents. If it appears that documents are missing from the document package (as determined by those listed in the collection order) the bank must immediately notify the party from whom the documents were received.

- Collection documents may be sent directly to the collecting/presenting bank or through an intermediary bank called a correspondent bank. The drawee is to be presented the documents in the form in which they were received from the principal. However, the remitting and collecting banks may affix stamps or rubber stamps, make endorsements, or attach a cover letter to the document package. If an incomplete or incorrect address of the drawee is shown on the collection order, the collecting bank may, without obligation or responsibility, attempt to find the correct address. The banks must make presentation of documents without delay. If a collection remains unpaid or a bill of exchange is not accepted and the collecting bank receives no new instructions within 90 days, it may return the documents to the bank from which it received the collection order.

- If the documents call for payment in a specific currency, the banks must, unless otherwise instructed, collect payment for documents in that currency. The collecting bank may not accept partial payments from the drawee unless otherwise instructed in the collection order.

4.3.3 Financing under the Collection

- **Financing Provided by the Remitting Bank to the Exporter**

Financing provided by the remitting bank to the exporter usually takes the form of export bill of exchange purchasing under documentary collection. The exporter hands the bill of exchange and the full set of shipping documents over to the remitting bank for the advance payment before the proceeds are collected, i.e., the remitting bank makes a loan to the exporter against the bill of exchanges and documents under a collection, the guarantee of which is the proceeds of selling goods to the buyer.

The risk for advance made by the remitting bank under a collection is greater than that under a L/C, for the collection is based on the commercial credit of the importer, especially for D/A terms, the importer can get the documents from the collecting bank only by its acceptance of the bill of exchange, in the case of non-payment by the importer at the maturity date and at the same time the financed exporter is insolvency, then the remitting bank will have to assume the loss.

- **Financing Provided by the Collecting Bank to the Importer**

  > **Import bill of exchange advance**(进口押汇)

Import bill advance means the collecting bank uses the documents especially the title document as a pledge to effect payment to the exporter for the importer before the importer actually pays. It usually involves great risks for banks, and is generally used under D/P term. The financing of import bill of exchange advance is granted on case basis, and can only be used to pay outwards to the exporter.

  > **Trust receipt**(凭信托收据借单提货)

Under the term of D/P at a fixed time after sight, when the goods and documents have both arrived at the destination, but the bill of exchange is not mature, the importer is eager to obtain the goods, then the importer may sign a written undertaking to the collecting bank to borrow the documents of title in advance and obtain the goods from shipping company in order to warehouse or sell them.

The so-called "*Trust Receipt*" is a written guaranty provided by the importer to the collecting bank for the purchase of borrowing B/L from the latter, in which the importer declares that he will take delivery of the goods, declare to the customs, store the goods, take out insurance on and push sales of the goods as the consignee of the collecting bank, and acknowledge the title to the goods and proceeds of the sale belonging to the collecting bank and with guarantee to make the payment on the date due.

Since this is an operation of "trust", the legal title to and real owner of the goods remains with the collecting bank, but the physical possession of the goods is being turned over to the trustee in the hope that he will turn over the proceeds of any sale to the entruster. It is risky for the collecting bank to release documents to the importer against T/R, for the importer may not pay after obtaining the goods. Consequently, trust receipt financing, as the term implies, requires a great degree of trust in reputation, creditworthiness, honesty of the customer acting as the trustee. Usually trust receipt is not used solely by banks, but as a means to guard against risks in financing business by which to guarantee the legal ownership of goods for banks.

> **Delivery of goods against bank guarantee**(提货担保)

When the goods arrived at the destination port before the documents, the buyer may obtain a bank guarantee from the collecting bank and submit it to the carrier in order to obtain the goods for sale. It is rather common for the goods to arrive in importer's country earlier than the documents by mail if the distance between trade countries is not far away from each other. Under such circumstances, the buyer cannot pay to redeem the documents and cannot pick up goods from the carrier, but with the shipping guarantee issued by the collecting bank to the carrier, the importer can take over the goods. By issuing the bank guarantee, the collecting bank will bear the risks of non-payment and losing the goods title and stand the claim from the carrier as stated in the bank guarantee.

★ Key Words

Collection(托收)

The Principal/Drawer(委托人)

The Collecting/Presenting Bank(代收行/提示行)

The Remitting Bank(托收行)

The Drawee(付款人)

Principal's representative in case of need(需要时的委托人代理)

Clean Collection(光票托收)

Documentary Collection(跟单托收)

Documents against payment (D/P)(付款交单)

D/P at sight(即期付款交单)

D/P at a fixed time after sight(远期付款交单)

Documents against acceptance (D/A)(承兑交单)

Direct Collection(直接托收)

Import bill of exchange advance(进口押汇)

Trust receipt(凭信托收据借单提货)

Delivery of goods against bank guarantee(提货担保)

★ Exercise

一、单选题(Exclusive Choice Question)

1. (　　) is the creditors in the collection.
   A. The drawer　　　　　　　　　　B. drawee
   C. remitting bank　　　　　　　　　D. collecting bank

2. Which bank plays the role of accepting the commission of remitting bank to present the bill of exchange and collect the payment? (　　)
   A. Remitting bank　　　　　　　　　B. Collecting bank
   C. Payment bank　　　　　　　　　　D. Correspondent bank

3. The collection is a kind of (　　).
   A. remittance way
   B. method to ensure the exporter can get payment
   C. commercial credit of payment
   D. way that exporter provide financing to importer

4. The bill of exchange used in collection is (　　).
   A. commercial bill, belongs to commercial credit
   B. commercial bill, belongs to bank's credit
   C. bank's bill, belongs to commercial credit
   D. bank's bill, belongs to bank's credit

5. One of the obligations of collection is (　　).
   A. to ensure that the goods are protected
   B. according to the instructions of the principal
   C. to check the contents of documents
   D. to guarantee for receiving payment

6. 托收行将单据寄到(　　),进口商接到通知后,前来银行取单。
   A. 己方银行　　B. 对方托收行　　C. 代收行　　D. 出口方银行

7. Principal 在托收业务中的意思是(　　)。
   A. 托收行　　　B. 卖方　　　　C. 代收行　　　D. 买方

8. 在托收方式下,下列对出口商最有利的交单条款是(　　)。
   A. 即期付款交单　　　　　　　　　B. 远期付款交单
   C. 承兑交单　　　　　　　　　　　D. 远期限付款交单,凭信托收据借单

9. 付款交单方式下,若货物先到而付款期限未到,买方可按下述方式提货(　　)。
   A. D/P at sight　　　　　　　　　B. D/P. T/R
   C. D/P. T/T　　　　　　　　　　　D. D/A. T/R

10. 付款交单凭信托收据借单是(　　)的融资。
    A. 进口商给予出口商　　　　　　　B. 托收行给予进口商
    C. 代收行给予出口商　　　　　　　D. 代收行或出口商给予进口商

二、多选题（Multiple Choice Question）
1. 进出口业务中用的支付方式有：（   ）。
   A. 付款交单　　　B. 汇款　　　C. 信用证　　　D. 托收
2. 托收结算方式下出口商面临的风险有：（   ）。
   A. 开证行拒付　　　　　　　　B. 进口商破产倒闭
   C. 进口国发生内乱或战争　　　D. 进口未申领到进口许可证
3. 托收行在向代收行寄出跟单托收项下单据前的处理手续应包括：（   ）。
   A. 审核托收申请人制填的申请书　　B. 核对单据的种类和份数
   C. 审核单据内容是否与合同相符　　D. 缮制出口托收委托书
4. 采用托收方式结算时出口商应注意：（   ）。
   A. 考察进口商的资信和经营作风　　B. 了解进口国的贸易和外汇管制
   C. 了解托收行的资信　　　　　　　D. 出口合同争取采用 CIF 条件成交
5. 托收结算方式下银行免责的情况有：（   ）。
   A. 单据在寄送中的延误所引起的后果
   B. 不可抗力所引起的后果
   C. 单据不相符所引起的后果
   D. 由于疏忽没有按委托指示所引起的后果
6. 托收的交单方式有：（   ）。
   A. 付款交单　　　　　　　　B. 承兑交单
   C. 承诺付款交单　　　　　　D. 议付交单
8. 光票托收一般用于（   ）。
   A. 收取货款尾数　　　　　　B. 代垫费用
   C. 样品费　　　　　　　　　D. 其他贸易从属费

三、判断题（True or False）
1. 托收方式是顺汇方式。（   ）
2. 在托收业务中，当进口商没有能力付款时，托收行负有连带责任。（   ）
3. 当银行将发生的一些意外情况通知委托人时，委托人必须及时指示，否则，因此而发生的损失由委托人自行负责。（   ）
4. 代收行与付款人之间存在委托代理关系。（   ）
5. 银行在受理托收业务时，不用承担连带责任，因此，对于未按照申请书的指示而产生的后果，银行也不用对其过失负责。（   ）
6. 承兑交单，即 Document Against Payment，卖方开立的一定是远期汇票。（   ）
7. 承兑交单方式对进口方十分有利。（   ）
8. 托收通过银行进行，所以托收属于银行信用。（   ）
9. 托收的最大特点是"收妥付汇、实收实付"。（   ）
10. 付款交单（D/P）与承兑交单（D/A）都有一定的风险，一般说来，D/A 方式风险较小，更易为卖方所接受。（   ）

Chapter 5

Payment Method Ⅲ: L/C

Chinese Company A received an order from Company B of United States, which is required settlement by Letter of Credit. The issuing bank was City Bank New York Branch, and the advising bank was Industrial and Commercial Bank of China Shanghai Branch. The Letter of Credit required commercial documents, like Shanghai-New York Port to Port Ocean Bills of Lading, Commercial Invoice, Quality Certificate, Certificate of Origin, Packing list, etc. Do you know the main operation process of L/C? Letter of credit, which is called L/C for short, has been used for more than 150 years to facilitate trade by providing payment against presentation of documents relating to the transaction as specified in the credit, which are probably still the most versatile and effective means of securing payment and one of the most important method of financing. This chapter mainly introduces the definition, parties and procedures of L/C in international trade.

★ Learning Objectives

(1) To enable the readers to know the definition, characteristics and basic parties to L/C.

(2) To enable the readers to understand the types of L/C and master their proper usages.

(3) To enable the readers to master the procedures of L/C and the main contents of L/C.

(4) To enable the readers to understand the risks faced with the relevant parties to L/C and the possible ways to avoid such risks.

(5) To enable the readers to understand the financing function of L/C to the seller or the buyer.

(6) To enable the readers to be familiar with widely used international customs and practices like UCP600.

5.1 An Overview of L/C

In international trade, the importer and the exporter have little chance to know each other because they are so far away from each other. The importer expects the exporter to deliver goods in time but she herself hopes to pay after reselling the goods. In such a process, financing provided by her bank is needed. The exporter, however, hopes to get funds from the bank before delivery of goods and get proceeds in time after that. L/C is made on the bank's credit, and the issuing bank undertakes the primary responsibility for payment. L/C promotes the development of international trade by guaranteeing the proceeds as well as the documents and offering financial facilities to both sides.

 5-1

信用证的发展简史

信用证的前身可以追溯到12世纪。作为一种最简单的"商业信用证",其运作方式是以支付汇票换取所有权单据,这种支付要通过第三方"开证人"进行,开证人充当的是中介人角色。银行承担义务的现代商业信用证出现于19世纪,最早是芬兰进口商在1840年从巴西进口咖啡豆时使用的信用证。在其后不到一个世纪的时间里,国际商会制定了《跟单信用证统一惯例》,该惯例推动和规范了信用证在国际贸易结算中的应用。由于信用证很好地解决了国际贸易中买卖双方的风险分担问题,促进了国际贸易的发展,因此它被誉为国际贸易的"生命血液"。

信用证在我国出现已有二十多年的发展历史。改革开放之初我国已将国内信用证与商业汇票同时推出,但由于国内信用证不适应当时的国内信用和经济发展环境,我国国内信用证并没有获得实质性发展。随着我国国内贸易的日益发展,为促进商品流通,规范社会信用,改变企业间相互拖欠,减少困扰经济发展的三角债问题,保持我国社会主义市场经济的健康发展,1997年中国人民银行制定颁布了《国内信用证结算办法》,正式将信用证引入国内贸易结算,同期在国内贸易领域大力推广的还有票据类的国内结算工具,其中包括与国内信用证极其相似的银行承兑汇票。遗憾的是,在此后的十年时间里,国内信用证在与银行承兑汇票的同台竞争中,始终处于下风。银行承兑汇票以其高流通性、手续简便、规则成熟,最终赢得了几乎所有的细分市场。国内信用证仅是尝试性地开了个头,一直停留在银行的菜单状态,乏人问津,发展非常缓慢。直到2007年,随着我国市场经济的飞速发展,企业对银行支付结算服务的要求不断提高,国内信用证实现了跨越式发展;特别是2011年,由于国家宏观调控,各商业银行信贷规模紧张,银票贴现价格一路飙升,企业接受银行汇票的意愿降低,此时国内信用证因银行消化渠道多样,受信贷规模影响较小等特性得到了突飞猛进的发展,并逐渐被部分企业应用于日常的国内贸易结算中。

5.1.1 Definition of L/C

According to UCP600, L/C means any arrangement, however named or described, that is irrevocable and thereby constitutes a definite undertaking of the issuing bank to honour[①] a

---

[①] Here "honour" means: (1) to pay at sight if the credit is available by sight payment; (2) to incur a deferred payment undertaking and pay at maturity if the credit is available by deferred payment, or (3) to accept a bill of exchange drawn by the beneficiary and pay at maturity if the credit is available by acceptance.

complying presentation①.

In simple terms, an L/C is a written promise by the issuing bank to the beneficiary, under which the bank will pay a certain sum to the beneficiary if the beneficiary of the L/C provides the bank with specified documents within a prescribed period, which all comply with the terms and conditions of the L/C. Banks act as intermediaries to collect payment from the buyer in exchange for the transfer of documents that enable the holder to take possession of the goods. L/C provides a high level of protection and security to both the buyer and the seller engaged in international trade. The seller is assured that payment will be made by a party independent of the buyer so long as the terms and conditions of the credit are met, while the buyer is assured that payment will be released to the seller only after the bank has received the title documents called for in the L/C.

信用证，又称信用状，是银行有条件的付款承诺。在国际贸易中使用的信用证是指开证银行应申请人(一般是进口人)的要求并按其指示向第三方(一般是出口人)开立的载有一定金额、在一定期限内凭符合规定的单据付款的书面保证文件。根据《跟单信用证统一惯例》(UCP600)的规定，无论其如何命名或描述，信用证意指一项约定，该约定不可撤销并因此构成开证行兑现支付请求。

简而言之，信用证是开证行开给受益人的，在规定时间内凭符合信用证条款和条件的文件支付一定金额给受益人的书面承诺。银行作为中介机构承担着从买方收到货款从而转移单证给持有人以占有货物的作用。信用证为从事国际贸易的买卖双方提供了高水平的保护和安全。卖方保证独立于买方的一方付款只要满足信贷的条件，而买方保证将付款给卖方只要银行收到信用证项下要求的单证。

Regarding the Role of Banks

It is important to note that documentary L/C procedures are not infallible. Things can and do go wrong. Since banks act as intermediaries between the buyer and the seller, both look to the banks as protectors of their interests. However, while banks have clear cut responsibilities, they are also shielded from certain problems deemed to be out of their control or responsibility. Several instances:

1. Banks act upon specific instructions given by the applicant (the buyer) in the documentary L/C. The buyer's instructions left out of the L/C by mistake or omitted because "we've always done it that way" don't count. The buyer, therefore, should take great care in preparing the application so that it gives complete and clear instructions.

2. Banks are required to act in good faith and exercise reasonable care to verify that the documents submitted *appear* to be as listed in the L/C. They are, however, under no

---

① Here "A complying presentation" means a presentation that is in accordance with the terms and conditions of the credit, the applicable provisions of these rules and international standard banking practice. Presentation means either the delivery of documents under a credit to the issuing bank or nominated bank or the documents so delivered.

obligation to confirm the authenticity of the documents submitted.

3. Banks are not liable, nor can they be held accountable for the acts of third parties. Third parties include freight forwarders, forwarding agents, customs authorities, insurance companies, and other banks. Specifically, they are not responsible for delays or consequences resulting from Acts of God (floods, earthquakes, etc.), riots, wars, civil commotions, strikes, lockouts, or other causes beyond their control.

4. Banks also assume no liability or responsibility for loss arising out of delays or loss in transit of messages, letters, documents, etc.

5. Because banks deal in documents instead of goods, they assume no responsibility regarding the quantity or quality of goods shipped. They are only concerned that documents presented appear on their face to be consistent with the terms and conditions of the documentary L/C. Any disputes as to quality or quantity of goods delivered must be settled between the buyer and the seller.

6. So long as the documents presented to the banks appear on their face to comply with the terms and conditions of the L/C, banks may accept them and initiate the payment process as stipulated in the documentary L/C.

5.1.2 Characteristics of L/C

● **Primary Liability of the Issuing Bank to Make Payment**(开证行负有第一性付款责任)

The issuing bank undertakes to effect payment by opening an L/C, quite independent of whether the applicant is bankrupt or is in fault or not, provided the documents presented by the beneficiary are in compliance with the terms and conditions of the L/C. The major difference between a collection and an L/C lies in that the former is based on a trader's credit while the latter on a banker's credit and the issuing bank is irrevocably bound to honour as of the time it issues the credit.

Banks are required to act in good faith and exercise reasonable care to verify that the documents submitted appear to be as listed in the L/C. They are, however, under no obligation for the form, sufficiency, accuracy, genuineness, falsification or legal effect of any document, or for the general or particular conditions stipulated in a document or superimposed. Moreover, banks also assume no liability or responsibility for loss arising out of delays or loss in transit of messages, letters, documents, and assume no liability for errors in translation or interpretation of technical terms and may transmit L/C terms without translating them. However, if a nominated bank determines a presentation to be complying and forwards the documents to the issuing bank, the issuing bank must honour or negotiate, or reimburse that nominated bank, even if the documents have been lost in transit.

● **The Credit Is Independent and Self-sufficient**(信用证是独立的自足性文件)

Although an L/C is issued on the basis of the contract, such L/C by its nature is a separate transaction from the sales or other contracts on which it may be based, for the sales contract shall be only binding on the importer and the exporter, while the L/C is an engagement between the issuing bank and the beneficiary which should abide by the L/C application and related international customs to regulate the obligations and rights of the involved parties. The terms of an L/C are independent of the underlying transaction even if an L/C expressly refers to that transaction.

According to UCP600, the undertaking of a bank to honour, to negotiate or to fulfill any other obligation under the L/C is not subject to claims or defenses by the applicant resulting from its relationships with the issuing bank or the beneficiary.

● **Dealing with Documents Only**(纯单据业务)

It is important to remember that all parties in the L/C transaction deal with documents, but not goods. When banks receives the documents submitted by the beneficiary, they examine the documents to make sure whether the terms and conditions are fulfilled and are not in a position to verify whether the goods supplied by the beneficiary actually conform to those specified in the L/C or in the documents. As long as the documents presented by the beneficiary are in compliance with the terms and conditions of the L/C, the issuing bank or the nominated bank should honour or negotiate. Therefore, to avoid unnecessary costs, delays, and disputes in the examination of documents, the applicant and beneficiary should carefully consider which documents should be required, by whom they should be produced and the time frame for presentation.

Abusing the Characteristics of Documentary L/C

The opportunity for fraud does exist under documentary L/C. As the banks only deal with documents but not goods, the seller has the opportunity to present fraudulent documents for payments. It's advisable for the exporter and the importer to know his/her counterpart and banks involved and to exercise caution and common sense in making decisions. Following are some fraud examples of abusing the characteristics of documentary L/C.

1. The seller has reported receiving and advice and confirmation of a documentary L/C from nonexistent banks. The perpetrator of the fraud attempts to get the seller to ship the goods and present documents for payment to the nonexistent bank. By the time the seller is aware of the fraud, the "buyer" has received the goods and filed away.

2. The buyer has reported receiving the empty container or container filled with sand instead of the goods they ordered. By the time she received the shipment, the bank has already paid the "seller".

3. Some buyers of commodity have reported being defrauded by the seller providing fraudulent shipping documents, evidencing shipment on a nonexistent ship.

5.1.3 International Rules and Customs for L/C

In order to facilitate the flow of international trade at a time when nationalism and protectionism posed serious threats to the world trading system, ICC (International Chamber of Commerce) first introduced UCP (Uniform Customs and Practice for Documentary Letter of Credit) in 1933 to alleviate the confusion caused by individual countries' promoting their own national rules on L/C practice, which is the universally recognized set of rules governing the use of the documentary L/Cs in international trade. Up to now, UCP has experienced the versions of 1951, 1962, 1974, 1983, 1993 and 2006. The majority of banks in most countries around the world have adopted the UCP as a code to standardize conditions under which bankers are prepared to issue L/Cs and the interpretation of L/C practice. The current version is UCP 600, approved by the ICC Commission on Banking Techniques and Practice during its meeting from 24th to 25th October, being put into use on July 1, 2007. All definitions and general documentary requirements referred to in this chapter are in accordance with UCP600 unless otherwise stated.

在民族主义和保护主义严重威胁世界贸易体系构成的情况下，为方便国际贸易的流动，国际商会在1933年首次规定《跟单信用证统一惯例》，这是国际贸易中公认的规则。到目前为止，跟单信用证经历了1951年、1962年、1974年、1983年、1993年和2006年几个版本。大多数国家的银行采用《跟单信用证统一惯例》作为银行办理信用证业务的依据。目前的版本是UCP600，于2007年7月1日正式实施。除非另有说明，本章所有涉及的定义和一般单证要求均按照UCP600。

However, as anyone ever working with an L/C knows, there is plenty of disagreement between all parties concerned, such as banks, account parties, and beneficiaries. Sometimes the UCP just doesn't clarify a situation the way you think it should. To help address some of this confusion, the International Chamber of Commerce Banking Commission created the International Standard Banking Practice (ISBP), which is not intended to amend the UCP and is rather a guide as to how the rules should be applied in a day-to-day working environment. Therefore, the references to related stipulations of L/Cs in practical work should be based on both of them, and it should also be remembered that in some instances this may differ from national law.

5.1.4 Contents and Form of L/C

● **Contents of L/C**(信用证的内容)

In practice, though the forms of L/C issued by banks may be different among countries all over the world, the basic contents are quite similar. It usually includes the following items: (1) details on the L/C itself, including the L/C Number, the issuing date, the expiry date and place, and the presentation period, etc.; (2) the form and type of L/C, say whether it can be transferable or should be confirmed by the advising bank, etc.; (3) basic parties, including the issuing bank, the beneficiary, the applicant, the advising bank, etc.; (4) bill of exchange clause, including the drawer, the drawee, and the payee of the bill of exchange; (5) settlement conditions, including sight payment, deferred payment, acceptance of bill of exchange and negotiation; (6) items on goods, shipping documents, transport and insurance; (7) L/C amount and currency; (8) additional conditions; (9) reimbursement of the paying, accepting and negotiating bank; and (10) the notation of the L/C subject to UCP600.

If an L/C is issued by SWIFT MT700, then the L/C usually includes the following items (see Table 5.1):

Table 5.1 Credit Items by SWIFT MT700

M	27	Sequence of total	合计次数
M	40A	Form of Documentary Credit	信用证类别
M	20	Documentary Credit Number	信用证编号
O	23	Reference to Pre-Advice	预告摘要
O	31C	Date of Issue	开证日期
M	31D	Date and Place of Expiry	到期日及地点
O	51s	Applicant Bank	申请开证银行
M	50	Applicant	申请人
M	59	Beneficiary	受益人
M	32B	Currency Code, Amount	币别代号、金额
O	39	Amount Specification	金额说明
M	41D	Available with __ by __	由____银行使用,使用方式为____
O	42	Drafts at __ Drawn on __	汇票期限____付款人____
O	43P	Partial shipment	分运
O	43T	Transshipment	转运
O	44	Shipment/Dispatch/Taking in charge from/at __ for Transportation to __	由____转运至____
O	45A	Shipment of (goods)	货物叙述与交易条件
O	46A	Documents Required	所需单据
O	47A	Additional Conditions	附加条件
O	71B	Charges	费用
O	48	Period for Presentation	提示期间
M	49	Confirmation Instructions	保兑与否提示
O	53s	Reimbursement Bank	偿付银行
O	78	Instructions to the Pay/Acc/Neg Bank	对付款/承兑/议付银行之提示
O	57s	Advise through Bank	收电银行以外的通知银行
O	72	Bank to Bank Information	银行间备注

注:M/O 为 Mandatory 与 Optional 的缩写,前者为必要项目,后者为任意项目。

● **Issuance Forms of L/C**(信用证的开立形式)

A letter of credit can be opened at the request of the applicant by means of airmail or telecommunication, which depends on how the L/C will be forwarded to the advising bank.

➢ **By airmail**(信开本信用证)

The issuing bank airmails the original L/C through an advising bank. The airmail way costs the least to the applicant, but it is the slowest means for sending an L/C to the beneficiary. International airmail may take several days to a few weeks to reach the advising bank from date of posting. An L/C issued by airmail when received by the advising bank should be checked against the specimen signature and is rarely used nowadays as a result of the development of telecommunication technology.

➢ **By telecommunication**(电开本信用证)

Issuance by telecommunication has taken the forms of issuance by cable, telex or SWIFT in history. As a cheap, efficient and safe way to issue an L/C, SWIFT is widely used in international banking business and communication. Issuance by telecommunication consists of two forms: short cable and full text cable.

A short cable is a combination of an airmail L/C and a preliminary advice by teletransmission (such as SWIFT). The issuing bank firstly teletransmits a pre-advice, which does not show the full details of the L/C to the advising bank and follows it by a mail confirmation. The teletransmission states "details to follow" (or words of similar effect) or states that the mail confirmation is to be the operative L/C instrument, and the teletransmission will not be deemed to be the operative L/C. The issuing bank should forward the mail confirmation to confirm the brief cable informing the advising bank of issuance of the L/C without delay. The short cable costs more than airmail, but it has the advantage of giving the exporter some advance information about the L/C and provides assurance that an L/C has been opened. The beneficiary often has to pay a fee for pre-advising and advising separately.

For full text cable, the full particulars of the letter of credit are sent to the advising bank by teletransmission. In recent documentary L/C operations, an authenticated teletransmission will be deemed to be the operative L/C instrument or the operative amendment, and no mail confirmation should be sent. If a mail confirmation should nevertheless be sent, it will have no effect and the advising bank or notifying bank will have no obligation to check such mail confirmation against the operative L/C or amendment received by teletransmission. The full text cable costs more to the applicant than airmail or short cable, but it is the fastest means for the L/C to reach the beneficiary.

 5-2

按照开立手段的不同,信用证可分为信开本信用证和电开本信用证。信开本信用证

是指开证行以书信格式缮制并通过邮寄方式送达通知行的信用证，一般是一式两份或两份以上；电开本信用证是开证行用电讯方式开立和通知的信用证，可分为电报方式、电传方式和 SWIFT 方式，目前以 SWIFT 方式居多。信开本信用证的样本如下：

THE ROYAL BANK OF CANADA
BRITISH COLUMBIA INTERNATIONAL CENTRE
1055 WEST GEORGIA STREET, VANCOUVER, B.C. V6E 3P3, CANADA

CONFIRMATION OF TELEX/CABLE PRE-ADVISED　　　　DATE: APR 8, 2015

TELEX NO. 4720688 CA　　　　　　　　　　　　　　PLACE: VANCOUVER

IRREVOCABLE DOCUMENTARY CREDIT	CREDIT NUMBER: 98/0501-FTC	ADVISING BANK'S REF. NO.
ADVISING BANK: SHANGHAI A. J. FINACE CORPORATION 59 HONG KONG ROAD SHANGHAI 200002, CHINA	APPLICANT: JAMES BROWN & SONS # 304-310 JALAN STREET, TORONTO, CANADA	
BENEFICIARY: HUAXIN TRADING CO., LTD. 14TH FLOOR KINGSTAR MANSION, 676 JINLIN RD., SHANGHAI, CHINA	AMOUNT: USD46,980.00 (US DOLLARS FORTY SIX THOUSAND NINE HUNDRED AND EIGHTY ONLY)	

EXPIRY DATE: MAY 15, 2015　　FOR NEGOTIATION IN APPLICANT'S COUNTRY

GENTLEMEN:
WE HEREBY OPEN OUR IRREVOCABLE LETTER OF CREDIT IN YOUR FAVOR WHICH IS AVAILABLE BY YOUR DRAFTS AT SIGHT FOR FULL INVOICE VALUE ON US ACCOMPANIED BY THE FOLLOWING DOCUMENTS:
+ SIGNED COMMERCIAL INVOICE AND 3 COPIES
+ PACKING LIST AND 3 COPIES, SHOWING THE INDIVIDUAL WEIGHT AND MEASUREMENT OF EACH ITEM.
+ ORIGINAL CERTIFICATE OF ORIGIN AND 3 COPIES ISSUED BY THE CHAMBER OF COMMERCE.
+ FULL SET CLEAN ON BOARD OCEAN BILLS OF LADIG SHOWING FREIGHT PREPAID CONSIGNED TOORDER OF THE ROYAL BANK OF CANADA INDICATING THE ACTUAL DATE OF THE GOODS ON BOARD AND NOTIFY THE APPLICANT WITH FULL ADDRESS AND PHONE NO. 77009910.
+ INSURANCE POLICY OR CERTIFICATE FOR 130 PERCENT OF INVOICE VALUE COVERING: INSTITUTE CARGO CLAUSES (A) AS PER I.C.C. DATED1/1/1982.
+ BENEFICIARY'S CERTIFICATE CERTIFYING THAT EACH COPY OF SHIPPING DOCUMENTS HAS BEEN FAXED TO THE APPLICANT WITHEIN 48 HOURS AFTER SHIPMENT.

COVERING SHIPMENT:				
4 ITEMS TEMS OF CHINESE CERAMIC DINNERWARE INCLUDING: HX1115 544SETS, HA2012 800SETS, HX4405 443SETS AND HX4510 245SETS DETAILS IN ACCORDANCE WITH SALES CONFIRMATION SHHX98027 DATED APR. 3, 2015. [ ]FOB/[ ]CFR/ [X]CIF/ [ ]FAS TORONTO CANADA				
SHIPMENT FROM SHANGHAI	TO VANCOUVER	LATEST APRIL 30, 2015	PARTIAL SHIPMENTS PROHIBITED	TRANSSHIPMENT PROHIBITED
DRAFTS TO BE PRESENTED FOR NEGOTIATION WITHIN 15 DAYS AFTER SHIPMENT, BUT WITHIN THE VALIDITY OF CREDIT. ALL DOCUMENTS TO BE FORWARDED IN ONE COVER, BY AIRMAIL, UNLESS OTHERWISE STATED UNDER SPECIAL INSTRUCTIONS.				
SPECIAL INSTRUCTIONS: ALL BANKING CHARGES OUTSIDE CANADA ARE FOR ACCOUNT OF BENEFICIARY + ALL GOODS MUST BE SHIPPED IN ONE 20' CY TO CY CONTAINER AND B/L SHOWING THE SAME. + THE VALUE OF FREIGHT PREP AID HAS TO BE SHOWN ON BILLS OF LADIG. + DOCUMENTS WHICH FAIL TO COMPLY WITH THE TERMS AND CONDITIONS IN THE LETTER OF CREDIT SUBJECT TO A SPECIAL DISCREPANCY HANDLING FEE OF USD35.00 TO BE DEDUCTED FROM ANY PROCEEDS.				
DRAFT MUST BE MARKED AS BEING DRAWN UNDER THIS CREDIT AND BEAR ITS NUMBER; THE AMOUNTS ARE TO BE ENDORSED ON THE REVERSE HEREOF BY NEG. BANK. WE HEREBY AGREE WITH THE DRAWERS, ENDORSERS AND BONA FIDE HOLDER THAT ALL DRAFTS DRAWN UNDER AND IN COMPLIANCE WITH THE TERMS OF THIS CREDIT SHALL BE DULY HONORED UPON PRESENTATION. THIS CREDIT IS SUBJECT TO THE UNIFORM CUSTOMS AND PRACTICE FOR DOCUMENTARY CREDITS (2006 REVISION) BY THE INTERNATIONAL CHAMBER OF COMMERCE PRBLICATION NO. 600.				
DAVID JONE AUTHORIZED SIGNATURE			YOURS VERY TRULY, JOANNE SUSAN AUTHORIZED SIGNATURE	

5.1.5 Parties Involved in an L/C

● **The Applicant**(开证申请人)

According to UCP600 Article 2, applicant means the party on whose request the L/C is issued, and it is the buyer/importer that initiates the L/C process by applying to her bank to open an L/C naming the seller as the beneficiary. The buyer, therefore, may be called the buyer in commercial terms, the importer in economic terms, and the applicant in banking terms.

> **Obligations**

The applicant is liable for timely payment to the issuing bank provided there is no discrepancy between the documents and the L/C and the documents are consistent with one another.

It is essential that the application for the L/C be in conformity with the underlying sales contract between the buyer and the seller, and the buyer's instructions to the issuing bank must be clear with respect to the type of L/C, the amount, duration, required documents, shipping date, expiration date, and the beneficiary. Any requirement of the applicant should be satisfied by certain documents and be clearly indicated when making L/C application. The applicant bears the risks of any ambiguity in its instructions to issue or amend an L/C. Besides, the applicant should hand in cash deposit or provide counter guarantee to the issuing bank, the amount of which is based on the L/C worthiness of the applicant.

> **Rights**

On the other hand, the applicant has the rights to examine documents upon receiving them from the issuing bank, and also has the rights to refuse payment provided discrepancies were found and to return the documents to the issuing bank.

● **The Issuing Bank**(开证行)

When a bank issues a letter of credit at the request of the applicant or on its own behalf, it is called the issuing bank or opening bank. The issuing bank is usually the buyer's bank in international transaction.

> **Obligations**

By issuing a letter of credit, the issuing bank is irrevocably bound to honour as of the time it issues the L/C provided that the stipulated documents were presented. The undertaking of the issuing bank is irrevocable and final, which means the issuing bank can not execute the rights of recourse after its actual payment.

An issuing bank undertakes to reimburse a nominated bank that has honoured or negotiated a complying presentation and forwarded the documents to the issuing bank, whose obligation is independent of the issuing bank's undertaking to the beneficiary. If a nominated bank determines that a presentation is complying and forwards the documents to the issuing bank or confirming bank, whether or not the nominated bank has honoured or negotiated, an issuing bank or confirming bank must honour or negotiate, or reimburse that nominated bank, even when the documents have been lost in transit between the nominated bank and the issuing bank or confirming bank, or between the confirming bank and the issuing bank.

> **Rights**

Upon receiving the buyer's application, the issuing bank has the rights to check the L/C application, determines whether cash security is necessary, and scrutinizes the contents of the application to see whether they are generally consistent with national and international banking and legal requirements. If there is any discrepancy in the documents submitted, the issuing bank has the rights to refuse to pay the negotiating or paying bank, or the beneficiary.

 5-3

信用证开证行的付款责任

1. 开证行对受益人和指定银行的付款责任

受益人是信用证最初始的受益者，也是信用证业务能够发起的根本原因。

关于开证行对指定银行（包括保兑行、议付行、承兑行、付款行）的付款责任，UCP600 在第 7 条 C 款中规定，指定银行承付或议付相符交单并将单据转给开证行之后，开证行即承担偿付该指定银行的责任，开证行偿付指定银行的责任独立于开证行对受益人的责任。这说明开证行承担两个付款责任：一是针对受益人；二是针对指定银行，而且上述两个付款责任是相互独立的，也就是说开证行对指定银行的付款责任不受受益人行为瑕疵的影响。即使受益人出现了欺诈行为，如果指定银行按照开证行的指示承付或议付了相符单据，而且指定银行没有参与，亦不知晓受益人的欺诈行为，开证行仍然承担向指定银行付款的责任。

2. 开证行对第二受益人的付款责任

银行界和法律界对这个问题存在较大分歧。在银行界，一般认为开证行与可转让信用证的第二受益人并没有直接的法律关系，也有人认为第二受益人的权益同 D/P 托收相差无几。因此，银行对为第二受益人办理转让信用证项下的打包放款等贸易融资业务心存芥蒂。但是法律界普遍认为信用证转让是开证行对第二受益人做出的新的、独立的付款承诺，第一受益人将信用证部分转让给第二受益人后，第二受益人参与到信用证业务中来，成为信用证的当事人之一，因此信用证开证行的付款责任也分为两部分：对第一受益人承担未转让部分的付款责任；对第二受益人承担已转让部分的付款责任。在开证行的行为损害第二受益人的利益时，第二受益人可以根据转让信用证向开证行索偿。

3. 开证行对正当持票人的付款责任

UCP600 第九条 A(IV) 分条中关于开证行与保兑行的责任中规定：对于议付信用证，开证行应根据受益人依照信用证出具的汇票及/或提交的单据向出票人及/或正当持票人无追索权地履行付款责任。UCP 将开证行对正当持票人的付款责任删除，这意味着 UCP600 确认了开证行付款责任限于受益人和指定银行。UCP 排除了开证行对正当持票人的付款责任是否意味着开证行不再承担这种责任呢？

UCP 是规范信用证业务操作的重要文件，但 UCP 并不能解决信用证业务纠纷的一切问题，UCP 没有触及的问题需要在信用证法律、票据法等民事法律的框架内解决。为了保证票据的流通性，各国的票据法律均保护正当持票人的合法权益。因此，即使 UCP 排除了开证行对正当持票人的付款责任，但是在票据法的框架中，开证行仍然需要承担对正当持票人的付款责任。

综上所述，在UCP600的框架之下，信用证的开证行承担向受益人（含第二受益人）和指定银行的付款责任；在票据法律之下，开证行还承担向汇票的正当持票人付款的责任。

（资料来源：王腾.信用证开证行究竟向哪些人承担付款责任？[OL].中国贸易金融网，2014-03-18）

● The Advising Bank（通知行）

Advising bank or transmitting bank is usually the correspondent bank of the issuing bank in the seller's/exporter's country, verifying the authenticity of L/C and any amendment, and forwarding them to the beneficiary. The obligation of the advising bank, if it is not a confirming bank, is limited to accurately transmit the terms and conditions of L/C and check the apparent authenticity of the L/C and assumes no other liability to the beneficiary.

If the advising bank cannot establish such apparent authenticity, it must inform without delay the bank from which the instructions have been received that it has been unable to establish the authenticity of the L/C. If the advising bank elects nevertheless to advise such an L/C, it must inform the beneficiary that it has not been able to establish the authenticity of the L/C. In practice, the advising bank is of a big help to the beneficiary in examining the terms and conditions of the L/C.

● The Beneficiary（受益人）

The seller receives notification (advice) of the credit from the advising bank, complies with the terms and conditions of the credit, and gets paid. The seller is the beneficiary of the documentary credit. The seller, therefore, may be called the seller in commercial terms, the exporter in economic terms, and the beneficiary in banking terms. They are all one and the same.

➢ Obligations

In order to get payment under L/C, the beneficiary has to fulfill the specified obligations according to the terms and conditions of the L/C and only against the stipulated documents will he be paid under the L/C. The beneficiary is also responsible for the accuracy and authenticity of the documents and the goods conforming to the contract.

➢ Rights

The beneficiary has the rights to examine an L/C upon receipt of it according to the sales contract and may require amendment or even reject the L/C if the terms and conditions in the L/C are not in accordance with the sales contract. After shipment, the beneficiary can claim payment on nominated banks with the complying presentation of documents.

● Confirming Bank（保兑行）

Confirming bank is the bank that adds its confirmation to an L/C upon the issuing banks' authorization or request. Usually, a bank of higher reputation in the beneficiary's country, frequently the advising bank, is asked to add its confirmation to the L/C issued by an issuing bank of lower reputation. When there exits great political risk or strict foreign exchange control in the issuing bank's country, a bank outside the importer's country will also be asked to add its confirmation.

According to the UCP600, confirmation means a definite undertaking of the confirming bank in addition to that of the issuing bank, to honour or negotiate (without recourse, if the L/C is available by negotiation with the confirming bank) a complying presentation. Therefore, a confirming bank is irrevocably bound to honour or negotiate as of the time it adds its confirmation to the L/C, making it to undertake the same obligations assumed by the issuing bank (responsible for an L/C independently and payment without recourse) and offers a double promise to pay to the beneficiary.

However, a bank has the rights to refuse to add its confirmation to an L/C. Moreover, if a bank is authorized or requested by the issuing bank to add its confirmation to an L/C but is not prepared to do so, it must inform the issuing bank without delay.

Sometimes the advising bank or some other banks will add their confirmation at the request of the beneficiary without authorization or instructions from the issuing bank, constituting a "silent confirmation". In this case, the beneficiary and the confirming bank make an independent agreement. According to the UCP600, confirmation is only added to an irrevocable L/C at the request or authorization of the issuing bank. Without the authorization or request by the issuing bank, an L/C may not be confirmed. Therefore, if a bank "confirms" an L/C based on a "silent confirmation agreement", the bank will not be considered the "confirming bank" by the issuing bank, and hence acquires no rights of claiming reimbursement from the issuing bank.

 5-4

保兑行挑剔拒付的案例

2014年2月18日,信用证受益人S公司向其代理交单银行M银行交来该信用证项下单据,编号BPXXXX10,金额USD3870396.80。经审核单证相符后,M银行于当日向保兑行A银行寄单索汇。2月23日,M银行收到A银行MT799称:"我们对单据进行了审核,发现以下不符点:1.装箱单没有签署;2.汇票显示收款人为'China M Banking Corp Ltd.',但汇票由'China M Banking Corporation'背书。我们将持单等待你行的进一步指示。请尽快授权我行将单据寄送开证行或做出其他指示。"

对于保兑行所提的第一个不符点,M银行认为不成立。信用证46A对装箱单的要求是:"两份由受益人签署的装箱单",而客户提交的装箱单已经清楚地盖有受益人公司的印章。根据ISBP745第a35款的规定,"签字无需手写。单据的签署也可以使用摹样签字(如预先印就或扫描的签字)、穿孔签字、印戳、符号(如印章)或任何机械或电子的证实方式"。由此可见,保兑行的第一条拒付理由是不成立的。对于保兑行提出的第二个不符点,M银行认为是保兑行的故意挑剔。虽然背书章中缺少了"LTD"的字样有失严谨,但并不会导致人们产生"China M Banking Corp Ltd."和"China M Banking Corporation"是两个不同银行的歧义,而且 ICC 在 TA590REV 案例中也明确指出,汇票作为开证行要求提交的单据应与信用证 46A 中要求提交给申请人的单据区分开来,特别是即期汇票,仅仅为银行自己保留的支付命令,对不符点的认定可相应放松。由此看来,保兑行提出的第二个不符点显然过于挑剔。

为了节省时间尽快解决问题,M 银行立即通过电话与 A 银行进行了交涉,明确表明 M 银行不接受上述所提的两个不符点,请其尽快履行保兑行的责任,凭相符单据付款。A 银行最终认可了 M 银行的交单为相符交单,同时不再要求 M 银行就其 MT799 发授权寄单电报。2014 年 2 月 24 日,M 银行收到 A 银行的 MT799 称:"我们今天已按照你行指示通过快递将单据寄往开证行请求承付。"同年 3 月 4 日,M 银行收到该 BP 项下款项,金额 USD3867627.52。

- **Nominated Bank**(指定银行)

Nominated bank means the bank with which the L/C is available or any bank in the case of an L/C available with any banks. Unless the L/C stipulates that it is available only with the issuing bank, all L/Cs must nominate the bank which is authorized to pay, to incur a deferred payment undertaking, to accept bill of exchange or to negotiate. In a freely negotiable L/C, any banks can be seen as nominated banks.

  ➢ **Paying bank/accepting bank**(付款行/承兑行)

The issuing bank may designate another bank, in most cases the advising bank, to effect payment or acceptance under an L/C. Such a bank is referred to as the paying bank or accepting bank. The paying bank may refuse to pay if the documents presented are inconformity to the L/C. Once the paying bank has made the payment to the beneficiary, it will lose its rights of recourse to the beneficiary, for as the drawee bank of bill of exchanges drawn under the L/C; its payment will discharge the bill of exchange. After the payment, the paying bank can turn to the issuing bank, confirming bank or reimbursing bank, if any, for reimbursement.

NOTE: Neither the paying bank nor the accepting bank is obligated to pay or accept under an L/C. That is to say, a bank may not be elected to act as the paying bank if there is no such arrangement in the correspondent agreement between the issuing bank and the paying bank.

- **Negotiating bank**(议付行)

According to the UCP600, negotiation means the purchase by the nominated bank of bill of exchanges (drawn on a bank other than the nominated bank) and/or documents under a complying presentation by advancing or agreeing to advance funds to the beneficiary on or before the banking day on which reimbursement is due to the nominated bank.

  ➢ **Obligations**

In essence, a negotiating bank under a negotiation L/C must purchase the bill of exchanges drawn on another bank and/or documents under a complying presentation, an unauthorized negotiation or mere examination of documents. Without honouring them, a bank doesn't constitute a negotiation and the relevant bank is not a negotiating bank but rather a remitting bank and can't be protected by UCP600. The negotiating bank must examine the documents with reasonable care to ascertain whether or not they appear, on their face, to be in compliance with the terms and conditions of the L/C.

> **Rights**

Since the negotiating bank advances or agrees to advance funds to the beneficiary before the drawee bank pays, it becomes the *bona fide* holder of a bill of exchange and can claim reimbursement from the issuing bank or confirming bank or nominated reimbursing bank after negotiation. If the bill of exchange is dishonoured by the issuing bank, the negotiating bank has the rights of recourse to the beneficiary.

● **Claiming Bank**(索偿行)

When a bank effects payment, acceptance or negotiation according to the instruction of the issuing bank, it is entitled to request the issuing bank or the bank nominated by the issuing bank to cover the payment made. Such a paying bank, accepting bank, or negotiating bank, which claims reimbursement from the reimbursing bank, is called the claiming bank.

If an L/C states that reimbursement is to be obtained by the claiming bank on another party (say the reimbursing bank), the L/C must state if the reimbursement is subject to the ICC rules for bank-to-bank reimbursements and a claiming bank shall not be required to supply a certificate of compliance with the terms and conditions of the L/C to the reimbursing bank. If not reimbursed by the reimbursing bank, the claiming bank is entitled to obtain the reimbursement from the issuing bank. If there is any loss of interest for reimbursement not provided on first demand by a reimbursing bank, the issuing bank will be responsible for the loss. An issuing bank's undertaking to reimburse a claiming bank is independent of the issuing bank's to the beneficiary.

● **Reimbursing Bank**(偿付行)

Reimbursing bank, also called the clearing bank, is the bank named in the documentary L/C from which the paying bank, accepting bank or negotiating bank (claiming bank) may request cover after paying or negotiating the documents in compliance with the L/C. It is usually the bank located in the clearing center of the L/C currency, say the clearing center of the USD is New York, and with which both the issuing bank and the claiming bank maintain current accounts. The purpose of designating a reimbursing bank in an L/C is for the convenience of payment or clearing between the issuing bank and the nominated banks.

Similar to what we have discussed in the claiming bank, a reimbursing L/C should state whether the reimbursement is subject to the ICC rules for bank-to-bank reimbursements. If without such statement in an L/C, an issuing bank must provide a reimbursing bank with a reimbursement authorization that conforms to the availability stated in the L/C.

It should be noticed that the payment made by the reimbursing bank is just a simple payment for the issuing bank without further obligations to examine the documents. If the issuing bank refuses to pay after examining the documents presented by the claiming bank, the reimbursing bank can ask for the refund from the claiming bank of any reimbursement which has been made together with interest. In addition, the reimbursing bank's charges should be for the account of the issuing bank. If the charges are for the account of the beneficiary, the issuing bank should indicate so in the L/C and in the reimbursement authorization, and the charges shall be deducted from the amount due to a claiming bank when reimbursement is made. If no reimbursement is made, the reimbursing bank's charges remain the obligations of the issuing bank.

5.2　Types of L/C

L/Cs can take different forms, and they can fall into different types according to different classification.

5.2.1　According to whether Accompanied by Commercial Documents

- **Clean L/C**(光票信用证)

Commercial documents are not necessary for a clean L/C, which only requires clean bill of exchange, i.e. bill of exchange not accompanied by any commercial documents for payment. Under a clean L/C, the documents of title to goods are sent by the financial institutions to the creditor. Only the bill of exchange drawn on the creditor is offered to the bank for purchase. Neither the financial institutions nor the bank retain control over the goods covered by the transaction. For the bank, it remains an unsecured advance. For this reason, a clean L/C is normally not found in commercial transactions. They are generally used in non-trade settlement or in payment in advance by means of the L/C. The most commonly used clean L/C is traveler's L/C as introduced below.

- **Documentary L/C**(跟单信用证)

A documentary L/C requires presentation of specified documentation before payment is made. The bank will pay or accept or negotiate the bill of exchange only if the accompanied documents are in order and the shipment has been made as specified. Typically the documents requested in an L/C are (1) commercial invoice; (2) transport document such as bill of lading or airway bill; (3) insurance policy; (4) inspection certificate; and (5) certificate of origin.

As we mentioned above, letters of credit deal in documents but not goods, so a documentary L/C provides more guarantee for the seller to get paid than a clean L/C. In practice, documentary L/C is actually used more often.

5.2.2 According to whether Confirmed by Another Bank

In UCP600 Article 2, it is clearly pointed out that L/C means any arrangement that is irrevocable and thereby constitutes a definite undertaking of the issuing bank to honour a complying presentation. An L/C is irrevocable even if there is no indication to that effect. Therefore, an L/C issued according to the UCP600 is considered to be irrevocable unless otherwise stipulated. An irrevocable documentary credit constitutes a firm contractual obligation on the part of the issuing bank to honour the terms of payment of the L/C as issued. The buyer and issuing bank cannot amend or cancel the credit without the express approval of the seller.

Payment under an irrevocable documentary credit is guaranteed by the issuing bank. However, from the seller's perspective, this guarantee may have limited value as the issuing bank may be (1) in a foreign country; (2) beholden to the buyer; (3) small and unknown to the seller; or (4) subject to unknown foreign exchange control restrictions. The seller, therefore, might wish that another, more local bank add its guarantee (confirmation) of payment to that of the issuing bank. Within the category of irrevocable credits there are two further options for the buyer and the seller. These are the irrevocable unconfirmed credit and the irrevocable confirmed credit.

- **Confirmed Irrevocable L/C**(不可撤销保兑信用证)

Confirmation means a definite undertaking of confirming bank, in addition to that of the issuing bank, to honour or negotiate a complying presentation. Confirmed L/C carries the commitment to pay of both the issuing and the advising banks. The advising bank adds its undertaking to pay to that of the issuing bank, and its commitment is independent of that of the issuing bank. Therefore, when documents conforming to the requirements of the confirmed documentary L/C are presented in a timely manner, the payment from the advising bank to the seller is final in all respects as far as the seller is concerned.

When a confirmation is added to an irrevocable L/C by another bank, the L/C becomes a confirmed irrevocable L/C. Under such an L/C, both the issuing bank and the confirming bank undertake to pay the beneficiary against the specified documents, which cannot be amended or cancelled without the consents of the issuing bank, the confirming bank, the beneficiary and the applicant. Hence, confirmed irrevocable L/C gives the seller the greatest protection of a double assurance getting paid, since the sellers can rely on the commitment of two banks to make payment. In accordance with the additional risk assumed by the banks, however, confirmed irrevocable L/C is more expensive than unconfirmed L/C. It is used when the seller does not have confidence whether the issuing bank can effectively guarantee payment, and most frequently in transactions involving buyers in developing countries. Therefore, if the issuing bank is considered to be a first class bank, there may not be any need to have its L/C confirmed by another bank.

Confirmation is usually given by a bank in the exporting country, which can eliminate the political and transfer risks in the importing country from the perspective of the exporter. Moreover, in case of dispute, the competent courts of the confirming bank's country have exclusive jurisdiction and the laws of that country shall apply. If an L/C is unconfirmed, on the other hand, disputes are dealt with by the courts of the issuing bank's country.

Usually, there is a special instruction in the confirmed irrevocable L/C, requiting the advising bank to add confirmation. If the advising bank confirms the L/C, it must pay without recourse to the seller when the documents are presented, provided they are in order and the L/C requirements are met.

- **Unconfirmed Irrevocable L/C**(不可撤销非保兑信用证)

Distinctly, an unconfirmed irrevocable L/C is an irrevocable L/C with another bank's confirmation added to the issuing bank's definite undertaking to pay the beneficiary.

5.2.3 According to the Mode of Availability

- **Sight L/C**(即期信用证)

In a confirmed sight credit, the value of the L/C is available to the beneficiary as soon as the terms and conditions of the L/C have been met (as soon as the prescribed document package has been presented to and checked by the confirming bank). When foreign exchange is at issue, several days may pass between the time of beneficiary's presentation of documents and the actual transfer of funds to the beneficiary's account. In a sight credit (unconfirmed), the value of the credit is made available to the beneficiary once the advising bank has received the funds from the issuing bank.

If a bill of exchange is used, it must be drawn on the party stated in the L/C, which could either be the issuing bank or any other nominated paying bank. If no other paying bank is nominated in the L/C, then the issuing bank is the paying banks, and when asking for payment, the beneficiary must take into account the time of sending the documents to the issuing bank. The payment of the paying bank is final and without recourse to the beneficiary, so the beneficiary of such an L/C normally can obtain the payment immediately after submitting complying documents, thus reducing the risks of foreign exchange fluctuations and the non-payment by the buyer. Sometimes, bill of exchange is not necessary in order to avoid the stamp duty.

This kind of L/C is usually marked with: "*this L/C is to expire on or before (date) at place and is available with issuing bank or advising bank/other bank by payment at sight against the beneficiary's bill of exchange at sight drawn on nominated paying bank and the documents detailed herein*".

- **Acceptance L/C**(承兑信用证)

In an acceptance L/C, the beneficiary presents the required document package to the bank along with a usance bill of exchange drawn on the issuing, advising, or a third bank for the value of the L/C. Once the documents have made their way to the buyer and found to be in order, the bill of exchange is accepted by the bank upon which it is drawn (the bill of exchange is now called an accepted bill of exchange) and it is returned to the seller who holds it until maturity. The seller has the option of selling the accepted bill of exchange by discounting its value. The buyer pays the bill of exchange at maturity to its holder.

> **Banker's acceptance L/C**(银行承兑信用证)

In a banker's acceptance L/C, a usance bill of exchange drawn on the issuing bank or any other nominated drawee bank by the beneficiary is essential, and the drawee of the bill of exchange should be banks only. Having fulfilled the requirements of the L/C, the beneficiary can present the bill of exchange(s) and the stipulated documents to the advising bank, who in turn forwards the bill of exchange(s) and documents to the issuing bank or the nominated accepting bank for acceptance, by which the drawee bank promises to pay when the bill of exchanges mature. After acceptance, the beneficiary can choose to hold the bill for payment at maturity or to discount the accepted bill to get immediate payment. Bills of exchange drawn under an acceptance L/C usually have a term of 60 to 180 days.

When the issuing bank accepts the bill of exchange and obtains the documents, it will not release them to the applicant until the applicant redeems the documents at maturity. The purpose of an acceptance L/C, however, is to give the importer time to make payment by using a time bill of exchange, so when both documents and goods have arrived at destination, the applicant may submit a Trust Receipt (T/R) to the issuing bank to borrow the documents and pick up the goods as the trustee of the issuing bank. If the applicant can resell the goods before payment falls due, she can use the proceeds to pay the bill of exchange. In this way, the applicant avoids the necessity of borrowing money to finance the transaction.

> **Buyer's acceptance L/C**(买方承兑信用证)

Buyer's acceptance L/C is also called usance L/C payable at sight, for according to the contract, payment to the seller should be at sight but the L/C requires a usance bill of exchange which is payable at sight to the beneficiary. Under the buyer's acceptance L/C, the beneficiary can get payment at sight, while the usance bill of exchange provides financing to the applicant. So in the L/C, we can find a clause reading as "*uaance bill of exchange can be negotiated at sight, discounting charges and acceptance commission are for the buyer's account.*" By discounting the accepted time bill of exchange, the applicant can make payment under the L/C.

● **Deferred Payment L/C**(延期付款信用证)

In a deferred payment L/C, the buyer accepts the documents and agrees to pay the bank after a set period of time. Essentially, this gives the buyer time (a grace period) between delivery of the goods and payment. The issuing bank makes the payment at the specified time, when the terms and conditions of the credit have been met. Under a deferred payment L/C, the beneficiary does not receive payment when he presents the documents, but at a later date, for instance after B/L date or presentation of documents. On the contrary, the applicant gains possession of the documents before becoming liable for payment.

This kind of L/C was originally generated for transactions of capital goods, the payment period of which may last for several years, while the discounting period provided by banks is usually no more than six months. Under this condition, bills of exchange can hardly be discounted to get financed. Moreover, drawing a bill of exchange entails the stamp duty in some European countries.

With time going on, the use of deferred payment L/C is not simply for the need of transactions of capital goods, but mainly for the purpose of avoiding the stamp duty. In this case, a commercial invoice can be used as a payment certificate. So a deferred payment L/C is in some way equivalent to an acceptance L/C, except for the absence of a bill of exchange. A deferred payment L/C could also be used in transactions involving food or drugs that require inspection prior to import and approval by a government agency. In this case the bank will release the documents to the importer/buyer against a trust receipt. The bank holds the title documents to the goods and still owns the merchandise. Once the goods have been approved by the government agency, the bank transfers the titles documents to the buyer, charges the buyer's account, and pays the seller.

As to the term of deferred payment, there are the following cases: (1) "...*payment will be effected at XXX days after presentation of documents*"; (2) "...*payment will be effected at XXX days after the date of shipment*"; or (3) "...*payment will be effected at XXX days after our receiving the documents*".

To the exporter, a deferred payment L/C is not so secure and convenient as an acceptance L/C, for under an acceptance L/C, the beneficiary obtains an accepted bill of exchange that can be readily negotiated or discounted and can be protected against the *Negotiable Instrument Laws*. But for the applicant of the L/C, she is more willing to ask for the issuance of a deferred payment L/C for both longer payment period and less constraints by the *Negotiable Instrument Laws*.

● **Negotiation L/C**(议付信用证)

A negotiation L/C refers to the L/C under which the issuing bank authorizes other nominated banks to purchase the bill of exchanges and/or documents presented by the beneficiary. Negotiation L/C is not the best for the beneficiary, for the payment by the negotiating bank is with recourse and the beneficiary has to wait for the final examination of the documents and payment from the issuing bank.

From the definition of negotiation, we can see that a "negotiation L/C" should have the following premises to be effective: (1) the L/C must indicate "available by negotiation"; (2) the negotiating bank should have gotten the authorization from the issuing bank; (3) only the complying presentation of documents can get advance funds from the negotiating bank; and (4) if there is a bill of exchange involved, the bill of exchange should be drawn on a bank other than the nominated bank.

A negotiation L/C can be divided into two types: the restricted negotiation L/C and free negotiation L/C, according to whether there is a restriction on the nominated negotiating bank.

➢ **Restricted negotiation L/C(限制议付信用证)**

In a restricted negotiable L/C, the authorization from the issuing bank to pay the beneficiary is restricted to a specific nominated negotiating bank. It is usually marked with "this L/C is restricted with XXX bank by negotiation". The negotiating bank usually is the issuing bank's branch or correspondent bank. In such an L/C, the beneficiary is deprived of the right to choose the negotiating bank at his own option and thus is disadvantageous to him especially when the nominated negotiating bank is far away from where he is located.

➢ **Free /Open negotiation L/C(自由/公开议付信用证)**

In a free negotiation L/C, the authorization from the issuing bank to pay the beneficiary is not restricted to a specific nominated negotiating bank. Any bank can be a nominated bank as long as the bank is willing to negotiate the bill of exchanges and/or documents. The issuing bank usually indicates "*this L/C is available with any bank by negotiation*" on the L/C and an engagement clause like "*we hereby engage with the drawers, endorsers and/or bona fide holders that bills of exchange drawn and documents presented in conformity with the terms of this L/C will be duly honoured on presentation*" will be marked on the back of the L/C.

Table 5.2 shows the comparison of the L/Cs with different availability.

Table 5.2 Comparison of the L/Cs with different availability

	sight L/C	deferred L/C	acceptance L/C	restricted negotiation L/C	free negotiation L/C
draft	with/without	without	with	sight-without time-with	sight-without time-with
tenor of draft	sight		time	sight/time	sight/time
drawee	paying bank		accepting bank	issuing bank	issuing bank
time of payment	sight	deferred	due date	sight minus interest	sight minus interest
restricted or free	R	R	R	R	F
right of recourse	without	without	without	with	with

5.2.4 Straight L/C

A straight L/C conveys a commitment by the issuing bank to only honour bills of exchange or documents as presented by the beneficiary of the L/C and expires at the counter of the issuing bank, which means the obligation of the issuing bank is extended only to the beneficiary with no commitment or obligation to persons other than the named beneficiary in honouring bills of exchange and documents. It is quite normal for banks to discount bills of exchange and documents of a beneficiary for immediate payment, but under a straight L/C the issuing bank has no formal obligation to such a discounting bank.

The beneficiary of the L/C is supposed to deal directly with the issuing bank in presenting bills of exchange and documents under the terms of the L/C. Straight L/C is usually advised to the beneficiary by the issuing bank directly. It is of greatest advantage to the applicant, because she does not incur a liability to pay the beneficiary until her own bank views the documents of the L/C. This kind of L/C is typically used in domestic trade and for standby L/Cs. In both situations, confirmation or negotiation is considered unnecessary.

The engagement of the issuing bank in a straight L/C may be expressed as: *"We hereby agree with the Beneficiary that all Bills of exchange drawn under and/or documents presented hereunder will be duly honoured by us provided the terms and conditions of the L/C are complied with and that presentation is made at this office on or before the expiry date"*.

5.2.5 Anticipatory L/C

An anticipatory L/C, also known as a red clause L/C, is an obligation on the part of an issuing bank to guarantee advance payments made by a confirming bank or any other nominated bank to the beneficiary prior to presentation of the documents. An anticipatory L/C provides funds to assist manufacturers in paying for labor and materials used in manufacturing or to middlemen who need financing to conclude a transaction. Ultimately, it is a form of financing provided by the buyer to the seller and is at the specific request of the applicant when the applicant would be willing to make special concession of this nature.

For the beneficiary, the benefit of an anticipatory clause L/C lies in the financing provided for preparing the goods, while if the beneficiary is unable to perform his obligation under the L/C, he is liable for repayment of the advance, plus the interest. For the applicant, this kind of arrangement will expose her to the final repayment to the issuing bank if the beneficiary fails to present the documents required under the L/C, and the applicant would also be liable for all costs, such as interest or foreign exchange hedging cost incurred by the issuing bank, or any other nominated advancing banks.

A clause authorizing advance payment will state the amount of the authorized advances, which may be for up to the full amount of the L/C, and any terms and conditions of the advances if any. The advance payment clause is usually expressed as: *"The negotiating bank is hereby authorized to make advances to you to the extent of..., against your receipt for the amount advanced which must state the advance is to be used to pay for the purchase and shipment of the merchandise for which this L/C is issued and be accompanied by your written undertaking to deliver documents in conformity with the L/C terms to the negotiating bank on or before the latest date for negotiation. The advance with interest is to be deducted from the proceeds of the bill of exchanges drawn under this L/C. We hereby undertake the payment of such advances, with interest, should they not be repaid to the negotiating bank by you on or before the latest date for negotiation".*

T/T can also be used to make advance payment to the beneficiary. The difference between T/T and the anticipatory L/C is that the applicant may hand in only a part of cash deposit needed to open an anticipatory L/C under the L/C line approved by the issuing bank, while in T/T the importer should hand in all the money needed to make advance payment to the remitting bank without any financing available.

5.2.6　Transferable L/C

According to UCP600 Article 38, a transferable L/C means an L/C that specifically states it is *"transferable"*, and terms such as *"divisible"*, *"fractionable"*, *"assignable"* and *"transmissible"* do not render the L/C transferable. If such terms are used, they shall be disregarded. Therefore, a transferable L/C is usually marked as: *"Irrevocable Transferable Documentary L/C"*, *"This L/C is transferable"*; or *"Transfer to be allowed"*.

A transferable L/C is used by a "middleman" who acts as an intermediary between the buyer and the seller to earn a profit for structuring the transaction. The buyer opens a documentary L/C naming the intermediary as the beneficiary. The intermediary then transfers both the obligations to supply the goods and part of the proceeds of the credit to the actual supplier. In the process, the intermediary commits little or no funds to the transaction. This form of payment is often used in situations where the intermediary does not wish the buyer and the actual supplier to know each other's identity.

A transferable L/C may be made available in whole or in part to another beneficiary (second beneficiary) at the request of the beneficiary (first beneficiary). In other words, under a transferable L/C, the first beneficiary may transfer the L/C to one or more second beneficiaries. In fact, the first beneficiary usually is not the manufacturer or original supplier of the goods, but a middleman. A transferable L/C is designed to meet the requirements of international trade. It enables a middleman receiving payment from a buyer under a documentary L/C to transfer his claim under the L/C to his own supplier. In this way, he can carry out transactions with only a limited outlay of his own funds.

A transferable L/C can be transferred only under the terms stated in the original credit. However, the intermediary may transfer the L/C with the following changes: (1) the name and address of the intermediary may be substituted for that of the original buyer (applicant of the credit); (2) unit prices and the total amount of the credit may be reduced to enable the intermediary an allowance for profit; (3) the expiration date, the final shipment date, and the final date for presentation of documents may all be shortened to allow the intermediary time to meet obligations under the original credit; or (4) insurance coverage may be increased in order to provide the percentage amount of cover stipulated in the original credit.

Since the ultimate buyer and the actual seller/supplier are separated by the intermediary there is the question of how to deal with amendments. Do amendments by the buyer get sent (advised) to the second beneficiary? The intermediary, therefore, must establish, irrevocably, at the time of the request for transfer of the credit, and prior to the actual transfer of the L/C, whether the transferring bank may advise amendments to the seller (second beneficiary). Options for transfer rights on amendments include full or partial transfer of the credit with (1) retaining the rights on amendments; (2) partial waiver of rights on amendments; and/or (3) waiver of rights on amendments. If the transferring bank agrees to the transfer, it must advise the seller (second beneficiary) of the intermediary's amendment instructions.

Transferring bank means a nominated bank that consents to the nomination by the issuing bank and transfers the L/C or, in an L/C available with any bank, a bank that is specific all authorized by the issuing bank to transfer and that transfers the L/C. A transferable L/C can only be transferred once, and second beneficiaries may not transfer it further. For the first time, UCP600 clearly states that an issuing bank may be a transferring bank and presentation of documents by or on behalf of a second beneficiary must be made to the transferring bank. The L/C that has been made available by the transferring bank to a second beneficiary is the transferred L/C.

Since the transferable L/C must be clearly marked "transferable", the buyer knows that the first beneficiary is not the ultimate supplier and is relying upon the credit as the financing instrument. This L/C is generally for use only by more sophisticated traders. In this form of L/C both the buyer and ultimate supplier may feel at a disadvantage not knowing each other and placing their trust in an intermediary who did not have the financing to conclude the transaction on his/her own.

5.2.7 Back-to-Back L/C

It may happen that an L/C in favor of the beneficiary is not stated to be transferable; meanwhile, the beneficiary himself is just a middleman and needs to purchase them from another supplier. In this case, a back-to-back letter of credit can be used as an alternative to the transferable L/C.

As the name implies, a back-to-back L/C is actually two distinct documentary L/Cs: (1) a documentary L/C opened by the buyer naming the seller as the beneficiary; and (2) second documentary L/C opened by the seller naming the actual supplier of the goods as the beneficiary.

A back-to-back L/C is used in situations where the original credit is not transferable and where the bank is willing to open the second L/C at the request of the seller. In a back-to-back L/C, the primary L/C is received by the exporter from the opening bank, used as security to establish a second letter of credit drawn on the exporter in favor of his supplier. So a back-to-back documentary L/C process actually involves two separate L/Cs: one opened by the buyer in favor of the seller, and one opened for the account of the seller naming the actual supplier of the goods as the beneficiary. The first beneficiary of the first L/C becomes the applicant for the second L/C, who is responsible to the bank for payment regardless of whether or not he himself is paid under the first L/C. The terms and conditions of a back-to-back L/C should be based on the primary L/C so as to enable the beneficiary of the primary L/C to produce and surrender the documents in accordance with the terms and conditions of the L/C. Since the seller is the applicant for the second credit, the seller is responsible to the bank for payment regardless of whether or not he himself is paid under the first credit.

Because the issuing bank of a back-to-back L/C only holds the primary L/C as an agent, and whether the primary L/C will be performed solely depends on the middleman's L/C worthiness. Many banks are reluctant to issue back-to-back L/C due to the level of risks to which they are exposed, while a transferable L/C will not expose them to higher risks than under the original L/C. In fact, most banks will refuse to open such an L/C unless they have extreme confidence in the seller's L/C worthiness and ability to perform.

Since the first L/C names the seller as the beneficiary, the buyer is unaware of the supplier other than the seller. This L/C is generally used by more sophisticated traders. The more paperwork and parties involved in the transaction, the greater the possibility for problems.

With back-to-back L/C, the second L/C should be worded so as to produce the documents (apart from the commercial invoice) required by the primary L/C within the time limits set by the primary L/C, in order that the primary beneficiary under the first L/C may be able to present his documents within the given period.

> **Comparison of the transferable L/C and back-to-back L/C**
>
> Both of the transferable L/C and back-to-back L/C are generated for the reason of a middleman involved in the international transaction. And some items can be modified both under a transferable L/C and a back-to-back L/C, such as the unit price and the amount

of L/C can be reduced; the expiry date, the period for presentation, or the latest shipment date or given period for shipment can be curtailed; the insurance percentage can be increased, and the name of applicant can be replaced by the middleman.

The difference between a transferable L/C and a back-to-back L/C is quite obvious. Firstly, in back-to-back L/C operation, the original L/C and the back-to-back L/C are two wholly independent L/Cs with wholly independent issuing bank undertakings, while the transferred L/C derives not only its existence from the original transferable L/C, but also its utilization. Secondly, under a transferable L/C, the transferring bank is authorized and designated by the issuing bank, while for a back-to-back L/C, the middleman can freely choose the issuing bank of the new L/C. Thirdly, the transferable L/C can only be transferred once, while in case of more than one middleman involved in transaction, back-to-back L/Cs can be issued in turn to satisfy the needs of transferring among several different middlemen.

5.2.8 Revolving L/C

A revolving documentary L/C is an obligation on the part of an issuing bank to restore a L/C to the original amount after it has been utilized, without the need for amendment.

The revolving L/C is used in situations where the buyer and the seller agree that goods will be shipped on a continuing basis and the parties to the credit wish to establish one credit to handle all the shipments rather than individual letters of credit for each shipment. The amount of a revolving L/C is renewed or reinstated to the original amount after it has been utilized without specific amendments to the L/C. The L/C must state that it is a revolving L/C and it may revolve either automatically or subject to certain provisions.

A revolving L/C is designed to facilitate ongoing relationships between buyers and sellers where buyers wish to purchase either a set maximum value of product per period of time, a certain maximum value of product, or as many products as the seller can produce or supply, and where parties to the L/C wish to establish one L/C to handle all the shipments rather than to establish individual L/C for each shipment. Revolving L/C is useful to avoid the need for repetitive arrangements for opening or amending letters of credit. It can revolve in relation to time or value.

A revolving L/C can be cumulative[①] or non-cumulative. If an L/C is "non-cumulative", portions not used in the prescribed period cease to be available, as do all subsequent portions. A cumulative revolving L/C is usually stated as: "*this L/C is*

---

① Here "cumulative" means that amounts from unused or incompletely used portions may be carried forward and utilized in a subsequent period.

revolving at USD 20000 coveting shipment of goods per month cumulative operation from May 2004 to September 2004 inclusive up to a total amount of USD 100000". While a non-cumulative revolving L/C is usually stated as: "this L/C is revolving for amount drawn there under up to a maximum amount of USD 200000 per month non-cumulative from October 2004 to December 2004".

- **Revolving around Time**

If the L/C is time revolving, once utilized, it is re-instated for further regular shipments until the L/C is fully drawn. For example, such an L/C may be stated as "This is a monthly revolving L/C which is available for up to the amount of USD 15000 per month, and the full L/C amount will be automatically renewed on the 1st day of each succeeding calendar month. Our maximum liability under this revolving L/C does not exceed USD 90000 being aggregate value of six months". Usually the issuing bank will specify the overall amount undertaken by her to maintain a control on the obligations of herself under the L/C.

- **Revolving around Value**

If the L/C revolves in relation to value, once utilized and paid, the value can be reinstated for further drawings. In an L/C that revolves in relation to value, the amount is reinstated upon utilization within a given period. For example, such an L/C may be stated as "This L/C is revolving for three shipments only. Each shipment should be effected at one month interval. The amount of each shipment is not exceeding USD 50000. The total value of this revolving L/C does not exceed USD 150000".

Such a revolving L/C may provide for automatic reinstatement immediately upon presentation of the specified documents, or reinstatement only after receipt by the issuing bank of the required documents or another stated condition.

➢ **Automatic revolving**

It may be stated as: "This L/C shall be renewable automatically twice for a period of one month each for an amount of USD 50000 for each period making a total of USD 150000".

➢ **Periodic revolving (semi-automatic revolving)**

It may be stated as: "Should the negotiating bank not be advised of stopping renewal within 5 days, the unused balance of this L/C shall be increased to the original amount on the 8th day after each negotiation".

➢ **Notice revolving (non-automatic revolving)**

It may be stated as: "The amount shall be renewable after each negotiation only upon receipt of issuing bank's notice stating that the L/C might be renewed".

NOTE: An L/C for the full value of the goods to be shipped but requiring specific quantities to be shipped weekly or monthly and allowing part-shipments is not a revolving credit. It is a credit available by installments.

5.2.9 Reciprocal L/C

A reciprocal L/C is mostly used in a barter trade, a trade of processing of incoming materials, a counter trade, or a compensation trade. In the above modes of trade, there are usually two transactions and L/Cs involved. The applicant of one L/C (the original L/C) may assume the position of the beneficiary of the other one (the reciprocal L/C), and the beneficiary of the first L/C is the applicant of the second.

Let's take the processing trade with customer's materials in China for example. The exporter of finished goods in China is also the importer of the materials needed. Similarly the exporter of the materials is the importer of the finished goods. Since the finished goods are produced by using the imported materials, in order to control the possible risks of nonpayment of the finished goods by the importer, it is very important to specify the time when the two L/Cs are to be effective. As the exporter of finished goods, we usually issue a usance L/C to import necessary materials (the first L/C), while requiring the importer of the finished goods to issue a sight payment L/C (reciprocal L/C) to us, and the tenor of the bill of exchange under the usance L/C generally matches the processing cycle of the exported finished goods. The advising bank of the first L/C is usually the issuing bank of the second L/C.

The first L/C is usually stated as: "*This L/C is available by bill(s) of exchange drawn on us at XXX days after bill of lading date. Payment will be effected by us on maturity of the bill(s) of exchange against the above-mentioned documents and our receipt of the L/C opener's advice stating that a reciprocal L/C in their favor issued by XXX Bank on your account available by sight bill(s) of exchange has been received by and found acceptable to them*".

5.2.10 Traveler's L/C

While a large number of tourists use traveler's cheques and credit cards, some of them still prefer to carry a traveler's L/C, even though drawings can only be done from banks specified by the issuing bank. Traveler's L/C is another form of credit instrument to be used to avoid both the trouble and risks of carrying a large sum in cash when a tourist travels abroad.

A tourist, when applying for a traveler's L/C, will be called upon to inform the issuing bank of particular places he/she plans to visit. The issuing bank then advises its branches or correspondents located in the places of the L/C issued and sends each of them a specimen of the beneficiary's signature. In some cases, a document known as a "letter of indication" containing a specimen of the beneficiary's signature may be issued. The issuing bank may require the applicant to pay the full L/C amount at the time of issue, or may permit a "bill of exchange as presented" basis for settlement. As soon as the L/C is issued, the traveler will be given a list of branches and correspondents of the issuing bank throughout the world from which drawings under this L/C can be made. The letter of indication and the L/C should be instructed to be kept separate at all times. The L/C addressed to "the branches or correspondents of the bank", will imply an authority to encash bills of exchange drawn hereunder, designate the drawee bank, fix the total amount available and its currency, set the expiry date, and bear the number and date of the L/C.

The reimbursement method of the traveler's L/C is the same as other commercial L/Cs, such as claim on the issuing bank or the reimbursing bank.

The paying bank will check the authorized signatures of the issuing bank on the L/C to ensure the authenticity of the document when enchasing the L/C. Each drawing is recorded on the back of the L/C together with the paying bank's stamp and date, so as to make certain that the L/C limit will not be exceeded. A bill of exchange drawn on the issuing bank and signed by the beneficiary is to be paid by the paying bank after verifying the beneficiary's signature to be identical with that shown in the letter of indication. The bill of exchange is then sent by the paying bank to the issuing bank for reimbursement.

As forgery has been frequently committed on the traveler's L/C these days, the paying agents are, therefore, extremely cautious when asked to make payment. The present trend is that several leading banks no longer issue the traveler's L/C as some of their paying correspondents abroad have refused to make payment on many occasions, despite the fact that their agency arrangements with the issuing bank stipulate provision of such services.

5.3 Procedures of Documentary L/C

The documentary L/C procedure involves the step-by-step exchange of documents giving title to the goods for either cash or a contracted promise to pay at a later time. The procedures of a documentary L/C operation are summarized as follows, which involve three major groups of steps, namely issuance, amendment, utilization and settlement. The procedures of a documentary L/C operation are illustrated in the following chart:

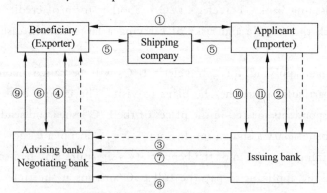

Chart 5.1　The flow Chart of an L/C Operation Process

(Note: The broken lines stand for the flow of modifying the original L/C, if necessary)

Stage 1: The seller and the buyer sign a commodity contract, specifying a documentary L/C as the means of payment.

Stage 2: The buyer applies an L/C to her bank.

Stage 3: The issuing bank issues an L/C after receiving the buyer's applicant.

Stage 4: The advising bank or negotiating bank advises the seller of the L/C.

Stage 5: The shipping company ships the goods, issuing related shipping documents to the carrier (either the seller or the buyer).

Stage 6: The seller submits the documents stipulated in the L/C to the advising bank or negotiating bank.

Stage 7: The advising bank or the negotiating bank sends the documents submitted by the seller to the issuing bank.

Stage 8: The issuing bank makes payment after receiving the documents sent from the advising or negotiating bank and making sure that the documents strictly comply with the L/C.

Stage 9: The advising bank or negotiating bank makes payment to the seller after receiving the payment from the issuing bank.

Stage 10: Upon the issuing bank's correspondent bank(s) having made payment to the seller, the issuing bank presents the buyer to achieve documents against payment or acceptance. The buyer makes payment or acceptance after receiving the issuing bank's presentation.

Stage 11: The issuing bank releases the documents to the buyer after it receiving her payment.

5.3.1 Issuance

Now we will learn more about the process of the buyer's applying for a documentary L/C at the issuing bank and the issuing bank's issuance of the L/C and formal notification of the seller through the advising bank.

- **Step 1: The buyer and seller agree on the terms of their commodity contract: (a) specifying a documentary L/C as the means of payment; (b) naming an advising bank (usually the seller's bank); and (c) listing required documents.**

If the importer has decided to accept the exporter's offer, under the agreed terms, after signifying her acceptance or signing the purchase contract, she must apply to the issuing bank for opening a documentary L/C in favor of the exporter. The purchase contract is the basis for opening an L/C, even if the latter is independent of the former in implementation by banks. It is the contents of the contract between the buyer and the seller that determines the contents of an L/C.

In order to avoid any disputes in a contract providing payment by a documentary L/C, the types of the documentary L/C, a list of required documents, a named advising bank and other relevant stipulations must be specified. A clearly and unambiguously stated business contract is the basis for the beneficiary to fulfill his obligations and get paid.

> **Contract Provision**
>
> When the buyer and the seller agree to use a documentary L/C for payment in the purchase/sale of goods, they are well-advised to insert a payment provision in their contract to that effect. The following is a sample payment clause in a business contract.
>
> - PAYMENT: To secure payment, the BUYER NAME shall have ISSUING BANK NAME open an IRREVOCABLE documentary L/C naming SELLER as beneficiary.
>
> The documentary credit is to be CONFIRMED by CONFIRMING BANK NAME. The documentary credit must remain valid for NUMBER OF MONTHS after issuance and be available AT SIGHT against presentation of the following documents:
>
> 1. ...
> 2. ...
> 3. etc.
>
> The cost of the credit is to be paid by BUYER NAME.
>
> The credit shall be subject to the Uniform Customs and Practice for Documentary Credits (2007 Revision), International Chamber of Commerce, Publication Number 600.
>
> The items in small capital letters are the variables. As with all legal matters it is best to consult with an experienced attorney for exact wording to best reflect your individual transaction.

- **Step 2: The buyer applies to her bank (issuing bank) and opens a documentary L/C naming the seller as beneficiary based on specific terms and conditions that are listed in the credit.**

An L/C is opened at the request and on the instructions of the applicant. The applicant should instruct a prime local bank to issue such an L/C within the time limit specified in the contract. When the importer applies for the issue of a documentary L/C, she is requesting her bank to make a promise of payment to the supplier. Obviously, the bank will generally only agree to this request if it can rely on reimbursement by the applicant. As a rule, the goods underlying the L/C cannot be accepted as the sole security, since that would involve the bank in excessive risks outside its special field. Applicant must therefore either have adequate funds in her account with issuing bank or have been granted an L/C line to cover the amount.

Since a documentary L/C is a pledge by the bank to make payment to the seller, the bank will want to evaluate the creditworthiness of the buyer. If the buyer's credit and relationship with the bank is excellent, the bank will issue a L/C for the full value. If the buyer's relationship is good, but perhaps not excellent, the bank will require that the buyer pledge a percentage of the value of the documentary L/C in cash funds. If the buyer's relationship with the bank is less established, the bank will require that the buyer pledges

100 percent of the value of the documentary L/C in cash funds in advance. The deposits, plus other fees and charges, can be expensive and may discourage importers from using the L/C in payment. Also in times of the devaluation or falling market price in the importing country, quite often the importer will request discounts before opening an L/C.

The applicant must file an application for L/C. The application for an L/C, which should be strictly based on the underlying business contract between the seller and the buyer, can be seen as a contract on the L/C business between the applicant and the issuing bank. Although a particular L/C may have its own terms and conditions, the essential contents of an application usually includes the following items: (1) signature of the applicant; (2) the full name and address of the beneficiary; be sure to make it correct and complete, or it may result in improper presentation of documents for the seller; (3) the amount of the L/C and currency used, which should be in compliance with the business contract, and the words "about", or "approximate" used may indicate a 10% more or less tolerance allowed of the drawing amount from that stated; (4) expiry date and place; (5) availability of the L/C, e. g. by sight payment, deferred payment, acceptance, or negotiation and the nominated banks; (6) a brief description of the goods, including details of quantity and unit price, if any; (7) the documents required; if the applicant has any requirements for the beneficiary to fulfill, then she should specify the documents to meet such requirements and if an L/C contains a condition without stipulating the document to indicate compliance with the condition, banks will deem such condition as not stated and will disregard it; (8) the requirements on the shipment, freight and insurance; (9) the period of time after the date of shipment within which the documents must be presented for payment, acceptance, or negotiation; and (10) the way the L/C is to be opened and whether or not the documentary L/C is transferable or confirmed.

 5-5

信用证欺诈的表现形式和形成原因

1. 信用证欺诈的表现形式

根据最高人民法院《关于审理信用证纠纷案件若干问题的规定》,信用证欺诈是指受益人伪造单据或者提交记载内容虚假的单据;受益人恶意不交付货物或者交付的货物无价值;受益人和开证申请人或者其他第三方串通提交假单据,而没有真实的基础交易以及其他进行信用证欺诈的情形。由此可见,信用证欺诈行为包括:(1)受益人欺诈。欺诈者以受益人或第二受益人的身份,用伪造的单据、假冒伪劣货物、倒签提单等欺诈开证行、通知行、议付行和申请人。(2)申请人和受益人串通欺诈。表现为申请人与受益人互相勾结,编造虚假的或根本不存在的买卖关系,由所谓的买方申请开立信用证,由所谓的卖方向开证行提交伪造的单据骗取银行的信用证付款,之后双方分赃,此时银行就成为信用证欺诈风险的受害者。(3)申请人欺诈。表现为申请人用伪造、变造信用证,行骗商业银行和受益人。

2. 信用证欺诈的形成原因

（1）信用证奉行独立性原则。国际商会《跟单信用证统一惯例》（UCP600）第 4 条"信用证与合同"、第 5 条"单据与货物、服务或履约行为"、第 34 条"关于单据有效性的免责"等条款都表明了信用证与基础合同无关，银行处理的只是单据，对单据有效性不负责任。信用证的这一独立性原则在一定程度上给欺诈行为造成了可乘之机。

（2）信用证的法律制度不健全助长了信用证欺诈行为。实际业务中涉及诉讼的法律问题相对复杂，国内国际社会法律对欺诈制裁不力，各国立法不同使欺诈者容易逃脱罪责，这些都是信用证欺诈存在的重要根源。特别是 UCP600 第 7 条"开证行责任"、第 8 条"保兑行责任"及第 12 条"指定"都保证了开证行和保兑行在单证相符的前提下，都要对信用证里被指定的付款行和议付行进行承付，而法律制度中的善意第三人受到法律保护。这样在欺诈发生时，如果信用证中的指定银行不知情而根据信用证要求完成了议付、承兑、付款行为，开证行和保兑行也要完成承付责任，这在一定程度上助长了信用证欺诈行为。

（3）单据的可伪造性给信用证欺诈提供了方便。商业发票由卖方制作，欺诈极其容易；保险公司签发保险单完全依赖于投保方的诚实告知，托运人、投保人的不诚实陈述会导致保险单据内容不真实；承运人也可能与受益人勾结倒签提单、预借提单、通过保函换取清洁提单，或者受益人干脆伪造提单，造成提单欺诈。

（4）国际贸易中买卖双方有时互不了解，当事人不熟悉国际惯例，还有中间商和可转让信用证的存在，给虚假卖方从事欺诈行为提供了便利。

（资料来源：原擒龙，夏霖.商业银行对信用证欺诈风险的防范[J].金融论坛，2009 年第 12 期）

- **Step 3**：**The issuing bank opens a documentary L/C according to the instructions of the applicant.**

The issuing bank will undertake the first-line responsibility of payment once an L/C is issued, so it should find out the L/C information of the applicant, and examine the business contract, issuance agreement, procedure of guarantee, market demand variation of imports, L/C information of the beneficiary and import license, etc., which are related to the issuance of the L/C. And after careful examination of the above-mentioned factors and the application, if the issuing bank decides to open an L/C, the contents of the L/C should be strictly based on the L/C application. Then, the buyer and the issuing bank will sign an agreement to open a documentary L/C. The credit must be written and signed by an authorized person of the issuing bank.

It is advisable to avoid non-documentary conditions when issuing an L/C, for if an L/C contains a condition without stipulating the documents to indicate compliance with the condition, banks will deem such condition as not stated and will disregard it, and hence such kind of requirements can't form any restriction on the fulfillment of the exporter.

The wording in a documentary L/C should be simple but specific. The more detailed the documentary credit is, the more likely the seller will reject it as too difficult to fulfill.

It is also more likely that the banks will find a discrepancy in the details, thus voiding the L/C, even though simpler terms might have been found to be in compliance with the L/C. The buyer should, however, completely and precisely set forth the details of the agreement as it relates to L/C terms and conditions and the presentation of documents.

The issuing bank should also make sure if the documentary L/C requires documents impossible for the seller to obtain, or requires the beneficiary to submit a document, the performance or production of which is totally dependent on a third party not controlled by the beneficiary (other than a transport document, an insurance document or an inspection certificate, etc.). The documentary L/C should not require documents that the seller cannot obtain; nor should it call for details in a document that are beyond the knowledge of the issuer of the document. The documents specified should be limited to those required to smoothly and completely conclude an international commodity transaction.

- **Step 4: The issuing bank sends the L/C to the advising bank named in the L/C to inform the beneficiary and perhaps also add its confirmation to the L/C.**

The issuing bank usually sends the original documentary L/C to the seller (called the beneficiary) through an advising bank, which may be a branch or correspondent bank of the issuing bank. The seller may request that a particular bank be the advising bank, or the buyer's bank may select one of its correspondent banks in the seller's country.

Upon receipt of the L/C from the issuing bank, the advising bank will examine the L/C and then inform the seller that the L/C has been issued. The advising bank, however, examines the terms of the L/C itself; it does not determine whether the terms of the L/C are consistent with those of the contract between the buyer and the seller, or whether the description of goods is correctly stated in accordance with the contract. By advising the L/C to the beneficiary, the advising bank entails to prove the apparent authenticity of the L/C and accurately reflect the terms and conditions of the L/C.

If the advising bank is simply "advising the L/C", it is under no obligation or commitment to make payment, and it will so advise the seller. The obligation of the advising bank, if it is not a confirming bank, is limited to the accurate transmission of the terms and conditions of the L/C and it assumes no other liability to the beneficiary. But in some cases the advising bank confirms (adds its guarantee to pay) the seller, where it becomes the confirming bank, thereby committing itself to make payment to the beneficiary the same as the issuing bank.

5.3.2 Amendment

Amendment is the process whereby the terms and conditions of a documentary L/C may be modified after the L/C has been issued, especially when the stipulation of the L/C does not comply with the business contract, which may greatly affect the export and import of the goods.

- **Step 5: The seller examines the documentary L/C, and requires an amendment of the L/C if necessary.**

When the seller receives the documentary credit it must be examined closely to determine if the terms and conditions (1) reflect the agreement of the buyer and seller; and (2) can be met within the time stipulated. Upon examination, the seller may find problems:

> The seller might disagree with the terms and conditions. For example, the transaction price listed in the credit may be lower than the originally agreed upon price, or perhaps the seller has specified that the total price is to include shipping, whereas the seller originally quoted a price without shipping.

> The seller might find himself unable to meet specific requirements of the L/C. For example, the time may be too short to effect shipment, or certain documents may not be available.

If the seller still wants to proceed with the transaction, but with modification to the terms of the credit, he should immediately report to the buyer and request him to instruct the issuing bank to make the necessary amendments.

Amendments must be authorized by the buyer and issued by the issuing bank to the seller through the same channel as the original documentary L/C. This can be an involved undertaking so any amendments should be initiated only when necessary and as soon as a problem is identified. Moreover, partial acceptance of an amendment is not allowed and the beneficiary shall give notification of rejection of such acceptance and require the importer to make another amendment. According to UCP600, Article 10 (a), however, an L/C can neither be amended nor cancelled without the agreement of the issuing bank, confirming bank if any, and the beneficiary. That is to say, the amendment takes effect with respect to the issuing bank from the time it issues the amendment, the confirming bank from the time it extends its confirmation to the amendment and the beneficiary when he shows acceptance of the amendment or the documents presented conform to the L/C and to any not yet accepted amendment.

A checklist for the seller's examination of the L/C

1. ❑ The buyer's and seller's names and addresses are correct.
2. ❑ The amount of the L/C is in accordance with the contract, including unit prices, shipping charges, handling costs, and total invoice amounts.
3. ❑ The merchandise description is consistent with the contract.
4. ❑ The L/C's payment availability agrees with the contract conditions.
5. ❑ The shipping, expiration, and presentation dates allow sufficient time for processing the order, shipping the merchandise, and preparing the documents for presentation to the bank.

6. ❑ Partial or transshipments are specified correctly.
7. ❑ The point of dispatch, taking charge of the goods, loading on board, or of discharge at final destination are as agreed.
8. ❑ Insurance coverage and party to pay charges are as agreed.
9. ❑ Instructions on whom the drafts are to be drawn, and in what tenor (maturity dates), are correct.
10. ❑ The L/C is confirmed or unconfirmed as agreed.
11. ❑ There are no unacceptable conditions.
12. ❑ The specified documents can be obtained in the form required.
13. ❑ The issuing (or confirming) bank is known to the seller.

5.3.3 Utilization and Settlement

Utilization refers to the procedure for seller's shipping of the goods, the transmission of documents from the seller to the buyer through the banks, and the transfer of the payment from the buyer to the beneficiary through the banks (settlement). Settlement (a subpart of utilization) concerns the different ways in which payment may be effected to the beneficiary from the buyer through the banks.

• **Step 6: The seller ships the goods to the buyer, obtains the title documents from the shipping firm/agent and prepares other documents required in the L/C, and presents all the documents as required by the L/C to the nominated bank.**

Before the seller presents the documents to his bank, he must ensure that they meet all the requirements laid down in the L/C. All the documents called for must be present (completeness); they must not contravene any stipulation of the L/C (correctness); they must not be at variance with each other (consistency).

According to the UCP600, Article 14 (g), a document presented but not required by the L/C will be disregarded and may be returned to the presenter. The beneficiary must present the documents to the bank specified in the L/C for settlement. In a free negotiation L/C, however, the beneficiary can present the documents to any bank for negotiation. After the settlement, the advising bank may become a paying bank, an accepting bank, or negotiating bank, depending on the manner in which the L/C is available.

Document Checklist Prior to Submission to the Bank
1. ❑ Do all the documents refer to the same order and the same L/C?
2. ❑ Are the documents presented in the correct number and in complete sets?
3. ❑ Are the name and address of the shipper correct?
4. ❑ Are the name and address of the buyer/consignee correct?

5. ☐ Are the issuer name and address correct?
6. ☐ Does the description of the goods, unit price, and total price match the description in the L/C?
7. ☐ Is the description of the goods, unit price, and total price consistent from document to document?
8. ☐ Does the invoice total not exceed the amount available in the L/C?
9. ☐ Is the country of origin of the goods listed and as specified in the documentary L/C?
10. ☐ Is the country of destination of the goods listed and as specified in the documentary L/C?
11. ☐ Do all the dimensions, weights, number of units and markings agree on all documents?
12. ☐ Have all the necessary documents been certified or legalized?
13. ☐ Are the invoice numbers and documentary L/C numbers correct and listed in the proper places?
14. ☐ Is the bill of exchange legally signed?
15. ☐ Does the bill of exchange have to be endorsed?
16. ☐ Does the insurance document cover all the risks specified in the L/C?
17. ☐ Has the insurance document been properly endorsed?
18. ☐ Are the documents being presented within the validity period?
19. ☐ Is the bill of lading "clean", without notations?
20. ☐ If the bill of lading has an "*on deck*" notation, does the L/C allow for it?
21. ☐ If the bill of lading is a charter party bill, does the L/C allow for it?
22. ☐ Is the notify address in the bill of lading correct?
23. ☐ Is the bill of lading endorsed?
24. ☐ Are corrections properly initialed by their originator?

• **Step 7: The nominated bank reviews the document package making certain the documents are in conformity with the terms and conditions of the L/C and pays the seller according to the terms of the L/C.**

According to the UCP600 Article 14 (a), the nominated bank acting on its nomination, the confirming bank, if any, and the issuing bank must examine a presentation to determine, on the basis of the documents alone, whether or not the documents appear on their face to constitute a complying presentation. That is, no matter whether it is the paying bank, accepting bank, or negotiating bank, the principle for the nominated bank's decision as to whether or not to accept the documents will be based strictly on the principle that the documents themselves and the timing of their presentation must be in compliance with terms and conditions of the L/C. Moreover, the nominated bank acting on its nomination, the confirming bank, if any, and the issuing bank shall each have a maximum of five banking days following the date of presentation to determine if a presentation is complying with terms and conditions of the L/C.

After examination, if the documents and the L/C are both in order, the nominated bank, say the negotiating bank, will negotiate the documents, i.e., giving the value for the bill(s) of exchange or documents.

The key issue is that the documents presented by the seller must be in conformity with the stipulation of the documentary L/C. Once again, banks deal in documents, but not goods. The banks, therefore, are seeking conformity of the documentation to the wording of the L/C and not of the goods to the documents. The bottom line is that if the seller's documents are not prepared in accordance with the terms and conditions of the L/C, the bank is under no obligation to pay the seller for the shipment.

Discrepancies with Documents & Bank Options

Perhaps the greatest problem associated with documentary L/C is discrepancies with documents as they are prepared, presented, and reviewed by sellers, buyers, and the banks. All parties have the obligations to check the documentation to make certain it is in order and all parties are at risk for failing to do so properly.

Banks have up to five banking days following the receipt of documents to examine and notify the party from which it received the documents of their acceptance or non-acceptance. If a bank involved in the transaction finds discrepancies in the documents, it has several options:

- ✓ The advising or confirming bank can refuse to accept the documents and return them to the seller (the beneficiary) so that they can be corrected or replaced. According to the UCP600 Article 16 (c), when a nominated bank acting on its nomination, a confirming bank, if any, or the issuing bank decides to refuse to honour or negotiate, it must give a single notice to that effect to the presenter, stating that the bank is refusing to honour or negotiate and each discrepancy in respect of which bank refuses to honour or negotiate. The notice should also state that the bank is holding the documents waiting further instructions from the presenter, or that the issuing bank is holding the documents until it receives a waiver from the applicant and agrees to accept it. Alternatively, the bank may state in the notice that it is returning the documents or is acting in accordance with instructions previously received from the presenter. The notice must be given by telecommunication or other expeditious means no later than the close of the fifth banking day following the day of presentation.

> ✓ If the issuing bank doesn't think the discrepancy is material to the transaction, it can ask the buyer (the applicant) for a waiver for the specific discrepancy, but it must do so within five banking days.
> ✓ The advising or confirming bank can remit the documents under approval to the issuing bank for settlement.
> ✓ The issuing or confirming bank can return the incorrect document(s) directly to the seller for correction or replacement and return directly to the issuing or confirming bank.
> ✓ The bank can proceed with payment to the seller but require a guarantee from the seller to reimburse the bank if the issuing bank does not honour the documents as presented.
>
> If there is a discrepancy, the buyer and the seller must communicate directly and then inform the banks of their decision. In the case of serious discrepancies, an amendment to the L/C may be necessary.
>
> The seller may request the opening bank to present the documents to the buyer on a collection basis. However, the buyer may refuse to accept the merchandise and be responsible for shipping and insurance costs.

- **Step 8: The nominated bank sends the documents to the issuing bank by mail or by courier or other telegraphic means, claiming reimbursement as agreed between them.**
- **Step 9: The issuing bank examines the documents and reimburses the negotiating bank.**

Before effecting the payment, the issuing bank must examine the documents, and if it finds discrepancies with the documents, it will refuse to take over them and hence refuse to pay. On principle, the basis for the issuing bank to examine the documents and the L/C should be the same as that for the negotiating bank.

As discussed above, the issuing bank must determine on the basis of the documents alone whether they appear on their face to be in compliance with the terms and conditions of the L/C. If not, the issuing bank may refuse to take over the documents. If an issuing bank decides to refuse to honour, as we have discussed above in step 7, it should also abide by the regulation in the UCP600 Article 16 (c) on the notice of dishonour. If an issuing bank fails to act in accordance with the provisions of the above mentioned article, it shall be precluded from claiming that the documents do not constitute a complying presentation.

When an issuing bank determines that a presentation does not comply, it may have the following options to deal with the documents: (1) refuse to accept the documents and return them to the advising bank so that the beneficiary can correct them and present them again in the validity period of the L/C; (2) in its sole judgment approach the applicant for a waiver of the discrepancies, and if the applicant elects to accept it, the issuing bank will reimburse the negotiating bank without further hesitation; (3) on the request of the beneficiary, present the discrepant documents to the buyer for a collection instead; or (4) authorize the nominated bank to pay, negotiate or accept with reserve or against indemnity, with which the bank can claim refund from the beneficiary if dishonoured by the applicant.

When the issuing bank receives the documents forwarded by the nominated bank and determines that they are in compliance with the L/C, it must reimburse the bank from which the documents were received according to their arrangement. If the issuing bank and the nominated bank maintain an account with each other, then the amount reimbursed can be credited or debited directly to the account. In case of a documentary L/C issued in a currency of a third country or they have no account with each other, settlement is a little more complex, and a reimbursing bank located in the respective currency area may be employed to transfer the amount owed on demand of the nominated bank. The reimbursement can be made by T/T or by airmail.

- **Step 10: The issuing bank sends the documents to the buyer who redeems the documents and takes possession of the shipment.**

When the issuing bank asks for the applicant to redeem the documents, the applicant has the rights to examine the documents and make sure they comply with the L/C before effecting reimbursement to the issuing bank. The fair reason to refuse to pay is that the documents are not on the face in compliance with the terms and conditions of the L/C or inconsistent with each other.

When the goods have arrived at the destination, the applicant can pick up goods by the bill of lading from the carrier. Even if the goods do not conform to the description of the L/C and the contract, the applicant cannot claim refund from the issuing bank provided the documents presented comply with the terms and conditions of the L/C, and should ask for compensation from the exporter, the carrier or the insurer according to the different conditions instead.

Reading material

Best Practice When Dealing with an L/C

Best practice when dealing with an L/C starts before it is received. Firstly the exporter should consider whether it is necessary to use an L/C, or if another method of payment could be acceptable. If it is decided that an L/C is necessary, the terms and conditions of the L/C should be agreed upon at the contract negotiation stage with the importer. The following issues should be considered: (1) who will pay the bank charges; (2) will the L/C be payable at sight or will there be an L/C period; (3) should the L/C be confirmed (if this is the case this must be stipulated when it is opened); (4) what documentation will be requested under the L/C; and (5) the date up to which the L/C will be valid and how many days to be allowed for presentation of documents (normally 21 days).

In order to ensure that all these points are considered, the exporter should provide their suggested L/C wording to the buyer as early as possible during the sales negotiations. If this is agreed on and built into the sale and purchase contract, there is less likelihood that goods or payment will be delayed due to problems with the L/C.

Even when the above steps are followed, it is essential to check the L/C as soon as it is received. The following is a checklist to be reviewed immediately on receipt of a letter of credit: (1) Is the L/C subject to UCP600? (2) Can the goods be shipped within the period set by the L/C? (3) Do any documents need to be legalized? (4) Can the mode of transport specified be used? (5) Can shipment be made from the port/airport specified? (6) Are the prices correct?

Check that the L/C terms conform with the underlying sales contract and in particular that: (1) the names and addresses of both the opener and the beneficiary are complete and correct; (2) the L/C is irrevocable on the part of the overseas bank (under UCP600 this is the case unless stated otherwise); (3) drawings under the L/C will be either negotiable or payable in China rather than abroad; (4) the description, price and quantity of the goods are in accordance with the terms of the contract.

The exporter should send a copy of the L/C to their shipping and forwarding agent. If there are any terms or conditions within the L/C which cannot be met, arrangements must be made, immediately, for the L/C to be amended. Only the applicant (the buyer) can instruct the bank to amend the L/C. This will take time and there will also be a cost involved, but is better than the alternative of leaving the L/C as it is and risking rejection of the documents when they are presented.

Once the exporter is certain that all the terms and conditions in the L/C can be met, care must be taken to compile all the documentation correctly. It must be remembered that the documents must be in strict compliance with the L/C since the bank's mandate to pay depends entirely on the correctness of the documentation.

Should the documents be rejected, the exporter has the following options: (1) correct documents; (2) instruct the advising bank to request the issuing bank for permission to pay despite the discrepancies; (3) offer the bank an indemnity if they will pay despite the discrepancies; or (4) send documents to the issuing bank on a collection basis. Options one and two are the best as the security of the L/C is maintained. With the third option, the exporter may have to repay the money if the importer refuses to pay for discrepant documents, and under the final option the security is lost.

 5-6

<h3 style="text-align:center">信用证项下"单单"、"单证"不符点的种类</h3>

不符点是指受益人提交的单据表面上有和信用证条款不符的部分，违背了信用证要求的"单证相符"、"单单相符"特性，从而很可能导致出口商遭受银行拒付。概括而言，信用证项下不符点主要有：

1. 实质性不符点。一般是指制单前就已经形成或者是由于出口企业违约造成的不符点，如货物出运错过规定的装船期等情况，若要改证不仅会增加出口企业的费用，还会大大延误出运时间，因此出口商只能选择不符点交单。信用证中的"软条款"也是产生实质性不符点的一个原因，比如信用证中有条款规定"检验证书必须由开证人派员检验合格，出具证书"，由于品质主动权掌握在对方手中，若遇市场行情有所变化，则开证人完全可以人为制造检验证书中的不符点而拒绝付款。

2. 非实质性不符点。一般指在制单过程中人为造成的单证不一致、单单不一致的不符点，对出口商履约无任何实质性影响。如单据的种类、份数和单据本身的项目不符合信用证要求，出口商没有在信用证有效期内及时将单据送交议付银行，或单据的文字内容未按信用证的要求和国际惯例填写，例如英文大小写的问题或明显的笔误和印刷错误等，以上表现均为非实质性不符点。一般来说银行不能以非实质性不符点为由拒付。

3. 审单时常见的不符点。银行审单时常见的不符点主要有：信用证方面，如信用证已超过期限，未按信用证所规定的单据提交，单据份数有误等；汇票方面，如期限与信用证不符，出票人未签字，付款人不正确等；提单方面，如信用证价格条款为 CIF 或 CFR 但提单上未注明"运费已付"，收货人名称/被通知人名称与信用证规定不符，信用证规定"禁止转运"但实际发生了转运等；商业发票方面主要有发票的货物描述与信用证不相符，发票中列入了信用证中不允许的费用，发票上的贸易术语与信用证上的不一致等；保险单据方面，如保险单据日期迟于装运单据日期，保险险别跟信用证中的规定不相符，还有检验证书、装箱单等单据中也会出现不符点。另外还会存在单据之间唛头和号码不一致，需要签字的单据没有签字，单据之间内容相互矛盾等不符点。

（资料来源：李燕.信用证项下如何审证和处理不符点的问题[J].对外经贸实务，2012年第1期）

5.4 Risks under L/C and Protection

Although the L/C has promoted international trade and financing, it may incur great risks due to many uncontrollable factors involving the importer and the exporter, shipping company, and insurance company at home and abroad. Therefore, risks should be considered when the L/C is to be issued.

● **Risks of Market**(市场风险)

The international market is constantly changing. Some salable commodities become dull of sale within a very short period of time, which directly affects the importer's ability to pay. Therefore, there exists fund risk and market risk in the L/C settlement method.

● **Risks of Fraudulence**(欺诈风险)

As we have seen, L/C enjoys a peculiar status in the payment cycle. Because they guarantee the underlying commercial transaction, they have to be a legally independent vehicle from that transaction. However, documentary L/C is not foolproof. There are layers of protection for both the buyer and the seller, but opportunities for fraud do exist. Many of the opportunities for fraud center on the fact that banks deal in documents but not goods, and therefore the seller has the opportunity for presenting fraudulent documents. Seller's fraud is mainly in forms of his obtaining the proceeds of the L/C by faking bills of lading while goods are not loaded at all, or sub-standard goods or even rubbish are inside the correct packing cases. Alternatively, and frequently much cheaper, if he can obtain an entire set of forged backing documents, including the bill of lading, he may present them to the bank negotiating the L/C and obtain payment.

As a reminder, it is always best to know your counterpart and the banks involved and to exercise caution and common sense in making decisions.

The situations listed below are extremely uncommon, but do exist.

➢ Sellers have reported receiving an advice or a confirmation of a documentary L/C from non-existing banks. The perpetrator of the fraud attempts to get the seller to ship goods and present documents for payment to a bank that does not exist. By the time the seller is aware of the fraud, the "*buyer*" has received the goods.

➢ Buyers have reported receiving empty crates or crates filled with sand instead of the merchandise they ordered. By the time they received the shipment the banks had already paid the "*supplier*".

➢ Buyers have reported receiving defective merchandise from sellers. While there may be some latitude for interpretation of what constitutes "*defective*", it is clear that some suppliers have purposefully shipped incorrect or substandard goods.

➢ Buyers have reported being short-shipped. In some cases buyers have ordered a valuable commodity sold by weight and were shortchanged by being charged for the gross weight rather than the net weight. They were charged the commodity price per kilogram for the packing materials.

➢ Buyers of commodities, especially gray market goods, have reported being defrauded by the seller's providing fraudulent shipping documents, evidencing shipment on a nonexistent ship.

The best way to avoid fraud is to have a detailed investigation about the L/C worthiness of the prospective wader.

● **Risks of Clauses**(软条款风险)

From the perspective of the exporter, the risks of clauses refer to the "trapped clauses"

or "soft clauses" in the L/C, which will make it hard for the exporter to fulfill his obligations under the L/C. The examples are as follows:
- > *"Shipment can only be effected upon receipt of applicant's shipping instructions through L/C opening bank nominating the name of carrying vessel by means of subsequent L/C amendment."*
- > *"Cargo receipt issued and signed by authorized signatories of the applicant, whose signature must be in conformity with our records, certifying that the goods have been received in good order, showing the quantity, value of goods, date of delivery and L/C number."*
- > *"Shipping advice issued by the applicant whose signature must be in conformity with L/C issuing bank records, showing the name of vessel and approving the date of shipment."*

All the above mentioned clauses and the documents required by them cannot be controlled by the beneficiary himself, which will adversely affect the presentation of documents by the beneficiary and further lead to the dishonour by the issuing bank or the applicant.

To avoid such soft clauses, the exporter should firstly pay more attention to establishment of the clauses in the sales contract, which should be elaborate, comprehensive and concise. Secondly, after receiving the L/C from the advising bank, the exporter should carefully examine the contents to see if there is any clause contradictory to the sales contract or hard to fulfill, and require amendments if necessary.

● **Risks of Controlling the Title to Goods**(控制货物所有权的风险)

In some circumstances, the L/C may specify that *"1/3 original B/L and one set of non-negotiable documents to be sent to applicant within 3 days after shipment by DHL"*, or *"beneficiary certificate stating original B/L of one set carried by the captain of the vessel"*. Such clauses are quite risky for both the exporter and the issuing bank, because it is quite possible for the importer to obtain the goods with the original B/L sent directly to her without making payment at maturity.

5.5 Financing under L/C

5.5.1 Financing Provided to the Exporter

● **Packing loan**(打包贷款)

Packing loan is known as a kind of pre-shipment financing method, by which the exporter may use the L/C as collateral to apply for a loan so as to prepare or manufacture the exported goods under the L/C. It can help the exporter without sufficient funds to conclude an international transaction and smoothly fulfill the obligations under the transaction.

Normally the period of packing loan provided by the bank will last from the date of getting the loan to the date of negotiating or no longer than 21 days after the expiry date of the L/C and the amount will not exceed 90% of the L/C total amount. The source of returning the loan comes from the proceeds under the L/C, so the provision of a packing loan is solely based on the L/C itself.

In order to control the risks involved in packing loan, the financing bank should pay attention to the following issues: (1) the L/C worthiness of the issuing bank, the applicant and the exporter; (2) careful examination on the L/C to avoid the possible "soft clauses" which will hinder the collection of proceeds under the L/C; (3) the financing bank should be in the position of advising bank and negotiating bank, and the bank giving a packing loan also can not follow the operation of the L/C, such as amendment on amount, extension on L/C; (4) keeping itself informed of how the loan is being used by the exporter and urging the exporter to arrange for shipment and present the documents for negotiation in time; (5) making a careful study on the characteristics, quality and quantity of the commodity, being sure that the goods can be shipped within its latest delivery time and documents presented for negotiation can meet the requirements of the L/C; and (6) keeping an eye on the trade background and its market under the L/C; etc.. The quality of the exported products and production or performance capacity of the supplier should be taken into account by the bank because all these have close relationship to the completion of an L/C. The bank should also be kept informed about the market, because the market is changeable, and the operation of an L/C will last more than one month. When the margin of the exported goods is rather small or even none, the exporter will probably not execute the L/C. In addition, the foreign exchange rate is also a factor affecting the gain of the export.

- **Export bill purchase**(出口押汇)

Export bill purchase means the negotiating bank, on the demand of the exporter, provides the in-transit financing to him using the documents presented as collateral after shipping the contracted goods. The bank can be seen as purchasing the complying documents provided by the beneficiary and hence financing the exporter to get the necessary funds. If the documents and bills are rejected by the issuing bank and importer, the negotiating bank retain the right for recourse. Export bill purchase is the most widely used short-term export financing method.

Under a usance L/C, the financing bank will only purchase the bill accepted by the issuing bank. If the documents and bills are dishonoured by the issuing bank, the negotiating bank can enforce the rights of recourse to the beneficiary.

When granting loans to the beneficiary by this method, the negotiating bank should pay attention to the following factors: (1) the L/C worthiness of the beneficiary, the applicant and the issuing bank; (2) whether the L/C contains "soft clause" which may lead to the discrepancies in documents presented by the beneficiary; (3) whether all the original B/Ls are presented by the beneficiary when negotiating; and (4) whether the L/C restricts the documents to be negotiated in some other banks than the financing bank.

- **Bill discounted**(票据贴现)

Bill discounting is to sell a usance bill already accepted by the drawee but has not yet fallen due to a financial institution at a price less than its face value. Similar to the export bill purchase, the bill discounted can also be enforced the rights of recourse to the beneficiary when dishonoured by the issuing bank.

When a bank starts an operation of bill discounting, it must examine the information about the applicant carefully including her account, acceptor's name, address, maturity and amount. Under an L/C, the bank has to check the documents to see if they are in conformity with the L/C. The bank can only discount the bill when the documents are in conformity with the L/C and the bill is accepted by a reputable bank.

Discount rate for export bill will be made by the bank. Usually banks like to make the discount rate on the base of Libor plus certain points. In some countries with developed international financial market, the discounted bills can be rediscounted by the central bank or sold in the market.

- **Discounting against export commercial invoice**(出口商业发票贴现)

As a newly developed financing business, discounting against export commercial invoice evolves from the financing function of international factoring business. It means that under the cash on delivery payment term, the exporter can use the commercial invoice as a pledge to get financing from the banks. Since the financing banks will bear great risks under this kind of financing method, the business is not as popular as the above-mentioned financing methods.

- **Anticipatory L/C**(预支信用证)

Anticipatory L/C is a documentary L/C with a special condition incorporated into it that authorizes the nominated bank to make advances to the beneficiary before presentation of the documents. It is one of the ways of financing for export. The anticipatory L/C is often used to provide a seller with funds prior to shipment. Therefore, it is of value to middlemen and dealers in area of commerce that require a form of pre-financing when a buyer would be willing to make special concession of this nature.

5.5.2 Financing Provided to the Importer

- **Approval of L/C line by the issuing bank**(开证授信额度)

A documentary L/C issuance can be regarded as a financing arrangement for the customer, and the way of financing is to pay the beneficiary stated in the L/C. Since under the L/C business, the issuing bank undertakes the primary or first-line responsibility of payment, it bears great risks without 100% cash deposit from the applicant when issuing an L/C outward, so business of L/C is a contingent liability of a bank. Thus banks will only agree to open the L/C when they are sure that they can get reimbursement from the applicant of the L/C.

Based on the L/C worthiness of the applicant, the issuing bank will usually approve an L/C line for her. Under the approved L/C line, the issuing bank will charge less or even no cash deposit for issuing an L/C for the importer, which will greatly reduce the occupation of the importer's funds and thus benefit her cash flow, therefore, it can be seen as a way to provide financing to the applicant by the issuing bank.

The L/C line, therefore, should be made through a comprehensive analysis on the applicant, counter guarantee provided, the background of underlying transaction and the market demand variation in importing country, etc. As to the L/C worthiness of the applicant, the issuing bank should examine strictly the operational conditions and profits, financial status, turnover of funds, the correspondence with the issuing bank, and the applicant's ability to pay when approving the L/C line, and shall revise the L/C line in time according to any change of the applicant's operational condition and fund availability.

L/C line approved by the issuing bank can be divided into two forms: general L/C limit and one time L/C limit. From the first kind of L/C line, the applicant can use repeatedly to ask for issuing an L/C. While the second L/C line is approved by the issuing bank toward one transaction upon the applicant's requirements and can be used only once.

- **Import bill advance**（进口押汇）

When documents arrive at the issuing bank, the importer has to make payment in order to obtain the title documents. But the case may be that the importer has no sufficient money or has another lucrative way to utilize the funds and hence require the bank to effect payment to the beneficiary upon presentation of the required documents before she herself actually pays.

The amount of payment is usually within the L/C line approved by the issuing bank to the applicant. The term of financing is usually not exceeding 90 days and should match with the time needed to resell the imported goods, for the major source of fund used to return the loan is the sales income of the imported goods. When the issuing bank makes payment to the beneficiary and gets the documents, it usually delivers the documents to the applicant by her payment or the trust receipt.

- **Trust receipt**（T/R）（信托收据）

As a way of releasing documents to the applicant after making payment outward by the issuing banking, trust receipt is actually a kind of arrangement of the title document between the issuing bank and the applicant, by which the issuing bank acting as the trustor and the true owner of the goods lends the title document to the importer (trustee) or entrusts her to take care of and resell the goods and repay the issuing bank from the proceeds of selling the goods at maturity.

The L/C line for trust receipt is on case basis and generally included as some percentage within the L/C line approved by the issuing bank to open an L/C. Trust receipt is seldom granted alone and usually serves as a way to protect the issuing bank from risks under the import bill advance and delivery of goods against bank guarantee.

- **Delivery the goods against bank guarantee**(银行担保)

When the distance between the trading partners is not far from each other, it is quite common for the goods to arrive earlier than the documents. In order to avoid demurrer charge and other possible expenses of goods, the buyer may obtain a bank guarantee from the issuing bank and submit it to the carrier to obtain the goods for sale.

By issuing the bank guarantee, the bank may bear the risks of non-payment of the buyer when documents arrived and assume the loss claim from the carrier. Therefore, the bank will require the applicant to provide necessary counter guarantee, and since the applicant has already obtained the goods from the carrier before actually making payment by the bank guarantee, the issuing bank must require the importer to fulfill her obligations as follows before issuing a shipping guarantee: (1) to transfer the fund as per the invoice in copy into an escrow account of the issuing bank; (2) to give up the right of dishonour in case of discrepancies on the documents when documents arrive at the issuing bank; (3) to redeem the shipping guarantee from the shipping company by original B/L to return to the bank within 7 working days after the arrival of the original B/L; (4) to be fully responsible for any loss of the shipping guarantee issued by the bank. However, all those mentioned above are not fully ensure the bank to be free from the risk, because there is a possibility that third party who holds the original bill of lading to take goods does not make a presentation or the bank does not receive the bill of lading from the negotiating bank.

5.6 Introduction to UCP600

This revision of the *Uniform Customs and Practice for Documentary Credits* (commonly called "UCP") is the sixth revision of the rules since they were first promulgated in 1933. It is the fruit of over three years of work by the International Chamber of Commerce's Commission (ICC) on Banking Technique and Practice.

ICC, which was established in 1919, had as its primary objective to facilitate the flow of international trade at a time when nationalism and protectionism posed serious threats to the world trading system. It was in that spirit that the UCP were first introduced to alleviate the confusion caused by individual countries' promoting their own national rules on L/C practice. The objective, since attained, was to create a set of contractual rules that would establish uniformity in that practice, so that practitioners would not have to cope with a plethora of often conflicting national regulations. The universal acceptance of the UCP by practitioners in countries with widely divergent economic and judicial systems is a testament to the rules' success.

In May 2003, the International Chamber of Commerce authorized the ICC Commission on Banking Technique and Practice (Banking Commission) to begin a revision of the *Uniform Customs and Practice for Documentary Credits*, ICC Publication 500.

A range of individuals and groups contributed to the current revision, which is entitled UCP 600. These include the UCP Drafting Group, which sifted through more than 5000 individual comments before arriving at this consensus text; the UCP Consulting Group, consisting of members from more than 25 countries, which served as the advisory body reacting to and proposing changes to the various drafts; the more than 400 members of the ICC Commission on Banking Technique and Practice who made pertinent suggestions for changes in the text; and ICC national committees worldwide which took an active role in consolidating comments from their members. ICC also expresses its gratitude to practitioners in the transport and Insurance industries, whose perceptive suggestions honed the final draft.

As with other revisions, the general objective was to address developments in the banking, transport and insurance industries. Additionally, there was a need to look at the language and style used in the UCP to remove wording that could lead to inconsistent application and interpretation.

When work on the revision started, a number of global surveys indicated that, because of discrepancies, approximately 70% of documents presented under letters of credit were being rejected on first presentation. This obviously had, and continues to have, a negative effect on the letter of credit being seen as a means of payment and, if unchecked, could have serious implications for maintaining or increasing its market share as a recognized means of settlement in international trade. The introduction by banks of a discrepancy fee has highlighted the importance of this issue, especially when the underlying discrepancies have been found to be dubious or unsound. Whilst the number of cases involving litigation has not grown during the lifetime of UCP 500, the introduction of the ICC's *Documentary Credit Dispute Resolution Expertise Rules* (DOCDEX) in October 1997 (subsequently revised in March 2002) has resulted in more than 60 cases being decided.

To address these and other concerns, the Banking Commission established a Drafting Group to revise UCP 500. It was also decided to create a second group, known as the Consulting Group, to review and advice on early drafts submitted by the Drafting Group. The Consulting Group, made up of over 40 individuals from 26 countries, consisted of banking and transport industry experts. Ably co-chaired by John Turnbull, Deputy General Manager, Sumitomo Mitsui Banking Corporation Europe Ltd, London and Carlo Di Ninni, Adviser, Italian Bankers Association, Rome, the Consulting Group provided valuable input to the Drafting Group prior to release of draft texts to ICC national committees. The Drafting Group began the review process by analyzing the contents of the official

Opinions issued by the Banking Commission under UCP 500. Some 500 Opinions were reviewed to assess whether the issues involved warranted a change in, an addition to or a deletion of any UCP article. In addition, consideration was given to the content of the four Position Papers issued by the Commission in September 1994, the two Decisions issued by the Commission concerning the introduction of the euro and the determination of what constituted an original document under UCP 500 sub-article 20(b) and the decisions issued in DOCDEX cases. During the revision process, notice was taken of the considerable work that had been completed in creating the *International Standard Banking Practice for the Examination of Documents under Documentary Credits* (ISBP), ICC Publication 645. This publication has evolved into a necessary companion to the UCP for determining compliance of documents with the terms of letters of credit. It is the expectation of the Drafting Group and the Banking Commission that the application of the principles contained in the ISBP, including subsequent revisions thereof, will continue during the time UCP 600 is in force. At the time UCP 600 is implemented, there will be an updated version of the ISBP to bring its contents in line with the substance and style of the new rules. The four Position Papers issued in September 1994 were issued subject to their application under UCP 500; therefore, they will not be applicable under UCP 600. The essence of the Decision covering the determination of an original document has been incorporated into the text of UCP 600. The outcomes of the DOCDEX cases were invariably based on existing ICC Banking Commission Opinions and therefore contained no specific issues that required addressing in these rules. One of the structural changes to the UCP is the introduction of articles covering definitions (article 2) and interpretations (article 3). In providing definitions of roles played by banks and the meaning of specific terms and events, UCP 600 avoids the necessity of repetitive text to explain their interpretation and application. Similarly, the article covering interpretations aims to take the ambiguity out of vague or unclear language that appears in letters of credit and to provide a definitive elucidation of other characteristics of the UCP or the credit. During the course of the last three years, ICC national committees were canvassed on a range of issues to determine their preferences on alternative texts submitted by the Drafting Group. The result of this exercise and the considerable input from national committees on individual items in the text is reflected in the content of UCP 600. The Drafting Group considered, not only the current practice relative to the documentary credit, but also tried to envisage the future evolution of that practice. This revision of the UCP represents the culmination of over three years of extensive analysis, review, debate and compromise amongst the various members of the Drafting Group, the members of the Banking Commission and the respective ICC national committees. Valuable comment has also been received from the ICC Commission on Transport and Logistics, the Commission on Commercial Law and Practice and the Committee on Insurance. It is not appropriate for this publication to provide an explanation as to why an article has been worded in such a way or what is intended by its incorporation into the rules. For those interested in understanding the rationale and interpretation of the articles of UCP 600, this information will be found in the Commentary to the rules, ICC Publication 601, which represents the Drafting Group's views.

 5-7

UCP 的产生和发展

在信用证诞生之初，有关信用证的规则往往是约定俗成的，条款极不稳定，解释也五花八门，难以统一。它的作用仅仅局限于约定的当事人之间，十分不利于信用证技术的推广和应用。在信用证初期实践过程中，各国银行往往从自身利益出发来解释信用证条款，各国缺乏对信用证条款的统一规范解释，因此信用证业务极其混乱。

有关信用证最早的明文规则出在第一次世界大战后的美国。第一次世界大战末期，美国已经扮演了全球物资供应商的角色，国际贸易额迅速上升，美国银行业国际贸易结算得益于国际贸易的繁荣而兴旺，那时信用证是国际贸易结算的主要方式。然而，由于信用证结算缺乏统一的规则，美国银行业在战后的经济萧条中遭受了严重损失。鉴于此，1920年银行、金融界会议在美国纽约召开，会议讨论草拟了信用证规则 Regulations Affecting Export Commercial Credits。之后，欧洲国家纷纷效仿，相继制定出本国的信用证规则，但是由于各国各行其是，互不统一，在国际贸易结算中信用证运作仍然无所适从。

1920年，国际商会在巴黎成立，以着手解决信用证业务中存在的问题，可以说，国际商会的成立对统一各国信用证条款解释起了重要作用。1933年UCP第一个版本最终以国际商会第82号出版物《商业跟单信用证统一惯例》的方式公布。随着国际贸易、运输、保险及通信技术的不断发展，该统一惯例先后经过六次修订并定名为《跟单信用证统一惯例》沿用至今，依次形成1951年的第151号出版物、1962年第222号出版物、1974年第290号出版物、1983年第400号出版物、1993年第500号出版物。这期间，有些国家还把UCP融入国内立法。

然而，贸易环境迅速变化，通信、运输、保险技术的进步日新月异，ICC在关于UCP500的4个意见书的前言中说："国际商会银行技术委员会遗憾而且关切地注意到，在UCP500实施以后，一些银行错误地解释和应用UCP500的一些条文。由于未能正确地运用这些条文，其结果严重妨碍了按照UCP500开立的跟单信用证的使用。"为了维持跟单信用证的活力，ICC针对UCP500的适用条款，先后发布了200多条咨询意见、60多个DOCDEX裁决意见、4个意见书、2个政策声明和1个ISBP，但UCP500还是显得与实际不相适应，拒付率的飙升就是一个最有力的说明，在UCP600出台前，信用证的拒付率已经上升为70%左右。为此，2002年ICC正式启动了UCP500的修订工作，并于2006年底正式完成并通过了最新版本的《跟单信用证统一惯例》，即UCP600。

Useful Words & Expressions for Issuing an L/C

● **Types of L/C**

(1) Sight L/C (L/C by sight bill of exchange) 即期信用证

(2) Time or Usance L/C 远期信用证

(3) Irrevocable L/C 不可撤销信用证

(4) Confirmed L/C 保兑信用证

(5) Unconfirmed L/C 不保兑信用证

(6) Transferable L/C 可转让信用证

(7) Back-to-back L/C 背对背信用证

(8) L/C without recourses 无追索权信用证

(9) L/C with recourses 有追索权信用证

(10) Documentary L/C 跟单信用证

(11) Clean L/C 光票信用证

(12) Anticipatory L/C 预支信用证

① Clean Anticipatory Payment L/C 全部预支信用证

② Partial Anticipatory Payment L/C 部分预支信用证

③ Red Clause L/C 红条款信用证

④ Green Clause L/C 绿条款信用证

(13) Revolving L/C 循环信用证

① Automatic Revolving L/C 自动循环信用证

② Non-automatic Revolving L/C 非自动循环信用证

③ Cumulative Revolving L/C 可积累循环信用证

④ Non-cumulative Revolving L/C 不可积累循环信用证

(14) Deferred payment L/C 延付信用证/预支信用证

(15) Traveler's L/C 旅行信用证

● **Amount of the L/C**

(1) amount RMB¥…金额：……人民币

(2) up to an aggregate amount of Hongkong Dollars…累计金额最高为港币……

(3) for a sum/sums not exceeding a total of GBP…总金额不得超过英镑……

(4) to the extent of HKD…总金额为港币……

(5) for the amount of USD…金额为美元……

(6) for an amount not exceeding total of JPY…金额的总数不得超过……日元的限度

(7) 金额一般规定为发票的 100%，此项用"100%"表示即可。(例如：凭全额发票金额的……信用证付款 By 100%…L/C)

- **Validity of L/C**

(1) 常用的即期信用证表达方法：

Sight L/C；L/C at sight；L/C payable by bill of exchange at sight；L/C to be available by bill of exchange at sight.

(2) 常用的远期信用证表达方法(以见票后 30 天议付的信用证为例)：

30 days L/C；L/C at 30 days；L/C at 30 days after sight；L/C available by bill of exchange at 30 days after sight.

- **Time arrival of L/C**

(1) 信用证的到达时间一般用下列不定式短语来表达：to reach the Sellers 30 days before the date/time of shipment。

(2) 信用证有效期及议付地点。此项内容的填写一般也用不定式短语表达：to remain valid for negotiation in…till…after the final date of shipment。（例如：议付有效期至上述装运期后 15 天在中国到期；e.g. "to remain valid for negotiation in China till the 15th day the final date of shipment"或"to remain valid for negotiation in China within 15 days after shipment"。）

NOTE：支付条款基本句式：By 100% confirmed, irrevocable, transferable, divisible sight L/C to reach the Sellers 30 days before the date of shipment and to remain valid for negotiation in China till the 15th day after the final date of shipment.（凭全额发票金额的、保兑的、不可撤销的、可转让的、可分割的即期信用证。信用证应于装运期前 30 天送达卖方，其议付有效期延至上述装运期后 15 天在中国到期。）填写合同时，可根据具体情况对以上基本句式做适当的增减调整。

- **Signing date and place**

一般的格式为：Done and signed in…On this…day of…，在介词 in 后填上地点，在 this 后填日，在 of 后填入月和年。（例如：2008 年 3 月 20 日于北京；e.g. Done and signed in Beijing on this/the 20th day of March 2008.）

- **The Stipulations for the shipping documents**

(1) available against surrender of the following documents bearing our credit number and the full name and address of the opener 凭交出下列注明本证号码和开证人的全称及地址的单据付款。

(2) bills of exchange to be accompanied by the documents marked(×)below 汇票须随附下列注有(×)的单据

(3) accompanied against to documents hereinafter 随附下列单据

(4) accompanied by the following documents 随附下列单据

(5) documents required 单据要求

(6) accompanied by the following documents marked(×)in duplicate 随附下列注有(×)的单据一式两份

(7) bills of exchange are to be accompanied by… 汇票要随附(指单据)……

● **Bill of exchange**

(1) the types of bills of exchange 汇票种类

① available by bill of exchange at sight 凭即期汇票付款

② bill of exchange to be drawn at 30 days after sight 开立见票后 30 天付款的汇票

③ sight bill of exchange 即期汇票

④ time bill of exchange 远期汇票

(2) drawn clauses 出票条款（注：即出具汇票的法律依据）

① all drafts drawn under this credit must contain the clause "Bills of exchange drawn Under Bank of... credit No...dated..."本证项下开具的汇票须注明"本汇票系凭……银行……年……月……日第……号信用证下开具"的条款。

② bills of exchange are to be drawn in duplicate to our order bearing the clause "Drawn under United Malayan Banking Corp. Bhd. Irrevocable Letter of Credit No... dated July 1 2,2007"汇票一式两份，以我行为抬头，并注明"根据马来西亚联合银行 2007 年 7 月 1 2 日第……号不可撤销信用证项下开立"。

③ bill(s) of exchange drawn under this credit to be marked："Drawn under...Bank L/C No....Dated (issuing date of credit)"根据本证开出的汇票须注明"凭……银行……年……月……日（按开证日期）第……号不可撤销信用证项下开立"。

④ bills of exchange in duplicate at sight bearing the clauses "Drawn under...L/C No...dated..."即期汇票一式两份，注明"根据……银行信用证第……号，日期……开具"。

⑤ bill(s) of exchange so drawn must be in scribed with the number and date of this L/C 开具的汇票须注上本证的号码和日期。

⑥ bill(s) of exchange bearing the clause："Drawn under documentary credit No... (shown above) of...Bank"汇票注明"根据……银行跟单信用证……号（如上所示）项下开立"

● **Invoice**

(1) signed commercial invoice 已签署的商业发票

① in duplicate 一式两份

② in triplicate 一式三份

③ in quadruplicate 一式四份

④ in quintuplicate 一式五份

(2) beneficiary's original signed commercial invoices at least in 8 copies issued in the name of the buyer indicating (showing/evidencing/specifying/declaration of) the merchandise,country of origin and any other relevant information 以买方的名义开具、注明商品名称、原产国及其他有关资料，并经签署的受益人的商业发票正本至少一式八份。

(3) Signed attested invoice combined with certificate of origin and value in 6 copies as required for imports into Nigeria. 已签署的、连同产地证明和货物价值的、输入尼日利亚的联合发票一式六份。

(4) combined invoice is not acceptable 不接受联合发票

(5) 4% discount should be deducted from total amount of the commercial invoice 商业发票的总金额须扣除4%的折扣

(6) invoice must be showed: under A/P No....date of expiry 19th Jan. 2001 发票须表明:根据第××号购买证,到期日为2001年1月19日

- **Amendment to an L/C**

(1) partial amendment 更改一部分

(2) whole amendment 更改全部

(3) to amend an L/C 更改(修改)信用证

(4) to amend as follows 做如下更改(修改)

(5) to make an amendment 更改

(6) to propose all amendment 建议更改

(7) to introduce an amendment 执行更改

(8) to suggest an amendment to an L/C 提出更改信用证的建议

- **Bill of Lading**

(1) full set shipping (company's) clean on board bill(s) of lading marked "Freight Prepaid" to order of shipper endorsed to...Bank, notifying buyers 一整套(公司的)清洁已装船提单应注明"运费付讫",作为以装船人指示为抬头、背书给……银行,通知买方

(2) bills of lading made out in negotiable form 做成可流通形式的提单

(3) clean on board ocean bills of lading to order and endorsed in blank marked "Freight Prepaid" notify: importer (openers, accountee) 清洁装船提单空白抬头并空白背书,注明"运费付讫",通知(进口人,开证人)

(4) full set of clean on board bills of lading/cargo receipt made out to our order/to order and endorsed in blank notify buyers M/S...Co. calling for shipment from China to Hamburg marked "Freight prepaid"/"Freight Payable at Destination" 全套清洁装船提单/货运收据作成以我(行)为抬头/空白抬头、空白背书,通知买方……公司,要求货物自中国运往汉堡,注明"运费付讫"/"运费在目的港付"

(5) bills of lading issued in the name of... 提单以……为抬头

(6) bills of lading must be dated not before the date of this credit and not later than Aug. 15, 2007 提单日期不得早于本证日期,也不得迟于2007年8月15日

(7) bill of lading marked notify: buyer, "Freight Prepaid" "Liner terms" "received for shipment" B/L not acceptable 提单注明通知买方、"运费预付"、按"班轮条件"、"备运提单"不接受

(8) non-negotiable copy of bills of lading 不可议付的提单副本

- **Risks and Coverage**

(1) free from particular average (F.P.A.) 平安险

(2) with particular average (W.A.) 水渍险(基本险)

(3) all risk 一切险(综合险)

(4) total loss only (T.L.O.) 全损险

(5) War risk 战争险

(6) cargo (extended cover) clauses 货物（扩展）条款

(7) additional risk 附加险

(8) from warehouse to warehouse clauses (W/W Clause) 仓至仓条款

(9) theft, pilferage and non-delivery (T.P.N.D.) 盗窃、提货不着险

(10) rain fresh water damage 淡水雨淋险

(11) risk of shortage 短量险

(12) risk of contamination 沾污险

(13) risk of leakage 渗漏险

(14) risk of clashing & breakage 碰损、破碎险

(15) risk of odour 串味险

(16) damage caused by sweating and/or heating 受潮受热险

(17) hook damage 钩损险

(18) loss and/or damage caused by breakage of packing 包装破裂险

(19) risk of rusting 锈损险

(20) risk of mould 发霉险

(21) strike, riots and civil commotion (S.R.C.C.) 罢工、暴动、民变险

(22) risk of spontaneous combustion 自燃险

(23) deterioration risk 腐烂变质险

(24) inherent vice risk 内在缺陷险

(25) risk of natural loss or normal loss 途耗或自然损耗险

(26) special additional risk 特别附加险

(27) failure to delivery risk 交货不到险

(28) import duty risk 进口关税险

(29) on deck risk 仓面险

(30) rejection risk 拒收险

(31) aflatoxin risk 黄曲霉毒素险

(32) fire risk extension clause-for storage of cargo at destination Hongkong, including Kowloon, or Macao 出口货物到香港（包括九龙或澳门在内）存仓火险责任扩展条款

(33) survey in customs risk 海关检验险

(34) survey at jetty risk 码头检验险

(35) institute war risk 协会战争险

(36) overland transportation risks 陆运险

(37) overland transportation all risks 陆运综合险

(38) air transportation risk 航空运输险

(39) air transportation all risk 航空运输综合险

(40) air transportation war risk 航空运输战争险

(41) parcel post risk 邮包险

(42) parcel post all risk 邮包综合险

(43) parcel post war risk 邮包战争险

(44) investment insurance (political risks) 投资保险(政治风险)

(45) property insurance 财产保险

(46) erection all risks 安装工程一切险

(47) contractors all risks 建筑工程一切险

(48) Insurance Policy (or Certificate) 保险单(或凭证)

(49) marine insurance policy 海运保险单

(50) specific policy 单独保险单

(51) voyage policy 航程保险单

(52) time policy 期限保险单

(53) floating policy (or open policy) 预约保险单

● **Stipulations for insurance**

(1) ocean marine cargo clauses 海洋运输货物保险条款

(2) ocean marine insurance clauses(frozen products) 海洋运输冷藏货物保险条款

(3) ocean marine cargo war clauses 海洋运输货物战争险条款

(4) ocean marine insurance clauses (woodoil in bulk) 海洋运输散装桐油保险条款

(5) overland transportation insurance clauses (train, trucks) 陆上运输货物保险条款(火车、汽车)

(6) overland transportation insurance clauses (frozen products) 陆上运输冷藏货物保险条款

(7) air transportation cargo insurance clauses 航空运输货物保险条款

(8) air transportation cargo war risk clauses 航空运输货物战争险条款

(9) parcel post insurance clauses 邮包保险条款

(10) parcel post war risk insurance clauses 邮包战争保险条款

(11) livestock&poultry insurance clauses (by sea, land or air)活牲畜和家禽的海上、陆上、航空保险条款

(12) …risks clauses of the P.I.C.C. subject to C.I.C. 根据中国人民保险公司的保险条款投保……险

(13) marine insurance policies or certificates in negotiable form, for 110% full CIF invoice covering the risks of War&W.A. as per the People's Insurance Co. of China dated 1/1/2001. with extended cover up to Kuala Lumpur with claims payable in(at) Kuala Lumpur in the currency of bill of exchange (irrespective of percentage)作为可议付格式的海运保险单或凭证按照到岸价的发票金额110%投保中国人民保险公司2001年1月1日的战争险和基本险,负责到吉隆坡为止。按照汇票所使用的货币在吉隆坡赔付(无免赔率)

(14) insurance policy or certificate covering F.P.A. including the risk of War and risks of S.R.C.C. as per I.C.C. dated…and institute War clauses dated…and institute S.

R.C.C. clauses dated…按照×年×月×日伦敦保险学会条款和×年×月×日学会战争险条款,以及×年×月×日学会罢工、暴动、民变险条款投保平安险、战争险和罢工、暴动、民变险

(15) this insurance must be valid for a period of 60 days after arrival of merchandise at inland destination 本保险扩展到货物到达内地的目的地后60天有效

(16) insurance policy or certificate covering W.A.（or F.P.A.）and war risks as per ocean marine cargo clause and ocean marine cargo War risk clauses of the People's Insurance Company of China dated 1/1/1981 保险单或凭证根据中国人民保险公司1981年1月1日的海洋运输货物保险条款和海洋运输货物战争险条款投保水渍险（或平安险）和战争险

(17) insurance policy/certificate covering all war, mines risks 保险单/凭证投保一切险、战争险、地雷险（注：mines 解释为地雷,属于战争险的负责范围,可以接受）

(18) W.A. this insurance must be valid for period of 60 days after the discharge of goods 水渍险在货物卸船后60天有效

(19) insurance policy issued of endorsed to order…for the face value of invoice plus 10% coveting including war with 15 days after arrival of goods at destination, only against F.P.A and T.P.N.D. 按发票面值加10%投保战争险,货物到达目的地后15天有效,仅负责平安险和盗窃提货不着险的保险单开给或背书给……

(20) insurance policy or certificate issued by an insurance Co. with W.P.A. clause covering the merchandise for about 10% above the full invoice value including unlimited transshipment with claims payable at Singapore 由保险公司签发的保险单或凭证按发票总金额另加10%投保水渍险,包括非限定转船的损失,在新加坡赔付

(21) covering all eventual risks 投保一切意外风险

(22) covering all marine risks 投保一切海运风险

(23) marine insurance policy including "both to blame" collision clauses and fully covering the shipment 海运保险单包括负责船舶互撞条款和全部货载

(24) insurance…including deviation clauses 保险……包括绕道条款

(25) covering overland transportation all risks as per overland transportation cargo insurance clauses（train, trucks）of the People's Insurance Company of China dated… 按照中国人民保险公司×年×月×日陆上运输货物保险条款（火车、汽车）投保陆上运输一切险

(26) covering air transportation all risk as per air transportation cargo insurance clauses of P.I.C.C. 按照中国人民保险公司×年×月×日航空运输货物保险条款投保航空运输一切险

(27) insurance policy or certificate covering parcel post all risks including war risks as per parcel post insurance clauses and parcel post War risk insurance clauses of the People's Insurance Company of China dated… 保险单或凭证按照中国人民保险公司×年×月×日邮包保险条款和邮包战争险条款投保邮包一切险和邮包战争险

(28) covering all risks including War risks as per ocean marine cargo clauses and air transportation cargo insurance clauses and ocean marine cargo War risk clauses and air transportation cargo War risk clauses of the People's Insurance Company of China dated… 按照中国人民保险公司×年×月×日海洋运输货物保险条款、航空运输货物保险条款、海洋运输货物战争险条款和航空运输货物战争险条款投保海空联运一切险和战争险

(29) covering all risks as per ocean marine cargo clauses and overland transportation cargo Insurance clause (train, truck) of P.I.C.C. dated… 按照中国人民保险公司×年×月×日海洋运输货物保险条款和陆上运输货物保险条款(火车、汽车)投保海陆联运一切险

(30) covering all risks including War risks as per overland transportation cargo insurance clauses (train, truck) and air transportation cargo insurance clauses and air transportation cargo war risk clause and War clauses (for cargo transportation by rail) of the People's Insurance Company of China dated… 按照中国人民保险公司×年×月×日陆运货物保险条款(火车、汽车)、空运货物保险条款、空运货物战争险条款和铁路货运战争条款投保陆空联运一切险和战争险

(31) including shortage in weight in excess of 0.5% (with 0.5% franchise) on the whole consignment 包括短量损失0.5%的绝对免赔率(0.5%相对免赔率),按全部货物计算

(32) including risk of breakage and clashing 包括破裂或凹瘪险

(33) including risk of chipping&denting 包括碎裂或凹弯险

(34) including risk of bad odor 包括恶味险

(35) including damage by hooks, oils, muds and contact with other cargo (insured value) 包括钩损、油污、泥污及与他物接触所致的损失(以保险价值为限)

(36) including damage caused by rain flesh and/or water, internal combustion (total or partial loss) 包括淡水雨淋、自燃所致的损失(包括全部或部分损失)

(37) including loss and/or damage caused by sea water, fresh-water, acid, grease 包括海水、淡水、酸蚀、油脂所致的损失

(38) including T.P.N.D. loss and/or damage caused by heat, ship's sweat and odour, hoop-rust, breakage of packing 包括盗窃提货不着、受热船舱发汗、串味、铁箍锈损、包装破裂所致的损失

(39) including damage caused by infestation mould 包括虫蛀霉烂的损失

(40) including damage due to rough handling during transit subject to C.I.C. 按照中国保险条款包括运输途中操作不当所致的损失

(41) including loss and/or damage from any external cause as per C.I.C. 按照中国保险条款包括外来原因所致的损失

(42) including damage by slings, stains, grease, acids 包括吊具、斑污、油脂、酸蚀造成的损失

(43) excluding risk of breakage 不包括破碎险

(44) including the breakage does not cover the goods remarked in the invoice as

originally damage 包括破碎险,但不负责发票所示之货物的原残损失

（45）excluding natural loss in weight 不包括途耗短量的损失

（46）including 60 days after discharge of the goods at port of destination（or at station of destination）subject to C.I.C. 按照中国保险条款货物在目的港卸船（或在目的地车站卸车）后60天为止

（47）including W.A.&risk of fire for 60 days in customs warehouse after discharge of the goods at port of destination subject to C.I.C. 按照中国保险条款投保水渍险和火险,在目的港卸货后存入海关仓库60天为止

● **Certificate of Origin**

（1）certificate of origin of China showing 中国产地证明书

① stating 证明

② evidencing 列明

③ specifying 说明

④ indicating 表明

⑤ declaration of 声明

（2）certificate of Chinese origin 中国产地证明书

（3）certificate of origin shipment of goods of...origin prohibited 产地证,不允许装运……的产品

（4）declaration of origin 产地证明书（产地声明）

（5）certificate of origin separated 单独出具的产地证

（6）certificate of origin "form A" "格式A"产地证明书

● **Packing List and Weight List**

（1）packing list detailing the complete inner packing specification and contents of each package 载明每件货物之内部包装的规格和内容的装箱单

（2）packing list detailing... 详注……的装箱单

（3）packing list showing in detail... 注明……细节的装箱单

（4）weight list 重量单

（5）weight Notes 磅码单（重量单）

（6）detailed weight list 明细重量单

（7）weight and measurement list 重量和尺码单

● **Inspection certificate**

（1）certificate of weight 重量证明书

（2）certificate of inspection certifying quality & quantity in triplicate issued by C.I.B.C. 由中国商品检验局出具的品质和数量检验证明书一式三份

（3）inspection certificate 检验证书

（4）plant quarantine certificate 植物检疫证明书

（5）fumigation certificate 熏蒸证明书

（6）certificate stating that the goods are free from live weevil 无活虫证明书（熏蒸除

虫证明书)

(7) sanitary certificate 卫生证书

(8) health certificate 卫生(健康)证书

(9) analysis certificate 分析(化验)证书

(10) tank inspection certificate 油仓检验证明书

(11) inspection and testing certificate issued by C.I.B.C. 中国商品检验局签发之检验证明书

(12) certificate of aflatoxin negative 黄曲霉毒素检验证书

(13) non-aflatoxin certificate 无黄曲霉毒素证明书

(14) survey report on weight issued by C.I.B.C. 中国商品检验局签发之重量检验证明书

- **Other documents**

(1) full set of forwarding agents' cargo receipt 全套运输行所出具之货物承运收据

(2) air way bill for goods consigned to…quoting our credit number 以……为收货人,注明本证号码的空运货单

(3) parcel post receipt 邮包收据

(4) parcel post receipt showing parcels addressed to…a/c accountee 邮包收据注明收件人:通过……转交开证人

(5) parcel post receipt evidencing goods consigned to…and quoting our credit number 以……为收货人并注明本证号码的邮包收据

(6) certificate customs invoice on form 59A combined certificate of value and origin for developing countries 适用于发展中国家的包括价值和产地证明书的格式59A海关发票证明书

(7) pure foods certificate 纯食品证书

(8) combined certificate of value and Chinese origin 价值和中国产地联合证明书

(9) a declaration in terms of FORM 5 of New Zealand forest produce import and export and regulations 1966 or a declaration FORM the exporter to the effect that no timber has been used in the packing of the goods, either declaration may be included on certified customs invoice 依照1966年新西兰林木产品进出口法格式第5条款的声明或出口人关于货物非用木器包装的声明,该声明也可以在海关发票中做出证明

(10) Canadian customs invoice(revised form) all signed in ink showing fair market value in currency of country of export 用出口国货币标明本国市场售价,并进行笔签的加拿大海关发票(修订格式)

(11) Canadian import declaration form 111 fully signed and completed 完整签署和填写的加拿大111号进口声明书

- **The Stipulation for Shipping Terms**

(1) loading port and destination 装运港与目的港

① dispatch/shipment from Chinese port to… 从中国港口发送/装运往……

② evidencing shipment from China to…CFR by steamer, in transit Saudi Arabia not later than 15th July, 2002 of the goods specified below 列明下面的货物按成本加运费价格用轮船不得迟于 2002 年 7 月 15 日从中国通过沙特阿拉伯装运到……

(2) date of shipment 装船期

① bills of lading must be dated not later than August 5, 2001 提单日期不得迟于 2001 年 8 月 5 日

② shipment must be effected not later than (or on) July 3, 2001 货物不得迟于（或于）2001 年 7 月 3 日装运

③ shipment latest date…最迟装运日期……

④ evidencing shipment/dispatch on or before…列明货物在×年×月×日或在该日以前装运/发送

⑤ from China port to…not later than 31st August, 2001 不迟于 2001 年 8 月 3 1 日从中国港口至……

(3) partial shipments and transshipment 分运与转运

① partial shipments are (not) permitted （不）允许分运

② partial shipments allowed (prohibited) 准许（不准）分运

③ without transshipment 不允许转运

④ transshipment at Hongkong allowed 允许在香港转船

⑤ partial shipments are permissible, transshipment is allowed except at…允许分运，除在……外允许转运

⑥ partial/*pro rata*, shipment/prorate shipments are permitted 允许分运/按比例装运

⑦ transshipment is permitted at any port against, through B/L 凭联运提单允许在任何港口转运

● **Date & Address of Expiry**

(1) valid in…for negotiation until…在……议付至……止

(2) bill(s) of exchange must be presented to the negotiating bank (or the drawee) not later than…汇票不得迟于……交议付行（受票行）

(3) expiry date for presentation of documents…交单满期日

(4) bill(s) of exchange must be negotiated not later than…汇票要不迟于……议付

(5) this L/C is valid for negotiation in China (or your port) until 15th, July 2007 本信用证于 2007 年 7 月 15 日止在中国议付有效

(6) bills of exchange must be negotiated within 15 days from the date of bills of lading but not later than August 8, 2007 汇票须在提单日起 15 天内议付，但不得迟于 2007 年 8 月 8 日

(7) this credit remains valid in China until 23rd May, 2007 (inclusive) 本证到 2007 年 5 月 23 日为止，包括当日在中国有效

(8) expiry date August 15, 2007 in country of beneficiary for negotiation 于 2007 年 8 月 15 日在受益人国家议付期满

（9）bill(s) of exchange drawn under this credit must be presented for negotiation in China on or before 30th August, 2007 根据本证项下开具的汇票须在 2007 年 8 月 30 日或该日前在中国交单议付

（10）this credit shall cease to be available for negotiation of beneficiary's bills of exchange after 15 August, 2007 本证将在 2007 年 8 月 15 日以后停止议付受益人之汇票

（11）expiry date 15th August, 2007 in the country of the beneficiary unless otherwise 除非另有规定,（本证）于 2007 年 8 月 15 日受益人国家满期

（12）bill(s) of exchange drawn under this credit must be negotiation in China on or before August 1, 2007, and after the date this credit expires 凭本证项下开具的汇票要在 2007 年 8 月 1 日或该日以前在中国议付,该日以后本证失效

（13）expiry(expiring) date... 满期日……

（14）...if negotiation on or before... 在……日或该日以前议付

（15）negotiation must be on or before the 15th day of shipment 自装船日起 15 天或之前议付

（16）this credit shall remain in force until 15th August 2007 in China 本证到 2007 年 8 月 1 5 日为止在中国有效

（17）the credit is available for negotiation or payment abroad until... 本证在国外议付或付款的日期到……为止

（18）documents to be presented to negotiation bank within 15 days after shipment 单据需在装船后 15 天内交给议付行

- **The Guarantee of the Opening Bank**

（1）We hereby engage with you that all bills of exchange drawn under and in compliance with the terms of this credit will be duly honored. 我行保证及时对所有根据本信用证开具与其条款相符的汇票兑付。

（2）We undertake that bills of exchange drawn and presented in conformity with the terms of this credit will be duly honored. 开具并交出的汇票,如与本证的条款相符,我行保证依时付款。

（3）We hereby engage with the drawers, endorsers and *bona-fide* holders of bill(s) of exchange drawn under and in compliance with the terms of the credit that such draft(s) shall be duly honored on due presentation and delivery of documents as specified (if drawn and negotiated with in the validity date of this credit). 凡根据本证开具与本证条款相符的汇票,并能按时提示和交出本证规定的单据,我行保证对出票人、背书人和善意持有人承担付款责任（须在本证有效期内开具汇票并议付）。

（4）provided such bills of exchange are drawn and presented in accordance with the terms of this credit, we hereby engage with the drawers, endorsers and *bona—fide* holders that the said bills of exchange shall be duly honored on presentation 凡根据本证的条款开具并提示汇票,我们担保对其出票人、背书人和善意持有人在交单时承兑付款

（5）We hereby undertake to honor all bills of exchange drawn in accordance with the terms of this credit. 所有按照本条款开具的汇票,我行保证兑付。

● **The Special Conditions**

（1）for special instructions please see overleaf 特别事项请看背面

（2）at the time of negotiations you will be paid the bill of exchange amount less 5% due to… 议付时汇票金额应少付 5%付给……（注：这种条款是开证行对议付行的指示）

（3）which amount the negotiation bank must authorize us to pay…该项金额须由议付行授权我行付给……（注：指佣金的金额）

（4）if the terms and conditions of this credit are not acceptable to you please contact the openers for necessary amendments 如你方不接受本证条款,请与开证人联系以作必要修改

（5）negotiations unrestricted/restricted to advising bank 不限制议付/限制通知行

（6）（the price）including packing charges（价格）包括包装费用

（7）all documents must be separated 各种单据须分开（即联合单证不接受）

（8）beneficiary's bills of exchange are to be made out for 95% of invoice value,being 5%commission payable to credit opener 受益人的汇票按发票金额的 95%开具,5%佣金付给开证人

（9）bills of exchange to be drawn for full CIF value less 5% commission,invoice to show full CIF value 汇票按 CIF 总金额减少 5%开具发票,须表明 CIF 的全部金额

（10）5% commission to be remitted to credit openers by way of bank bills of exchange in sterling pounds drawn on…this commission not to be showed on the invoice 5%佣金用英镑开成以……为付款人的银行汇票付给开证人,该佣金勿在发票上表明

（11）freight and charges to be showed on bill of lading etc. 提单等（单据）须标明运费及附加费

（12）cable copy of shipping advice dispatched to the accountee immediately after shipment 装船后,即将装船通知电报副本寄交开证人

（13）one copy of commercial invoice and packing list should be sent to the credit opener 15 days before shipment 商业发票和装箱单各一份须在装船前 15 天寄给开证人

（14）the beneficiary is to cable Mr X…stating L/C No., quantity shipped name & ETD of vessel within 5 days after shipment, a copy of this cable must accompany the documents for negotiation 受益人应在装船后 5 天内将信用证号码、装船数量、船名和预计开航日期电告……先生,该电报的副本须随同单据一起议付

（15）all documents except bills of exchange and B/L to be made out in name of A.B.C.Co. Ltd. and which name is to be shown in B/L as joint notifying party with the applicant 除汇票和提单外,所有单据均须作成以 A.B.C.有限公司为抬头,并以该公司和申请人作为提单的通知人

（16）signed carbon copy of cable required 要求（提供）经签署的电报复本

（17）both shipment and validity dates of this credit shall be automatically extended for 15 days at the date of expiry 本证的装船有效期均于到期日自动延长 15 天

(18) amount of credit and quantity of merchandise…percent more or less acceptable 证内金额与货物数量允许增减百分之……

(19) credit amount and shipment quantity…percent more or less allowed 证内金额与装运数量允许增减百分之……

(20) shipment samples to be sent direct by airmail to buyer before shipment 装运前须将装船货样直接航邮买方

(21) cable accountee name of steamer/carriage number, quantity of goods and shipment date(or E.T.A.)将船名/车号、货物数量及装船期(或预抵期)电告开证人

(22) all banking charges outside Hongkong are for account of accountee 香港以外的全部银行费用由开证人负担

(23) drawee Bank's charges and acceptance commission are for buyer's account 付款行的费用和承兑费用由买方负担

(24) port congestion surcharge, if any, is payable by openers in excess of this documentary credit amount against evidence 如果有港口拥挤费,超过本证金额部分凭证明由开证人支付

(25) amount of this credit may be exceeded by cost of insurance 本证金额可以超过保险费部分

(26) this letter of credit is transferable in China only, in the event of a transfer, a letter from the first beneficiary must accompany the documents for negotiation 本信用证仅在中国可转让,如实行转让,由第一受益人发出的书面(证明)须连同单据一起议付

(27) letter of guarantee and discrepancies are not acceptable 书面担保和错误单据均不接受

(28) admixture 5% max including organic matter such as weed and inorganic 杂质最高5%包括有机物(如杂草)和无机物

(29) include this symbol "丹" in the shipping marks on each side of the carton(that is four markings in one carton)包含有"丹"字记号的装船唛头刷在纸箱的每一面(即每个纸箱要刷四个唛头)

- **In Reimbursement**

(1) instruction to the negotiation bank 议付行注意事项

① the amount and date of negotiation of each bill of exchange must be endorsed on reverse hereof by the negotiation bank 每份汇票的议付金额和日期必须由议付行在本证背面签注

② this copy of credit is for your own file, please deliver the attached original to the beneficiaries 本证副本供你行存档,请将其随正本递交给受益人

③ without you confirmation thereon(本证)无需你行保兑

④ documents must be sent by consecutive/successive/succeeding airmails 单据须分别由连续航次邮寄(注:即不要将两套或数套单据同一航次寄出)

⑤ all original documents are to be forwarded to US by air mail and duplicate documents by sea-mail 全部单据的正本须用航邮,副本用平邮寄交我行

⑥ please dispatch the first set of documents including three copies of commercial invoices direct to US by registered airmail and the second set by following airmail 请将包括3份商业发票在内的第一套单据用挂号航邮寄至我行,第二套单据在下一次航邮寄出

⑦ original documents must be sent by registered airmail, and duplicate by subsequent airmail 单据的正本须用挂号航邮寄送,副本在下一班航邮寄送

⑧ all documents made out in English must be sent to our bank in one lot 用英文缮制的所有单据须一次寄交我行

(2) method of reimbursement 索偿办法

① in reimbursement, we shall authorize your Beijing Bank of China Head Office to debit our Head Office RMB Yuan account with them, upon receipt of relative documents 偿付办法,我行收到有关单据后,将授权你北京总行借记我总行在该行开立的人民币账户

② in reimbursement draw your own sight bill of exchanges in sterling on…Bank and forward them to our London office, accompanied by your certificate that all terms of this letter of credit have been complied with 偿付办法,由你行开出英镑即期汇票向……银行支取;在寄送汇票给我伦敦办事处时,应随附你行的证明,声明本证的全部条款已经履行

③ available by your bill of exchange at sight payable by US in London on the basis to sight bill of exchange on New York 凭你行开具的即期汇票向我行在伦敦的机构索回票款,票款在纽约即期兑付

④ in reimbursement, please claim from our RMB￥account held with your banking department Bank of China Head Office Beijing with the amount of your negotiation 偿付办法,请在中国银行北京总行我人民币账户中索回你行议付的款项

⑤ upon presentation of the documents to US, we shall authorize your head office backing department by airmail to debit the proceeds to our foreign business department account 一旦向我行提交单证,我行将用航邮授权你总行借记我行国外营业部账户

⑥ after negotiation, you may reimburse yourselves by debiting our RMB￥account with you, please forward all relative documents in one lot to US by airmail 议付后请借记我行在你行开立的人民币账户,并将全部有关单据用航邮一次寄给我行

⑦ all bank charges outside U.K. are for our principals account, but must claimed at the time of presentation of documents 在英国境外发生的所有银行费用,应由开证人负担,但须在提交单据时索取

⑧ negotiating bank may claim reimbursement by T/T. on the…bank certifying that the credit terms have been complied with 议付行须证明本证条款已履行,并按电汇条款向……银行索回货款

⑨ negotiating bank are authorized to reimburse themselves to amount of their negotiation by redrawing by airmail at sight on…bank attaching to the reimbursement bill of exchange their certificate stating that all terms of the credit have been complied with and that the original and duplicate bills of exchange and documents have been forwarded to US by consecutive airmail 议付行用航邮向……银行重开一份即期汇票索取议付条款；索偿汇票须附上证明，声明本证所有条款已履行，单据的正副本已由连续航次寄交我行

- **The Stipulations of "Uniform customs and Practice for documentary Credits"**

（1）except as otherwise stated herein 除本证另有规定外

（2）except so far as otherwise expressly stated 除非另有明确表示

（3）This credit is subject to…本证根据……解释

（4）uniform customs and practice for documentary credits 跟单信用证统一惯例

（5）International Chamber of Commerce Brochure No.600 国际商会第600号手册

（6）2007 revision 2007年修订本

（7）except as otherwise expressly stated herein, this credit is subject to uniform customs and practice for documentary credits 2006 Revision, International Chamber of Commerce, publication No.600 除另有规定外，本证根据国际商会第600号出版物《跟单信用证统一惯例》2007年修订解释

Useful Sentences for Issuing an L/C

1. Signed commercial invoices in five copies for value not exceeding the draft amount quoting import under the policy 2004—2009 non-negative policy and certifying goods are as per proforma invoice No. SY01-001 dated 9th January, 2008.

已签发的商业发票一式五份，价值不超过汇票金额，进口遵从2004—2009年非消极政策的规定，证明所有货物在编号为SY0-001，日期为2008年1月9日的形式发票项下的规定。

2. One non-negotiable set of documents should be forwarded through courier and relative courier receipt should be enclosed with the negotiable set of documents.

应向承运人提交一整套不可转让单据，相关承运人的收据应当同整套不可转让单据一起提交。

3. The full set of clean on board ocean B/L (three) original and two non-negotiable copies signed manually and to notify applicant. In the bill of lading it must be mentioned that 14 days free time for clearing the cargo should be allowed.

全套清洁已装船海运提单（三份）：原件及两份已经手签的不可转让副本，并通知开证申请人。海运提单中必须注明允许14天用于清点货物。

4. Beneficiary should inform the applicant the following details by fax directly after shipment within 10 days.

受益人应当在货物装船后10天内以传真形式告知开证申请人以下细节。

5. All documents must be in English unless specified otherwise and must mention our L/C No and date.

除有另外说明，所有单据均应使用英语，必须提及我方信用证编号和日期。

6. Import under OGL chapter V PARA 8 of the EXIM policy 2004—2009 must be mentioned on all the documents.

所有单据应注明：进口遵循2004—2009年OGL第五章第八段关于进出口银行的政策规定。

7. Free spare parts should be shipped and a copy of the invoice should be faxed after shipment.

免费备用配件应当一同装船，装船后应传真发票副本。

8. Materials to be packed in applicant's approved packing design already sent to the beneficiary.

原材料包装应采用已经发至受益人并得到开证申请人认可的包装设计。

9. Shipping mark, net weight, gross weight and country of origin should be mentioned in each box.

每箱都应注明唛头、净重、毛重和原产地国家。

10. Insurance to be covered by the applicant. 开证申请人负责投保。

11. Except as otherwise expressly stated this documentary credit is subject to UCPDC (2007), revision as published in ICC publication No. 600.

除另有规定外，此跟单信用证根据国际商会第600号出版物《跟单信用证统一惯例》(2007年修订版)进行解释。

12. We regret to say that we have not received your L/C related to the above mentioned Sales Confirmation until today.

我们遗憾地告诉你方，直到今天我方才收到你方有关上述销售确认书的信用证。

13. It is stipulated clearly in the Sales Confirmation that the relevant L/C must reach to us not later than the end of Aug. Although the reaching time of the L/C is overdue, we would like still to ship your goods in view of long standing friend relationship between us.

在确认书上清楚地规定有关信用证应不迟于8月底到达我处。虽然你方信用证到达的期限已过，但鉴于我们之间的长期友好关系，我们仍愿装运你方订货。

14. However, we can not make shipment of your goods within the time stipulated in the Sales Confirmation owing to the delay of the L/C. Therefore, the L/C needs to be extended as follows.

然而，由于信用证迟到，我们不能按销售确认书规定时间装运货物。因此，需将信用证延期如下。

15. Your kind attention is invited to the fact that we must receive your L/C amendment before Sept. 30. Otherwise, we will not be able to effect the shipment in time.

请注意我们要求在9月30日之前收到信用证修改。否则，我们无法如期装运货物。

16. B/L showing costs additional to freight charges are not acceptable.

除了运费以外，提单上不能显示其他费用。

17. Extra copy of invoice/or issuing banks file is required.

另外提交一份发票作为开证行留档。

18. A confirmation certificate is issued by the applicant's representative, whose name will be introduced by the issuing bank.

证明书由开证人代表出具,且签字要和开证行留存的相同。

19. Should the applicant waive the discrepancy, we will release documents to the opening. 如果开证人接受不符点,我们将放单给开证人。

20. Beneficiary must courier one set of non-negotiable documents to the applicant.

受益人必须快递一套副本单据给开证人。

21. If dated and signed after this date by competent authorities it must bears the mention issued retrospectively.

如果权威部门在该日期之后签署,则必须倒签。

22. We hereby engage with drawers and/or bona fida holders that bills of exchange drawn and negotiated in conformity with the terms of this credit.

开证行承诺汇票的出票人或善意持票人将在单证相符的情况下得到议付。

23. Third party, Short Form, and Chartered party B/L will not be acceptable.

不接受第三方提单、简式提单和租船提单。

24. We have today instructed our Bank, the Frank Bank in New York, to open in your favor a confirmed, irrevocable letter of credit with partial shipment and transshipment allowed clause, available by bill of exchange at sight, against surrendering the full set of shipping documents.

我们今天已通知纽约弗兰克银行,开立以你方为抬头的、保兑的、不可撤销的允许分运和转船的信用证,凭即期汇票并附全套装运单据向议付行议付。

25. The goods have already been bought from the manufacturer for our account, and we are anxious to know when you can arrange for a credit under new import license.

我们已从厂家购得此货,请速告,按新的进口许可证规定,你方何时可开出信用证。

26. Provided such bills of exchange are drawn and presented in accordance with the terms of this credit, we hereby engage with the drawee, endorsed and bona fide holders that the said bills of exchange shall be honored on presentation.

凡根据本信用证的条件开出并提示的汇票,本行保证对出票人、背书人及善意持有人付款。

27. Bills of exchange drawn under this credit must be negotiated in China on or before April 28, 2008 after which this credit expires.

此信用证的汇票必须在2008年4月28日之前在中国议付,此日之后汇票期满。

28. Complete set of not less than two clean Ocean Bills of Lading to order and blank endorsed.

不少于两份的全套清洁、空白抬头、空白背书的海运提单。

29. The L/C has been received this date, but without necessary amendment. Again, we must ask you to refer to our telex of February 20, 2008 in which our request was made to you regarding the following clause to be amended.

信用证今日收到,但未作修改。我们必须再一次提请你方注意我们2008年2月20日的电传,请你方对下述条款进行修改。

30. After we have checked the L/C carefully, we request you to make the following amendments:

(1) The quantity should read: 1000 M/T(5% more or less at Seller's option);

(2) Partial shipments are allowed.

我们在认真审核了信用证之后,请求你方作如下修改:

(1) 数量为:1000公吨(允许5%溢短装,由卖方决定);

(2) 允许分批装运。

31. 修改信用证受益人

如来证将受益人写错,要求开证人将受益人的名称改正:Letter of Credit No. XXX fails to conform with Contract No. XXX in respect of the name of beneficiary, Our correct name should be…Please make the necessary amendment.

信用证第×××号内的受益人名称与合同不符,我方正确的名称应为×××,请做必要的修改。

32. 来证类型与合同不符

如来证的类型与合同不符时:We regret to find that the L/C No. XXX is irrevocable credit. This is not in conformity with the clause in Sales Contract No. XXX, which calls for opening irrevocable and transferable credit. We have to request you to amend the credit to read irrevocable and transferable as soon as possible.

我们遗憾地发现,你方开具的第×××号信用证仅是不可撤销的信用证,这与第×××号销售合同的规定不符。该合同规定开立的是不可撤销的和可转让的信用证。我们请你方尽快将上述信用证修改为不可撤销的和可转让的信用证。

33. 修改信用证金额

We find that the amount of your L/C is insufficient, because the premiums for Dark and Special colors are not included therein. Therefore, please increase the amount of the L/C to $56800.

我们发现由于信用证金额未包括深特色加价,因此信用证金额不足,请将信用证金额增至$56800。

Checking the figure in L/C No. XXX up with the total value in S/C No. XXX, we find that there is a deficiency of USD XXX in your credit. Please instruct the opening bank to make up the deficiency by cable/telex/fax.

信用证第×××号经与销售合同第×××号核对时,发现该证金额缺少×××美元,请通知开证行用电报、电传或传真补充所缺金额。

34. 修改信用证品名(或规格、数量、包装、单价、合同号码及目的港口等)

L/C No. XXX fails to conform with S/C No. XXX in respect of the name of goods (or specifications/quantity/packing/unit price/Contract No./port of destination). Will you please amend the name of goods (or specifications/quantity/packing/unit price/

Contract No./port of destination) to read…

信用证第×××号的品名(规格/数量/包装/单价/合同号/目的港)与第×××号销售确认书不符。请将证内的品名(规格/数量/包装/单价/合同号/目的港)修改为……

35. 要求准许转运或分批装运

Please amend the L/C to read "Partial shipments and transshipment allowed".

请将信用证修改为允许分批装运和转船。

As there is no direct vessel for your port during month of…we have to ship via Hong Kong. Please cable/telex amendment your credit to allow transshipment at Hong Kong, so that the goods may be shipped in time.

由于在某月份内无直达船开往你方港口,我方不得不经香港转船。请用电报或电传将信用证修改为准许在香港转船,以便及时装运。

L/C No. XXX. We find that partial shipments are not allowed. It is clearly not in conformity with S/C No. XXX. In order to enable US to ship your order on board in time, we must ask you to amend your credit by cable/telex to allow partial shipments immediately.

我方发现信用证第×××号不允许分批装运,这显然与销售确认书不相符,为了及时将你方所订货物装船,务请即用电报或电传将信用证改为准许分批装运。

36. 增加溢短装条款

…there is no more or less clause as mentioned in S/C No. XXX on your L/C No. XXX. Please insert the wording "5% more or less is allowed" after both the total value and the quantity to be delivered in the credit.

你方开具的信用证×××号没有按照销售确认书第×××条的规定列明溢短装条款。请在信用证内的总金额及数量后加上允许增减5%的字样。

37. 修改保险条款

L/C No. XXX requires us to cover the goods against All Risks and War Risk for 150% of invoice value. As this is not in conformity with clause…in S/C XXX calls for coverage of All Risks and War Risk for 110% of invoice value, we have to request to make the necessary amendment.

信用证第×××号要求我方按发票金额的150%投保一切险和战争险,这与第×××号销售确认书第×××条规定不符,该条规定为按发票金额的110%投保一切险和战争险。望你方作必要的修改。

38. 展延装运期

Please extend the shipment date and the validity of your L/C No.111 to the end of Jan. and Feb.15, 2006 respectively, and see to it that the amendment advice will reach us before the end of Dec. 2005.

请将信用证111号的装运船和议付期分别延长至2006年1月底和2月15日,并请注意把修改书于2005年12月底前寄达我们这里。

As there is no direct vessel for your port during the time of shipment stipulated in

L/C No. XXX under the circumstances, we have to ask you to amend L/C to extend the time of shipment and the validity of the credit to…and…respectively.

由于无直达船在第×××号信用证规定的期限内开往你方港口,在这种情况下,我方不得不要求你方修改信用证,将装运期及有效期分别延长至某日和某日。

We have received your L/C No. 111 covering the above-mentioned contract. But on checking up its clauses, we find that it calls for shipment to be effected not latter than Nov. 10, 2005, whereas the contract stipulates shipment Dec. 2005. Please extend the shipment date to the Dec. 15th 2005 and validity to the 31st of Dec.

上述合约项下的信用证第111号已收到。但是经过核对条款,发现该证规定装运期不迟于2005年11月,而合约规定装运期为2005年12月,为此请把该证装运期延长至2005年12月15日,议付期延长至12月31日。

39. 修改数量条款

Please amend the foregoing L/C to read piece length in 30 yards instead of 40 yards.

请把上述信用证条款中匹长40码改为30码。

40. 修改规格条款

We would draw your attention to the fact that the construction of our Art. No. 3100S is 32×32～78×65 whereas your credit calls for 30×30～78×65. Therefore, you are requested to amend the credit according to the stipulation of the contract.

我们提请贵方注意,我方坯布的规格为32×32～78×65,而贵方信用证却规定30×30～78×65,故请按照合约规定修改信用证。

41. 特别条款

Documents have to be presented with 14 days after the date of issue of the bills of lading or other shipping documents.

单据必须在提单或其他装船单据签发日期之后14天内提示。

★ Exercise

一、单项选择(Exclusive Choice Question)

1. Which of the following parties shall enjoy the right of recourse after the bank payment to the L/C's beneficiary? (   )

    A. Negotiation bank   B. Issuing bank
    C. Confirming bank   D. Reimbursing bank

2. Checking the L/C is based on the contents of(   ).

    A. the UCP600 and contract   B. Insurance policy
    C. commercial invoice   D. Bill of lading

3. According to the UCP600, the primacy payer of the L/C is (   ).

    A. importer   B. issuing bank
    C. negotiation bank   D. Advising bank

4. In fact, using buyer's usance L/C is using the funds of (   ).

A. exporter B. importer
C. issuing bank D. negotiation bank

5. Generally, the most appropriate L/C for perennial quantitative trading is (　　).
   A. Back to back L/C B. revolving L/C
   C. transferable L/C D. confirmed L/C

6. 下列哪项不属于"正确"制单所要求的"三相符"原则？(　　)
   A. 单据与信用证相符 B. 单据与货物相符
   C. 单据与单据相符 D. 单据与贸易合同相符

7. 信用证支付方式下，银行处理单据时不负责审核(　　)。
   A. 单据与有关国际惯例是否相符 B. 单据与信用证是否相符
   C. 单据与国际贸易合同是否相符 D. 单据与单据是否相符

8. 来证规定："Documents to be presented within 14 days after the date of B/L, but in any event within the credit validity."假设最迟装运期为9月10日，实际装运日为9月6日，信用证有效期为9月25日，出口商最迟应在(　　)交单。
   A. 9月5日 B. 9月20日 C. 9月24日 D. 9月14日

9. 在结算方式中，按出口商承担风险从小到大的顺序排列，应该是(　　)。
   A. 付款交单托收、跟单信用证、承兑交单托收
   B. 跟单信用证、付款交单托收、承兑交单托收
   C. 跟单信用证、承兑交单托收、付款交单托收
   D. 承兑交单托收、付款交单托收、跟单信用证

10. 可转让信用证在使用时，转让行不可以改变(　　)。
    A. 有关商品品质规格的条款
    B. 信用证总金额
    C. 商品单价
    D. 装运期和信用证有效期

11. 以下关于可转让信用证说法错误的是(　　)。
    A. 可转让信用证适用于中间商贸易
    B. 信用证可以转让给一个或一个以上的第二受益人，而且这些第二受益人又可以转让给两个以上的受益人
    C. 未经过信用证授权的转让行办理，受益人自行办理的信用证转让业务视为无效
    D. 可转让信用证中只有一个开证行

12. 一份信用证规定有效期为2015年11月15日，装运期为2015年10月，未规定装运日后交单的特定期限，实际装运货物的日期是2015年10月10日。根据《UCP600》规定，受益人应在(　　)前向银行交单。
    A. 2015年11月15日 B. 2015年10月31日
    C. 2015年10月15日 D. 2015年10月25日

13. 某开证行2010年3月1日(周一)收到A公司交来的单据，根据《UCP600》规定，

最迟的审单时间应截至（　　）。

A. 2010年3月5日　　　　　　B. 2010年3月6日

C. 2010年3月7日　　　　　　D. 2010年3月8日

14. A银行开立一份信用证，委托B银行作通知行，由于B银行无法直接通知给受益人，经联系受益人后，A银行将信用证发送给C银行，由C银行通知受益人。在此业务中，上述哪家银行是《UCP600》认可的通知行？（　　）

A. A银行　　　　　　　　　　B. B银行

C. C银行　　　　　　　　　　D. B银行和C银行

二、多选题（Multiple Choice Question）

1. 某贸易公司的工作人员因为粗心大意，没有发现信用证上的公司名称与公司的印章名称不一致，信用证上的是ABC Corporation，而印章上则是ABC，其所制作的单据都加盖的印章，请问这种情况下（　　）。

A. 开证行有权拒付　　　　　　B. 开证行应该如期付款

C. 双方可协商解决　　　　　　D. 以上都不对

2. 对开信用证经常用于（　　）。

A. 易货贸易　　B. 一般贸易　　C. 加工贸易　　D. 服务贸易

3. 采用信用证结算方式，银行拒付的理由只能是（　　）。

A. 单证不符　　　　　　　　　B. 单单不符

C. 货物与合同不符　　　　　　D. 货物与信用证不符

4. 指出下列信用证条款中属于软条款信用证性质的是（　　）。

A. 商业发票需开证申请人签署

B. 货物样品寄交开证申请人认可并作为议付条件之一

C. 商检证书由开证申请人签发，并作为议付单据之一

D. 信用证规定货物清关后银行才支付货款

E. 承运船只由买方指定，船名以信用证修改书的方式通知，交单时必须提交信用证修改书

5. 在信用证支付方式下，外贸单证工作主要有（　　）等方面的内容，它贯穿于合同履行的全过程。

A. 审证　　　　B. 制单　　　　C. 审单　　　　D. 交单

E. 存档

6. 对于信用证与合同关系的表述正确的是（　　）。

A. 信用证的开立以买卖合同为依据

B. 信用证业务的处理不受买卖合同的约束

C. 有关银行办理信用证业务应适当考虑合同

D. 合同是审核信用证的依据

7. 可转让信用证被转让时，（　　）可以变动。

A. 信用证金额　　　　　　　　B. 商品单价

C. 商品的品质规格　　　　　　D. 最迟装运日

8. 进口商申请开立信用证的程序包括（　　）。
   A. 递交有关合同副本及附件　　　　B. 填写开证申请书
   C. 缴付保证金　　　　　　　　　　D. 支付开证手续费
   E. 在开证申请书背面签字

9. 某公司分别以 D/P at 90 days after sight 和 D/A at 90 days after sight 两种支付条件对外出口了两批，这两笔业务具有以下那些特点：（　　）。
   A. 前者是进口商在到期日付清货款才可以取得货运单据，后者是进口商在见票时承兑后即可取得货运单据
   B. 前者没有遭进口商拒付的风险，而后者存在这种风险
   C. 前者的风险比后者大
   D. 后者的风险比前者大

10. 下列说法正确的是：（　　）。
    A. 根据《UCP600》规定，信用证如未规定有效期，则该证可视为无效
    B. 国外开来信用证规定货物数量为 3000 箱，6/7/8 月，每月均匀装运。我出口公司于 6 月份装运 1000 箱，并收妥款项。7 月份由于货未备妥，未能装运。8 月份装运 2000 箱。根据《UCP600》规定，银行不得拒付
    C. 在信用证支付方式下，受益人只要在信用证规定的有效期内向银行提交符合信用证规定的全部单据，银行就必须履行付款义务（必须满足单单相符，单证相符）
    D. 假如受益人要求开证申请人将信用证的有效期延长一个月，在信用证未规定装运期的情况下，同一信用证上的装运期也可顺延一个月

三、判断题（True or False）

1. 信用证的开立说明了开证行接受了开证申请人的要求，因此信用证体现了开证行对开证申请人的承诺。（　　）
2. 跟单信用证开立的基础是销售合约，因此信用证下当事人不仅受信用证条款的约束，而且同时受销售合约条款的约束。（　　）
3. 信用证有效期是指受益人能够利用信用证的最迟期限，这个期限是指受益人向出口地银行提示单据最迟的日期。（　　）
4. 对受益人来说，保兑行和开证行承担同样的责任，他可以要求其中任何一个银行履行付款责任，但是他首先要服从信用证条款的规定。（　　）
5. 即期付款信用证可以是开证行自己付款，也可以由其他银行付款；可以要求受益人提供汇票，也可以不要求提供汇票。（　　）
6. 对开信用证即背对背信用证，是一种从属信用证，这种信用证是受益人把开证行开给他的信用证用作支持其往来银行开给其供货商的另一信用证。（　　）
7. 《UCP600》规定，L/C 项下可以开立以开证申请人为受票人的汇票。（　　）
8. 开证申请人以开证申请书与开证行订立契约关系，信用证一经开出，申请人有义务付款赎单，无论单据是否相符。（　　）
9. 循环信用证可省去开证申请人多次开证的麻烦和费用支出，因此适用于分批的均

匀交货的合同。（　　）

10．延期付款信用证中，受益人必须出具远期汇票及随附单据向开证行或者指定银行索款。（　　）

四、案例分析题（Practice）

1．某出口公司收到国外开来的一份不可撤销议付信用证，正准备按信用证规定发运货物时，突然接到开证行的通知，声称开证申请人已经倒闭。

试问：出口公司应如何处理？为什么？

2．我国 A 公司向加拿大 B 公司以 CIF 术语出口一批货物，合同规定4月份装运。B 公司于4月10日开来不可撤销信用证，此证按《UCP600》规定办理。证内规定：装运期不得晚于4月15日。此时我方已来不及办理租船订舱，立即要求 B 公司将装期延至5月15日。随后 B 公司来电称：同意展延船期，有效期也顺延一个月。我 A 公司于5月10日装船，提单签发日5月10日，并于5月14日将全套符合信用证规定的单据交银行办理议付。

试问：我国 A 公司能否顺利结汇？为什么？

3．Is It A Right Decision?

Bank A in Norway opened L/C No. 7636 to purchase working gloves of size 10 from China. After examining the documents presented by the export company, the negotiating bank found no mistake in these documents and sent them to the issuing bank. Half a month later, the issuing bank made a refusal of payment arguing that the size of the gloves shown on the documents was not in accordance with that in the original sales contract.

The truth is that the size specified in the original contract was "size 10- 1/2", but the L/C said "size 10". For the sake of convenience, the export company did not ask for amendment but prepared the goods according to the contract but furnished the documents according to the requirement of the L/C. In order to help the applicant make customs clearance, the beneficiary issued another invoice showing "size 10 -1/2" and informed the applicant that the working gloves shipped were all of that size. In the end, the importer made the payment.

Chapter 6

Other Methods of International Settlement

An exporter from London and an importer from Egypt signed a business contract, which demanded the exporter to open the performance bond by the bank, for 5% of the cost. Therefore, the exporter commissioned the National Westminster Bank to open a demand guarantee in which the beneficiary is the importer, and provides the bank with the counter guarantee. Later the importer request the payment for the National Westminster bank as the exporter failed to perform the contract. However, the exporter got a ban from the local court that demand the National Westminster bank shall not pay, and the bank apply to repeal this ban. Will the court support the requirement of the bank? What are the risks of demand guarantee? How to control the risks? In this chapter, we will learn other methods of international settlement including letter of guarantee, stand by letter of credit, international factoring and forfaiting.

★ Learning Objectives

(1) To enable the readers to know the definition of bank guarantee, and basic parties to bank guarantee.

(2) To enable the readers to understand the open procedure, functions and contents of bank guarantee.

(3) To enable the readers to know the definition, nature and features of standby letter of credit.

(4) To enable the readers to know the definition, basic process of international factoring.

(5) To enable the readers to know the definition of forfaiting, and understand its application in international trade.

6.1 Bank's Letter of Guarantee(L/G)

In dealings with the international economic transactions, the two sides were in different countries or regions, lack of necessary understanding and trust between each other. This may lead to a crisis of credit. So if there is a guarantee filing to connect different countries of both parties, to eliminate the distrust between each other, the development of international economic will be promoted. This is the main reason why the letter of guarantee was born. Basically a banker's letter of guarantee gives the beneficiary certainty over receiving agreed payments if the principal fails to meet her contractual obligations.

6.1.1 Definition of L/G

L/G is a written undertaking made by the guarantor at the request of the applicant to the beneficiary, guaranteeing that the applicant will perform obligations under the contract signed between the applicant and the beneficiary. It may also be defined as the irrevocable obligation of the bank to pay a sum of money in the event of non-performance of the contract by the principal. Distinguished from an L/C, a bank guarantee is an undertaking which will be brought into effect by the guarantor, namely, the bank, only if the principal fails to pay or perform, and so the bank is secondarily liable to the beneficiary. However, under a payment guarantee, it is stipulated that the bank undertakes to pay, provided the documents presented are in compliance with the terms and conditions of the guarantee. In that case, the issuing bank is primarily liable to the beneficiary.

银行保函(the banker's letter of guarantee, L/G)是指银行或其他金融机构作为担保人, 根据委托人的申请, 以第三者的身份保证委托人如未对受益人履行某项契约的义务时, 向受益人有条件地支付一定金额的经济赔偿责任的书面担保。简言之, 银行保函就是银行向受益人开立的保证文件。

6.1.2 Parties to An L/G

● **The Beneficiary**(受益人)

The beneficiary is the person in whose favor the guarantee is issued. He is secured against the risk of the principal's not fulfilling her obligations towards the beneficiary in respect of the underlying transaction for which the demand guarantee is given.

● **The Principal**(委托人)

The principal is the person at whose request the L/G is issued. While recognizing the needs of the beneficiary, the principal can expect on the grounds of equity and good faith to be informed in writing. This should help to eliminate a certain level of abuse of guarantees through unfair demands by beneficiaries.

● **The Guarantor**(担保人)

The guarantor is a bank or a financial institution which issues an L/G undertaking to make payment to the beneficiary in the event of default by the principal against the presentation of a written demand and other specific document.

● **The Instructing Party**(指示人)

The instructing party is a bank or a financial institution or any other body or person that issues a counter guarantee acting on the instruction of a principal in favor of a bank or a financial institution commonly located in the beneficiary's country instructing the latter to issue an L/G on behalf of the former's principal in favor of a specified party named therein.

银行保函：进口贸易中不可忽视的一把利器

提到进口贸易，大家首先想到的是信用证。但是，信用证仅仅是买方向卖方提供了银行信用作为担保，并不适用于卖方要向买方提供担保的场合。在多年的进口贸易实践中，我们发现，银行保函正是能够解决这一问题的一把利器，然而在实际工作中，银行保函并没有得到应有的重视，甚至是一直被忽视。随着我国国际贸易的不断发展，熟练掌握与运用保函规则，提高保函实务操作能力，是广大国际贸易从业人员亟待解决的问题。

不可否认，信用证一直牢牢占据着国际贸易结算的主导地位，但是仅仅采用信用证方式结算对买方来说仍然存在着较大风险。比如，按照信用证规定，卖方提交了与信用证要求一致的单据后买方必须付款，但单据一致并不代表也不能保证卖方交货的数量和质量与合同要求一致，数量短少和以次充好的现象时有发生。虽然买方可以在合同中要求卖方提交国家或国际商检机构出具的商检证书来证明商品的数量和质量，但是由于国际贸易项下合同内容多样、条款各异，所涉及商品的质量标准和技术规范各不相同，商检证书无法满足买方对不同商品的不同要求，而且更重要的是，商检证书无法从根本上保证实际到货与证书不一致时买方能够得到赔偿。因此，买方为了保证自己的利益不受损害，通常会在合同中要求留一部分尾款待质保期结束后再支付给卖方，但是很多货物的质保期相当长，越来越多的公司特别是大公司为了资金的回笼周转不能接受这种等同于押现金的做法。这种情况下，双方可以在合同中约定卖方向买方提交一份银行保函保证交货的数量和质量与合同要求一致，这个保函可以作为买方开出信用证的前提条件，也可以作为信用证项下单据之一与其他单据一起提交，甚至可以在卖方要求支付尾款时提交。只要卖方交货的数量和质量与合同要求不一致，买方就可以向担保银行索赔而得到赔款，这样不仅买方的利益得到了有效保障，卖方也避免了长时间的资金无法回笼问题，达到了买卖双赢。特别是我们工作中进口的很多是大型成套设备，除了设备作为商品与货币的交换之外，还涉及设备的安装调试和人员培训等诸多有偿服务，因此，要求卖方提交银行保函以保障买方利益就更加必要了。

（资料来源：张伟伟.银行保函：进口贸易中不可忽视的一把利器[J].对外经贸实务，2012年第4期）

6.1.3 Types of L/G

The main types of the bank L/G are tender bond, performance bond and repayment guarantee, but in practice there are also guarantees for repayment of money borrowed by the account party, for payment due under a lease, and for deferred payment of equipment under a project, etc.

- **Tender Guarantee, Tender Bond, or Bid Bond**(投标保函)

A tender guarantee is an undertaking given by a bank at the request of a tender in favor of a party inviting tender abroad, whereby the guarantor undertakes, in the event of default by the principal in the obligations resulting from the submission of tender, to make payment to the beneficiary within the limits of a stated sum of money. The guarantor will pay the total amount stated in the guarantee on first demand, if the beneficiary of the guarantee informs him that the offer is withdrawn before its expiry date or the tenderer has failed to accept the contract awarded or the bid bond is not replaced by a performance bond after the contract has been awarded. The bank's liability depends upon the precise wording of the guarantee. In tender bond, the beneficiary is the party inviting the tender who is entitled to get compensation if the tenderer fails to meet his obligations arising from the submission of tender. The principal is the party tendering who will meet his obligations arising from the submission of tender which is guaranteed by the bank. The guarantor is the bank, which should meet its commitment in compliance with the terms of the guarantee without becoming involved in possible disputes between the beneficiary and the principal resulting from the tender transaction. As a rule, the guarantee charge collected by the bank is 1%～5% of the guaranteed amount. The period of validity is usually between three and six months until the signing of the contract or issuing a performance bond.

- **Performance Guarantee or Performance Bond**(履约保函)

A performance guarantee is an undertaking given by a bank (the guarantor) at the request of a supplier of goods or service or a contractor (the principal) to a buyer or an employer (the beneficiary), whereby the guarantor undertakes to make payment to the beneficiary within the limits of a stated sum of money in the event of default by the supplier or the contractor in due performance of the terms of a contract between the principal and the beneficiary. In performance bond, the beneficiary is the party awarding the contract, who is entitled to get compensation if the supplier or other contractors fail to perform the contract. The principal is the party to whom the contract has been awarded and who is guaranteed by the bank to perform the contract in compliance with its terms. The guarantor is the bank which guarantees the principal to perform the contract in accordance with its terms. The guaranty fee is usually 10% of the contract amount. The bond remains valid for the full amount until complete performance of the contract. The period of validity may be one year, two years or even longer.

- **Repayment Guarantee**(还贷保函)

A repayment guarantee is an undertaking given by a bank (the guarantor) at the request of a supplier of goods or service or other contractor (the principal) to a buyer or an employer (the beneficiary), whereby the bank undertakes to make payment to the beneficiary within, the limits of a stated sum of money in the event of default by the principal to repay, in accordance with the terms and conditions of a contract between the principal and the beneficiary, any sum or sums advanced or paid by the beneficiary to the principal. The beneficiary in repayment guarantee is the party making advance payment. He wants to be sure that this advance payment will be repaid to him if the principal fails to perform the contract. The principal is the party who receives advance payment or down payment from the beneficiary and it's guaranteed by the bank to return the payment to the beneficiary if he fails to perform the contract. The guarantor is the bank which guarantees the principal to make repayment in accordance with the terms.

- **Leasing Guarantee**(租赁保函)

The guarantee bank guarantees to the beneficiary that the lessee will pay the rent in accordance with the terms and conditions of the lease agreement. Should the lessee fail to pay the rent within the time limit as stipulated in the lease agreement the bank undertakes to effect payment for the unpaid rent plus defaulted interest, if any.

- **Advance Payment Guarantee**(预付款保函)

This guarantee is issued at the request of the exporter to the importer (the beneficiary) when the advance payment is required of the latter. The guarantee ensures the repayment of the advance by the exporter in the event of the non-performance of his contractual obligations. It is a little like the repayment guarantee under the contract guarantees. The guaranteed amount is the amount of the advance payment, which is, as a rule, automatically and proportionally reduced by each following shipment. A utilization of the related documentary L/C is usually recognized as an evidence of delivery. The validity of the advance payment guarantee should be limited in such a way that it expires on the date when the covered performance is made. It should enter into force only after receipt of such an advance payment. Therefore, a clause to this effect should be embodied in the guarantee whenever available.

 6-2

中国承包商在利比亚履约保函和预付款保函的处置

利比亚的国内局势已不再是悬念,卡扎菲政府已经倒台,美英法等支持下的"利比亚全国过渡委员会"建立新政府只是时间问题。但如何应对和妥善处理卡扎菲政府时期中国承包企业为承包工程开出的预付款保函和履约保函,则是当前中国承包企业乃至中国政府相关职能部门所要面对的挑战。

利比亚相关银行提出保函延期及不延期即付款要求,意味着国内开具保函的银行或选择付款,或选择继续为中国在利比亚企业承担部分担保义务。据商务部统计,在卡扎菲政府未被推翻前,利比亚两家银行共向中国进出口银行、中国银行、中国建设银行提出11笔保函延期要求,总金额4.97亿美元,其提出的保函延期要求涉及中土集团、中水电集团、北京建工等7家企业的8个项目,其中进出口银行收到6笔,涉及金额2.25亿美元;中国银行收到4笔,涉及金额2.3亿美元;建设银行收到1笔,涉及金额3185万美元,利比亚有关银行的延期要求主要针对已到期和即将到期的保函。其中,利比亚撒哈拉银行就7笔保函、利比亚共和国银行就1笔保函提出"不延期即付款"的要求,其余3笔仅提出延期要求。

按照"工程预付款"承包商向开证行提供的担保书的约定,中方承包商如果未能履行合同且不退还业主支付的预付款,业主可以向承包商索赔预付款的本金和利息。本次利比亚动乱之初,中国企业大举撤离,导致许多在建工程被迫中断,且主要集中在基础建设领域。2011年3月25日,利比亚撒哈拉银行已向葛洲坝集团、中国水利水电建设集团公司、宏福建工等公司针对预付款保函进行索赔,对每家企业的索赔额度均达数亿元。

利比亚银行对我国企业提出的这两种选择(赔偿预付款本金和利息或将预付款保函延期)都将对我方企业不利。若选择赔偿,会给中国企业造成巨大损失;若选择保函延期,等同于新开保函,基于利比亚目前的国内形势,中国的反担保银行很难做出抉择。从承包方的角度分析,即使开立保函的银行同意对以往开立的保函进行延期,也会给承包方及战后索赔带来非常大的困难,因为业主手中有承包方的见索即付的履约保函和/或预付款保函,会使承包商失去索赔谈判的胜算筹码。

利比亚内战结束后,项目业主必然会要求承包方先回到工地复工,而后再谈损失赔偿;在这种情况下谈判,承包方完全处于被动的地位,索赔成功的比例大幅度降低;执政的新政府也会要求承包方先复工,然后对前政府签订的合同进行审核,如若业主借机凭借手中的保函对承包方的不履约行为提出索赔,将会使国内承包商遭受巨大损失。

(资料来源:南锦林.中国承包商在利比亚履约保函和预付款保函的处置[J].中国商报,2011)

6.1.4 Procedure of L/G

A guarantee may be issued directly or indirectly to the beneficiary if the beneficiary is located in a foreign country.

- A direct guarantee occurs when the client (customer) authorizes the bank to issue a guarantee directly to the beneficiary. The procedure is shown in the Chart 6.1:

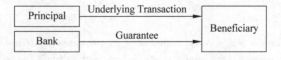

Chart 6.1 The Procedure of Direct Guarantee

- An indirect guarantee is a guarantee where a second bank is involved. This bank (usually a foreign bank located in the beneficiary's country of domicile) will be requested by the initiating bank to issue a guarantee in return for the latter's counter-guarantee. Thus the initiating bank protects the foreign bank from the risk of a loss which could result from the beneficiary submitting a claim under the foreign bank's guarantee. The initiating bank must formally pledge to pay that amount claimed by the beneficiary under the guarantee upon demand by the guaranteeing bank. Indirect guarantees are mainly used in connection with international business. The procedure chart is as follows (see Chart 6.2):

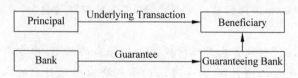

Chart 6.2　The Procedure of Indirect Guarantee

6.1.5　Contents of L/G

The contents of a guarantee are the most important part of the guarantee. All illustrations for the issue of guarantees and amendments thereto and guarantees and amendments themselves should be clear and precise and should avoid excessive details.

A guarantee generally contains the following clauses: ① the principal; ② the beneficiary; ③ the guarantor; ④ the underlying transaction requiting the issue of the guarantee[①]; ⑤ the amount of the guarantee[②]; ⑥ the expiry date and/or expiry event of the guarantee[③]; ⑦ the terms for demanding payment[④]; and ⑧ any other provisions such as the reduction of the amount, the governing law and jurisdiction.

 6-3

银行保函的基本内容

基本内容	解释及应注意的问题
保函的编号和开立日期	保函编号的作用是为了便于银行内部业务管理，保函的开立日期在许多情况下即为保函的生效日期
保函当事人的完整名称和详细地址	其中担保行的地址涉及保函的法律适用性问题及受益人的交单地点和保函本身的到期地点。受益人名称和地址不得有误，否则，通知行或转开行无法及时通知或转开

---

　① Since the bank guarantee is independent of the underlying transaction, a precise definition of how the principal defaulted on the contract in question is not necessary, and the beneficiary's claim is all that is needed to elicit payment.

　② The amount payable under a guarantee shall be reduced by the amount of any payment made by the guarantor in satisfaction of a demand in respect thereof.

　③ According to ICC NO. 458, expiry date shall be on a specified calendar date or on presentation to the guarantor of the documents specified for the purpose of expiry. If both an expiry date and an expiry event are specified in a guarantee, the guarantee shall be expired on whichever of the expiry date or expiry event occurs first.

　④ In ICC No. 458, any demand for payment under guarantee shall be in writing and shall be supported by a written statement stating that the principal is in breach and other documents as specified in the guarantee.

续表

基本内容	解释及应注意的问题
保函所依据的基础交易合同的内容	交易合同是保函担保的标的物,即担保人的责任范围。保函中必须说明交易合同的基本内容、合同编号、开立日期、签约双方、有无修改等
保函的性质	保函的性质即保函与基础交易合同的关系,从属性保函和独立性保函的法律性质不同,担保行所承担的责任和对受益人的赔付条件是不同的,在保函中应明确
保函金额	保函的金额是银行的担保限额,必须明确,大小写应保持一致
保函的有效期限和终止到期日	保函的有效期是受益人索偿要求送达担保函的最后期限。保函的终止到期日是担保行解除其担保责任的最后期限
当事人的权利和义务	保函当事人的责任和义务、索赔文件、仲裁等各种条款
索偿条件	受益人向担保行提出索偿的方式和路线
其他条款	如保函金额随申请人履约进度递减的规定等

6.1.6 Differences between L/G and L/C

- The undertaking of the issuing bank under an L/C is to pay, accept and pay bill of exchange or negotiate bill of exchange and/ or documents, or to fulfill any other obligations under the L/C provided documents presented are in compliance with the terms and conditions of the L/C. It is always used for financing the international trade. An L/G is properly operative only if the principal failed to fulfill his obligations. Their purpose is different from that of an L/C.

- All L/Cs must clearly indicate whether they are available by sight payment, deferred payments, acceptance or negotiation. But there is no such stipulation in an L/G. Presentation of documents under an L/C must be made to the nominated bank, the confirming bank or the issuing bank which will pay, accept, or negotiate it according to the stipulations in the L/C. The bank authorized to pay, accept or negotiate may be at the location of the beneficiary or at the issuing bank as indicated in the L/C. But documents presented under L/G shall be presented to the guarantor before the expiry date at the place of issue. Otherwise the demand shall be refused by the guarantor. If the documents presented are in compliance with the terms of the guarantee, the guarantor will pay it accordingly no matter whether the relative contract is fulfilled.

- Unlike the L/C, there is no confirming bank, negotiating bank or paying bank likewise under the L/G as under the L/C. Under L/G there is only an issuing bank. If an L/G is issued on the basis of a counter guarantee, according to ICC No. 458, the instructing party undertakes to pay the guarantor on presentation of the documents in conformity with the terms of the counter guarantee which by nature is separate transaction from the guarantee to which they relate and the

- instructing party is in no way concerned with or bound by such guarantee. A confirmed L/C bears not only the undertaking of the issuing bank but also that of the confirming bank. Documents will be presented either to the issuing bank or to the confirming bank.
- An L/C is issued by a bank at the request of its customer, and there is no definition about and explanation of the word "bank" in UCP600. An L/G may be issued by a bank, an insurance company or any other body or person acting on the instructions of a principal as stipulated in ICC No.458.
- The expiry date under an L/C means documents must be presented on or before this date. Every L/C must stipulate an expiry date and a place for presentation of documents for payment, acceptance or a place for presentation of documents for negotiation. The place may be either in the beneficiary's country or at the location of the issuing bank or at any other place as stipulated in the L/C. In addition to the expiry date for presentation of documents, every L/C which calls for a transport document should also stipulate a specified period of time after the date of shipment during which presentation must be made in compliance with the terms and conditions of the L/C. But according to ICC No.458, the expiry date shall be on a specified calendar date or upon presentation of a document of an expiry event as specified in the L/G.
- UCP600 does not stipulate the governing law and jurisdiction. If there are any disputes under an L/C, where the disputes shall be settled is a complex problem. Under L/G Publication No.458, the governing law and jurisdiction are all clearly indicated, which means that the governing law shall be the place of business of the guarantor or instruction party. In case of more than one place of business, it is the place where the guarantee or counter guarantee is issued.

 6-4

银行保函"见索即付"风险的一则案例

安徽省某建筑公司与澳大利亚签署一工程承包合同。国内某银行接受了申请人的申请并为其开立了履约保函,保函条款规定:"只有在中方承包公司违约的情况下,受益人方可提出索赔",付款条件为无条件的见索即付。然而在合同的实际履行中,因业主资信不好,资金筹措困难,多次拖延付款,且施工材料到位不及时,致使我承包公司流动资金周转困难,长期停工待料,工程无法按期完成。最后,尽管工程以高标准、高质量完成,被澳政府视为样板工程,但却遭业主以中方拖延了交工时间而违约,向担保行提出索赔。因保函条款规定"见索即付",我担保银行不得不予以偿付,使国内建筑公司承担了损失。

由案例可以得出:对保函是否附加赔付的条件和要求,会直接影响保函担保人的索赔风险。有条件保函是指在保函条款中对索赔的受理限定了条件,只有这些条件满足后,担保银行才会履行其支付义务。无条件保函又称"见索即付"保函,是指担保银行只要在保函有效期内接到受益人所提交的符合保函条款的书面索赔通知后,担保银行就必须履行无条件的支付义务,而不论基础交易合同的执行情况如何,也不论受益人本身是否履行了合同中规定的义务。见索即付保函中,申请人和担保银行面临较高的风险,可能会由于受益人的恶意索赔而陷于被动,但目前国际工程保函中见索即付保函所占的比例较大。

中国承包商在与境外业主就保函格式进行谈判时,应尽量在保函格式中删除"无条件"等描述,同时增加索赔的条件,例如在索赔条款中要求业主通过银行向保函担保行提出索赔,受益人须提供申请人未履约情况的说明及第三方机构出具的鉴定证明材料等,从而达到约束业主的目的。

6.2　Standby L/C

6.2.1　Definition of Standby L/C

A standby documentary L/C is an obligation on the part of an issuing bank to pay a beneficiary in the case of the nonperformance of the applicant.

备用信用证又称商业票据信用证、担保信用证,是指开证行根据开证申请人的请求对受益人开立的承诺某项义务的凭证。即开证行保证申请人未能履行其应履行的义务时,受益人只要凭备用信用证的规定向开证行开具汇票(或不开汇票),并提交开证申请人未履行义务的声明或证明文件,即可取得开证行的偿付。

Standby L/C is used as support where an alternative, less secure, method of payment has been agreed and the main purpose is to provide L/C assurance. Should the exporter fail to receive payment from the buyer he may claim under the standby L/C? Generally speaking, standby L/C can be used to guarantee the following forms of payment or performance: ① payment of bills payable after sight; ② repayment of bank advances; ③ payment for goods delivered; ④ delivery of goods in accordance with contract; and/or ⑤ fulfillment of contracts for work and materials, etc. In simple terms, a standby L/C is an obligation on the part of an issuing bank to pay a beneficiary in the case of the nonperformance of the applicant.

Standby L/C are originally used in the United States, where they take place of guarantees, which under the laws of most US states may not be issued by banks. But in Europe, too, the use of this type of L/C is increasing. Standby L/C is often used in the United States as a legal form of bank guarantee. Standby L/C can be seen as a kind of guarantee-type instruments because of their documentary character governed by UCP too. In 1999, the International Chamber of Commerce publishes rules for operating standby L/C, namely ISP98 (*International Standby Practices*). At present, a standby L/C may be subject to either the UCP600 or the ISP98.

In a standard commercial documentary L/C the issuing bank has an obligation to pay the beneficiary based on the performance of the beneficiary (the beneficiary's fulfillment of the terms and conditions of the L/C). In a standby documentary L/C the issuing bank is obligated to pay the beneficiary based on the nonperformance of the applicant. A standby documentary L/C is generally obtained and held in reserve or paid out only as a result of noncompliance with some underlying contract between the parties involved. Therefore, Standby documentary L/C is also called "nonperforming L/C", because they are only used as a backup payment method if the collection on a primary payment method is past due.

Exporters may be asked to provide a standby documentary L/C as a requirement of working on complicated infrastructure projects abroad or as an assurance under a contractual obligation that they will perform as agreed. If the goods are provided, or the service performed, as agreed, the standby documentary L/C will expire unused. The exporter must also be certain that the documents submitted are exactly as required in the documentary L/C.

6.2.2 Characteristics and Types of Standby L/C

● Characteristics

Firstly, from the definition, we can see that the most obvious characteristic of a standby L/C is to be used as a backup payment method or a tool to compensate the beneficiary when the collection on a primary payment method is past due or the applicant proves to be not performing the obligations under the underlying transaction, and that is why this kind of L/C is called "standby L/C".

Secondly, similar to a commercial L/C, a standby L/C is also independent in nature and irrevocable in form. When dealing with a standby L/C, the issuing bank is in no way concerned with or bound to the sales or other contracts on which it may be based, even if any reference whatsoever to it is included in the L/C. When asking for payment, once the beneficiary presents the required documents by the L/C, the issuing bank should make payment to him.

Finally, a standby L/C is also documentary. The documents presented under a standby L/C, however, are quite different from those under a commercial L/C. Under a commercial documentary L/C, the beneficiary can only get paid by the complying presentation of documents showing that he has fulfilled the obligations and complied with the terms of the L/C. While under a standby L/C, the documentation for payment is much simpler. Certain documents are likely to be required to obtain payment including: the standby L/C itself; a sight bill of exchange for the amount due acting as a demand for payment; a copy of the unpaid invoice; proof of dispatch and a signed declaration from the beneficiary stating that payment has not been received by the due date and therefore reimbursement is claimed by the L/C. So a commercial documentary L/C issued as per

UCP600 usually contains details on the required documents to ensure the beneficiary's fulfillment of obligations under the contract, and the standby L/C issued as per ISP98 has no such strict requirements on documents. Even if a standby L/C is issued according to UCP600, the stipulations on shipping documents in UCP600 should be marked not applicable to the standby L/C for the sake of circumspection.

NOTE: The standby L/C serves as a back-up or secondary means of payment, though it is recognized as a primary obligation of the issuing bank. In both types of usage, commercial or standby L/C alike, the underlying purpose of the issuing bank is to pay for goods supplied or services furnished, as required by the contract between the parties. The difference in application can be expressed by saying that the commercial documentary L/C is activated by the "performance" of the beneficiary. The standby L/C, by contract, supports the beneficiary in the event of a "default".

● **Types**

The usage of standby L/C is similar to that of bank guarantee and the specific contents and clauses may vary according to the requirements of the underlying transactions. Basically, the common types of standby L/C include performance standby L/C, advance payment standby L/C, bid bond/tender bond standby L/C, counter standby L/C, financial standby L/C, direct pay standby L/C, insurance standby L/C and commercial standby L/C, etc.

6.2.3 Differences between Standby L/C and L/C

- According to different Practice. The standby letter of credit is opened according to ISP 98 (*International Standby Practice* 1998), and documentary letter of credit is opened according to UCP 600. Even open the standby letter of credit according to the provisions of UCP600 art. 4, applicability of the uniform customs and practice for documentary letter of credit terms and conditions are also different.
- Require different documents. Issued by the standby letter of credit are generally only by the beneficiary of the applicant fails to perform the contract written statements or documents for payment basis, and documentary letter of credit in strict accordance with the requirements of the L/C usually shipping documents as the basis of payment.
- Documentary L/C is the primary responsibility of payment bank guarantee certificate, and the standby L/C is a secondary payment commitments. Documentary L/C is the beneficiary bank payment after delivery obligations, while the standby L/C is when the applicant fails to performance by the applicant. Visibly, although the standby L/C applicant forms to see Mr. Pay the first payment of duty, but their intention is essentially secondary.
- Function and purpose are different. Standby L/C with a variety of purposes,

widely applicable to various forms of financing or performance, such as for borrowing, bidding, the performance and credit business, or pay for damages, can also be used for issuing commercial paper, etc. Documentary L/C only commonly used in the import and export trade in goods. So the standby L/C has more extensively applicable scope. In Europe, documentary L/C has been reducing, and around the world, standby letter of credit business is growing.

- Operation process and business process are different. Standby L/C is often the case with credentials' general use: the debtor defaults and documentary L/C is the corresponding import and export business with the settlement of tools. On some other specific processing, there are a lot of details in the ISP98 rules, also different from the UCP600 contains.

6.2.4 Differences between Standby L/C and L/G

- Standby L/C is applicable to the ISP98 rules, while undertaking applies to guarantee law related countries, as well as the International Chamber of Commerce for Guarantee ICC325 and ICC458, unless L/G clear statement on the basis of the ISP98 rules to open.
- According to the different payment. Standby L/C is the beneficiary and the applicant fails to submit draft performance when the claim of a written statement. And the L/G and interest submitted order, usually, guarantee bank by the beneficiary statement of claim and prove that the applicant in writing of the default of payment.
- Revocable different nature. Standby L/C is irrevocable, but does not rule out a special statement revocable. But the bank L/G is irrevocable, because revocable bank guarantee has no guarantee effect.
- Bank payment responsibility is different. The issuing bank of standby L/C has primary responsibility for payment, but for the secondary obligor; while the bank L/G to guarantee bank as well as village with primary responsibility, also can be secondary payment responsibility.

6.3 International Factoring

In recent years, we have witnessed very difficult market conditions and recessional trends in international trade as the traditional "seller's market" has given way to "buyer's market". In order to expand business, more and more exporters have been adopting Open Account (O/A) or Documents against Acceptance (D/A). To avoid possible risks incurred by using the above two methods of payment, a new method of payment and financing for international trade, namely international factoring, comes into being.

Since the 1960s factoring has been increasingly widely used in international trade. Factoring is a form of trade financing that allows sellers to trade overseas essentially on an open account basis. With the founding of Factors Chain International (FCI) in l968 in Holland and the issuance of UNIDROIT Convention on international factoring (Ottawa, 28 May, 1988), the important position of international factoring in international trade and financing was established. As a new method of financing for international trade, international factoring has been widely used in recent 20 years. According to the statistics issued by FCI, since 1990s, the annual average volume of international factoring amounts to 30 billion US dollars. Factoring volume continues to grow and out performance most other sectors of the banking and financial services industry.

 6-5

中国国际保理等待"破零"

2013年3月中国服务贸易协会商业保理专业委员会刚成立时,天津还是商业保理公司的大本营。之后短短两年多的时间里,商业保理公司在全国遍地开花。特别是2012年12月商务部发布试点通知以后,商业保理公司数量迅猛增长。

在2015年国际保理CEO圆桌会议上,中国服务贸易协会商业保理专委会副主任兼秘书长韩家平表示,"据预测,到2020年全球进口市场90%都将以赊销、赊购的方式来做。"可以想象,以后进口和出口环节对保理的需求是非常大的。从全球市场来看,国际保理业务占全球保理业务总额的18%左右,国内保理业务约占82%的比例。2009—2013年,国际保理业务的增速是国内保理业务的2倍,潜力比国内保理还大。不过,他同时表示,目前国内商业保理公司中,几乎还没有一家真正开展过国际保理业务,"将来我国国际保理业务的增长空间非常大"。

不过,当前银行虽然开展国际保理业务,但覆盖的多是大中型企业,中小企业难以获得银行保理支持。与银行保理相比,商业保理公司提供的保理服务,更有助于财务制度不规范的中小企业处理应收账款,同时降低企业的财务管理费用。此外,商业保理不要求企业提供固定资产抵押和反担保措施,符合中小企业应收账款较多、固定资产较少的特点,更能满足中小企业的融资需求。

(资料来源:李前.国际保理等待"破零"[J].进出口经理人,2015年第6期)

6.3.1 Definition of International Factoring

International factoring is a complete financial package that combines credit protection, account receivable bookkeeping, and collection services. When an exporter and an importer enter into an international transaction contract in which O/A or D/A has been agreed upon, the exporter and an international factor can establish an agreement, under which the factor purchases the exporter's accounts receivable, normally without recourse, and assumes the responsibility for the importer's financial ability to pay. If the importer goes bankrupt or is unable to pay its debts for credit reasons, the factor will pay the exporter.

国际保理业务的全称是国际保付代理业务,简称保理或出口代理,在我国大陆又称为代理融通、包销代理、承购应收账款业务等。它是指保理商从其客户(出口商)手中,购进通常以发票表示的对债务人的应收账款,并负责信用销售控制、销售分户账户管理和债权回收业务。它主要是为承兑交单、赊销设计的。

In simple terms, factoring is the purchase of claims, arising from sales of goods, by a specialized company known as factoring company or factor. The essence of factoring is the discounting of acceptable accounts receivables on a non-recourse notification basis. Factoring is in fact a three-party transaction between a financial institution and a business entity selling goods or providing services to foreign debtor. The factor acts as a manager of exporter's sales and provides his client with finance based on the level of sales, and on the other hand, evaluates the importer's credit worthiness either by himself or with the aid of his correspondent or agent so as to ensure the final payment. The essence of factoring is the discounting of acceptable accounts receivables on a non-recourse notification basis.

The primary services offered are credit investigation, credit approval, assumption of credit risk, account receivable bookkeeping, and collection of matured accounts.

The essence of factoring is the discounting of acceptable accounts receivable on a non-recourse and notification basis. Accounts receivable are sold outright to the factor, who assumes the responsibility for collection as well as the risk of credit losses without recourse to the client. Customers are notified to remit directly to the factor. Clients are thus able to eliminate or reduce the need for L/C, bookkeeping and other related administrative activities.

6.3.2　Parties to International Factoring

- **The Exporter or Supplier**(出口商或供应商)

The exporter is the seller in the sales contract. The exporter assigns the benefit of the sales contract to a financial house, called the factor, which advances the purchase price for the goods or services provided, minus his charges.

- **The Importer or Debtor**(进口商或债务人)

The importer is the buyer in the purchase contract. The importer is responsible for paying for the goods or services provided by the seller.

- **The Exporter's Factor**(出口商保理)

The exporter's factor is the party who is willing to purchase the invoice representing the exporter's claim according to the factor agreement.

- **The Importer's Factor or Correspondent Factor**(进口商保理或代理保理商)

The importer's factor provides the services as the agent of the export factor.

6.3.3 Types of International Factoring

- **Maturity Factoring & Advanced Factoring**(到期保付代理&融资保付代理)

In maturity factoring, after the export factor purchased the receivables from the exporter, he does not reimburse the exporter immediately but confirms and undertakes to pay the exporter without recourse when the relevant bills of exchange fall due. In advanced factoring (also called standard factoring), when the export factor purchased the receivables from the exporter, it shall reimburse the exporter immediately without recourse.

- **Disclosed Factoring & Undisclosed Factoring**(公开型保理&隐蔽型保理)

Under disclosed factoring, the factors are responsible for collecting the exporter's receivables subsequent to purchasing the same from the exporter, and the exporter informs the importer of paying the importer factor. In contrast, under undisclosed factoring, after selling the receivables to the factor, the exporter is still responsible for collecting receivables, and then transfers the same to the factor. Undisclosed factoring is often applied when the exporter wants to avoid being known by the importer that international factoring is used due to his lack of current capital.

- **Two-factor System & Single Factor System**(双保理&单保理)

Two-factor system involves an export factor and an import factor, in which, the exporter and the export factor establish an agreement under which the receivables are purchased by the export factor, then the export factor and the import factor enter into an agency agreement, under which, the receivables are transferred to the import factor who is responsible for collecting from the importer the receivables. Two-factor system requires that both the export factor and the import factor are members of FCI. If it is the case, both the exporter and the importer only have to contact the factor in his/her country, which can reduce costs and improve working efficiency as the differences in legal system, business customs and languages are all avoided. Nowadays, most of the international factoring business in Europe and North America is in this system. The single factor system involves only one factor, and it is the primary model of international factoring. Now, it is mainly used in domestic factoring.

- **Non-recourse Factoring & Recourse Factoring**(无追索权保理&有追索权保理)

Under non-recourse factoring, the factor has no rights of recourse to the approved receivables. When the debtor is unable or refuses to pay, the factor bears losses resulting from bad debt. In practice, most of the Factorings are non-recourse. Under recourse factoring, the factor presents recourse right to the approved receivables. When the debtor is unable or refuses to pay, the factor can claim to the supplier to refund the paid receivable amount.

● **Full Service Factoring & Partial Service Factoring**(全套服务保理&部分服务保理)

Under full service factoring, the factor is to perform all the functions of financing for the supplier, accounts receivables ledgering, collection of receivables and protection against default in payment by debtors. While under partial service factoring, the factor only provides partial of the above mentioned four types' functions.

6.3.4 Procedures of International Factoring

In accordance with *UNIDROIT Convention on International Factoring and General Rules for International Factoring* (Version: FCI October 2001, which went into effect for all new invoices as of 1st July 2002), the procedures of international factoring are shown in Chart 6.3 as follows:

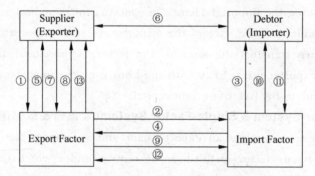

Chart 6.3   The Procedure of International Factoring

Step 1: The exporter and the importer enter into an international commercial contract, under which, O/A or D/A is agreed upon, and the exporter informs a factor in his country of the content of the contract and requires the factor to provide international factoring service and to authorize the importer a credit amount.

Step 2: The export factor informs a factor in the importer's country of the transaction and the import factor undertakes to have a status enquiry of the importer and to evaluate the importer's credit. If the importer is of sound credit, the import factor will authorize him a credit amount.

Step 3: The import factor investigates the debtor's standing of credit.

Step 4: The import factor notifies the export factor of the information on the creditworthiness of the debtor and the approved credit line.

Step 5: The export factor notifies the supplier of the result of the investigation and the approved credit line.

Step 6: If the importer agrees to purchase from the exporter goods or service, the exporter commences to supply the goods or service. After obtaining relevant shipping documents endorsed "the receivables are to be transferred to the export factor", the exporter transfers relevant invoice with articles of transferring to the importer.

Step 7：The exporter delivers a copy of the invoice to the export factor, and the export factor informs the import factor of the details of the invoice.

Step 8：If the exporter requires financing, the export factor can pay the exporter about 80% of the invoice value.

Step 9：The import factor transfers the invoice copy to the import factor.

Step 10：The import factor begins to dun the importer for payment several days before the due time of the invoice, and the importer is responsible for paying the import factor when the invoice falls due.

Step 11：The import factor delivers the payment to the export factor. Should the importer failed to effect payment 90 days after the due time of the invoice, the import factor is liable for paying the export factor.

Step 12：The export factor reimburses the exporter the balance after deducting the principal and the interest of the financing (if have) and the relevant fees.

Step 13：The factors are responsible for recourse and claim from the exporter should the latter be unable to pay on time or reject to paying, and the export factor is liable for reimbursing the exporter in accordance with the contracted time.

6.3.5 Application of International Factoring

Through using international factoring, the factors can offer the following services to the importers and exporters：

- **Credit Approval**(信贷审批)

The factor acts as the client's credit department to evaluate the importer's credit standing to determine a credit line for his client's customer so that he can exercise the function of pre-approving orders prior to shipment. If the importer appears not to be a reliable one as a result of this evaluation, the factor will not approve this transaction.

- **Credit Protection**(信用保护)

By purchasing the client's accounts receivable without recourse, factoring can protect the clients from risk of loss so long as the merchandise quality, quantity and terms meet the requirements of the business contract between the client and his customer. However, the client takes full responsibility if the goods are claimed to be defective or any disputes occur concerning the shipment.

- **Management of account receivable**(应收账款管理)

Upon shipment, the client invoices his customer and sends a copy to the factor. The invoice indicates that it is payable to the factor. At maturity of the invoice, the factor will collect payment from the client's customer.

- **Financing**(融资)

The factor may grant financing to the client prior to the maturity of the invoice by purchasing the latter's account receivable. Usually, the factor pays his client ahead of the maturity date of the accounts receivables, and the amount is usually up to a maximum of 80% of factored sales. Typically, the supplier can get paid in cash immediately after selling the accounts receivables to the factor. The advantages of factoring finance are as follows: (1) injection of working capital to finance expansion; (2) more finance available than from bank borrowing; (3) suppliers can be paid promptly so the seller can doubly benefit from reducing costs by taking advantage of prompt payment discounts and improving his credit standing with suppliers; and (4) no loss of equity and no formal funding limit.

6.3.6 Advantages of International Factoring

International factoring has many advantages over other payment methods of international trade, and the greatest one is that it allows both exporters and importers to trade on O/A terms without risks.

International factoring is also a method of obtaining finance and enhancing liquidity. The use of factors to provide prepayments for the sale of goods and services in an international context is necessary to increase the volume of international trade. Further, what factoring does in essence is to introduce intermediaries between the buyer and the seller where the communication between them may be difficult due to differences in language, culture or trading practices. The factor can facilitate trade in such situation and undertake the burdensome obligation of debt collection across national borders. Thus, international factoring can be used to effectively finance and facilitate International trade.

International factoring is used by exporters who sell on open account or documents against acceptance terms. International factoring eases much of the credit and collection burden created by international sales. By outsourcing the credit function, exporters can convert the high fixed cost of operating an international credit department into a variable expense. Commissions paid to the factor are based on sales volume so costs fluctuate with actual sales, lowering operating costs during slow sales periods. In addition to relieving exporters of the time-consuming administrative burden of approving credit and collecting export sales, international factoring lets exporters safely offer their foreign customers competitive open account terms. Financing is provided by means of advances against outstanding accounts receivable. In summary, international factoring provides the following benefits to exporters:

- Increasing sales in foreign markets by offering competitive terms of sale;
- Protection against credit losses on foreign customers;
- Accelerating cash flow through faster collections;
- Lower costs than the aggregate charges for L/C transactions;
- Liquidity to boost working capital;

- Enhancing borrowing potential and an opportunity to make use of supplier discounts.

Obviously, there are also advantages for importers. Until quite recently the L/C was the most universally accepted method to control international trade, in the sense of assuring that the exporter would ship in accordance with the sales contract or the purchase order and that the importer would honor her financial obligations. Yet, while this method (or "term of sale") had considerable merit when goods were moving slowly and at irregular intervals along shipping lanes, the L/C places a financial burden on importers, which in most cases is no longer tolerated. In summary, international factoring provides the following benefits to importers:

- Purchasing on convenient? "open account" terms;
- No need to open L/C;
- Expanding purchasing power without blocking existing lines of credit;
- Orders can be placed swiftly without incurring delays, L/C opening charges, negotiation charges, etc.

6.3.7 Compassion between International Factoring and Traditional Payment Method

国际保理业务与传统结算方式的比较

项目 种类	国际保理业务	汇付	托收	信用证
债权风险保障	有	无	无	有
进口商费用	无	有	有	有
出口商费用	有	有	有	有
进口商银行抵押	无	无	无	有
提供进口商的财务灵活性	较高	较高	一般	较低
出口竞争力	较高	较高（货到付款）	一般	较低

 6-6

中行：双保理——让"死"钱变"活"钱

盐城市对外贸易有限公司多年来向美国出口凉鞋，与美国进口商建立了稳定的贸易往来。然而自今年年初以来，金融危机让美国进口商的资金周转遇到困难，提出了延长付款期限的要求。盐城市对外贸易有限公司为了保住订单，不得已接受进口商延迟付款的要求，但是随之而来的问题是，自身的流动资金面临周转压力。正在情急之时，中行江苏省分行的保理业务，解决了企业资金周转难题。在这项业务中，这家企业将产品出口后获得的应收账款，"转卖"给了中行江苏省分行，并从中行获得了资金融通；中行凭借广泛的代理行网络，与进口商所在地的保理商合作，将应收账款再次转让，即通过出口双保理业务为客户提供了应收账款的解决方案。提出办理申请后，盐城市对外贸易有限公司在中行获得了30万美元保理额度。随后，公司装船发货，中行江苏省分行立即为其融资，将此次出口的13770美元货款付给企业，并按照当日汇率为企业办理结汇，不仅解决了企业的资金周转问题，而且提高了企业抗风险能力和市场竞争力，使其在金融危机中，订单不降反增，与进口商进一步巩固了合作关系。

中国银行公司金融总部国际结算模块的产品总监程军介绍："出口双保理业务可以帮助出口商争取更有竞争力的付款条件，而且还以预支方式为出口商提供融资便利，缓解流动资金被应收账款占压的问题，改善其现金流状况并规避风险。进口商的资信调查、账务管理和账款催收都由保理商负责，这样也减轻了出口商的业务负担和管理成本。"2009年1～5月，中国银行为出口外贸企业提供出口双保理业务近10亿美元，同比增长40%以上，继续保持全球第一，为外贸企业有效规避了风险，使其获得充裕的流动资金。

（资料来源：中行：双保理——让"死"钱变"活"钱[N/OL].人民网——《人民日报》，2009-6-8，http://www.sinotf.com/GB/Trade_Finance/Factoring/2009-06-08/2MMDAwMDAyODM2MA_2.html）

6.4 Forfaiting

In order to further minimize risks resulting from deterred payment such as interest rate risk, credit risk and political risk, exporters may consider forfaiting. As a form of non-recourse financing, forfaiting is operated by discounting an exporter's future receivables without recourse basis.

6.4.1 Definition of Forfaiting

The word "forfaiting" comes from the French word "forfait", and thus convey the idea of surrendering rights, which is of fundamental importance in forfaiting. This expression is rendered by "forfaitierung" in German, "le forfaitage" in French, "la forfetizzazione" in Italian and "la forfetizacion" in Spanish. Simply speaking, forfaiting is the term generally used to denote the purchase of obligations falling due at some future date, arising from deliveries of goods and services without recourse to any previous holder of the obligation. The bank, i.e., the purchaser of the receivables, becomes the entity to the importer who is obliged to pay its debt. It is a method of finance which exporter could collect cash in advance by transferring the receivable and bank guaranteed long-dated bill to banks. After the transferring, the banks have no right to recover the debt if the receipts cannot be exercised when become mature.

6.4.2 Characteristics of Forfaiting

The characteristics of forfaiting are stipulated as follows:
- The goods involved in forfaiting are usually capital goods.
- Forfaiting is a medium-term business in the sense that only those with maturities from six months to five or six years are to be considered. However, every forfaiter will impose his own limits, to be determined largely by market conditions and his assessment of the risks involved in a particular transaction.
- The purchase of bills of exchange or promissory notes falling due on some future date by forfaiter is without recourse to any previous holder if the drawee of the bill of exchange/maker of the promissory note fails to pay it at maturity.
- Forfaiting is a relatively expensive and attractive alternative to other forms of export financing for the exporter. By forfaiting the exporter wishes to pass all risks and responsibilities for collection to the forfaiter in exchange for immediate cash payment. The exporter virtually converts his credit-based sale into a cash transaction.
- Unless the credit standing of the importer is first class, any forfaiting bill must carry a collateral security in the form of an "aval" ①or an unconditional and irrevocable bank guarantee acceptable to the forfaiter ensuring the holder there of that the importer will pay it at maturity. The fulfillment of this condition is of the utmost importance in view of the non-recourse aspect of the business, for the forfaiter can only rely on this form of bank guarantee as his sole security in the event of non-payment of the obligor.
- The purchase of bills in forfaiting is carried out by discounting, namely by deduction of the interest in advance for the immature draft. Discounting takes place the moment the forfaiter has received the bill of exchange, i.e., the agreed discounting interest for the corresponding maturities is deducted from the nominal amount and the net amount is paid by the forfaiter. Discounting rate in forfaiting is higher because the forfaiting bank bears more risks than the discount bank.

6.4.3 Parties to Forfaiting

● **The Exporter**(出口商)

The exporter refers to the seller under the sales contract. When the exporter extends

---

① An "aval" can be regarded in international practice as an irrevocable and unconditional guarantee to pay on the due date, as if the guarantor had been the obligor. It is the most suitable form of security. The aval is written directly on each promissory note or bill of exchange with the words "per aval" and the signature of the availing party. Its simplicity and clarity, together with its inherent abstractness and transferability avoid many of the complications to be found with guarantee.

credit to the importer, the exporter may apply for the finance from a forfaiter. Upon purchase by the forfaiter, the exporter may obtain the net proceeds in advance after deducting the interest and commissions.

- **The Importer**(进口商)

The importer refers to the buyer under the sales contract, and the payer of the L/C instruments that the exporter and the importer have agreed to use to evidence the debts. When the instruments mature, the importer should pay the holder.

- **The Forfaiting Bank/Forfaiter**(包买商)

The forfaiting bank is a bank in the seller's country which buys the bills or notes at their discounted value from the seller and agrees to waive any rights of recourse it may have against the seller should the buyer or the guaranteeing bank default.

- **The Importer's Bank**(出口地银行)

The importer's bank serves as the guarantor. It is usually an internationally acknowledged bank. Unless the importer is a first-class obligor of undoubted standing, any forfeit must carry a security. The series of debts are usually guaranteed by the importer's bank, which is known to the forfaiter and well acquainted with the credit standing of the importer. Typically, it issues an L/G to provide guarantee for the instruments. Bills or notes guaranteed by a bank not only alleviate the risks of the forfaiter, but also enables him to have the bills or notes rediscounted in a secondary market.

6.4.4 Procedure of Forfaiting

Chart 6.4 It clearly shows how forfaiting operates below.

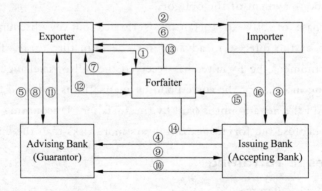

Chart 6.4　The Procedure of Forfaiting

Step 1: The exporter contracts a forfaiter and comes to a preliminary agreement on the amount, maturity of the paper and discount rate, because the exporter will add the discounting interest and other charges in his selling price and the importer needs to calculate the cost of funding.

Step 2: The exporter and the importer sign a sales contract.

Step 3: The importer applies for a letter of credit to the issuing bank.

Step 4: The issuing bank issues a letter of credit and sends it to the advising bank.

Step 5: The advising bank notifies the L/C to the exports.

Step 6: The exporter delivers the goods to the importer.

Step 7: The exporter concludes a forfaiting agreement with the forfaiter, which states the details of the forfaiting transaction, the discount rate, and the fees to be charged, the latest date of transfer and delivery of the instruments.

Step 8: The exporter presents the full set of documents including the draft to the advising bank.

Step 9: The advising bank delivers the full set of documents to the issuing bank and requires it to accept draft.

Step 10: The issuing bank accepts the draft and delivers it to the advising bank, meanwhile the issuing bank delivers the documents to the importer.

Step 11: The advising bank returns the accepted draft to the exporter.

Step 12: The exporter submits documents required by the forfaiter to forfaiter.

Step 13: The forfeiter pays to the exporter according to the forfaiting agreement.

Step 14: The forfeiter claims to the accepting bank at maturity.

Step 15: The accepting bank pays to the forfeiter.

Step 16: The importer pays to the accepting bank.

6.4.5 Advantages and Disadvantages of Forfaiting

Because of the characteristics of forfaiting, the exporter can minimize possible risks involving political issues, currency rate, interest rate and importer's credit by taking the advantages of the forfaiting service. Forfaiting involves no interest rate risk for the exporter. The rate of discount applied by the forfaiter is fixed, and subsequent changes in the general level of interest rates do not affect the discount. Under forfaiting, there is no risk of fluctuations in the exchange rate and no changes in the status of the debtor. All exchange risks, buyer risks, and country risks are removed. Also under forfaiting, there are no credit administration and collection problems and related risks and costs.

However, it may be difficult to find an institution that will be willing to be prepared to guarantee the importer's liabilities. Sometimes the guarantor institution may charge a high commitment fee if the buyer is not considered undoubted.

6.4.6 Difference between Factoring and Forfaiting

Although both factoring and forfaiting are the discounting of account receivables on a non-recourse basis, they have the following differences:

- Factoring is suitable for the financing of the export of consumer goods sold on a short term (usually less than one year) and involving smaller amount of money.

Forfaiting is used for the financing of capital goods exports sold on a medium or long term (usually two to five years, even to ten years) and involving larger amount of money.

- Factoring does not need the guarantee of the importer's bank while forfaiting must be guaranteed by the words "per aval" or standby L/C or L/G made by the importer's bank.
- In factoring, the exporter need not negotiate with the importer beforehand, however, prior to reaching a forfaiting agreement the exporter must negotiate with the importer to reach an agreement.
- Factoring usually does not cover and transfer the political risks while a forfaiter must bear these risks.

★ Key Words

Banker's Letter of Guarantee(银行保函)   Accessory L/G(从属性保函)
Independent L/G(独立保函)   Payment Guarantee(付款保函)
Deferred Payment Guarantee(延期付款保函)
Advance Payment Guarantee(预付款保函)
Leasing Guarantee(融资租赁保函)   Tender Guarantee(投标保函)
Performance Guarantee(履约保函)   Retention Guarantee(留置金保函)
Loan Guarantee(借款保函)   Overdraft Guarantee(透支保函)
Standby Letter of Credit(备用信用证)   International Factoring(国际保理业务)
Factor(保理商)   Protection against Bad Debts(坏账担保)
Unapproved Receivables(未核准应收账款)
Collection from Debtors(债款催收)
Maintenance of the Sales ledger(销售分户账管理)
Forfaiting(福费廷)   Forfaiter(包买商)
Discount Rate(贴现率)
Factors Chain International, FCI(国际保理商联合会)
International Standby Practice 1998(《国际备用信用证惯例》)
Code of International Factoring Customs(《国际保理业务管理规则》)
The Unidroit Convention on International Factoring(《国际保理业务公约》)

★ Exercise

一、单选题(Exclusive Choice Question)

1. The Application for L/G represents a certain legal obligations and responsibilities ( ).

    A. between the applicant and the guarantor bank
    B. between the applicant and the advising bank

C. between the applicant and the beneficiary

D. between the guarantor bank and reissuing bank

2. This guarantee is issued at the request of the exporter to the importer (the beneficiary) when the advance payment is required of the latter. The guarantee ensures the repayment of the advance by the exporter in the event of the non-performance of his contractual obligations. This L/G is called(   ).

  A. Tender Guarantee   B. Performance Guarantee

  C. Retention Guarantee   D. Advance Payment Guarantee

3. Which situation below does not need a confirming bank? (   )

  A. The credit of guarantor bank is poor.

  B. The credit of applicant is poor.

  C. The nation of guarantor bank is foreign exchange shortage.

  D. The guarantor bank's country is political and economic instability.

4. The applicant of Tender Guarantee is (   ).

  A. the tender's government   B. the tender

  C. the bidder   D. the winning bidder

5. Which one is the pioneer of forfaiting business? (   )

  A. The American commercial banks

  B. Zurich, Switzerland Bankers Association

  C. Bank of China

  D. The British commercial banks

6. 以下不属于保函申请人的主要责任是(   )。

  A. 严格按照合同的规定履行自己义务,避免保函项下发生索偿和赔偿

  B. 索偿时应按保函规定提交符合要求的索偿证明或有关单据

  C. 承担保函项下的一切费用和利息

  D. 在担保行认为必要时,预支担保保证金,提供反担保

7. 以下不属于备用信用证和跟单信用证相同点的为(   )。

  A. 两者形式相似

  B. 两者都属银行信用

  C. 两者都凭符合信用证规定的凭证或单据付款

  D. 两者的用途相同

8. 以下关于备用信用证的说法不正确的是(   )。

  A. 开立备用信用证的目的是由开证行向受益人承担第一性的付款责任

  B. 若申请人未能履约,则由银行负责向受益人赔偿经济损失

  C. 若申请人按合同规定履行了有关义务,受益人就无需向开证行递交违约声明

  D. 备用信用证常常是备而不用的文件

9. 以下(   )不是保理融资的特点。

  A. 融资比例较高   B. 绝对没有追索权融资

C. 融资条件低、手续简便　　　　　D. 融资额度灵活
10. 福费廷商包买票据时买断的风险不包括(　　)。
　　A. 欺诈风险　　　B. 市场风险　　　C. 商业风险　　　D. 汇率风险

二、多选题(Multiple Choice Question)
1. 下列可成为银行保函申请人的是(　　)。
　　A. 投标人　　　　B. 招标人　　　　C. 卖方　　　　D. 买方
2. 银行保函可以解决交易中存在的如下问题(　　)。
　　A. 买方怀疑卖方的交货能力
　　B. 卖方怀疑买方的支付能力
　　C. 买卖双方的资金不足
　　D. 在合约的执行过程中,因一方的违约导致另一方的损失
3. 备用信用证与保函的主要区别在于(　　)。
　　A. 保函与备用信用证受到不同国际惯例的约束
　　B. 保函一定会有付款行为发生,而备用信用证不一定
　　C. 保函有独立性保函和从属性保函之分,备用信用证无此区别
　　D. 保函有负第一性付款责任的,也有负第二性付款责任的,而备用信用证总是负第一性付款责任
4. 保函的基本内容中,保函有效期包括(　　)。
　　A. 保函生效期　　B. 保函失效期　　C. 最迟交单期　　D. 最迟装运期
5. 下面关于备用信用证的说法正确的是(　　)。
　　A. 备用信用证是不可撤销的
　　B. 备用信用证的开证行履行其责任和义务的前提是"单证相符"
　　C. 备用信用证独立于交易合同之外
　　D. 备用信用证自开立时起即对开证行具有约束力
6. 进口类保函包括(　　)。
　　A. 付款保函　　　B. 承包保函　　　C. 延期付款保函　　D. 租赁保函
7. 银行保函的作用是(　　)。
　　A. 以银行信用代替或补充商业信用
　　B. 推动国际贸易等各种经济交往的发展
　　C. 可以促进交易顺利进行
　　D. 使交易一方可以避免因对方违约而遭受损失的风险
8. 以下属于备用信用证基本内容的是(　　)。
　　A. 备用信用证的编号和开立日期
　　B. 备用信用证的有效期
　　C. 索偿时受益人所需要提供的文件或单证及提示方式
　　D. 货物简要名称、数量、单价及包装
9. 根据保函与基础合同的关系来划分,银行保函可以分为(　　)两类。
　　A. 从属性保函　　　　　　　　　　B. 有追索权保函

C. 独立性保函　　　　　　　　　D. 无追索权保函

10. 以下关于保理表述正确的是（　　）。
　A. 银行对出口商无追索权
　B. 融资比例通常为发票金额的80%
　C. 融资期限一般180天（半年）以内，属于短期融资
　D. 又称为票据买断

三、判断题（True or False）

1. 签发保函意味着担保行承担了一项确定的负债。因此，担保行出于自身利益的考虑，在签发保函之前往往要对申请人的资信情况及财务状况、担保品及反担保措施、项目可行性及效益、保函申请书或委托担保协议等内容进行详尽的审查。（　　）

2. 独立性保函中担保人承担第一性的偿付责任，即担保人的偿付责任独立于申请人在交易合同项下的义务。（　　）

3. 保函的修改必须经有关当事人一致同意后方可进行，任何一方单独对保函条款进行修改都视为无效。（　　）

4. 任何一份银行保函都有保兑行这一基本当事人。（　　）

5. 银行在为申请人开立银行保函时，为了控制自身风险，往往都要求申请人提供反担保。（　　）

6. 银行保函的修改必须经有关当事人一致同意后，由受益人向担保行提出书面的修改申请。（　　）

7. 银行保函的应用范围要远远大于普通的跟单信用证，可以用于保证任何一种经济活动中任何一方履行其不同的责任与义务。（　　）

8. 保函的担保期限即保函的有效期，只有在保函的有效期内，担保行才承担保证责任。所以受益人必须在规定的期限内向担保行提出赔付要求，否则担保行可以不付款或不履行赔偿义务。（　　）

9. 在向受益人赔付后，担保行有权向申请人或反担保人索偿。如果申请人不能立即偿还担保行已支付的款项，担保行有权处置保证金或抵押品；如果处置后仍不足抵偿，担保行自行承担该损失（对没有抵偿部分仍有追索权）。（　　）

10. 福费廷可使出口商获得高达100%的融资额度，而且不占用出口商在银行的授信额度。（　　）

四、实务操作题（Practice）

说明以下未加保兑的转开保函的业务流程。

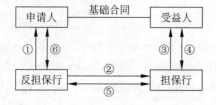

Chapter 7

Documents Used in International Settlement

Mr. Zhang is a clerk of company A which exporting products to foreign countries. This company will export a lot of products to the United States, and the method of payment is documentary L/C. The L/C requires to provide the following documents: Commercial Invoice one original and three copies; Packing List one original and three copies; Full set of clean Bill of Lading marked "freight prepaid" and the consignee writes: "TO THE ORDER OF BANK OF AMERICA"; Marine Insurance Policy one original and one copy, whose coverage is 110% of the invoice value and against all risks, etc.. What is the function of these documents? How to prepare these documents to conform the L/C? This chapter mainly deals with issues related to documents, which refer to a set of certificates or papers used in international settlements.

★ Learning Objectives

(1) To enable the readers to understand the concept, function and types of documents.

(2) To enable the readers to understand the functions and contents of commercial invoice.

(3) To enable the readers to master the main categories of transport documents, and understand the content of bill of lading.

(4) To enable the readers to understand the main contents of insurance policy.

(5) To enable the readers to understand other accompanied documents.

7.1 Documents

As we know, in the international trade, the relevant parities deal with documents instead of goods. Therefore, it is important to once again mention that the technical name for L/C is documentary L/C and, along with documentary collections, that documents are at the heart of all forms of international payment. As with all matters involving money and payments, the form and content of these documents is of great importance to all parties to the transaction. Subtle differences between forms and subtle changes in wording can mean the difference between a successful transaction and an unsuccessful one.

International trade is exchange of goods and services across national boundaries. Because the buyer and the seller are from different countries, the commodities and services can't be exchanged with currency simply and directly. Document act as a medium of exchange. They are the documents and evidence in the import and export against which the buyer and the seller deliver, ship, insure and inspect the goods and make settlement.

单据,也称货运单据、商业单据,是出口方应进口方和其他有关方的要求必须备妥并提交的、完整地代表货物所有权的各种货运单据。

Business documents mainly include two kinds: import documents and export documents. They are largely identical but with minor differences. We will introduce export documents (on L/C terms) in this chapter. Export documents mainly include Commercial Invoice, B/L, Insurance Policy, Certificate of Origin, Customs Declaration, Bill of Exchange, Packing List, Inspection Certificate, Customs Declaration, Shipping Advice and Beneficiary Certificate, etc.

Particularly, the export documents should be made out according to the order of the date of documents and based on the L/C. That means all information should be in compliance with that in the L/C. The general principle for the making of export documents is "Four Consistencies", namely consistency between L/C and contract, between documents and L/C, between documents and documents, between documents and goods. The documents should be correct, integrated, duly, concise and neat.

International trade process mainly includes the following steps as shown in Figure 7.1: (1) the buyer and the seller sign the sales contract and agree on the method of payment; (2) If the settlement way is L/C, the buyer will entrust the issuing bank to open an L/C; (3) the seller will deliver the goods after reviewing the L/C is correct, and make out the relevant documents; and (4) the issuing bank makes the payment after reviewing.

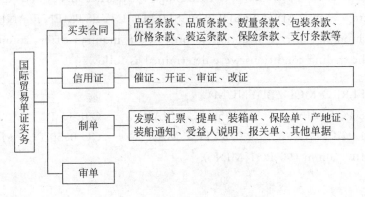

Figure 7.1 International Trade Process

> **Documentation Consistency Checklist**
> The following is a list of points of consistency buyers, sellers, and banks should all be aware of when preparing, presenting, and checking documents for documentary L/C and documentary collection transactions:
> 1. Name and address of shipper
> 2. Name and address of buyer/consignee
> 3. Issuer name and address
> 4. Description of the goods, quantities, units
> 5. Country of origin of the goods
> 6. Country of destination of the goods
> 7. Invoice numbers, documentary L/C numbers
> 8. Certifications
> 9. Legalizations
> 10. Shipping marks and numbers
> 11. Net weight, gross weight, volume
> 12. Number of crates, cartons, or containers

We will take the business transaction between JINZHOU HOTIY MINERAL CORPORATION and TAIWAN SHUANGSHENT INVESTMENT AND TRADING CO., LTD on FERRO MOLYBDENUM as an example to illustrate the procedure of the making of export negotiating documents and the contents of each document.

Example 7-1

In November 2007, JINZHOU HOTIY MINERAL CORPORATION determined the export price of FERRO MOLYBDENUM through the market survey and cost accounting. After consulting with TAIWAN SHUANGSHENT INVESTMENT AND TRADING CO. LTD (through contract negotiation process of inquiry, offer, counter-offer and acceptance), the trading conditions were determined as follows:

> 品名：钼铁(FERRO MOLYBDENUM)
> 规格：MO 58 PCT MIN.,   SI 1.50 PCT MAX.,   C 0.15 PCT MAX.,
> 　　　S 0.10 PCT MAX.,   P 0.05 PCT MAX.,   CU 0.50 PCT MAX.,
> 　　　SIZE 10～60mm (90 PCT MIN.)
> 唛头：无
> 数量：40MTS
> 单价：USD 55.50/MT CIF KAOHSIUNG, TAIWAN

装运港/目的港：从中国任意港口到高雄港
装运条款：2012年1月21日前，不允许分批装运但可以转船
包装：40包，底部带有卸货槽的标准包装袋
保险：由卖方按发票金额的110%投保伦敦保险协会条款的ICC(A)险和协会战争险、协会罢工险
付款条件：不可撤销即期信用证付款，该信用证应于2011年12月20日之前到达卖方

According to the Sales Contract, the L/C has been issued in the stipulated time, as shown in Document Instance 7-1.

Document Instance 7-1

Msg Type：700（Issue of a Documentary L/C）
Destination Bank：BANK OF CHINA, JINZHOU BRANCH
Sequence Total　　＊27　1/1
Type of Documentary L/C　　＊40A　IRREVOCABLE
Letter of L/C Number　　＊20　CDMS2011U/5539
Date of Issue　　31C　　071218
Date and Place of Expiry　　＊31D　　120205 CHINA
Applicant Bank　　51D　　TAIWAN COOPERATIVE BANK, TAIWAN
Applicant　　＊50　　SHUANGSHENT INVESTMENT AND TRADING CO., LTD
PEACE ROAD MARSHALL ISLANDS MH 96890, KAOHSIUNG
Beneficiary　　＊59 JINZHOU　HOTIY　MINERAL CORPORATION
HOTIY BUILDING, 37-2　VICTORY STREET, JINZHOU CITY, LIAONING, CHINA
Currency Code, Amount　　＊32B　　USD1287600,00
Available with…by…　　＊41D　ANY BANK BY NEGOTIATION
Percentage L/C Amount Tolerance　　＊39A　00/00
Drafts at　　42C　AT SIGHT
Drawee　　42D　TACBTWTP563：TAIWAN COOPERATIVE BANK, TAIWAN
Partial Shipments　　43P　　NOT ALLOWED
Transshipment　　43T　　ALLOWED
Shipping on Board/Dispatch/Packing in Charge at/from　　44E　　CHINESE MAIN PORT
Transportation to　　44B　　KAOHSIUNG PORT
Latest Date of Shipment　　44C　　120121
Description of Goods or Services　　45A
40 MTS OF FERRO MOLYBDENUM WITH MO CONTAINED 58 PCT APPROXIMATED AT UNIT PRICE USD55.50 PER KG OF MOLYBDENUM CONTAINED IN FERRO MOLYBDENUM
SPECIFICATION：
MO 58 PCT MIN., SI 1.50 PCT MAX., C 0.15 PCT MAX.,
　　S 0.10 PCT MAX., P 0.05 PCT MAX., CU 0.50 PCT MAX.,
SIZE 10—60 MM (90 PCT MIN.)

CIF KAOHSIUNG,TAIWAN PER INCOTERMS 2000

Documents Required   46A

+ SIGNED COMMERCIAL INVOICE IN TRIPLICATE.

+ FULL SET OF ORIGINAL CLEAN ON BOARD OCEAN BILLS OF LADING MADE OUT TO ORDER OF TAIPEI FUBON COMMERCIAL BANK, AND BLANK ENDORSED, MARKED "FREIGHT PREPAID" AND NOTIFY PARTY HONGDA UNITED STEEL CORPORATION WITH FULL ADDRESS 658 LUCK ST. JIA HSING KANGSHAN JENN,KAOHSIUNG HSIEN,TAIWAN.

+ PACKING LIST IN 3 TRIPLICATES.

+ FULL SET OF MARINE INSURANCE POLICY OR CERTIFICATE IN NEGOTIABLE FORM AND BLANK ENDORSED FOR FULL CIF VALUE PLUS 10 PERCENT COVERING INSTITUTE CARGO CLAUSES (A), INSTITUTE WAR CLAUSES (CARGO) AND INSTITUTE STRIKES CLAUSES (CARGO).

+ CERTIFICATE OF ORIGIN (FORM A) IN 2 COPIES.

+ VESSEL'S AGE CERTIFICATE ISSUED BY THE SHIPPING COMPANY OR ITS AGENT.

+ BENEFICIARY'S CERTIFICATE STATING THAT TWO COMPLETE SETS OF COMMERCIAL INVOICE, PACKING LIST, NON-NEGOTIABLE SHIPPING DOCUMENTS HAS BEEN FAXED TO THE APPLICANT AT FAX NO.12-77581 WITHIN 3 DAYS AFTER SHIPMENT DATE.

+ BENEFICIARY'S CERTIFICATE STATING ONE COPY OF SHIPPING ADVICE HAS BEEN FAXED TO THE APPLICANT AT FAX NO. 12-77581 WITHIN 3 DAYS AFTER SHIPMENT DATE.

Additional Instructions   47A

1. THIRD PARTY DOCUMENTS EXCEPT COMMERCIAL INVOICE AND DRAFT ARE ACCEPTABLE.

2. ALL DOCUMENTS MUST INDICATE THIS L/C NO.：CDMS2011U/5539 AND CONTRACT NO.：03HL21401

3. SHIPMENT EFFECTED BEFORE L/C ISSUING DATE IS ACCEPTABLE.

4. DELY PENALTY：

+ IN CASE OF BENEFICIARY (SELLER) EFFECTING THE SHIPMENT LATER THAN THE LATEST SHIPMENT DATE OF THIS L/C, THE DELAY PENALTY WILL BE DEDUCTED FROM THE PROCEEDS AT PAYMENT DIRECTLY   AS FOLLOWING ONCE IT IS DELAYED FOR：

A)1—15 DAYS LATE：0.1 PCT OF TOTAL INVOICE VALUE

B)16 DAYS LATE AND OVER：0.2 PCT OF TOTAL INVOICE VALUE

Charges   71B

ALL BANKING CHARGES OUTSIDE THE OPENNING BANK ARE FOR BENEFICIARY'S ACCOUNT.

Period for Presentation   48

DOCUMENTS MUST BE PRESENTED WITHIN 7 DAYS AFTER THE DATE OF ISSUANCE OF THE TRANSPORT DOCUMENTS BUT WITHIN THE VALIDITY OF THE L/C.

Confirmation Instructions   *49   WITHOUT

Instructions to the Paying/Accepting/Negotiating Bank   78

1. ALL DOCUMENTS UNDERE THIS L/C MUST BE SENT BY COURIER SERVICE TO US AT NO.60, DONGFA MEN STREET HSINCHU CITY TAIWAN R.O.C.

续表

2. DISCREPANT DOCUMENT FEE OF USD 50.00 OR EQUAL CURRENCY WILL BE DEDUCTED FROM DRAWING IF DOCUMENTS WITH DISCREPANCIES ARE ACCEPTED. 3. UPON RECEIPT OF ALL DOCUMENTS AND DRAFT IN CONFORMITY WITH THE TERMS AND CONDITIONS OF THIS L/C, WE SHALL REMIT THE PROCEEDS TO THE BANK DESIGNATED BY YOU. **Sender to Receiver Information   72** THIS IS THE OPERATIVE INSTRUMENT SUBJECT TO UNIFORM CUSTOMS AND PRACTICE FOR DOCUMENTARY L/Cs, 2007 REVISION, INTERNATIONAL CHAMBER OF COMMERCE PUBLICATION NO. 600. 72 SENDER TO RECEIVER INFORMATION "Advising Through" Bank   57A: BANK OF CHINA, JINZHOU BRANCH ******** other wordings between banks are omitted ********

（资料来源：锦州和泰钼铁有限公司提供）

Normally, documents can also be classified into 4 groups by different issues: (1) business documents issued by sellers, buyers or other traders, for facilitating trade and payment; (2) transport documents issued by carriers, certifying that the goods have been loaded on board or dispatched or taken in charge; (3) insurance documents issued by the insurers, which are the evidence of insurance contract signed between the insurer and the insured; (4) official documents issued by state authorities, which required to meet both the exporting and importing countries' customs or foreign exchange regulations.

7.2 Invoice

There are many forms of invoice: Commercial Invoice, Customs Invoice, Consular Invoice, and Proforma Invoice, etc.

7.2.1 Commercial Invoice

The commercial invoice is the key accounting document describing the commercial transaction between the buyer and the seller. It is a document giving details of goods, price, quantity and shipment. Its primary function is to indicate to the buyer the sale of goods at its price terms on the part of the seller and to check the price and the goods bought on the part of the buyer. Sometimes it is used by the buyer as an evidence for making payment or clearance of the goods or as a voucher to enter into his account book.

商业发票是卖方开立的凭以向买方索取货款的价目清单，是装运货物的总说明。

The buyer, seller, and bank(s) should all carefully check for discrepancies in the invoice. The details specified therein should not be inconsistent with those of any other documents, and should exactly conform to the specifications of the L/C.

The commercial invoice mainly includes the following elements: (1) name and address of the seller; (2) name of "Commercial Invoice"; (3) name and address of the buyer[①]; (4) invoice number; (5) order or contract number; (6) date of issuance; (7) marks & Nos.; (8) quantity and description of the goods; [②] (9) amount, which should include unit price, total price, other agreed upon charges, and total invoice amount; [③] (10) shipping details, which includes weight of the goods, number of packages, etc.; (11) port of loading and port of discharge or place of receipt and place of delivery; (12) L/C No. and Issuing Bank, if used L/C; (13) details of freight and insurance charges where applicable; (14) any other information as required in the documentary L/C (e.g., country of origin); (15) the seller's signature. Here is the commercial invoice example according to the Document Instance 7-2.

Document Instance 7-2

锦州和泰矿物有限公司
JINZHOU HOTIY MINERAL CORPORATION
HOTIY BUILDING, 37-2 VICTORY STREET, JINZHOU CITY, LIAONING, CHINA

COMMERCIAL INVOICE

TO:
INVOICE NO.:   HSF120120
SHUANGSHENT INVESTMENT AND TRADING CO., LTD
PEACE ROADMARSHALL   DATE: 15 JAN., 2012
ISLANDS MH 96890, KAOHSIUNG   S/C NO.:   03HL21801
                                           L/C NO.: CDMS2011U/5539

FROM XINGGANG PORT, CHINA TO KAOHSIUNG PORT, TAIWAN

---

① Unless otherwise stipulated in the documentary L/C, the commercial invoice must be made out in the name of the applicant (buyer). The exception: In a transferable documentary L/C the invoice may be made out to a third party.

② In transaction involving a documentary credit it is vitally important that the description of the goods in the commercial invoice correspond precisely to the description of goods in the documentary credit.

③ In transactions involving a documentary L/C, the amount should match exactly (or at least should not exceed) the amount specified in the L/C. Banks have the right to refuse invoices issued for amounts in excess of the amount stated in the L/C. For this, as well as other reasons, the invoice should be made out in the same currency as the L/C amount. There are exceptions. If the L/C does not stipulate the quantity in a stated number of units (i.e., it does not state units such as piece, set, box, dozen, or gross), or unless the L/C stipulates that the quantity of the goods specified must not be exceeded or reduced, a tolerance of 5% more or 5% less quantity is permitted, provided the total amount does not exceed the amount of the L/C. If a documentary L/C specifies "about" in relation to the currency amount and quantity of merchandise, in which case the invoice may specify an amount equal to plus or minus 10 percent of the stipulated amount of the L/C.

续表

MARKS & NOS.	DESCRIPTIONS	QUANTITIES	UNIT PRICE	AMOUNT
N/M	FERRO MOLYBDENUM MO：58.00PCT SI：0.42PCT C：0.024 PCT S：0.082 PCT P：0.040 PCT CU：0.24 PCT SIZE 10—60MM(90 PCT MIN)	40MTS	US55.50 PER KG OF MOLYBDENUM CONTAINED IN FERRO MOLYBDENUM CIF KAOHSIUNG,TAIWAN PER INCOTERMS 2000	USD1287600.00

TOTAL：
SAY US DOLLARS ONE MILLION TWO HUNDRED AND EIGHTY-SEVEN THOUSAND SIX HUNDRED ONLY

锦州和泰矿物有限公司(章)
JINZHOU HOTIY MINERAL CORPOARATION

 7-1

做好商业发票声明文句缮制要注意的问题

（一）认真研究贸易伙伴国海关通关文件规定，做好归类总结

商业发票是进口商通关的重要文件，出口商要做好商业发票的缮制，首先要认真研究贸易伙伴国海关通关文件的规定，正确认识信用证对单据的规定。只有这样，缮制声明文句才能做到正确和完整，单证才能一致。各贸易伙伴国海关通关文件规定既有相似性，又有一定的差异性。日本、智利、秘鲁、阿拉伯国家、美国及挪威等海关均要求商业发票注明价值的分解，便于进行海关估价。澳大利亚、新加坡、泰国、孟加拉国等海关均要求商业发票注明原产地或制造商名称。还有的国家海关对两者均有要求。

（二）随时掌握贸易伙伴国认证商业发票的新政策，做到灵活应对

由于越来越多的贸易伙伴国针对信用证业务提出认证商业发票的要求，出口商要随时掌握有关商业发票的新政策，灵活应对才有备无患。目前的趋势是，涉及需要办理领事认证的国家范围正在逐步扩大。传统需要进行发票领事认证的国家一般是中东和南美国家，如阿联酋、阿曼、沙特、埃及、阿根廷及智利等。目前，亚洲、非洲国家信用证对单据认证的使用频率也越来越高。阿尔及利亚、埃塞尔比亚、利比亚、韩国、印度尼西亚、印度等海关对商业发票有认证的要求。

此外，各贸易伙伴对单据认证的内容规定多、差异大，出口商要准确把握，灵活应对。黎巴嫩要求，认证产地证须同时认证发票。伊朗则规定，产地证不必和发票一起认证。利比亚要求，单独认证发票须附贸促会出具的产地证副本，供使馆参考，供使馆参考的产地证须在右上角注明"不需认证，供使馆阅"字样。

（三）仔细审核信用证声明文句，防范风险

出口商收到信用证后，需对照合同条款、惯例，尤其还要对照中国的有关法律法规，仔细审核单据声明文句条款。如果信用证对商业发票要求不合理，出口商难以办到，不可能办到，要坚决提出改证。如至巴拿马某信用证要求发票进行使领馆认证，出口商将面临不能收汇的风险。因巴拿马在中国并无使领馆，故出口商是不可能完成该任务的。该信用证要修改，删掉此要求或者同意其他国家（如墨西哥）代办使领馆认证。

（四）特别关注中东和孟加拉国开来的信用证，做到缮制无遗漏无错误

信用证对商业发票的声明文句要求往往不止一处，应全面通读信用证，尤其是单据要求（45A）和附加条件（46A）两个项目，单据要求大多出现在这里。要特别关注中东和孟加拉国的信用证，注意阅读其46A，该条会隐藏多处单据要求。出口商要逐一列明声明文句，是要证实原产地在中国、注明CIF的分解，或者是无以色列物质证明等，做到缮制无遗漏。此外，还要做到内容缮制无错误，即that后面的宾语从句内容正确，无多文字，无少文字。前信用证要求："Made in China" must be sticked on each pair and the invoice must certify to this effect。出口商下列商业发票的声明文句缮制是错误的：We hereby certify that "Made in China" has been sticked on each pair and the invoice must certify to this effect。后半句（从and开始）是信用证要求发票要缮制声明文句，直接复制在发票上属画蛇添足之举。

（资料来源：姜燕.信用证项下商业发票声明文句的缮制解析[J].对外经贸实务.2014.01.）

7.2.2　Other Invoice

In order to abide by regulations of control on foreign trade and foreign exchange, importers of some countries probably call for other forms of invoices as follows:

- A Consular Invoice is sometimes the precondition for import declaration obtained by the exporter from the consular in exporting country or neighboring countries. Such invoices, mostly required by the Latin American countries, are used by customs official of the entry country to verify the value, quantity, country of origin, and nature of the merchandise. The certificate and legalization of such invoices made by the consulate take more time than the normal commercial invoice. The consular invoice of each country will have its own form and content. Certain elements are likely to be included in all consular invoices: (1) name and address of the seller; (2) name and address of the buyer; (3) date of issuance; (4) country of origin of the goods shipped; (5) country of final destination of the goods; (6) quantity and description of the goods; (7) shipping details including weight of the goods, number of packages, and shipping marks and numbers.

领事发票是出口方根据进口国驻出口国领事馆制定的固定格式填写并经领事馆签章的发票。

- Pro-forma Invoice is issued in advance by the exporter for the importer to apply to their authority for import license. Actually, it is a form of "offer" or "quotation" to the buyer which shows the intention of the exporter to conclude the contract with the buyer. Once the pro-forma invoice is accepted by the buyer wholly, it will become a formal contract between the buyer and the seller. In such case, a commercial invoice will be made out for payment.

形式发票是在没有正式合同之前,经双方签字或盖章之后产生法律效力的充当合同的文件,它包括产品描述、单价、数量、总金额、付款方式、包装、交货期等。

- A customs invoice, normally prepared by the exporter, is a special invoice required by the importing customs for the purpose of determining the value and origin of the imported goods. It is also called certified invoice, combined certificate of value and origin, etc, which is necessary evidence for the goods entry with a levy of lower import duty or even free of duty. The same as the consular document, it determines the basis of calculating import duty and serves to prevent dumping of imports at low prices (lower than its domestic price). The customs of importing country uses it also for statistical purposes and checking origin of goods. The customs invoice of each country will have its own form and content. Certain elements are likely to be included in all customs invoices. Here is an example of Canada Customs Invoice, including the following elements: (1) vendor, name and address of the seller; (2) date of direct shipment to Canada, date and number of B/L; (3) order reference, e. g., number of contract, order and invoice, etc.; (4) consignee, name and address of the buyer of Canada; (5) purchaser's name and address; country of transshipment; country of origin of goods; (6) transportation: give mode and place of direct shipment Canada, e. g., "From Guangzhouo To Quebec, Canada By Sea"; (7) conditions of sales and terms of payment, e. g., "CIF Toronto By L/C At Sight", "FOB Guangzhou By D/P at sight"; (8) currency of settlement, which should be in the same currency as stated in the invoice; (9) number of packages; (10) specification of commodities and of packages, marks and numbers, general description and characteristics, say grade or quality; (11) quantity; (12) unit price; (13) total weight, which is composed of net weight and gross weight; (14) invoice total; (15) if any of above-mentioned fields are included on and attached commercial invoice, check this box; (16) exporter's name and address; (17) originator (name and address); (18) Departmental ruling; (19) domestic freight charges; (20) ocean or international freight; (21) insurance cost; (22) export packing cost.

海关发票是根据某些进口国海关的规定,由出口商填制的一种特定格式的发票,它的作用是供进口商凭以向海关办理进口报关、纳税等手续。

7.3 Transport Documents

7.3.1 Marine Bill of Lading

A marine bill of lading, sometimes named ocean bill of lading or port-to-port bill of lading(B/L for short) is a document issued by a carrier or its authorized agents, to a shipper and used primarily in international sales of goods where the carriage of goods is by sea. Definitions of the Bill of Lading vary from country to country. Broadly, a bill of lading is a document issued by a carrier to a shipper, signed by the captain, agent, or owner of a vessel, furnishing written evidence regarding receipt of the goods, the conditions on which transportation is made, and the engagement to deriver goods at the prescribed port of destination to the lawful holder of the bill of lading.

海运提单是证明海上运输合同和货物已由承运人或其代理人接管或装运,以及承运人保证凭此交付货物的单据。

- **Functions of Marine B/L**

Marine B/L performs a number of functions. Generally, it is (1) a receipt for the goods shipped, issued by a carrier that an identifiable consignment of goods has been received by him for shipment, or actually loaded on board his ship. The B/L as a receipt will show the quantity and condition of the cargo loaded, ship's name, port of loading, the destination, details of date and so on; (2) a document of title to the goods, the possession of which is equivalent in law to possession of the goods and the holder of the bill of lading is able to obtain delivery of the goods at the port of destination, and during transit, the goods can be sold merely by endorsing the bill of lading; and (3) evidence of the terms of the contract to deliver it as freight.

- **Types of Marine B/L**

B/L normally are issued in three or more originals to prevent from loss through mail or courier services. One of the full set of original B/L is used for picking up the goods; the other will be automatically null and void. There are number of types of B/L:

➢ **On Board (Shipped) B/L vs. Received for Shipment B/L**(已装船提单和装要备运提单)

"On board" is a notation on a B/L indicating that the goods have in fact been loaded on board or shipped on a named vessel. This notation may be made by the carrier or his agent, the master of the ship or his agent. Since on board B/L provides better guarantee for the consignee to receive the cargo at the destination, the importer will normally require the exporter to produce on board B/L and most bill of lading forms are preprinted as "On board". Most of B/L are shipped on board B/L by pre-printed wording "shipped on board in apparent good order and condition".

Received for shipment B/L state that the goods have been received for shipment, and do not indicate the actual date of loading. A received for shipment B/L indicated by wording "received in apparent good order and condition" is just a receipt, not a document of title to the goods, which grew up because with the development of the liner services it became the custom for the ship owner to receive the cargo some hours or even days before it was actually loaded.

> **Named consignee, Blank and Order B/L**(记名提单、空白提单和指示提单)

A Named consignee B/L, called also non-negotiable B/L, indicates that the shipper will deliver the goods to a named consignee, which can not be transferred from one to another. The consignee only needs to identify himself to claim the goods. It is often used when payment for the goods has already been made in advance or in cases where the goods are shipped on open account. A straight B/L, therefore, cannot be transferred to a third party.

The blank B/L means that there is no definite consignee of the goods. There usually appear in the box of consignee words like to "bearer". Anyone that holds the bill is entitled to the goods the bill represents. No endorsement is needed for the transfer of the blank B/L. Due to the exceedingly high risk involved, this kind of B/L is rarely used.

An order bill of lading called also negotiable B/L, is issued by the carrier to the order of shipper or consignee. This means that the carrier, ship-owner, charterer or master will deliver the goods at the port of destination not solely to the named consignee, but to any person designated by him. This negotiable B/L enables the order to transfer the title to the goods to anyone else by endorsement. The L/C may call for an order B/L that is: (1) to order blank endorsed or to order of shipper and blank endorsed; (2) to order of shipper and endorsed to order of "the named party" or (3) to order of "the named party". The order B/L is broadly used under L/C.

> **Clean B/L vs. Unclean B/L**(清洁提单和不清洁提单)

A clean B/L is one where the carrier has noted that the merchandise had been received in apparent good condition, usually with such words as "in apparent good order and condition" or "clean on board" etc.. Most forms of payment require a "clean" B/L in order for the seller to obtain payment under a documentary L/C.

A claused B/L is opposite of a clean bill of lading, which contains notations that specify a shortfall in quantity or deficient condition of the goods and/or packaging, for example, "one carton short" or "missing safety" indicated on the B/L.

> **Straight B/L vs. Transshipment B/L**(直达提单和转船提单)

Straight B/L is issued when the goods are shipped by one vessel directly from the loading port to the destination port without transshipment on the route.

Transshipment B/L is used when the goods have to be transferred from one ship to another at a named transshipment port. The carrier has full responsibility for the full journey, and these are documents of title if appropriate negotiable wording appears on the bill. On the form of L/C, it must be given that the transshipment is allowed or not.

➢ **Multi-modal B/L vs. Container B/L**（多式联运提单和集装箱提单）

Multi-modal B/L, also called combined transport B/L, is a B/L covering two or more modes of transport, such as shipping by rail and by sea. It evidences that the goods have been collected from a named inland place and have been dispatched to a port or inland container depot in the country of import. Even if an L/C prohibits transshipment, banks will accept a multimodal transport document that indicates that transshipment will or may take place, provided that the entire carriage is covered by one transport document, but it is necessary to put "or" or "and/or" between the names of the required transport documents. For example, if the goods are to be shipped by both sea and air, the L/C might specify "marine B/L and/or air waybill".

When goods are packed in containers, the shipping company will issue a B/L that acts as a receipt for containers. This kind of B/L can be issued to cover goods being transported on a traditional port-to-port basis, or they can cover transport from an inland container depot in the exporter's country to an inland container depot in the importer's country.

➢ **Liner B/L vs. Charter party B/L**（班轮提单和租船合约提单）

The liner B/L is issued by a shipping company in respect of the goods carried on a scheduled route to reserved berths at destination, thus the exporter can reasonably assume that his goods will reach the buyer's country by a fixed date. This kind of document fulfils all the normal functions of a B/L, including that of document of title.

The charter party B/L is issued by the carrier or its agent in the charter shipping. The terms of this kind of B/L are subject to the charter party between the ship-owner and charterer. Such a bill is usually marked subject to charter party, therefore it is not usually considered to be document of title. Unless authorized in the L/C, the charter party bill of lading is not acceptable in the L/C negotiation.

➢ **Short Form B/L vs. Long Form B/L**（简式提单和全式提单）

In a short form B/L (blank back B/L) the terms and conditions of carriage on the reverse (back) of the B/L are omitted, instead they are listed on a document other than the B/L. Otherwise stipulated in the L/C, a short form B/L is acceptable. The short form B/L saves the cost of printing (i.e., no printing on the back of the B/L) and if the terms and conditions of carriage change, there is no need to reprint the B/L form. In a long form B/L the terms and conditions of carriage are printed on the reverse (back) of the B/L. The long form B/L is commonly used in international shipping.

➢ Anti-Dated B/L, Advanced B/L and Stale B/L(倒签提单、预签提单和过期提单)

Under the L/C, if the actual date of the completion of shipment on the B/L is later than the date stipulated on the L/C, it is likely that the bank will refuse to negotiate. Therefore, in order to get his proceeds successfully from the bank, the consigner may request the carrier to sign on the B/L a date earlier than the actual loading date. This kind of B/L is called anti-dated B/L. Anti-dated B/L is issued by the carrier at the request of shipper so as to avoid non-acceptance by the bank when the actual shipment date is later than that stipulated in the L/C. Due to the risk of goods being rejected by the buyer arising from the issuance of such a B/L, it's advisable to avoid this malpractice even when it seems necessary in certain circumstances.

Advanced B/L refers to the "shipped on board B/L" issued by the carrier as the consigner requires when the loading is not actually completed. The purpose of issuing such a B/L is to negotiate payment with the bank in time within the validity of the L/C. It is also regarded as unlawful and risky and should be avoided.

In short-sea trades, for example within the Asian countries, it is not uncommon for the goods to arrive at the port of destination before the B/L. Under this circumstance the B/L is known as a stale B/L or late B/L. Stale B/L may cause demurrage[①].

NOTE: In order to assume no risk in any circumstance, bank are willing to accept shipped on board, clean, straight and order B/L.

● Contents of Bills of Lading

A B/L usually embodies the following details: (1) the name of shipper, usually the exporter or his agent; (2) the name of consignee; (3) the address of notify party, the person whom the shipping company will notify on arrival of the goods; (4) transport details, including place of receipt, ocean vessel voy. no. , port of loading, port of discharge, place of delivery, etc. ; (5) marks & Nos. ; (6) description of goods; (7) gross weight; (8) measurement; (9) number of original B/Ls; (10) the details of the freight; (11) the on board notation; (12) place and date of issue; (13) signed for or on behalf of the carrier. Here gives the Document Instance 7-3.

---

① The extra charges for storing goods or for parking containers at the port until the documents arrive are called demurrage, and can be very expensive.

Document Instance 7-3

		B/L NO.: TF12S68
Shipper: JINZHOU HOTIY MINERAL CORPORATION HOTIY BUILDING, 37-2 VICTORY STREET, JINZHOU CITY, LIAONING, CHINA		天津福祥海运有限公司 TIANJIN FUXIANG MARINE SHIPPING CO., LTD. BILL OF LADING DIRECT OR WITH TRANSHIPMENT
Consignee: TO ORDER OF TAIPEI FUBON COMMERCIAL BANK		SHIPPED on board in apparent good order and condition (unless otherwise indicated) the goods or packages specified herein and to be discharged at the mentioned port of discharge or as near thereto as the vessel may safely get and be always afloat.
Notify address: HONGDA UNITED STEEL CORPORATION 658 LUCK ST. JIA HSING KANGSHAN JENN, KAOHSIUNG HSIEN, TAIWAN.		The weight, measure, marks and numbers, quality, contents and value. Being particulars furnished by the shipper, are not checked by the carrier on loading.
Pre-carriage by	Place of receipt	The shipper, consignee and the holder of this bill of lading hereby expressly accept and agree to all printed, written or stamped provisions. Exceptions and conditions of this Bill of Lading, including those on the back hereof.
Vessel: SKY FORTUNE V.152E	Port of loading: XINGANG	
Port of discharges: KAOHSIUNG PORT, TAIWAN	Final destination:	IM WITNESS whereof the number of original Bills of Lading stated below have been signed, one of which being accomplished, the other to be void.
Container seal No. N/M CLHU3080892/833910/CY-CY/20'X1 CLHU3234806/833917/CY-CY/20'X1	Description of goods FERRO MOLYBDENUM L/C NO.: CDMS2011U/5539 S/C NO.: 03HL21801	Gross weight (kgs.) Measurement(m³) 40056.00 40.00

Total Number and kind of packages:
FORTY BAGS ONLY
                CLEAN ON BOARD
                                            18 JAN 2012		

REGARDING TRANSHIPMENT INFORMATION PLEASE CONTACT		Freight and charges FREIGHT PREPAID
	Prepaid at	Freight payable at	Place and date of issue TIANJIN 2012/01/18
Ex. rate	Total prepaid	Number of original B/Ls (THREE)	Signed for or on behalf of the Master as Agent AS AGENT FOR THE CARRIER: TFMS 李弘

 7-2

电子海运提单及其实现

电子海运提单(Electronic Bill of Lading, e-B/L)是将海运提单信息输入并保存到计算机上,代替纸质海运提单记载或体现海运提单的内容,并在承运人(Carrier)、货主(Consignor)或收货人(Consignee)等相关贸易参与方之间流转。它与海运提单具有相同的法律效力,而且转移其承载的物权及交付被运输货物的时候,通过电子签名识别与证明合法身份,其传输、接收、记录可以替代转让和背书传统海运提单的一般过程。与纸质海运提单不同的是,其发行形式和交付方式改变成了电子信息传递。因此,电子海运提单将以传统纸质海运提单包含的信息内容体现方式改变的同时,还应导致贸易习惯或法律的修订,从而保证其与纸质海运提单具有相同的功能。

随着IT技术的迅猛发展,计算机作为一种现代化的管理和通信手段正越来越深入地影响到社会的各个方面。在全球市场一体化的大趋势下,在国际贸易领域,贸易商们更多地使用计算机及网络来处理日常业务,以促进交易的迅捷和高效。作为证明承运人已接管货物和货物已装船的货物收据,承运人保证凭以交付货物和可以转让的物权凭证,以及海上货物运输合同成立的证明文件,海运提单是贸易领域最为重要的单证之一,其电子化的实现是整个贸易链电子化、无纸化的核心环节,历来备受业界关注。

在海上货物运输中,由于结汇方面的原因,有时在货物装船以后,提单不能迅速到达卸货港的收货人手中,尤其在装卸两港距离较近的情况下,有时船舶已经到达卸货港,但提单尚在邮寄的过程中,因而使得收货人没有相应的凭证提取货物。虽然在实践中,收货人也可以凭副本提单加保函提取货物,但收货人取得此种保函是有一定困难的。在电子提单下,由于所有的单证均以电子形式保存和流转,缩短了单证在传递过程中耽搁的时间,因而具有快速性的特点,有利于货主及时提货,尤其是在集装箱货物运输方式下,可以满足该种运输对货运单证流转的要求。同时电子单证不需要重复录入,便于审核,可以有效地提高单证的处理速度。提单的到达不会发生延迟,电子提单把传统提单的流转时间由几天至几十天缩短为几分钟,大大提高了流转速,减少了无单放货的需要,降低了承运人的营运风险,减少了贸易商为取得担保而支付的费用。

正是由于上述背景,尽管国际贸易惯例与规则修正成果并不足以支持电子海运提单的法律效力,仍然出现了Bolero等组织推出的众多商业计划,他们的经验教训为海运提单及其他贸易单证的电子化发展奠定了基础。

(资料来源:丁强、高爽.电子海运提单及其实现[J].国际商务——对外经济贸易大学学报,2007年第5期)

7.3.2 Sea Waybill

A sea waybill is a transport document covering port-to-port shipment. It is not a title document, non-negotiable and can not be endorsed, the carrier is allowed to deliver the goods merely to the consignee identified in the bill, no matter whether the consignee holds the originals or not, unlike the situation in the bill of lading.

海运单,是指证明海上货物运输合同和承运人接收货物或者已将货物装船的不可转让的单证。海运单的正面内容与提单的基本一致,但是印有"不可转让"的字样。

The key elements on a non-negotiable sea waybill are the same as stated on the section of marine B/L except the consignee must be a specific person, and on the surface, a sea waybill looks very like a marine B/L except for with words "not negotiable" and without the words "bill of lading".

Shipments stated in a sea waybill can be delivered by the carrier directly to the specified consignee without having to present originals. Indeed, it is convenient for the consignee to pick goods up, but no way for the exporters and banks to force importer to pay against original transport documents. So they are appropriate for shipments between associated companies, for shipments to an agent for sale at destination on an open account basis, and for organizations that have established mutual trust.

7.3.3 Airway Bill

An airway bill is a non-negotiable transport document covering transport of cargo from airport to airport, indicating that the goods have been accepted for carriage, and it must be signed or authenticated by the carrier or the named agent for or on behalf of the carrier.

航空运输单据是在航空运输方式下、由承运的航空公司或其代理人签发的运输单据,是发货人与承运人(或代理人)之间的运输合同。它有别于海运提单,并非代表货物所有权的物权凭证,是不可议付的单据。

The airway bill is both a contract for transportation between the carrier and the shipper and a receipt evidencing delivery of the shipments. An airway bill is also used for freight bill calculation, customs declaration, and offers specific information on handling of the shipment. Generally speaking, an airway bill contains the following elements: (1) name of the carrier with a signature identified as that of carrier or named agent for or on behalf of the carrier; (2) an indication that the goods have been accepted for carriage and the date of issuance or date of loading; (3) an indication of the actual date of dispatch if required by the documentary L/C, but if the actual date of dispatch is not required by the L/C, the issuance date of the document is deemed to be the date of shipment; (4) an indication of the airport of departure and destination; (5) appears on its face to be the original for shipper regardless of wording in the documentary L/C stipulating a full set of originals; (6) the terms and conditions of carriage or a reference to the terms and conditions of carriage in another source or document; (7) meets any other stipulations of the documentary L/C.

Since airway bills are issued in three originals, namely one for the issuing carrier, one for the consignee (buyer), and one for the shipper (seller), the documentary L/C should not require presentation in more than one original. Nor should it call for a "full set of original air waybills".

The airway bill must name a consignee (who can be the buyer), and it should not be required to be issued "to order" and/or "to be endorsed". Since it is not negotiable, and it does not evidence title to the goods, in order to maintain some control of goods not paid for by cash in advance, sellers often consign air shipments to their sales agents, or freight forwarders' agents in the buyer's country. Usually, the shipper will consign it to a trusted third party (if he agrees), such as the collecting bank, who will release the goods after receiving payment or a promise of payment made by importer.

The airway bill should not be required to indicate an "actual flight date" since IATA regulations specify that reservations requested by the shipper shall not be inserted under "Flight/Date".

7.3.4　Railway Bill

The railway bill serves as a receipt for goods and an evidence of the contract of carriage, but it is not a document of title to the goods. The consignee can obtain the goods from the carrier at the destination point without presentation of the railway bill.

铁路运输分为国际铁路联运和通往港澳的国内铁路运输,分别使用国际铁路货物联运单和承运货物收据。当通过国际铁路办理货物运输时,在发运站由承运人加盖日戳签发的运单叫"铁路运单"。铁路运单是由铁路运输承运人签发的货运单据,是收货人、发货人同铁路公司之间的运输契约。

The railway bill must be signed or authenticated and/or bear a reception stamp or other indication of receipt by the carrier or the named agent for or on behalf of the carrier. The signature, authentication, reception stamp, or other indication of receipt by the carrier must be identified on the face of the railway bill on the part of the carrier. If the goods are dispatched to Hong Kong by railway, a cargo receipt may be used. A cargo receipt is not a document of title, just an acknowledgement of receipt of goods for dispatch, so it is non-negotiable.

A cargo receipt contains the following elements: (1) date of issue; (2) name and address of the sender and the consignee; (3) name of the originating railway station/place designated for delivery; (4) ordinary description of goods and method of packing and, in the case of dangerous goods, its generally recognized description; (5) gross weight of goods or its quantity; (6) carriage charges; (7) requisite instructions for customs and other formalities.

7.4　Insurance Documents

Insurance document is a contract whereby the insurer (insurance company), on the basis of a premium paid, and undertakes to indemnify the insured against loss from certain risks or perils to which the cargo insured may be exposed. It is a document indicating the type and amount of insurance coverage in force on a particular shipment. As a title document, insurance document can be transferred. There are two types of endorsement by transferring insurance documents, i.e., blank endorsement and named endorsement. Most of endorsements are made in blank. There are often two important insurance documents: Insurance Policy and Insurance Certificate.

7.4.1　Insurance Policy

An insurance policy is a written legal contract between the insurance company and the party insured, containing all terms and conditions of the agreement (normally preprinted on the back side of the policy). It shows full details of the risks covered, so called also formal insurance document.

It is a legal evidence of the agreement to insure, which may be issued at the time when the contract is made, or on a later date.

保险单俗称大保单。一般是由保险人根据投保人的投保申请而逐笔签发的，它是一种正规的保险合同。

Claim against damage or loss: (1) the consignee should always note on the delivery document any damage or loss prior to signing for receipt of the goods; (2) copies of documents necessary to support an insurance claim include the insurance policy, bill of lading, invoice, packing list, and a survey report (usually prepared by a claims agent).

A typical insurance policy should include the following items: (1) name and address of the insurer; (2) name of the insured; (3) marks & Nos.; (4) quantity; (5) description of goods; (6) amount insured; (7) total amount insured; (8) premium; (9) rate; (10) per conveyance S.S; (11) slg. on or abt.; (12) from…to…; (13) conditions, risk insured against; (14) claim payable at; (15) the date and place of issuing the insurance policy; (16) the signature of the insurer.

The example of the insurance policy is showed as Document Instance 7-4:

Document Instance 7-4

PICC 中国人民保险公司 XX 分公司
The People's Insurance Company of China XX Branch

总公司设于北京　　一九四九年创立　　保单正本份数 3
Head Office Beijing　Established in 1949　No of Originals (THREE)

货物运输保险单
CARGO TRANSPORTATION INSURANCE POLICY

发票号（INVOICE NO.）：**HSF120120**　　保单号次（POLICY NO.）：**ATAE0042007B**
合同号（CONTRACT NO.）：**03HL21801**　　提单号（B/L NO.）：**TF12S68**
信用证号（L/C NO.）：**CDMS2011U/5539**
被保险人（THE INSURED）：**JINZHOU HOTIY MINERAL CORPORATION**

人民保险公司（以下简称本公司）根据被保险人的要求，由被保险人向本公司缴付约定的保险费，按照本保险单承保险别和背面所列条款与下列条款承保下述货物运输保险，特立本保险单。

THIS POLICY OF INSURANCE WITNESSES THAT THE PEOPLE'S INSURANCE COMPANY OF CHINA (HEREINAFTER CALLED "THE COMPANY") AT THE REQUEST OF THE INSURED AND INCONSIDERATION OF THE AGREED PREMIUM PAID TO THE COMPANY BY THE INSURED, UNDERTAKES TO INSURED THE UNDERMENTIONED GOODS IN TRANSPORTATION SUBJECT TO THE CONDITIONS OF THIS POLICY AS PER THE CLAUSES PRINTED OVERLEAF AND OTHER SPECIAL CLAUSES ATTACHED HEREON.

标记 MARKS & NOS.	包装及数量 QUANTITY	保险货物项目 DESCRIPTION OF GOODS	保险金额 AMOUNT INSURED
N/M	40 BAGS	FERRO MOLYBDENUM L/C NO.：CDMS2011U/5539 S/C NO.：03HL21801	USD1416360.00

总保险金额（TOTAL AMOUNT INSURED）：**SAY U.S. DOLLARS ONE MILLION FOUR HUNDRED SIXTEEN THOUSAND THREE HUNDRED AND SIXTY ONLY.**

保费　　　　费率　　　　　　　启运日期
PREMIUM：**AS ARRANGED** RATE**AS ARRANGED** DATE OF COMMENCEMENT**JAN 21,2012** PER 装载运输工具：
CONVEYANCE：**SKY FORTUNE V.152E**

自　　　　　经　　　　至
FROM **XINGANG PORT, CHINA** VIA _____ TO **KAOHSIUNG PORT, TAIWAN**

承保险别（CONDITIONS）：COVERING INSTITUTE CARGO CLAUSES(A), INSTITUTE WAR CLAUSES (CARGO) AND INSTITUTE STRIKES CLAUSES (CARGO).

所保货物，如发生保险单项下可能引起索赔的损失或损坏，应立即通知本公司下述代理人查勘。如有索赔，应向本公司提交保单正本（保险单共　**两**　份正本）及有关文件。如一份正本已用于索赔，其余正本自动失效。

IN THE EVENT OF LOSS OR DAMAGE WHICH MAY RESULT IN A CLAIM UNDER THIS POLICY, IMMEDIATE NOTICE MUST BE GIVEN TO THE COMPANY'S AGENT AS MENTIONED HEREUNDER. CLAIMS, IF ANY, ONE OF THE ORIGINAL POICY WHICH HAS BEEN ISSUED IN **TWO** ORIGINAL TOGETHER WITH THE RELEVENT DOCUMENTS SHALL BE SURRENDERED TO THE COMPANY. IF ONE OF THE ORIGINAL POLICY HAS BEEN ACCOMPLISHED, THE OTHERS TO BE VIOD.

Contact Name(s)：Mr Peter Hocapt.　Stanley Chen　Telephone：(886)223313998(24Hrs)

中国人民保险公司 xx 分公司
赔款偿付地点 CLAIM PAYABLE AT **KAOHSIUNG IN TAIWAN**　The People's Insurance Company of China xx Branch

出单日期
ISSUING DATE **JAN. 19 2012**　　　　　　　　　　　　　　Authorized Signature

7.4.2 Insurance Certificate

An insurance certificate is a document issued to the insured certifying that insurance has been effected. It contains the same details as an insurance policy except that the version of the provisions of the policy is abbreviated.

保险凭证俗称小保单,是保险人签发给被保险人,证明货物已经投保和保险合同已经生效的文件。它是一种简化了的保险单,保险凭证的正面依然载明了保险的基本项目,但背面未列保险条款,仅有相应声明。

 7-2

Notes on Insurance

- ✓ If the documentary L/C stipulates CIF (Cost, Insurance and Freight) or CIP (Cost and Insurance Paid) terms the seller is responsible for providing insurance against damage or loss to the shipment. More specifically, the seller is responsible for presenting an insurance document with the document package that evidences insurance cover.
- ✓ The L/C should name the specific type of insurance coverage required and any additional risks that are to be covered. The terms "usual risks" or "customary risks" should not be used as they will be ignored by the banks. The buyer should be specific as to what insurance document is required, the dates of coverage, and the amount of coverage.
- ✓ The insurance document is typically issued in duplicate and, if so, both originals must be presented with the document package.
- ✓ The insurance document must be issued by an insurance company or its agent. Cover notes issued by brokers are not acceptable unless authorized in the L/C. Banks will, unless otherwise stated in the L/C, accept an insurance certificate under an open insurance cover which is pre-signed by the insurance company or underwriter.
- ✓ The insurance document must indicate that the cover is effective at the latest from the date of loading of the goods on board a transport vessel or the taking in charge of the goods by the carrier, as indicated by the transport document (bill of lading, etc.).
- ✓ The insurance document must specify coverage for at least 110 percent of either: (a) the CIF or CIP value of the shipment, if such can be determined from the various documents on their face, otherwise, (b) the amount of the payment, acceptance, or negotiation specified in the documentary L/C, or (c) the gross amount of the invoice.

- ✓ The insurance currency (e.g., US dollars, Japanese yen, etc.) should be consistent with the currency of the documentary L/C.
- ✓ Even if the buyer has responsibility under the contract to insure the shipment, the seller still may wish to take out contingency coverage to cover the possibility that the insurance steps taken by the buyer are inadequate.
- ✓ If a documentary L/C calls for an insurance document specifying "insurance against all risks", the banks will accept an insurance document containing any "all risks" notation or clause, even if the document indicates that certain risks are excluded.

7.5 Other Documents

7.5.1 Packing List

A packing list is a document prepared by the shipper listing the kinds and quantities of merchandise in a particular shipment. The exporter or his agent (e.g., the customs broker or the freight forwarder) reserves the shipping space based on the gross weight or the measurement shown in the packing list.

装箱单是发票的补充单据,通常可以将其有关内容加列在商业发票上,它列明了信用证(或合同)中买卖双方约定的有关包装事宜的细节,便于国外买方在货物到达目的港时供海关检查和核对货物,但是在信用证有明确要求时,就必须严格按信用证约定缮制。

Packing list is also a type of certificate of fulfillment, presenting that the shipper have packed the goods in accordance with the terms of contract or suitable for the transport mode, so that the goods can arrive at the destination with perfect conditions. On the other hand, packing list is necessary for carrier to arrange loading, unloading and transshipment during transportation, for customs to verify the outgoing cargo and the incoming cargo, and for the importer to inventory the incoming consignment.

NOTE: The packing list is a more detailed version of the commercial invoice but without price information. The type of each container is identified, as well as its individual weight and measurements. The packing list is attached to the outside of its respective container in a waterproof envelop marked "packing list enclosed", and is immediately available to authorities in both the countries of export and import.

The packing list is a more detailed version of the commercial invoice but without price information. The type of each container is identified, as well as its individual weight and measurements. Generally speaking, the packing list should include the following elements: (1) name and address of the seller; (2) name of the "Packing List"; (3) name and address of the buyer; (4) invoice number; (5) order or contract number; (6) date of issuance; (7) quantities and descriptions of the goods; (8) shipping details including: weight of the goods, number of packages, and shipping mark & number; (9) quantity and description of contents of each package, carton, crate or container; (10) any other information as required in the documentary L/C. Here is the Packing List example according to the Document Instance 7-5.

Document Instance 7-5

锦州和泰矿物有限公司

JINZHOU HOTIY MINERAL CORPORATION

HOTIY BUILDING, 37-2 VICTORY STREET, JINZHOU CITY, LIAONING, CHINA

PCKING LIST

EXPORTER: JIZHOU HOTIY MINERAL CORPORATION HOTIY BUILDING, 37-2 VICTORY STREET, JINZHOU CITY, LIAONING, CHINA	INVOICE NO.: HSF110120	DATE: JAN. 15, 2012
	S/C NO.: 03HL21801	L/C NO.: CDMS2011U/5539
TO: SHUANGSHENT INVESTMENT AND TRADING CO., LTD PEACE ROAD MARSHALL ISLANDS MH 96890, KAOHSIUNG	TRANSPORT DETIALS: B/L NO: TF12S68 FROM: XINGANG PORT, CHINA TO: KAOHSIUNG, TAIWAN BY VESSVEL: SKY FORTUNE V.152E	
SHIPPING MARK	DESCRIPTION OF GOODS QUANTITY GROSS NET	
N/M	FERRO MOLYBDENUM MO: 58.00PCT MT KG KG SI: 0.42PCT C: 0.024 PCT 40MTS 40056KGS 40000KGS S: 0.082 PCT P: 0.040 PCT CU: 0.24 PCT SIZE 10—60MM(90 PCT MIN) PACKING: IN 1MT SUPER BAGS WITH BOTTOM DISCHARGE SPOUT TOTAL: 40 BAGS ONLY <div align="right">锦州和泰矿物有限公司(章) JINZHOU HOTIY MINERAL CORPOARATION</div>	

7.5.2 Certificate of Origin

A certificate of origin is an independent document issued by an authority, evidencing the goods originated from a particular country. It is the basic document for the customs clearance in importing country to levy the import duty.

原产地证明书是卖方应进口商的要求,自行签发或向特定的机构申请后由其签发的,证明出口商品的产地或制造地的一种证明文件。

The certificate of origin is typically required by the importer's country as a requirement for import processing. If you are the importer and your country requires such documentation, make sure that you specify in the documentary L/C the documentation as specified by your country's customs authority.

Buyers should avoid the use of such terms as "first class", "well-known", "qualified", "independent", "official", "competent", or "local" when referring to the certifying authority. It is preferable to specifically name the required certifying authority. Use of vague terminology (as above) will result in the bank's acceptance of any relevant document that appears "on its face" to be in compliance with the documentary L/C, so long as it was not issued (signed) by the beneficiary (the seller).

In certain countries the certificate of origin is prepared by the seller (the beneficiary to the documentary L/C) on a standard form and then certified (with a signature, stamp or seal) by the certifying authority. Certifying authorities most often used are city and regional chambers of commerce and chambers of commerce and industry.

The certification of origin is an alternative to the declaration or the certification and/or legalization of the commercial invoice. The certificate of origin is based on the rules of the country of origin.

The country of origin is the country where the goods are grown, produced or manufactured. The manufactured goods must have been substantially transformed in the exporting country as the country of origin, to their present form ready for export. Certain operations such as packaging, splitting and sorting may not be considered as sufficient operations to confer origin.

Four kinds of Certificate of Origin are generally adopted in our country: (1) certificate of Origin which is issued by CIQ (China Exit and Entry Inspection and Quarantine Bureau) or CCPTT (China Council for the Promotion of International Trade); (2) generalized System of Preference Certificate of Origin Form (GSP Form A) which is issued by CIQ, which may be used to get preferential import duties in countries that give us GSP preferential treatments, such as New Zealand, Canada, Japan, EU members, etc.; (3) certificate of Origin Textile Product issued by the local department of commerce to apply for quota, and when we export textiles to EU countries, this certificate together with Form A shall be submitted; (4) country Declaration for Export to America, which applies to quota commodities and falls into three forms: Form A (Single Country Declaration), Form B (Multiple Country Declaration) and Form C (Negative Declaration).

- **Certificate of Origin of the People's Republic of China**(一般原产地证明书)

Certificate of Origin of the People's Republic of China should include the following elements: (1) exporter, with the full name and detailed address of exporter ended with the name of one's country/region. The exporter should be the same as that in column No. 11; (2) certificate No.; (3) consignee, covering the full name and detailed address of the end consignee①; (4) means of Transport and route, which includes port of shipment and destination, date of shipment and means of transport; (5) country/region of destination; (6) for certifying authority use only; (7) marks and numbers; (8) number and kind of packages description of the goods; (9) H. S. Code;② (10) quantity; (11) number and date of the invoices; (12) declaration by the exporter; (13) place and date, signature and stamp of the certifying authority.

一般原产地证明书,简称产地证,是指中华人民共和国出口货物原产地证明书,它是证明中国出口货物符合《中华人民共和国货物原产地规则》,确实是中华人民共和国原产地的证明文件。

- **Generalized System of Preference Certificate of Origin Form A**(普惠制产地证表格 A)

In international trade, some importing countries require a certificate of origin to establish whether or not a preferential duty rate is applicable. A popular example of the certificate of origin is the Generalized System of Preference Certificate of Origin Form A, which is often called the GSP Form A.

A GSP certificate of origin Form A is a certificate used to obtain the treatment of preferential customs duty imposed by the developed country on the developing countries. China began to use it in 1978. It should include the following elements: (1) goods consigned from (exporter's business name, address, country); (2) goods consigned to (consignee's name, address, country); (3) means of transport and route (as far as known); (4) for official use; (5) item number; (6) marks and numbers of packages; (7) number and kind of packages & description of goods; (8) origin criterion; (9) gross weight or other quantity; (10) number and date of invoices; (11) place and date, signature and stamp of certifying authority; (12) declaration by the exporter. Here is an example of certificate of origin as shown in Document Instance 7-6.

普遍优惠制是发达国家对发展中国家向其出口的制成品或半成品货物时,普遍给予的一种关税优惠待遇的制度。凡享受普惠制待遇的商品,出口方一般应向给惠国提供原产地证书表格 A。

---

① The consignee usually is the importer of the business; notify party in the L/C or consignee on the B/L. Sometimes the L/C requires "Blank" here, "TO WHOM IT MAY CONCERN" or "TO ORDER" or " *** " is marked here.

② HS code is mainly used international materials and commercial products system of information classification and code.

Document Instance 7-6

1. Goods consigned from (Exporter's business name, address, Country) JINZHOU HOTIY MINERAL CORPORATION HOTIY BUILDING, 37-2 VICTORY STREET, JINZHOU CITY, LIAONING, CHINA	Reference No. 0013991 GENERALIZED SYSTEM OF PREFERENCES CERTIFICATE OF ORIGIN (Combined declaration and certificate) FORM A Issued in THE PEOPLE'S REPUBLIC OF CHINA (country) See Notes overleaf
2. Goods consigned to (Consignee's name, address, country) SHUANGSHENT INVESTMENT AND TRADING CO., LTD PEACE ROAD MARSHALL ISLANDS MH96890, KAOHSIUNG	
3. Means of transport and route (as far as known) FORM XINGANG PORT OF CHINA TO KAOHSIUNG, TAIWAN BY SEA.	4. For official use

5. Item number	6. Marks and numbers of packages	7. Number and kind of packages; description of goods	8. Origin criterion (see Notes overleaf)	9. Gross weight or other quantity	10. Number and date of invoices
1	N/M	40 (FORTY-BAGS) OF FERRO MOLYBDENUM ********************** L/C NO.: CDMS2011U/5539	"P"	40.0566MT	HSF120120 JAN.15, 2012

| 11. Certification
It is hereby certified, on the basis of control carried out, that the declaration by the exporter is correct.

JINZHOU JAN.18, 2008 (检验机构手签员签字)
Place and date, signature and stamp of certifying authority | 12. Declaration by the exporter
The undersigned hereby declares that the above details and statements are correct; that all the goods were produced in
CHINA
(country)
and that they comply with the origin requirements specified for those goods in the Generalized System of Preferences for goods exported to
TAIWAN
(importing country)
JINZHOU JAN. 18, 2012 (出口企业手签员签字)
Place and date, signature of authorized signatory |

7.5.3 Inspection Certificate

Inspection certificate is a document issued by an authority, indicating that the goods have been inspected prior to shipment and the results of the inspection. The purpose of Inspection Certificate is to ensure that the quality and quantity of merchandise have come up to the standard or specifications mentioned in sales contract.

商检证书是各种商品检验证书、鉴定证书和其他证明书的统称,是由中国出入境检验检疫局以国家行政机构的身份,对进出口商品进行检验和鉴定后对外签发的、具有法律效力的证书,它是证明卖方所交货物与合同规定是否相符的依据,也是报关验放的有效凭证。

Inspection certificates are generally obtained from neutral testing organizations, e.g., government entity or independent service company. Buyer should avoid the use of such terms as "first class", "well-known", "qualified", "independent", "official", "competent" or "local" when referring to an acceptable inspection authority. It is preferable to agree beforehand as to a specific inspection organization or entity and for the buyer to name the required certifying organization or entity in the documentary credit.

The most commonly used inspection certificates in international trade are as follows:
- Inspection Certificate of Quality;
- Inspection Certificate of Weight;
- Inspection Certificate of Quantity;
- Inspection Certificate of Analysis;
- Inspection Certificate of Veterinary;
- Inspection Certificate of Plant Quarantine;
- Inspection Certificate of Sanitary/Health;
- Inspection Certificate of Disinfection/Sterilization;
- Inspection Certificate of Temperature;
- Inspection Certificate of Fumigation;
- Inspection Certificate of Packing;
- Inspection Certificate on Damaged Cargo.

In documentary L/C transactions, an inspection certificate should include the following elements: (1) key details regarding the shipment, which should be in conformity with other documents (e.g., documentary L/C, commercial invoice); (2) date of inspection; (3) statement of sampling methodology; (4) statement of the results of the inspection; (5) the name, signature and/or stamp or seal of the inspection entity.

中华人民共和国出入境检验检疫
ENTRY-EXIT INSPECTION AND QUARANTITE
OF THE PEOPLE'S REPUBLIC OF CHINA

ORIGINAL

编号 No.: 2107012010906

共 1 页 第 1 页   Page 1 of 1

CERTIFICATE OF QUALITY

发货人 **JINZHOU HOTIY MINERAL CORPORATION**
Consignor **HOTIY BUILDING, 37-2 VICTORY STREET, JINZHOU CITY, LIAONING, CHINA**

收货人 **SHUANGSHENT   INVESTMENT AND TRADING CO., LTD**
Cosignee **PEACE ROA DMARSHALL ISLANDS MH 96890, KAOHSIUNG**

品名   标记及号码
Description of Goods **FERRO MOLYBDENUM**   Mark & No.   **N/M**

报检数量/重量
Quantity/Weight Declared **- 40-MT/-40 BAGS**

包装种类及数量
Number and Type of Packages **-40- BAGS**

运输工具
Means of Conveyance **BY SEA**

UPON THE APPLICATION OF THE CONSIGNOR, OUR INSPECTORS INSPECTED THIS LOT OF COMMODITY, THE DETAILS WERE AS FOLLOWS:

CONDITION OF GOODS: PACKED IN 1MT SUPER BAGS WITH BOTTOM DISCHARGE SPOUT AND SEALED WELL AFTER SAMPLING LOT IN ORDER.

SAMPLING: IN ACCORDANCE WITH THE STANDARD NO. ZB/T4010-94, 10 BAGS WERE OPENED AT THE FACTORY, FROM WHICH ABOUT 80 KGS OF REPRESENTATIVES WERE DRAWN ON 18 JAN, 2012 AND CRUSHED TO 10MM DOWN, OF WHICH 7KGS WERE MADE THOUGH MIXING & DEDUCTING AND RECRUSHED TO 2.8MM DOWN TO PREP ARE THE REQUIRED SAMPLE.

INSPECTION: THE ABOVE MENTIONED SAMPLE WAS INSPECTED ACCORDING TO THE CONTRACT AND OTHER RELEVANT STANDARDS WITH THE RESULTS AS FOLLOWS:

MO: 58.00PCT   SI: 0.42PCT   C: 0.024 PCT
S: 0.082 PCT   P: 0.040 PCT   CU: 0.24 PCT

SIZE 10--60MM (90 PCT MIN) CONCLUSION: THE QUALITY OF THIS LOT OF COMMODITY MEETS THE CONTRACT NO. HSF120120 AND THE L/C NO. CDMS2011U/5539

印章: 签证地点 Place of Issue **JINZHOU, CHINA**   签证日期 Date of Issue **JAN. 19, 2012**
Official Stamp   授权签字人 Authorized Officer **XXX** 签名 Signature **XXX**

我们已尽所知和最大能力实施上述检验,不能因我们签发本证书而免除卖方或其他方面根据合同和法律所承担的产品质量责任和其他责任。All inspections are carried out conscientiously to the best of our knowledge and ability. This certificate dose not in any respect absolves the seller and other related parties from his contractual and legal obligations especially when product quality is concerned.

B1001536

7.5.4 Export License

An export license is a document prepared by a government authority of a nation granting the right to export a specific quantity of a commodity to a specified country. This document is often required for the exportation of certain natural resources, national treasures, drugs, strategic commodities, and arms and armaments.

出口许可证是指商务部授权发证机关依法对实行数量限制或其他限制的出口货物签发的准予出口的许可证件。出口许可证制是一国对外出口货物实行管制的一项措施。

The export license of each country will have its own form and content. Certain elements are likely to be included in all export licenses: (1) name and address of the seller; (2) name and address of the buyer; (3) date of issuance; (4) validity date; (5) description of the goods covered by license; (6) name of country of origin; (7) name of country of ultimate destination.

Some countries require export licenses for virtually all commodities and products. The license is a means of control and taxation. In some cases the lack of an export license can be cited as a reason why goods cannot be shipped, even though payment has been made. Buyers should be especially careful about buying sensitive goods from countries with a demonstrated lack of rule by law.

The export license is typically the responsibility of the seller. However, if the buyer is dealing in sensitive goods, he should research the need for an export license beforehand. Failure to secure such a license can delay or prevent shipment and jeopardize the validity of a documentary L/C.

7.6 Documents Examination and Disposal of Discrepancies

案例 7-1

某年3月,美国Beyene公司出口一批货物给也门的Moham-ITledSofan公司,当时,进口商通过也门复兴开发银行开出信用证给美国出口公司,并指定美国欧文银行为该信用证的保兑银行。同年5月货物运出后,出口公司将单据提交给欧文银行请求付款,欧文银行发现提单中所载通知人名字系Mohamed Sofan公司而非Moham-ITledSofan公司,认为不符信用证规定,虽然欧文银行也曾向也门复兴开发银行请求授权其付款,但复兴开发银行坚持拒绝授权付款。

Beyene公司(受益人)认为通知人名字打错而遭开证行拒绝付款是开证行过分挑剔,即向法院起诉,要求保兑行付款并负担因其未按信用证付款而使原告所受之损失,欧文银行则以多项理由请求其地方法院驳回了原告的起诉。

Beyene公司不服地方法院的驳回,声称仅名字拼错不足以解除保兑行的付款责任并以此为理由再行上诉,上诉法院结果作了如下判决:

通常信用证条款要求受益人向开证行交付有关单据,使开证人相信他可以得到所购的货物才能据以付款。只要受益人严格遵照信用证条款履行,开证行或保兑行应承担"绝对付款的义务"。为维护开证行或保兑行的权益,其绝对付款义务,只有在信用证条款被严格遵守时才能发生。因此,银行对出口商的付款按承诺是严格建立在"单单相符,单证相符"的基础之上的。

(注:案例改写自国际贸易理论与实务,案例汇编 http://soft.studa.com。)

7.6.1 Documents Examination

Examining documents must be considered as a vital step in the whole transaction.

- Principles of of examining documents are as follows: (1) parties examining documents should be strict but with reasonable care; (2) all parties except the beneficiary have to complete examination within a reasonable period, normally up to seven banking days after receiving documents; (3) the documents must comply with terms and conditions of the credit; (4) the documents must be consistent with each other; (5) the parties involved only check documents clearly identified in the L/C, non-document conditions would be ignored.
- Procedure of examining documents differs from country to country and even from bank to bank. Procedure listed following can be considered as a reference or a recommendation:
  - ➢ Tosort and count types and numbers of documents received;
  - ➢ To write a receipt of documents package in duplicate, indicating the date of receipt, one of them should be returned to party from which the document are received;
  - ➢ To compare documents with the L/C. The sequence of comparison is firstly in vertical direction and then in horizontal direction. So-called "vertical" means that all documents are to be compared with L/C, in detail, items in various documents should be consistent with those stated in the credit. "Horizontal" means that all documents are to be compared with invoice. All discrepancies should be listed out during the comparison, and written down in the column of "discrepancies and action taken" on the list.

7.6.2 Documents Checklists

In the practice of international settlements, the seller/exporter/beneficiary has the responsibility of preparing and presenting documents in accordance with the terms of the documentary L/C or collection. If the documents are incorrect or inconsistent there is a risk of having them refused, wasting time and money, and possibly imperiling the transaction itself. The issuing (buyer's) bank has the responsibility of examining the documents package presented by the seller/beneficiary to make certain they are consistent with the documentary L/C or collection. The advising bank (often the confirming bank as well) has the responsibility of examining the documents presented by the issuing bank to determine if they are consistent with the requirements of the documentary L/C or collection. The buyer/importer/applicant first has the responsibility of listing documents that are required of the seller in the documentary L/C. Upon presentation by the bank the buyer examines documents for consistency and accuracy. Problems with documents often lead to problems securing goods from the shipping company or customs or receiving unwanted or incorrect goods.

The following are a series of checklists that can be used in document examination in the international settlements. They are not fully comprehensive as there are an almost infinite number of transaction variations possible, some of which require specialized procedures and documentation. Therefore, they should be viewed only as a general guide.

- **The Draft**

1. Is the name of the drawee correct?
2. Is the name of the payee correct?
3. Does the draft contain the "to the order of" notation?
4. Does the draft contain an expiration date?
5. Does the draft contain an unconditional instruction to pay?
6. Are the amounts in words and figures identical?
7. Is the draft drawn on the party named in the documentary L/C?
8. If the draft is made out to own order (ourselves), is it endorsed?
9. Does the draft contain any and all notations as stipulated in the L/C? (i.e., drawn under L/C number _____)?
10. Does the draft name the place and date of issue?
11. Does the draft bear the signature of the issuer?
12. Are the values of the draft, invoices, and the L/C consistent?

- **Commercial Invoice**

1. Is the invoice issued by the seller/beneficiary as named in the L/C?
2. Is the invoice issued to the buyer/applicant as named in the L/C?
3. Is the invoice issued to the correct address of the buyer/applicant as stated in the documentary L/C?
4. Does the description of the goods in the invoice correspond exactly to their description in the documentary L/C?
5. Does the quantity of the goods in the invoice correspond exactly to the quantities specified in the documentary L/C?
6. Does the value of the goods (unit price and total price) correspond exactly to the values specified in the documentary L/C?
7. Does the invoice amount not exceed the amount of the documentary L/C?

8. Is the invoice free of any unauthorized charges?

9. Does the currency used in pricing in the invoice match that of the documentary L/C?

10. Does the invoice state the delivery terms (e.g., CIF, EXW)?

11. Do the delivery terms stated in the invoice match those specified in the documentary L/C?

12. If required by the documentary L/C, is the invoice signed?

13. If required by the documentary L/C, does the invoice bear proper certifications, authorizations, or legalizations?

14. If required by the documentary L/C, does the invoice contain any special marks, numbers, or other notations?

- **The Transport Document(s)**

1. Does the transport document contain the correct consignee name and address as specified in the L/C?

2. Does the transport document contain an "on board" notation?

3. Does the transport document contain a notation naming the vessel?

4. Does the transport document contain a notation of the on board date?

5. Does the transport document name the correct port of loading and port of destination as stipulated in the documentary L/C?

6. Is the transport document "clean" (without notations for shortage, loss, or damage)?

7. If the transport document states "on deck" stowage, it is allowed by the L/C?

8. If required by the documentary L/C, is the "notify address" listed?

9. Was the transport document issued within the period specified in the documentary L/C?

10. Is the full set of originals being presented?

11. Is the transport document not a charter party document, unless authorized by the documentary L/C?

12. Is the transport document not a forwarder's transport document, unless authorized by the documentary L/C?

13. Is the quantity and description of the goods consistent with that contained in the documentary L/C?

14. Are the marks and numbers on the transport document consistent with those on other documents?

15. Are the freight payments terms consistent with those stipulated in the documentary L/C?

16. Does the transport document meet the stipulations of the documentary L/C with regard to transshipment?

17. Does the transport document meet all other stipulations of the documentary L/C?

● **Insurance Document**

1. Was the insurance document issued as either a policy or as a certificate as stipulated in the L/C?

2. Is the insurance document issued and signed by an insurance carrier, underwriter, or their agent (not by a broker)?

3. Does the insurance document cover all the risks specified in the L/C?

4. Does the insurance document cover the risks resulting from a) the particular mode of shipment, b) the transport route, or c) reloading or "on deck" storage, etc. ?

5. Does the insurance document indicate that cover is effective at the latest from the date of loading of the goods on board or the taking in charge of the goods by the carrier, as indicated by the transport document?

6. Is the information in the insurance document concerning mode of transport and transport route consistent with the documentary L/C?

7. Does the document specify coverage for at least 110 percent of either a) the CIF or CIP value of the shipment, or, if that information is not provided, b) the amount of the payment, acceptance or negotiation specified in the documentary L/C, or c) the gross amount of the invoice?

8. Is the currency of the insurance document consistent with the L/C?

9. Have all issued originals of the document been presented?

10. If endorsement is required, is the document properly endorsed?

● **Packing List**

1. Is the name and address of the seller as specified in the L/C?

2. Is the name and address of the buyer as specified in the L/C?

3. Is the date of issuance correct?

4. Are the invoice numbers, contract numbers, order numbers, and any other numbers correct and in conformity with the documentary L/C?

5. Is the quantity and description of the goods in conformity with the L/C?

6. Are all shipping details correct including: weight of the goods, number of packages, and shipping marks and numbers?

7. Is other information included as required (e.g., country of origin)?

● **Certificate of Origin**

1. Is the name and address of the seller as specified in the L/C?

2. Is the name and address of the buyer as specified in the L/C?

3. Is the date of issuance correct?

4. Is the quantity and description of the goods in conformity with the documentary L/C?

5. Is the country of origin named and in conformity with the documentary L/C?

6. Is the issuer named and in conformity with the documentary L/C?

7. Does the document bear the signature, stamp, or authentication of the issuer?

8. Is any other information included as required in the documentary L/C?

- **Inspection Certificate**

1. Does the inspection certificate contain key details of the consignor, consignee, and inspection entity?

2. Does the inspection certificate contain a description of the goods that is consistent with the description of goods in the L/C?

3. Does the inspection certificate contain the date of the inspection?

4. Does the inspection certificate contain a statement of the sampling methodology?

5. Does the inspection certificate contain a statement of the results of the inspection?

6. Does the inspection certificate contain the name, signature, and/or stamp or seal of the inspecting entity?

7.6.3 Disposal of Discrepancies

Discrepancies refer to that documents presented under a credit are missing or/and have one or more points which are not consistent with those in the L/C or in any other documents.

In the event of discrepancies, the security given by the L/C is largely lost, as a documentary L/C is undertaking of payment with prerequisite, where terms and conditions in the documents presented are on face consistent with those in the L/C.

The discrepancies, commonly not acceptable by the bank involved, are listed as follows:

✓ L/C expired

✓ Bill of exchange drawn on the buyer or a wrong party

✓ Bill of exchange payable on an undeterminable time

✓ Amount on the bill of exchange exceeding that of the L/C

✓ Description of goods on the invoice different from that sown in the L/C

✓ Being an unclean bill of lading

✓ No notation "shipped on board" in a marine bill of lading

✓ Place of loading on board/dispatch/taking in charge and destination being inconsistent with those stated in the L/C

✓ Bill of lading not showing the freight paid or not

✓ Late shipment

✓ Short shipment

✓ Goods shipped on desk

✓ Type of insurance document being rather than that required by the L/C

✓ Insurance risks covered not as specified in the L/C

✓ Under-insured

- ✓ Date of insurance issuance being later than that of transport document marks and package numbers inconsistent between documents
- ✓ Weight different between documents
- ✓ Documents inconsistent with each other
- ✓ Absence of documents called for in the L/C
- ✓ Instruments such as bill of exchange, insurance document and bill of exchange not endorsed correctly
- ✓ Absence of signature required on the documents
- ✓ Documents presentation not in time

Banks concerned have up to five banking days following the receipt of documents to examine and notify the party, from which it received the documents, of documents being order or not.

When a bank finding out discrepancies in the document, several options may be selected:

- ✓ The nominated bank or confirming bank in the interest of the beneficiary can point out the discrepancies and return them to beneficiary. If the beneficiary due to his apparent careless introduces discrepancies in creating documents, such as typing mistakes, spelling mistakes, whatever, he can correct or replace them;
- ✓ The nominated bank remits the documents with discrepancies continuously to the issuing bank, draws its attention to the discrepancies, and informs the latter that it has paid or negotiated under or against an indemnity in respect of such discrepancies. If the issuing bank decides to reject the documents, it must notice to the bank from which it received the documents by telecommunication, not later than the close of the seven banking days following the day of receipt of the documents;
- ✓ The nominated bank ask for an authorization from the issuing bank to pay, accept or negotiate at the request of the beneficiary;
- ✓ The nominated bank sends the documents with discrepancy, if not essential, to the issuing bank continuously, which effects his responsibility for payment, or acceptance, or negotiation, but in the meantime, asks for an guarantee from the seller or reimburse the proceeds if the issuing bank does not honor the documents at presentation.
- ✓ The nominated bank dispatches the documents with discrepancies continuously to the issuing bank without effecting his obligation of payment, or acceptance, or negotiation. That eventually changes a payment under documentary credit to that under documentary collection, which is subject to the Uniform Rules of Documentary Collection No.522.
- ✓ The issuing bank, if it feels that the discrepancies are not fatal to the transaction,

can confer with the buyer on a waiver for the specific discrepancies, but must do so within seven working days.
- ✓ The bank, which received the documents and found discrepancy, refuses to accept them. If the bank decides to refuse to accept the documents in the event of discrepancies, it has to: (1) notify the party, from which it received the documents, its decision by telecommunication or by other expeditions means, not later than the close of the fifth banking day following the day of receipt of the documents, otherwise, it has no right to refuse to effect its obligation; (2) points out all the discrepancies in respect of which it refuses the documents at one time; (3) state keeping documents at the disposal of presenter or send all documents directly back to the presenter.

In cases where the L/C expiry date is near and under circumstances beyond the exporter's control that a discrepancy has occurred, if the discrepancy will not adversely affect the importer in his imports and/or performance of the business, the exporter may inform the importer of the discrepancy and request him to confirm accepting the discrepancy by fax. At the same time, the exporter may request the importer to instruct his issuing bank to accept the discrepancy, rather than requesting an L/C amendment which costs more to both the importer and the exporter. The exporter may attach the fax confirming acceptance of the discrepancy to the documents for presentation to the bank. Nevertheless, not all the banks will accept a fax confirmation of acceptance of the discrepancy, particularly if the exporter does not maintain business accounts with the negotiating bank.

Generally speaking, problem of dishonor by the paying bank due to the discrepancy, if not fraudulent, can be solved in compromise by the seller or the buyer, for example, waiving discrepancies, cutting down price, changing by means of payment of collection, and so on.

★ Key Words

Commercial Invoice(商业发票)　　　　Customs Invoice(海关发票)
Proforma Invoice(形式发票)　　　　　Consular Invoice(领事发票)
Transport Documents(运输单据)　　　Marine Bill of Lading(海运提单)
Clean B/L(清洁提单)　　　　　　　　Unclean B/L(不清洁提单)
Received for shipment B/L(待运提单)　Shipped on board B/L(已装船提单)
Direct B/L(直达提单)　　　　　　　　Transshipment B/L(转船提单)
Through B/L(联运提单)　　　　　　　Straight B/L(记名提单)
Open B/L(不记名提单)　　　　　　　Order B/L(指示性提单)
Short form B/L(简式提单)　　　　　　Long form B/L(全式提单)
Liner B/L(班轮提单)　　　　　　　　Charter party B/L(租船提单)

Stale B/L(过期提单)   Anti-dated B/L(倒签提单)
Non-negotiable sea waybill(不可流通转让的海运单)
Multimodal Transport Document(多式运输单据)
Airway Bill(航空运单)   Railway Bill(铁路运单)
Insurance Policy(大保单)   Insurance Certificate(小保单)
Inspection Certificate(商品检验证明)   Certificate of Origin(原产地证明)
Generalized System of Preference,GSP(普惠制产地证)
Packing List(装箱单)

★ Exercise

一、单项选择(Exclusive Choice Question)

1. 发票上的货物数量应与信用证一致,如信用证在数量前使用"约"、"大约"字眼时,应理解为:(   )。
   A. 货物数量有不超过5%的增减幅度
   B. 货物数量有不超过10%的增减幅度
   C. 货物数量有不超过3%的增减幅度
   D. 货物数量不得增减

2. 信用证要求提供厂商发票的目的是:(   )。
   A. 查验货物是否已经加工生产
   B. 核对货物数量是否与商业发票相符
   C. 检查是否有反倾销行为
   D. 确认货物数量是否符合要求

3. 下列的保险的险别中文与英文翻译正确的是(   )。
   A. 偷窃、提货不着险条款 Fresh Water &/or Rain Damage Clause.
   B. 淡水、雨淋险条款 Shortage Clause.
   C. 碰损、破碎险条款 Clash & Breakage Clause.
   D. 受潮受热险条款 Intermixture & Contamination Clause.

4. 信用证中规定"PACKING LIST IN FIVE COPIES",则受益人提交的装箱单的份数为(   )。
   A. 5份副本   B. 1份正本4份副本
   C. 不需要提交正本   D. 5份正本至5份副本

5. 所谓"信用证严格相符"的原则,是指受益人必须做到(   )。
   A. 信用证和合同相符   B. 信用证和货物相符
   C. 信用证和单据相符   D. 合同和货物相符

6. 信用证上如未明确付款人,则制作汇票时,受票人应为(   )。
   A. 申请人   B. 开证银行   C. 议付行   D. 任何人

7. 某外贸公司的工作人员因为在审证过程中粗心大意,未能发现合同发票上的公司名称与公司印章的名称不一致,合同发票上的是 ABC Corporation,而印章上则是 ABC,

仅一词之差,此时又恰逢国际市场价格有变,在这种情况下(　　)。
　　A. 外商有权拒绝付款　　　　　　B. 责任在外商
　　C. 外商应按规定如期付款　　　　D. 拒付
8. 海运提单的签发日期是(　　)。
　　A. 货物开始装船的日期　　　　　B. 货物装船完毕的日期
　　C. 船只到达装运港的日期　　　　D. 船只离开装运港的日期
9. 采用信用证与托收相结合的支付方式时,全套货运单据应(　　)。
　　A. 随托收部分汇票项下　　　　　B. 随信用证的汇票项下
　　C. 直接寄往进口商　　　　　　　D. 留在卖方

二、判断题(True or False)
1. 如果合同和信用证中均未规定具体唛头,则填写发票时,"唛头"一栏可以空白不填。(　　)
2. 信用证要求 PACKING LIST TO BE MADE OUT IN NEUTRAL FORM,则装箱单中不能显示出具人名称。(　　)
3. 商业发票上的货物描述应详细,而装箱单的货物描述只需用商品品名。(　　)
4. 装箱单的主要作用是补充商业发票内容的不足,便于买方掌握商品的包装、数量及供进口国海关检查和核对货物。(　　)
5. 商业发票的日期应早于提单的日期。(　　)
6. 除非信用证另有规定,商业发票必须由信用证的受益人开立。(　　)

三、案例分析(Case Analysis)
1. 一份国外来证规定货物在 1 月、2 月份分两次装运(IN TWO SHIPMENTS)。出口公司在 1 月 31 日和 2 月 2 日分两次把货物装到同一航次的同一艘船上,取得两份提单(提单日期分别为 1 月 31 日和 2 月 2 日),当单据送交银行时,银行因为不符合信用证规定,拒绝支付货款。问:银行这样做是否合理?
2. 我国 A 公司向巴基斯坦 B 公司以 CIF 条件出口一批货物。国外来证中单据条款规定:"商业发票一式两份;全套清洁已装船提单,注明运费预付,做成指示抬头空白背书;保险单一式两份,根据中国人民保险公司 1981 年 1 月 1 日海洋运输货物保险条款投保一切险和战争险。"信用证内并注明"按 UCP600 办理"。
A 公司在信用证规定的装运期限内将货物装上船,并于到期日前向议付行交单议付,议付行随即向开证行寄单索偿。开证行收到单据后,来电表示拒绝付款,其理由是单证有以下不符点:
(1) 商业发票上没有受益人的签字;
(2) 正本提单是以一份组成,不符合全套要求;
(3) 保险单上的保险金额与发票金额相等,因此投保金额不足。
问:分析开证行单证不符的理由是否成立?并说明理由。

四、实务操作题(Practice)
1. 根据下列内容填制汇票一份。

ISSUING BANK: DEUTCHE BANK (ASIA) HONGKONG
L/C NO. AND DATE: 756/05/1495988, NOV. 20, 2014
AMOUNT: USD 1974500.00
APPLICANT: MELCHERS (H. K) LTD., RM. 1210, SHUNTAK CENTER, 200 CONNAUGHT ROAD, CENTRAL, HONGKONG
BENEFICIARY: CHINA NATIONAL ARTS AND CRAFTS IMP. & EXP. CORP. GUANG DONG (HOLDINGS) BRANCH.

WE OPENED IRREVOCABLE DOCUMENTS CREDIT AVAILABLE BY NEGOTIATION AGAINST PRESENTATION OF THE DOCUMENTS DETAILED HEREIN AND OF BENEFICIARY'S DRAFTS IN DUPLICATE AT SIGHT DRAWN ON OUR BANK.

INV. NO.: ITBE001121
DATE OF NEGOTIATION: DEC. 20, 2014

2. 根据下列国外来证及有关信息制作所要求单据。

AWC-14-522 号合同项下商品的有关信息如下：该批商品用纸箱包装，每箱装 10 盒，每箱净重为 75 千克，毛重为 80 千克，纸箱尺寸为 113cm×56cm×30cm，商品编码为 6802.2110，货物由"海华"轮运输出海。

FROM: HONGKONG AND SHANGHAI BANKING CORP., HONGKONG
TO: BANK OF CHINA, XIAMEN BRANCH, XIAMEN CHINA
TEST: 12345 DD.010705 BETWEEN YOUR HEAD OFFICE AND US. PLEASE CONTACT YOUR NO. FOR VERIFICATION.
WE HEREBY ISSUED AN IRREVOCABLE LETTER OF CREDIT
NO. HKH123123 FOR USD 844000.00, DATE 140705.
APPLICANT: PROSPERITY INDUSTRIAL CO. LTD.
342-3 FLYING BUILDING KINGDOM STREET HONGKONG
NO. 88 YILA ROAD 13/F XIANG YE BLOOK RONG HUA BUILDING, XIAMEN, CHINA
THIS L/C IS AVAILABLE WITH BENEFICIARY'S DRAFT AT 30 DAYS AFTER SIGHT DRAWN ON US ACCOMPANIED BY THE FOLLOWING DOCUMENTS:
1. SIGNED COMMERCIAL INVOICE IN TRIPLICATE.
2. PACKING LIST IN TRIPLICATE INDICATING ALL PACKAGE MUST BE PACKED IN CARTON/NEW IRON DRUM SUITABLE FOR LONG DISTANCE OCEAN TRANSPORTATION.
3. CERTIFICATE OF CHINESE ORIGIN IN DUPLICATE.
4. FULL SET OF CLEAN ON BOARD OCEAN MARINE BILL OF LADING MADE OUT TO ORDER AND BLANK ENDORSED MARKED "FREIGHT PREPAID" AND NOTIFY APPLICANT.
5. INSURANCE POLICY OF CERTIFICATE IN DUPLICATE ENDORSED IN BLANK FOR THE VALUE OF 110 PERCENT OF THE INVOICE COVERING FPA/WA/ALL RISKS AND WAR RISK AS PER CIC DATED 1/1/81.

续表

SHIPMENT FROM: XIAMEN, CHINA. SHIPMENT TO: HONGKONG
LATEST SHIPMENT: 31 AUGUST, 2014
PARTIAL SHIPMENT IS ALLOWED, TRANSHIPMENT IS NOT ALLOWED.
COVERING SHIPMENT OF:
COMMODITY AND SPECIFICATIONS   QUANTITY   UNIT PRICE   AMOUNT
1625/3D GLASS MARBLE   2000BOXES   USD 2.39/BOX   USD 4,780.00   CIF HONGKONG.
1641/3D GLASS MARBLE   1000BOXES   USD 1.81/BOX   USD 1,810.00
2506D   GLASS MARBLE   1000BOXES   USD 1.85/BOX   USD 1,850.00

SHIPPING MARK: P.7.
             HONGKONG
             NO. 1-400
    ADDITIONAL CONDITIONS:
5 PERCENT MORE OR LESS BOTH IN QUANTITY AND AMOUNT IS ALLOWED.
    ALL BANKING CHARGES OUTSIDE ISSUING BANK ARE FOR ACCOUNT OF BENEFICIARY.
    DOCUMENTS TO BE PRESENTED WITHIN 15 DAYS AFTER THE DATE OF ISSUANCE OF THE SHIPPING DOCUMENT BUT WITHIN THE VALIDITY OF THE CREDIT.
    INSTRUCTIONS:
NEGOTIATING BANK IS TO SEND DOCUMENTS TO US IN ONE LOT BY DHL.
    UPON RECEIPT OF THE DOCUMENTS IN ORDER WE WILL COVER YOU AS PER YOUR INSTRUCTIONS.
    L/C EXPIRATION: 15 SEP. 2014.
    THIS L/C IS SUBJECT TO UNIFORM CUSTOMS AND PRACTICE FOR DOCUMENTARY EDITS INTERNATIONAL CHAMBER OF COMMERCE PUBLICATION NO. 600.
    PLEASE ADVISE THIS L/C TO THE BENEFICIARY WITHOUT ADDING YOUR INFORMATION.
    THIS TELEX IS THE OPERATIVE INSTRUMENT AND NO MAIL CONFIRMATION WILL BE FOLLOWED.

Chapter 8

Non-trade Settlement

Li Lei wants to go to America to study for two months. He is now confusing to choose which kind of financial consumption between cash, traveler's checks and international credit card. In fact, there are different ways in which funds can be transferred from one country to another under non-trade transactions. When the tourist, merchants, delegations or other people go abroad, they need money to spend, to buy something, or to pay various expenses and charges there. The most common means to carry funds are cash, traveler's cheque, traveler's credit and credit card.

★ Learning Objectives

(1) To enable the readers to understand the main contents of the non-trade settlement.

(2) To enable the readers to understand the definition of Overseas Chinese Remittance.

(3) To enable the readers to understand the business knowledge of traveler's cheque and international credit card.

8.1 Non-trade Settlement

International trade settlement and non-trade settlement constitute the two main elements of the country's international settlement business. Import and export of goods make a country obtain the foreign exchange. Besides trade, foreign exchange earnings come from other different sources, such as transport, insurance, financial, cultural and other labor or services, as well as unilateral transfer payments and so on. With the development of China's economic reform and opening up, the progress of science and technology, transportation, finance and insurance industry, the expansion of foreign exchange and other international cultural and sports exchanges, the increased adaptation of non-trade settlement in China is improving its position in the whole international business, and getting more attention from people.

The contents of non-trade settlement include overseas Chinese remittance, traveler's cheque and credit cards.

8.2 Overseas Chinese Remittance

Overseas Chinese remittance is the inward remittance from abroad to home. Inward remittance from abroad refers to the settlement of funds in which the remitter of a foreign country or of Hong Kong, Macao, and Taiwan areas transfers the fund to a local bank via an overseas bank, and the paying bank shall credit the designated payee's account according to the instructions of the remitting bank. Since the outward remittance bank accepts the materials and remits the fund to the business department, the inward bank informs the payee and enters the fund into the payee's account. The inward remittance can be accomplished within about three working days.

侨汇是华侨汇款的简称。它是居住在国外的华侨、有中国血统的外国人、港澳同胞从国外或港澳地区寄回用以赡养内地亲属的汇款。

In order to guarantee that you can receive the remittance from abroad within 2 or 3 working days, the payee should inform the overseas remitter of your ID number, contact telephone number, deposit account (if any) for specification on the remittance letter, so that the bank can contact you when receiving the fund.

The way of remittance includes telegraphic transfer (T/T), mail transfer (M/T), and banker's demand draft (D/D), among which T/T and D/D are used most commonly.

Telegraphic transfer, the quickest settlement tool, helps speed up cash flow. Also, overseas Chinese remittance is easy to operate and involves relatively lower costs.

侨汇与侨乡的经济变化

中国国内亲属与海外华侨华人之间的血缘、地缘关系通过侨汇和信件已经非常牢固。至改革开放前期,来自海外的侨汇很少用于再生产,主要用于扶助国内侨眷的生活。对中国政府来说,在填补贸易差额方面没有偿还义务的侨汇外币收入作为非贸易外汇收入来源是极为重要的。在 1950 年至 1988 年的 39 年期间,中国对外贸易为顺差,顺差额为163.52 亿美元,而在 16 年期间逆差额达到了 224.77 亿美元,两者相抵,逆差额为 61.24亿美元。1950-1988 年同期的侨汇达到了 96.10 亿美元,即使同期外贸逆差额 61.24 亿美元以侨汇相抵,侨汇仍剩余 34.86 亿美元。由此可见,侨汇对中国的国际收支平衡起到了重要的作用。

此外,就国内亲属的侨汇用途来看,从 1862 年至 1949 年中华人民共和国成立,侨汇对企业的投资占整体的不到 4%。20 世纪五六十年代,侨汇 60% 用于生活费用,20% 用于建筑,10% 用于投资和公益事业,10% 用于冠婚葬祭。

正式将侨汇用于再生产必需等待中国进入商品经济时代。即:自 1979 年开始的改革开放时代,随着商品经济的发展,侨汇除了以往那种海外票汇之外,或寄物,或回乡时带回外币,以多种途径投入侨乡的的企业发展和生产发展。

(资料来源:山岸猛,司韦.侨汇与侨乡的经济变化(上)[J].南洋资料译丛,2010 年第 02 期)

8.3 Traveler's Cheque

8.3.1 Definition of Traveler's Cheque

Traveler's cheque is a bill of exchange of a bank or travel agency which is self-identifying and may be cashed at banks, hotels, etc., either throughout the world or in particular areas only. The self-identification is provided by obtaining the signature of the customer on the instrument at the time of issuance, with a second space for his signature being left blank until presentation for cashing, when the encashing agent requires signature in his presence. This gives reasonable safety, both for the traveler and for the party cashing the item. It is of prime importance that the cheque not be signed in the second space until it is to be cashed, and then actually before the person cashes it.

Traveler's cheque is in fixed, round, convenient amount. Their wider rang of acceptability makes them suitable for people taking comparatively smaller amounts when traveling from place to place and likely to require cash over weekends or holidays when banks are not open to negotiate drawings under traveler's credit.

旅行支票是没有指定付款人和付款地点,由大银行、大旅行社发行的固定金额、专供旅游者或其他目的的出国者使用的一种支付工具。

A traveler's cheque is a specially printed form of cheque issued by a financial institution in preprinted denominations such as $10, $20, $50, $100, $500 and $1000. The issuer commits himself to pay the stated sum to any payee and undertakes to repay the purchaser if the cheque is lost or stolen before it is cashed. Here is a sample of traveler's cheque (see Chart 8.1):

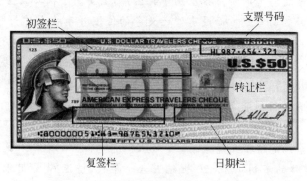

Chart 8.1

8.3.2 Parties to a Traveler's Cheque

There are five parties to a traveler's cheque, namely the issuer, the selling agent or office, the purchaser (or the holder), the paying agent or the person who encashes the cheque, and the transferee.

> **Issuer**

The issuer is a financial institution issuing the traveler's cheque. If the issuer is a bank, it is also called the issuing bank or the drawee bank, for the cheque is drawn on the issuer. The name and address of the issuer usually appear on the upper part of the cheque. A valid traveler's cheque ought to bear the printed facsimile of the issuer's authorized signature.

> **Selling agent or office**

The selling agent is one that sells the traveler's cheque. If the issuer sells the cheque by itself, then it is acting as the selling agent or office. If the issuer dispatches its traveler's cheques to their branches or correspondents in other counties for sale, the latter is acting as its selling agents.

A space is usually provided either on the face or on the reverse of the cheque for the selling agent to insert its name and address therein. All dispatches of the traveler's cheques are to be advised to their selling agent by the issuer. Receipt is to be acknowledged by telegram. Separate accounts should be kept by the selling agents to record the total amount of cheques they received and sold.

> **Purchaser (or holder)**

The purchaser is the person who buys a traveler's cheque from the issuer or its selling agent. When purchasing the cheque, he must sign his name thereon at the counter of the issuer or its selling agent, thereby making himself a holder of the instrument.

> **Paying agent**

The paying agent is one that undertakes by arrangement with the issuer to pay the latter's traveler's cheques when presented by the holder.

> **Transferee**

The transferee is one to whom the traveler's cheque is transferred. If the purchaser or the holder makes use of the traveler's cheque to pay a bill of any hotel or restaurant or an invoice of any shop, the hotel, restaurant or shop becomes the transferee.

8.3.3 Procedures of Traveler's Cheque Transaction

> **Purchase**

The traveler first fills out an application form in which the total amount and denominations needed are indicated, requesting the issuer or its selling agent to sell the traveler's cheque and record the number (each traveler's cheque is numbered) of the cheque to be sold on the customer's purchase receipt along with the purchaser's name and address. The purchaser signs his name on the face of each cheque in a designated place in the presence of the clerk of the bank teller and pays the amount equivalent to the total values of the cheque plus a small commission, usually one percent or less. The purchaser receives the cheques, together with a list of cheque's serial numbers of which it is advisable to be carried separately from the cheques.

> **Encashment**

Whenever the traveler desires to cash one or more of the traveler's cheques during a trip, he or she countersigns on each cheque in a designated place in the presence of the cashier of a store, a hotel or a bank. The cashier then compares this signature with that already signed thereon. If the two signatures are identical with each other, the cashier will encashes the traveler's cheque. If the countersignature differs slightly from the initial signature, the holder may be requested to endorse his name on the back of the cheque in the presence of the cashier. The encashment by the paying agent is subject to the endorsement which should be identical with the initial signature. Sometimes the submission of the presenter's passport or any other official identity document with his photograph affixed may be required.

> **Claims**

One of the most important characteristics of the traveler's cheque favorable to the purchaser is that in case the cheques are lost or stolen, they will be replaced. Once the cheque is lost or stolen, the loser should notify the issuer either directly or more often through one of its local selling agent. The issuer will replace the lost cheques as quickly as possible frequently within hours. Losers who fail to keep a separate listing of their cheque numbers, may encounter a time delay in getting the replaced cheques due to the fact that the issuer will seek to identify the missing cheque numbers from the computer records.

8.3.4 Advantages of the Traveler's Cheque

Firstly, traveler's cheque is safer than foreign bank notes and coins. If it has not been encashed, lost or stolen cheque will be soon replaced by the issuer. Secondly, traveler's cheque is readily encashable at banks, hotels, railway stations, airports and many commercial firms abroad because of their worldwide acceptability. Thirdly, different denominations of traveler's cheque facilitate its use by the traveler to meet his needs during a trip. Fourthly, traveler's cheques are not as bulky as an ordinary wallet full of bank notes for the same total amount. Finally, no time limit is set to the circulation of the traveler's cheque, for in general, no expiry date is specified on the cheque.

 8-2

旅行支票兑付相关法律问题分析与启示

境外商人林某持69张（每张面额1000美元）已经经过初签的旅行支票到某商业银行办理旅行支票兑付业务，银行经对林某当面逐一复签过的69张旅行支票核对无误后，当场兑付9000美元现金。同时对剩余面额合计6万美元的旅行支票办理托收，并将林某的护照复印留存备案。银行办理兑付、托收手续过程中，林某的女友尹某一直在现场。同年11月，尹某持已经由林某初签、复签且签名一致的另外10张面额合计1万美元的旅行支票到银行办理了第二笔托收业务。11月21日和12月5日，尹某持林某护照、托收申请书原件、尹某本人的身份证，先后两次到银行分别提取了6万美元和1万美元。次年8月，林某因未从尹某处得到前述款项，遂以"银行办理旅行支票业务违规、给其造成损失"为由向法院起诉要求银行向其赔付7万美元及相应利息。

银行在庭审中提出：林某从未到银行办理过纠纷所涉旅行支票的挂失业务，纠纷所涉面额合计为6万美元的旅行支票属于林某委托尹某代为到银行领取；纠纷所涉面额合计为1万美元的旅行支票属于林某将旅行支票转让给尹某后，由尹某自行到银行兑付；银行在办理这两笔业务过程中，是按照银行所规定的业务流程进行操作的，在客观方面不存在任何违反规定之处，在主观方面不存在任何过错。由于银行已经按照正常的业务操作规程支付了纠纷所涉的款项，故不应再次予以重复支付。同时提出要求追加尹某为本案诉讼当事人。

两个月后，法院以"被告未经旅行支票所有人林某亲自办理兑付手续而将相关款项支付给他人属违规操作，被告提出原告委托尹某代领的主张没有实据"为由做出一审判决，判决银行向林某全额承担赔付责任。银行不服，提起上诉。二审法院以一审判决认定事实不清、证据不足为由，裁定发回重审。原审法院重审再次判决银行败诉，理由是：被告未按照有关法律规定和兑现旅行支票的程序办理该笔业务，将原告林某的7万美元旅行支票兑付给了他人，属违规操作。因此而造成原告林某损失，应承担民事赔偿责任。被告提出原告委托尹某代领6万美元并将另1万美元的旅行支票转让给尹某的主张因无实据，不予支持。对于银行提出的追加尹某为诉讼当事人的主张，则以"尹某与本案非系同一法律关系"为由不予支持。

（资料来源：平一.旅行支票兑付相关法律问题分析与启示[J].中国城市金融，2010年第11期）

8.4　Credit Card

The credit card is a new way of payment to meet demands of the commodity economy. The development of credit card services is based on the popularization of computers and modern communication equipment. It is very convenient to use, with functions of withdrawal, transfer, inquiry, consumption, settlement and deposit, and is incomparably safe.

8.4.1 Definition of Credit Card

Credit cards are issued by banks to carefully selected customers with a certain line of credit based on the latter's financial status. By using these cards, commodities can be bought, hotel bills paid, air fares met without paying any cash in many regions of the world. In other words, credit cards are a short-term small amount consumer's credit extended by a bank. They are in effect used as a substitute for money. Stores, hotels or restaurants accepting the credit card for payment of commodities sold or services rendered are bound to have prearrangement with the card issuing bank.

信用卡是发卡银行对消费者提供短期消费信贷而发放的一种信用凭证。

The credit card is a piece of plastic card. The best known cards in the world are American Express card, Diners Club Card, Visa Card, Master Card, Federal Card, Million Card, JCB Card, etc.

There are many kinds of credit cards issued by commercial banks. They can be divided into the following types on different standards: (1)cards are divided into business cards and personal cards according to the issued targets and personal cards are divided into master cards and affiliated cards; (2) cards are divided into platinum cards, golden cards and ordinary cards according to grades; (3) cards are divided into international cards and local cards according to the area the cards can be used in.

8.4.2 Parties to a Credit Card

➢ **Cardholder**

An individual to whom a card is issued, or who is authorized to use an issued card.

➢ **Card Issuer**

Any association member of financial institution, bank, credit union, or company that issues, or causes to be issued, plastic cards to cardholders.

➢ **Acquirer**

A member that signs a credit card merchant agreement or disburses currency to a cardholder in a cash disbursement, and directly or indirectly enters the resulting transaction receipt into interchange.

➢ **Merchant**

An entity that contracts with merchant banks to originate transactions.

8.4.3 Procedure of Credit Card

When applying for a credit card, the card issuing bank or institution should investigate the annual income of the applicant as well as his credit standing. An entrance fee and/or an annual membership due are to be charged to the card holders. Some credit cards are given to the card holders free of any charge. A credit limit varying from institution to institution is usually allowed for each customer.

When making encashment under a credit card or using a credit card to pay a hotel bill or buy some commodities, the card holder should sign a sales slip and hand it together with his card to the paying bank, the hotel or the store. On receipt of the sales slip and the credit card, the bank teller or the clerk in the hotel or store must examine carefully whether the card is a valid or a forged one, whether it is expired or not, cheque the card with the black list airmailed by the card issuing bank and identify the signature on the sales slip with that appearing on the card. An authorization from the card issuing bank must be obtained as per arrangement between the issuing bank and the paying agent.

Sales slips are provided to record all the details of each transaction. A part of the required information is to be hand-written on the sales slip and the remaining to be obtained by processing the credit card and sales slip with an imprinter provided by the card issuing bank. The imprinter, while processing, will record on the sales slip the cardholder's account number, his name and card expiration date. Other information such as date, description of merchandise purchased or service rendered, total amount, etc. is filled in by the clerk on the sales slip. Afterwards the clerk presents the signed sales slip to the card issuing bank or to its local agent and receives payment less a discount ranging from one to several percent allowed to the bank as prearranged. The cardholder receives a monthly bill from the bank for his spending. He has the option of paying the bill in full within a grace period (usually twenty five days) without interest or drawing revolving credit with an interest usually higher than a 90 day's commercial paper discount rate.

Generally, the card issuing bank always maintains an account with the paying agent or the paying bank only for making payment under the credit card. The target balance of the account will depend upon the volume of the payment effected under the credit card.

国际信用卡如何使用

一、什么是国际信用卡?

国际发卡组织的会员(银行)发行的卡在该组织的特约商内都可以签账。这种卡都称为国际卡。众所周知,三大国际组织 VISA、MASTER、JCB。其中以 VISA 的市占率最高,其次为 MASTER,JCB 但是 JCB 在日本很好用,在其他地方就不一定了。虽然 JCB 也是国际卡,但是有些网络上面购物是不接受 JCB 的。

通常国际信用卡以美元作为结算货币,国际信用卡可以进行透支消费(先消费后还款),目前国际上比较常见的信用卡品牌主要是 Visa、Master Card 等,国内的各大商业银行也均有开办国际信用卡业务,您可以很方便地在银行柜台办理申请信用卡手续,但在国际信用卡内存款没有利息。

二、国际信用卡使用应该注意什么？

（一）尽量不在国外网站使用信用卡

在国外网站消费时候，不随意泄露自己的卡号、有效期等信息，建议先将信用卡绑定到 PayPal 上，然后使用 PayPal 进行支付，因为使用信用卡在网站上消费会透露卡号和日期，万一这两个信息被第三方恶意使用，将会带来不必要的损失，而使用第三方的 PayPal 支付则更能保护消费者利益，有时进行租用服务时，商家甚至不会知道你的 PayPal 账号，实在万不得已需要使用境外网站的网上支付功能时，建议选择知名度高、信誉良好的网站进行交易。

（二）调整信用卡的额度

银行给的信用卡额度都比较大，通常情况下是用不了这么多的信用额度，而万一信用卡丢失则会造成很多不必要的损失，因此个人可以手动调整信用卡的限额，比如在招商银行网上银行专业版中的信用卡额度调整中设置限额，这样改信用卡的消费额度就是限制在这个限额之内，风险就小很多了，当需要更多额度时候还可以手动修改回去。

（三）关闭信用卡的 ATM 取款功能

使用信用卡在 ATM 取款基本上没有什么用处，其利息也高得惊人，一旦信用卡失窃还会带来更多风险，因此建议关闭信用卡的取款功能。

（四）签名和密码哪个更安全

以签名作为信用卡的消费凭证是国际银行业的主流，从安全性角度来讲，这种信用卡不用设密码，仅凭签字就可消费，尤其是通过网上银行消费，一般只要知道持卡人姓名、卡号、信用卡到期日及查询密码就有可能被盗用。因此很多国内持卡人认为，密码比签名更安全。但是使用密码也有一些坏处，就是保管密码的责任则转嫁到了持卡人身上，也就意味着"损失自负"，一旦发生信用卡被冒用的事件，使用签名的持卡人的权益往往能得到更好的保护和补偿。

（五）信用卡丢失或被盗

申请信用卡前应该先了解银行的信用卡风险条款，不要申请一些高风险银行的信用卡，这些银行通常将信用卡风险转嫁至持卡人身上，将信用卡丢失被盗后的损失让持卡人承担。而好的银行则承诺会承担挂失前 48 小时内的被盗损失。因此，一旦用户发现卡片丢失、被盗等情况应该立即联系银行挂失。以招商银行的信用卡为例，在招商银行信用卡丢失或失窃后，以挂失时间为起算点，之前 48 小时内发生的被盗用损失，都可以向招行申请补偿，招行承担信用额度内被盗刷损失，普卡持卡人每年最高保障人民币 1 万元，金卡为 2 万元。值得注意的是，招行承担的损失不包括凭密码进行的交易。

（资料来源：http：//one.pingan.com/yizhangtonglicai/duihaoruzuo/jiayouzhan/1371798278540.shtml.）

8.4.4 Function of Credit Card

Though issued by different banks, the operation of cards is very similar. The standard credit card offers the following functions to clients who are considered as having standard creditworthiness.

> **Purchase Credit**

The cardholder may purchase merchandise or services with revolving credit under the credit limit at hotels, stores, restaurants, and other entertainment or shopping centers across the nation that bear the credit card's logo.

> **Cash Advance across the Nation**

The credit card holder may advance cash at the bank's outlets across the nation with the card and valid identification.

> **Interest on deposits**

Interest accrues on deposits on the credit card account at the rate for demand deposits.

> **ATM Cash Withdrawal**

The personal credit cardholder may withdraw cash on ATMs of the national network.

> **Overdraft Credit**

The cardholder may overdraw within the credit limit. He or she may also have the credit limit increased if certain requirements are met.

> **Telephone Banking**

Where telephone banking is offered, the cardholder may inquire into the account, change or request the password, and report a lost card by telephone.

> **Third-party Collection and Payment**

Most credit cards can pay telephone bills, rent, and housing or car mortgages on behalf of the cardholder. They may pay salaries on behalf of companies, non-profit organizations, and associations. They may settle securities account for the cardholder.

> **Credit Record**

The issuer offers the credit card as a payment device for the client. Holding a credit card signals credit worthiness.

★ Key Words

Non-trade settlement（非贸易的国际结算）　　Overseas Chinese Remittance（侨汇）
Traveler's cheque（旅行支票）　　Credit Card（信用卡）
Encashment（兑现）

★ Exercise

一、单项选择（Exclusive Choice Question）

1. 下列不属于非贸易结算内容的是（　　）。
 A. 国际商品进出口收支　　B. 旅游外汇收支
 C. 国际运输收支　　D. 保险费收支
2. 以下关于旅行支票的说法错误的是（　　）。
 A. 旅行支票属于一种有价证券，在兑付的过程中，银行既要谨慎处理以防范风险，又要保障持票人的正当权益

B. 购票人在购买支票时,必须在签发银行柜台当面签署名字,这是旅行支票的初签

C. 旅行支票的复签可以在取款时当面签署或事先签署,以便兑付行准确确定持票人的身份,安全兑付

D. 在旅行支票的持票人要求兑付时,银行会要求提供护照和购买合同

3. 以下不属于信用卡基本当事人的为( )。
   A. 发卡行   B. 持卡人   C. 特约商户   D. 中央银行

4. 以下关于信用卡免息期说法错误的是( )。
   A. 从银行记账日(也称账单日)至发卡银行规定的到期还款日之间为免息还款期
   B. 信用卡在用于透支消费等非现金交易时,享有免息期待遇
   C. 如果没能全额还款,银行需要收取所有未偿还的透支利息,而且还要罚息
   D. 透支现金同样享有免息待遇

5. 以下关于票汇的说法错误的是( )。
   A. 票汇是指汇款人到汇出行交款购买银行汇票,然后将汇票自带或邮寄给收款人,并由收款人持票向指定的解付行兑付票款的一种汇款结算方式
   B. 票汇的主要特点是费用低,但速度慢
   C. 票汇是汇出行填制一整套包括票汇总清单、票汇委托书、正副收条、汇款证明书及票汇通知书等套写格式,邮寄给解付行的汇款
   D. 解付行将汇票上的出票人签字、汇票通知书上的签字和汇出行签字样本核对相符后,办理解付

6. 以下不属于旅行支票特点的是( )。
   A. 面额固定   B. 不能挂失
   C. 兑取方便   D. 携带安全

7. 下列关于旅行信用证说法错误的是( )。
   A. 开证申请人和受益人同为一人   B. 不能转让
   C. 为跟单信用证   D. 业务已日益萎缩

8. ( ),持卡人可以享受信用卡免息期待遇。
   A. 持卡消费并偿还最低还款额
   B. 持卡提取现金
   C. 持卡消费并在规定的到期还款日之前全额归还欠款
   D. 持卡消费,但在到期日时约定还款账户内资金不够归还信用卡欠款

二、多项选择(Multiple Choice Question)

1. 以下哪些项目是非贸易结算的项目:( )。
   A. 银行收支   B. 旅游部门外汇收入
   C. 保险收支   D. 外币收兑

2. 侨汇的解付原则包括( )。
   A. 保护侨汇,优惠侨汇   B. 存款自愿、取款自由
   C. 可以积压   D. 解付侨汇付给现金

3. 信用卡的主要关系人包括（　　）。
   A. 发卡人　　　　B. 持卡人　　　　C. 特约商户　　　　D. 代办行
4. 信用卡的特点包括（　　）。
   A. 通用性　　　　B. 安全性　　　　C. 便利性　　　　D. 快捷性
5. 根据流通范围不同，信用卡分为（　　）。
   A. 国际卡　　　　B. 贷记卡　　　　C. 地区卡　　　　D. 借记卡

三、判断题（True or False）

1. 信用卡可以指定一个储蓄账户作为约定还款账户，银行会在到期还款日之前自动从约定还款账户内扣款来归还信用卡的欠款。（　　）
2. 旅行信用证目前在发达国家广泛使用。（　　）
3. 电汇迅速、便捷，收款人能在较短的时间里收到汇款，但是汇款人须承担较高的费用。（　　）
4. 旅行支票一旦遗失或被窃，只要符合发行银行的有关规定，挂失人就可得到退款或补发新的旅行支票。（　　）
5. 万事达卡国际组织是全球第一大信用卡国际组织。（　　）

附录 I

CDCS 考试

跟单信用证专家(Certified Documentary Credit Specialist, CDCS)考试

1. 考试简介:

跟单信用证专家(CDCS)是一个证明跟单信用证人员理论能力及实际业务操作能力的专业认证考试。它是在业内专家磋商基础上发展起来的,并保证此认证能够真实地对参考人员的业务能力进行考察。跟单信用证专家(CDCS)是由国际商会(ICC)授权,由英国金融服务学院(IFS)和国际金融服务协会(IFSA)开发并在全球共同推出的认证。CDCS 是对国际贸易、银行、金融等领域从业人员理论和操作水平的专业认证,代表着该领域的国际水平。中国大陆地区由中国贸促会(中国国际商会)培训中心负责考试报名工作。

2. 报名流程:

CDCS 考试采取网上报名的方式。报考人员可登录 www.ccoic.cn 点击"活动预告中"的"2015 年跟单信用证专家(CDCS)考试报名通知",浏览通知详情后根据个人情况选择相应的报名系统,进行网上报名。该中心只接受网上报名。

考生完成报名工作后即可进行汇款。该中心仅接受网上银行汇款,考生在汇款后需将电子汇款凭证截屏或拷贝后通过电子邮件发送至指定邮箱。汇款时,考生或代付款人必须在附言中注明考生姓名及考试名称。

考生报名成功后,该中心将以快递形式向考生发出以下资料:

(1) 复习材料 The Guide to Documentary Credits。在收到考生汇款一周内发出,如遇报名高峰期,寄送时间会延迟一周左右。

(2) 发票。发票在考生报名后一个月左右发出。

(3) 准考信或延考信。考前三周左右,考生可凭本人用户名和密码登录 IFS 官网下载打印准考信,并凭准考信参加考试。

3. 考试费用:

考生首次参加考试注册费(Registration)为 5400 元人民币,费用包括参加考试、购买考试复习材料、资料寄送费,不包括前去参加考试的食宿交通费用、培训费用或其他任何未列明的费用。

补考费(Resit)为 3700 元人民币。报名时要求注明本人前一次参加考试的 IFS 号码。如忘记自己的号码可向该中心致电咨询。

4. 考试时间

CDCS 考试每年两次,分别在 4 月和 10 月,报名截止日期分别为每年 1 月和 7 月底。

5. 考试地点：

北京、上海、广州、大连、长沙、成都、济南、合肥,具体地址另行公布。

6. 考题设置和评分标准：

CDCS考试时间为3小时,全英文考卷,共分为两个部分100道题,A部分包括60道选择题,以CDCS考试指导(The Guide to Documentary Credits)内容为基础。B部分包括三个部分：10个选择题,每题1分,共计10分；3个文件包题目,每个包括5道选择题,每题1分,共计15分；3个案例题,考生必须从10个选择中选出5个不符点选项,每选对1个得1分,选错不扣分。每个案例题全部正确将得5分,共计15分。B部分目的在于检测考生工作中的信息积累、对信用证的理解和判定等方面的技巧。

根据IFS最新通知,CDCS考试Part B部分通过比例由原来的70%调整为60%,A、B部分总分通过比例仍为70%。即如果考生能够获得Part B部分总分的60%及以上,将有资格进行A、B部分的总分加成,总分达到70%及以上者可以获得CDCS证书。

7. 考试形式：

闭卷、答题卡。

8. 证书寄送和补制

考后六周左右,IFS将公布考试结果,成绩显示"Distinction"和"Pass"的考生将获得CDCS证书。成绩显示"Fail"、"Fail Section"和"Did Not Sit"的考生未通过考核。证书将在考后约八周后寄送,如需要修改邮寄地址,考生须提前电话通知该中心工作人员。

9. 持证限制：

CDCS专家资格有效期为三年,如果希望延续,有两个途径：一是重新参加考试；二是积累学分,三年内积满24分,一年内最多不超过16分。

10. 考试难度：

☆☆☆☆☆

11. 考务咨询：

中国国际贸易促进委员会(中国国际商会)培训中心

电话：010-82217206；010-82217266

传真：010-82217272

邮件：peixun@ccoic.cn

地址：北京市西城区桦皮厂胡同2号国际商会大厦2层,100035

模 拟 题

Section A

1. If a L/C contains such words: "Will be automatically extended for a further year... AT LEAST 60 DYAS PRIOR TO THE 31ST DAY OF JANUARY OF THE FIRST YEAR OF THE CURRENT...NOTICE IS GIVEN", which of the following type does it belong to?

A. Commercial L/C

B. Automatically revolving L/C

C. Evergreen L/C

2. When the issuing bank receives the claim from the beneficiary and applicant's extension instruction by call at the same time, the issuing bank should:

A. reject the claim and notice the beneficiary

B. withhold the payment, waiting the written confirmation of extension from applicant

C. effect the payment and notice the applicant

3. Among the kinds of documentary credits subject to UCP600, from which can the beneficiary get two banks irrevocable undertaking to pay if complying documents are presented?

A. Irrevocable credit

B. Transferable credit

C. Confirmed credit

4. Which transport document of the following is not a goods title?

A. Bill of lading

B. Air waybill

C. Multimodal transport documents

5. Who must undertake the primary liability for payment under an irrevocable credit?

A. The issuing bank

B. The applicant

C. The nominated bank

6. A standby L/C is issued with statement that it is not operative, so this standby is ( ).

A. Not issued as an enforceable L/C

B. Revocable

C. Regarded as irrevocably issued

7. SB L/C issued to pay in default of the payment for the value of goods by the buyer. Which type of this SB L/C belongs to?

A. Performance SB L/C

B. Commercial SB L/C

C. Tender SB L/C

8. Issuing bank request the advising bank to advice the L/C on the condition that the advising bank do not confirm and do not sent notes of confirmation of the apparent authenticity. What should the advising bank do?

A. Do as requested, and it may advise L/C if it sent notice of the special commission to the beneficiary.

B. Do as requested, and it may advise L/C if it sent notice of the special commission to the beneficiary and the issuing bank.

　　C. Do not as requested, and it may advise L/C if it sent notice of the special commission to the beneficiary.

9. With reference to (　　), the expression "transhipment not allowed" is not a binding term under credit transaction.

　　A. air transportation

　　B. marine transportation

　　C. insurance policy

10. Silent confirmation is an arrangement made between (　　).

　　A. beneficiary and advising bank

　　B. issuing bank and advising bank

　　C. beneficiary and applicant

11. A credit can be transferred (　　).

　　A. from the first beneficiary to the second beneficiary

　　B. from the second beneficiary to the third beneficiary

　　C. from the applicant to the beneficiary

12. As for a freely negotiable credit, which bank acts as a transferring bank?

　　A. The advising bank

　　B. The specifically authorized bank

　　C. Any negotiating bank

13. Which of the following document is not acceptable when L/C prohibit transhipment?

　　A. B/L showing transshipment is effected and use trailers.

　　B. Railway bill showing change of modes of railway means.

　　C. Charter party B/L showing reserving the rights to transhipment.

14. L/C require documents including charter party B/L and contract of charter party, the confirming bank received charter party B/L and relative contract of charter party from the beneficiary. What should the confirming bank do with the contract?

　　A. Return the contract of charter party to beneficiary for amendment.

　　B. Disregarded and pass it to issuing bank without checking.

　　C. Check all the details against the L/C and other documents.

15. According to UCP600, a complying presentation is presented to the counter of issuing bank on Thursday April 1, the latest day on which the issuing bank must honor is(　　).

　　A. April 6

　　B. April 7

　　C. April 8

16. Of documentary credit and documentary collection in international trade, (　　) is better for the seller as it means a bank's irrevocable undertaking to pay.

A. the former

B. the latter

C. neither

17. Which abbreviation of the following is for uniform customs and practice for documentary credits?

A. UCP

B. URC

C. URDG

18. Which one means "free on board a vessel" at the loading port, for which the seller does not supply insurance documents?

A. FOB

B. CFR

C. FCA

19. A transferable L/C is available with any bank by negotiation. Which of the following is correct?

A. The transferring bank nominated by the issuing bank

B. The advising bank as the transferring bank

C. Any bank as the transferring bank

20. A transferable L/C amount is USD 85000.00, partial shipment allowed, first shipment for ×× sets is USD 65000.00, second shipment for ×× sets is USD 20000.00, insurance coverage must by 120%. Then the L/C is separately transferred to two second beneficiary. As following:

First Amount: USD 48750.00

Second Amount: USD 16000.00

For complying presentation the insurance coverage of the two presentations should be( ).

A. 160%   160%

B. 150%   150%

C. 160%   150%

21. According to Incoterms 2000, which of the trade terms below is recommended when the credit requires an air waybill marked freight prepaid to the airport of destination?

A. CFR

B. CPT

C. FCA

22. If an exporter is willing to release the shipping documents directly to the buyer, but wishes to retain some guarantee of payment should the buyer fail to pay on the due date, which of the following documentary credit best suits the exporter's needs?

A. Transferable

B. Standby

C. Revolving

23. Besides insurance company or its agent, the party who is also qualified to sign insurance document is (   ).

A. Underwriter

B. Broker

C. Proxy

24. Under ucp600, what is the minimum insurance amount acceptable when the credit requires the invoice amount be CIF USD1000?

A. USD1000

B. USD1100

C. USD1200

25. Insurance covers all risks and some of additional risks. Which of the following does not belong to the type of additional risks of institute cargo clause?

A. TPND

B. Institute war clauses

C. From warehouse to warehouse

26. A transferable credit, total amount is USD 20,000.00, partial shipment is not allowed. The first beneficiary transfer USD18,000.00 to a second beneficiary, and assign proceeds of USD 3000 to C. When the first beneficiary substitutes its own invoice and draft, the amount should be (   ).

A. USD 20,000

B. USD 17,000

C. USD 18,000

27. (   ) in collection transactions, when documents presented lack bills of exchange, the remitting bank, upon request of the drawer, may instruct either the collecting bank or the drawee to create the bills of exchange instead with proper requirements as to their form and wording.

A. Unless the remitting bank agrees

B. Unless the presenting bank agrees

C. No conditions needed

28. L/C requires one signed invoice in one original and three copies. Which of the following documents are acceptable?

A. One signed invoice issued by beneficiary and three unsigned copies

B. Four photocopies of invoice stating being original

C. Four invoice signed by beneficiary not stating being original

29. An EUCP credit, the expiry date is April 10, the notice of completeness is given on April 11, other documents are presented before the expiry date. Which of the following is correct?

A. Electronic records must be presented at the same time, should not be presented separately
B. Comply with the terms of L/C
C. Late Presentation

30. After L/C expired, the reimbursing bank received a claim from claiming bank and paid accordingly. On the other hand, the issuing bank also paid to the claiming bank directly. Hence, which bank should be responsible for the duplicate payment?
A. Reimbursing bank
B. Claiming bank
C. Issuing bank

Section B

Simulation 1

Instructions

You are the Document Checker at the nominated confirming bank.

Assumptions

1) Today's date is Monday 30 June XXXX.

2) All signatures where shown are original.

3) The documentary credit was opened correctly and duly passed authentication.

4) The documents are presented in the required number of originals and copies.

5) The documents are duly endorsed where required.

Supporting documentation

1) Documentary credit (MT 700)

2) Commercial invoice

3) CMR

Instructions to students

Identify the five discrepancies on the attached discrepancy checklist (document 1) then transfer your answers to the main answer sheet.

Discrepancy checklist

1.	Shipment not within period allowed.	
2.	Partial shipment effected.	
3.	Documentary credit overdrawn.	
4.	Documents do not evidence goods of Dutch origin.	
5.	No bill of exchange presented.	
6.	Amount on the commercial invoice incorrect.	
7.	Transport document not correctly issued to the order of the applicant.	
8.	Transport document not signed in accordance with UCP 600.	
9.	Transport document not stamped and signed by the shipper.	
10.	The invoice covers merchandise not called for in the documentary credit.	

MT 700

INCOMING SWIFT MT 700
FROM ISSUING BANK   MERHABA BANK, ISTANBUL, TURKEY
TO ADVISING BANK   ACB BANK, ROTTERDAM, THE NETHERLANDS

27: SEQUENCE OF TOTAL 1/1
40A: FORM OF DOCUMENTARY CREDIT IRREVOCABLE
20: DOCUMENTARY CREDIT NUMBER 2691010100029383
31C: DATE OF ISSUE   07 MAY XXXX
40E: APPLICABLE RULESUCPURR LATEST VERSION
31D: DATE AND PLACE OF EXPIRY
                            01 JULY XXXX, ROTTERDAM, THE NERHERLANS
50: APPLICANT   FACTORING A.S. ISTANBUL, TURKEY
59: BENEFICIARY   DE GROOT MACHINES B.V. HAARLEM, THE NETHERLANS
32: CURRENCY AND AMOUNT   EUR 180,000
41A: AVAILABLE WITH/BY   ACB BANK, ROTTERDAM
                            BY DEF PAYMENT
42P: DEFERRED PAYMENT DETAILS
                            180 DAYS FROM CMR DATE
43P: PARTIAL SHIPMENTS   NOT ALLOWED
43T: TRANSHIPMENT   NOT ALLOWED
44A: ON BOARD/DISP/TAKING CHARGE
                            HAARLEM, THE NETHERLANDS
44B: FOR TRANSPORTATION TO
                            HALKALI FREE ZONE, ISTANBUL, TURKEY, BY TRUCK
44D: SHIPMENT PERIOD   DURING MIDDLE OF JUNE XXXX
45A: DESCRIPTION OF GOODS AND
                            1 UNIT "DE GTOOT" BRAND ROTARY
/OR SERVIES   CUTTING MACHINE, TYPE 500, AND ALL
NECESSARY ACCESSORIES
                            CUSTOMS TARIFF NUMBER 8462.8000
                            DELIVERY TRERMS CIP HALKALI REEE ZONE, ISTANBUL, TURKEY

46A: DOCUMENTS REQUIRED + SIGNED COMMERCIAL INVOICE IN 3 FOLD INDICATING THE SERIAL NUMBER OF THE MACHINE AND CERTIFYING THAT THE MACHINE IS AND NOT USED BEFORE.
+ ORIGINAL CMR TRANSPORT DOCUMENT CONSIGNED TO THE ORDER OF FACTORING A.S., ISTANBUL, TURKEY AND MARKED FREIGHT PREPAID.

47A: ADDITIONAL CONDITIONS
DOCUMENTS ISSUED PRIOR TO THE ISSUE DATE OF THIS DOCUMENTARY CREDIT ARE NOT ACCEPTABLE.
ALL DOCUMENTS MUST SHOW THE NUMBER OF THIS DOCUMENTARY CREDIT. GOODS MUST BE OF DUTCH ORIGIN

71B: CHARGES
ALL BANKING CHARGES AND COMMISSIONS ARE FOR ACCOUNT OF APPLICANT.

48: PERIOD FOR PRESENTATION
10 DAYS

49: CONFIRMATION INSTRUCTIONS
CONFIRM

78: INSTR TO PAYG/ACCPTG/NEGOTG BANK WE SHALL REIMBURSE YOU ON THE
MATURITY DATE IN ACCORDANCE WITH YOUR INSTRUCTIONS WITH THE TERMS AND CONDITIONS OF THIS DOCUMENTARY CREDIT ARE DULY PRESENTED AT YOUR COUNTERS.

72: SENDER TO RECEIVER INFORMATION
PLEASE ACKNOWLEDGE RECEIPT BY SWIFT MT 730.

MESSAGE PASSED AUTHENTICATION

DE GROOT MACHINES B. V.

SPAARNE 1000   TEL：**31(0)235999999
1000 VC HAARLEM   FAX：**31(0)235888888
THE NETHERLANDS

COMMERCIAL INVOICE nr. 987

TO：

FACTORING A. S.   **ORIGINAL**

1，BAHAR SOKAK

ISTANBUL，TURKEY

Haarlem，25 June XXXX

DESCRIPTION OF GOODS：

1 UNIT"DE GROOT" BRAND ROTARY CUTTING MACHINE

TYPE 500

SERIAL NUMBER 2003

CUSTOMS TARIFF NUMBER 8462.8000

AND ALL NECESSARY ACCESSORIES

INCLUDING A SET OF FREE ADVERTISING AND PROMOTION MATERIAL

WE CERTIFY THAT THE MACHINE IS BRAND NEW AND WAS NOT USED BEFORE

CUTTING MACHINE PACKES ON 4 PALLETS

ACCESSORIES AND PROMOTIONAL MATERIAL PACKED IN 1 CARTON

PRICE：

ROTARY CUTTING MACHINE	EUR	180,000
ACCESSORIES	EUR	20,000
TOTAL CIP HALKALI FREE ZONE，ISTANBUL	**EUR**	**200,000**

Marks：2003 pallet numbers 1/5-4/5

Documentary Credit no. 2003. AC. 100

For and on behalf of

DE GROOT MACHINES B. V.

B. DE GROOT

Original for shipper (sender)

1 Sender (Name, Address, Country) DE GROOT MACHINES B.V. SPAARNE 1000 1000 VC HAARLEM THE NETHERLANDS	CMR **INTERNATIONAL CONSIGNMENT NOTE** This transport is, unless otherwise specified, subject to the Convention on the Contract for the International Carriage of Goods by Road (CMR)	
2 consignee FACTORING A.S. 1, BAHAR SOKAK ISTANBUL, TURKEY	16 carrier (Name, Address, Country) WINDMILL TRANSPORT B.V. RAAKS 2000 1000 VK HAARLEM. The Netherlands	
3 Place of delivery of the goods Place HALKALI FREE ZONE, ISTABUL Country TURKEY	17 consecutive carrier	
4 Place and date of taking in charge of the goods Place HAARLEM Country THE NETHERLANDS Date 21 JUNE XXXX	18 reserves and remarks by the carrier CMR nr. 100	
5 Documents enclosed		
6 marks & numbers 7 number of packages 8 packing type 9 Goods description 1 UNIT "DE GROOT" BRAND ROTARY CUTTING MACHINE TYPE 500 SERIAL NUMBER 2003 Marks: 2003 pallet numbers 1/5-4/5 4 wooden pallets Documentary Credit number: 2003. AC. 100	10 statistic number	
:::	11 gross weight 10,000 kg	
:::	12 volume 10cbm	
13 Instructions by the carrier (customs formalities)	19	Freight tariff and specifications
:::		
:::		
:::		
:::		
14 Reimbursement		
15 Freight instructions **FREIGHT PREPAID**	20 Special agreements	
25 truck/ lorry/ vehicle details REGISTRATION NUMBER: 51-BG-LN NATIONALITY: DUTCH		
21 Place and date of issue: HAARLEM, 10 JUNE XXXX	24 Goods received Date:	
22 Stamp and signature of shipper	23 *W. Mill* Stamp and signature of carrier	Stamp and signature of consignee

附录 II

UCP600 中文版

第一条 UCP 的适用范围

《跟单信用证统一惯例——2007 年修订本,国际商会第 600 号出版物》(简称"UCP")乃一套规则,适用于所有的其文本中明确表明受本惯例约束的跟单信用证(下称信用证)(在其可适用的范围内,包括备用信用证。)除非信用证明确修改或排除,本惯例各条文对信用证所有当事人均具有约束力。

第二条 定义

就本惯例而言

通知行指应开证行的要求通知信用证的银行。

申请人指要求开立信用证的一方。

银行工作日指银行在其履行受本惯例约束的行为的地点通常开业的一天。

受益人指接受信用证并享受其利益的一方。

相符交单指与信用证条款、本惯例的相关适用条款及国际标准银行实务一致的交单。

保兑指保兑行在开证行承诺之外做出的承付或议付相符交单的确定承诺。

保兑行指根据开证行的授权或要求对信用证加具保兑的银行。

信用证指一项不可撤销的安排,无论其名称或描述如何,该项安排构成开证行对相符交单予以交付的确定承诺。

承付指:

a. 如果信用证为即期付款信用证,则即期付款。

b. 如果信用证为延期付款信用证,则承诺延期付款并在承诺到期日付款。

c. 如果信用证为承兑信用证,则承兑受益人开出的汇票并在汇票到期日付款。

开证行指应申请人要求或者代表自己开出信用证的银行。

议付指指定银行在相符交单下,在其应获偿付的银行工作日当天或之前向受益人预付或者同意预付款项,从而购买汇票(其付款人为指定银行以外的其他银行)及/或单据的行为。

指定银行指信用证可在其处兑用的银行,如信用证可在任一银行兑用,则任何银行均为指定银行。

交单指向开证行或指定银行提交信用证项下单据的行为,或指按此方式提交的单据。

交单人指实施交单行为的受益人、银行或其他人。

第三条 解释

就本惯例而言:

如情形适用,单数词形包含复数含义,复数词形包含单数含义。

信用证是不可撤销的,即使未如此表明。

单据签字可用手签、摹样签字、穿孔签字、印戳、符合或任何其他机械或电子的证实方法为之。

诸如单据须履行法定手续、签证、证明等类似要求,可由单据上任何看似满足该要求的签字、标记、戳或标签来满足。

一家银行在不同国家的分支机构被视为不同的银行。

用诸如"第一流的""著名的""合格的""独立的""正式的""有资格的"或"本地的"等词语描述单据的出单人时,允许除受益人之外的任何人出具该单据。

除非要求在单据中使用,否则诸如"迅速地""立刻地"或"尽快地"等词语将被不予理会。

"在或大概在(on or about)"或类似用语将被视为规定事件发生在指定日期的前后五个日历日之间,起讫日期计算在内。"至(to)""直至(until、till)""从……开始(from)"及"在……之间(between)"等词用于确定发运日期时包含提及的日期,使用"在……之前(before)"及"在……之后(after)"时则不包含提及的日期。

"从……开始(from)"及"在……之后(after)"等词用于确定到期日期时不包含提及的日期。

"前半月"及"后半月"分别指一个月的第一日到第十五日及第十六日到该月的最后一日,起讫日期计算在内。

一个月的"开始(beginning)""中间(middle)"及"末尾(end)"分别指第一到第十日、第十一日到第二十日及第二十一日到该月的最后一日,起讫日期计算在内。

第四条 信用证与合同

a. 就其性质而言,信用证与可能作为其开立基础的销售合同或其他合同是相互独立的交易,即使信用证中含有对此类合同的任何援引,银行也与该合同无关,且不受其约束。因此,银行关于承付、议付或履行信用证项下其他义务的承诺,不受申请人基于与开证行或与受益人之间的关系而产生的任何请求或抗辩的影响。

受益人在任何情况下不得利用银行之间或申请人与开证行之间的合同关系。

b. 开证行应劝阻申请人试图将基础合同、形式发票等文件作为信用证组成部分的做法。

第五条 单据与货物、服务或履约行为

银行处理的是单据,而不是单据可能涉及的货物、服务或履约行为。

第六条 兑用方式、截止日和交单地点

a. 信用证必须规定可在其处兑用的银行,或是否可在任一银行兑用。规定在指定解行兑用的信用证同时也可以在开证行兑用。

b. 信用证必须规定其是以即付款、延期付款,承兑还是议付的方式兑用。

c. 信用证不得开成凭以申请人为付款人的汇票兑用。

di. 信用证必须定一个交单的截止日。规定的承付或议付的截止日将被视为交单的截止日。

ii. 可在其处兑用信用证的银行所在地即为交单地点。可在任一银行兑用的信用证其交单地点为任一银行所在地。除规定的交单地点外,开证行所在地也是交单地点。

e. 除非如第二十九条 a 款规定的情形,否则受益人或者代表受益人的交单应截止日当天或之前完成。

第七条 开证行责任

a. 只要规定的单据提交给指定银行或开证方,并且构成相符交单,则开证行必须承付,如果信用证为以下情形之一:

i. 信用证规定由开证行即期付款、延期付款或承兑;

ii. 信用证规定由指定银行即期付款但其未付款;

iii. 信用证规定由指定银行延期付款但其未承诺延期付款,或虽已承诺延期付款,但未在到期日付款;

iv. 信用证规定由指定银行承兑,但其未承兑以其为付款人的汇票,或虽然承兑了汇票,但未在到期日付款。

v. 信用证规定由指定银行议付但其未议付。

b. 开证行自开立信用证之时起即不可撤销地承担承付责任。

c. 指定银行承付或议付相符交单并将单据转给开证行之后,开证行即承担偿付该指定银行的责任。对承兑或延期付款信用证下相符合单金额的偿付应在到期日办理,无论指定银行是否在到期日之前预付或购买了单据,开证行偿付指定银行的责任独立于开证行对受益人的责任。

第八条 保兑行责任

a. 只要规定的单据提交给保兑行,或提交给其他任何指定银行,并且构成相符交单,保兑行必须:

i. 承付,如果信用证为以下情形之一:

a) 信用证规定由保兑行即期付款、延期付款或承兑;

b) 信用证规定由另一指定银行延期付款,但其未付款;

c) 信用证规定由另一指定银行延期付款,但其未承诺延期付款,或虽已承诺延期付款但未在到期日付款;

d) 信用证规定由另一指定银行承兑,但其未承兑以其为付款人的汇票,或虽已承兑汇票未在到期日付款;

e) 信用证规定由另一指定银行议付,但其未议付。

ii. 无追索权地议付,如果信用证规定由保兑行议付。

b. 保兑行自对信用证加具保兑之时起即不可撤销地承担承付或议付的责任。

c. 其他指定银行承付或议付相符交单并将单据转往保兑行之后,保兑行即承担偿付该指定银行的责任。对承兑或延期付款信用证下相符交单金额的偿付应在到期日办理,无论指定银行是否在到期日之前预付或购买了单据。保兑行偿付指定银行的责任独立于保兑行对受益人的责任。

d. 如果开证行授权或要求一银行对信用证加具保兑,而其并不准备照办,则其必须毫不延误地通知开证行,并叵通知此信用证而不加保兑。

第九条　信用证及其修改的通知

a. 信用证及其任何修改可以经由通知行通知给受益人。非保兑行的通知行通知信用及修改时不承担承付或议付的责任。

b. 通知行通知信用证或修改的行为表示其已确信信用证或修改的表面真实性,而且其通知准确地反映了其收到的信用证或修改的条款。

c. 通知行可以通过另一银行("第二通知行")向受益人通知信用证及修改。第二通知行通知信用证或修改的行为表明其已确信收到的通知的表面真实性,并且其通知准确地反映了收到的信用证或修改的条款。

d. 经由通知行或第二通知行通知信用证的银行必须经由同一银行通知其后的任何修改。

e. 如一银行被要求通知信用证或修改但其决定不予通知,则应毫不延误地告知自其处收到信用证、修改或通知的银行。

f. 如一银行被要求通知信用证或修改但其不能确信信用证、修改或通知的表面真实性,则应毫不延误地通知看似从其处收到指示的银行。如果通知行或第二通知行决定仍然通知信用证或修改,则应告知受益人或第二通知行其不能确信信用证、修改或通知的表面真实性。

第十条　修改

a. 除第三十八条另有规定者外,未经开证行、保兑行(如有的话)及受益人同意,信用证即不得修改,也不得撤销。

b. 开证行自发出修改之时起,即不可撤销地受其约束。保兑行可将其保兑扩展至修改,并自通知该修改时,即不可撤销地受其约束。但是,保兑行可以选择将修改通知受益人而不对其加具保兑。若然如此,其必须毫不延误地将此告知开证行,并在其给受益人的通知中告知受益人。

c. 在受益人告知通知修改的银行其接受该修改之前,原信用证(或含有先前被接受的修改的信用证)的条款对受益人仍然有效。受益人应提供接受或拒绝修改的通知。如果受益人未能给予通知,当交单与信用证以及尚未表示接受的修改的要求一致时,即视为受益人已作出接受修改的通知,并且从此时起,该信用证被修改。

d. 通知修改的银行应将任何接受或拒绝的通知转告发出修改的银行。

e. 对同一修改的内容不允许部分接受,部分接受将被视为拒绝修改的通知。

f. 修改中关于除非受益人在某一时间内拒绝修改否则修改生效的规定应被不予理会。

第十一条　电讯传输的和预先通知的信用证和修改

a. 以经过证实的电讯方式发出的信用证或信用证修改即被视为有效的信用证或修改文据,任何后续的邮寄确认书应该不予理会。

如电讯声明"详情后告"(或类似用语)或声明以邮寄确认书为有效信用证或修改,则该电讯不被视为有效信用证或修改。开证行必须随即不迟延地开立有效信用证或修改,其条款不得与该电讯矛盾。

b. 开证行只有在准备开立有效信用证或作出有效修改时,才可以发出关于开立或修改信用证的初步通知（预先通知）。开证行作出该预先通知，即不可撤销地保证不迟延地开立或修改信用证，且其条款不能与预先通知相矛盾。

第十二条 指定

a. 除非指定银行为保兑行，对于承付或议付的授权并不赋予指定银行承付或议付的义务，除非该指定银行明确表示同意并且告知受益人。

b. 开证行指定一银行承兑汇票或做出延期付款承诺，即为授权该指定银行预付或购买其已承兑的汇票或已做出的延期付款承诺。

c. 非保兑行的指定银行收到或审核并转递单据的行为并不使其承担承付或议付的责任，也不构成其承付或议付的行为。

第十三条 银行之间的偿付安排

a. 如果信用证规定指定银行（"索偿行"）向另一方（"偿付行"）获取偿付时，必须同时规定该偿付是否按信用证开立时有效的 ICC 银行间偿付规则进行。

b. 如果信用证没有规定偿付遵守 ICC 银行间偿付规则，则按照以下规定：

i. 开证行必须给予偿付行有关偿付的授权，授权应符合信用证关于兑用方式的规定，且不应设定截止日。

ii. 开证行不应要求索偿行向偿付行提供与信用证条款相符的证明。

iii. 如果偿付行未按信用证条款见索即偿，开证行将承担利息损失以及产生的任何其他费用。

iv. 偿付行的费用应由开证行承担。然而，如果此项费用由受益人承担，开证行有责任有信用证及偿付授权中注明。如果偿付行的费用由受益人承担，该费用应在偿付时从付给索偿行的金额中扣取。如果偿付未发生，偿付行的费用仍由开证行负担。

c. 如果偿付行未能见索即偿，开证行不能免除偿付责任。

第十四条 单据审核标准

a. 按指定行事的指定银行、保兑行（如果有的话）及开证行须审核交单，并仅基于单据本身确定其是否在表面上构成相符交单。

b. 按指定行事的指定银行、保兑行（如有的话）及开证行各有从交单次日起至多五个银行工作日用以确定交单是否相符。这一期限不因在交单日当天或之后信用证截止日或最迟交单日截至而受到缩减或影响。

c. 如果单据中包含一份或多份受第十九、二十、二十一、二十二、二十三、二十四或二十五条规制的正本运输单据，则须由受益人或其他表在不迟于本惯例所指的发运日之后的二十一个日历日内交单，但是在任何情况下都不得迟于信用证的截止日。

d. 单据中的数据，在与信用证、单据本身及国际标准银行实务参照解读时，无须与该单据本身中的数据，其他要求的单据或信用证中的数据等同一致，但不得矛盾。

e. 除商业发票外，其他单据中的货物、服务或履约行为的描述，如果有的话，可使用与信用证中的描述不矛盾的概括性用语。

f. 如果信用证要求提交运输单据、保险单据或者商业发票之外的单据，却未规定出单人或其数据内容，则只要提交的单据内容看似满足所要求单据的功能，且其他方面符合第十四条 d 款，银行将接受该单据。

g. 提交的非信用证所要求的单据将被不予理会,并可被退还给交单人。

h. 如果信用证含有一项条件,但未规定用以表明该条件得到满足的单据,银行将视为未作规定并不予理会。

i. 单据日期可以早于信用证的开立日期,但不得晚于交单日期。

j. 当受益人和申请人的地址出现在任何规定的单据中时,无须与信用证或其他规定单据中所载相同,但必须与信用证中规定的相应地址同在一国。联络细节(传真、电话、电子邮件及类似细节)作为受益人和申请人地址的一部分时将被不予理会。然而,如果申请人的地址和联络细节为第十九、二十、二十一、二十二、二十三、二十四或二十五条规定的运输单据上的收货人或通知方细节的一部分时,应与信用证规定的相同。

k. 在任何单据中注明的托运人或发货人无须为信用证的受益人。

l. 运输单据可以由任何人出具,无须为承运人、船东、船长或租船人,只要其符合第十九、二十、二十一、二十二、二十三或二十四条的要求。

第十五条 相符交单

a. 当开证行确定交单相符时,必须承付。

b. 当保兑行确定交单相符时,必须承付或者议付并将单据转递给开证行。

c. 当指定银行确定交单相符并承付或议付时,必须将单据转递给保兑行或开证行。

第十六条 不符单据、放弃及通知

a. 当按照指定行事的指定银行、保兑行(如有的话)或者开证行确定交单不符时,可以拒绝承付或议付。

b. 当开证行确定交单不符时,可以自行决定联系申请人放弃不符点。然而这并不能延长第十四条 b 款所指的期限。

c. 当按照指定行事的指定银行、保兑行(如有的话)或开证行决定拒绝承付或议付时,必须给予交单人一份单独的拒付通知。

该通知必须声明:

i. 银行拒绝承付或议付;及

ii. 银行拒绝承付或者议付所依据的每一个不符点;及

iii. a) 银行留存单据听候交单人的进一步指示;或者

b) 开证行留存单据直到其从申请人处接到放弃不符点的通知并同意接受该放弃,或者其同意接受对不符点的放弃之前从交单人处收到其进一步指示;或者

c) 银行将退回单据;或者

d) 银行将按之前从交单人处获得的指示处理。

d. 第十六条 c 款要求的通知必须以电讯方式,如不可能,则以其他快捷方式,在不迟于自交单之翌日起第五个银行工作日结束前发出。

e. 按照指定行事的指定银行、保兑行(如有的话)或开证行在按照第十六条 c 款 iii 项 a)发出了通知后,可以在任何时候单据退还交单人。

f. 如果开证或保兑行未能按照本条行事,则无权宣称交单不符。

g. 当开证行拒绝承付或保兑行拒绝承付或者议付,并且按照本条发出了拒付通知后,有权要求返还已偿付的款项及利息。

第十七条 正本单据及副本

a. 信用证规定的每一种单据须至少提交一份正本。

b. 银行应将任何带有看似出单人的原始签名、标记、印戳或标签的单据视为正本单据,除非单据本身表明其非正本。

c. 除非单据本身另有说明,在以下情况下,银行也将其视为正本单据:

i. 单据看似由出单人手写、打字、穿孔或盖章;或者

ii. 单据看似使用出单人的原始信纸出具;或者

iii. 单据声明其为正本单据,除非该声明看似不适用于提交的单据。

d. 如果信用证使用诸如"一式两份(in duplicate)"、"两份(in two fold)"、"两套(in two copies)"等用语要求提交多份单据,则提交至少一份正本,其余使用副本即可满足要求,除非单据本身另有说明。

第十八条 商业发票

a. 商业发票:

i. 必须看似由受益人出具(第三十八条规定的情形除外);

ii. 必须出具成以申请人为抬头(第三十八条 g 款规定的情形除外);

iii. 必须与信用证的货币相同;且

iv. 无须签名

b. 按指定行事的指定银行、保兑行(如有的话)或开证行可以接受金额大于信用证允许金额的商业发票,其决定对有关各方均有约束力,只要该银行对超过信用证允许金额的部分未作承付或者议付。

c. 商业发票上的货物、服务或履约行为的描述应该与信用证中的描述一致。

第十九条 涵盖至少两种不同运输方式的运输单据

a. 涵盖至少两种不同运输方式的运输单据(多式或联合运输单据),无论名称如何,必须看似:

i. 表明承运人名称并由以下人员签署:

* 承运人或其具名代理人,或

* 船长或其具名代理人。

承运人、船长或代理人的任何签字,必须标明其承运人、船长或代理人的身份。

代理人签字必须表明其系代表承运人还是船长签字。

ii. 通过以下方式表明货运站物已经在信用证规定的地点发送,接管或已装船。

* 事先印就的文字、或者

* 表明货物已经被发送、接管或装船日期的印戳或批注。

运输单据的出具日期将被视为发送,接管或装船的日期,也即发运的日期。然而如单据以印戳或批注的方式表明了发送、接管或装船日期,该日期将被视为发运日期。

iii. 表明信用证规定的发送、接管或发运地点,以及最终目的地,即使:

a) 该运输单据另外还载明了一个不同的发送、接管或发运地点或最终目的地,或者。

b) 该运输单据载有"预期的"或类似的关于船只,装货港或卸货港的限定语。

iv. 为唯一的正本运输单据、或者,如果出具为多份正本,则为运输单据中表明的全

套单据。

v. 载有承运这条款和条件,或提示承运条款和条件参见别处(简式/背面空白的运输单据)。银行将不审核承运条款和条件的内容。

vi. 未表明受租船合同约束。

b. 就本条而言,转运指在从信用证规定的发送,接管或者发运地点最终目的地的运输过程中从某一运输工具上卸下货物并装上另一运输工具的行为(无论其是否为不同的运输方式)。

c. i. 运输单据可以表明货物将要或可能被转运,只要全程运输由同一运输单据涵盖。

ii. 即使信用证禁止转运,注明将要或者可能发生转运的运输单据仍可接受。

第二十条　提单

a. 提单,无论名称如何,必须看似;

i. 表明承运人名称,并由下列人员签署:

*承运人或其具名代理人,或者

*船长或其具名代理人。

承运人,船长或代理人的任何签字必须标明其承运人,船长或代理人的身份。

代理人的任何签字必须标明其系代表承运人还是船长签字。

ii. 通过以下方式表明货物已在信用证规定的装货港装上具名船只:

*预先印就的文字,或

*已装船批注注明货物的装运日期。

提单的出具日期将被视为发运日期,除非提单载有表明发运日期的已装船批注,此时已装船批注中显示的日期将被视为发运日期。

如果提单载有"预期船只"或类似的关于船名的限定语,则需以已装船批注明确发运日期及实际船名。

iii. 表明货物从信用证规定的装货港发运至卸货港。

如果提单没有表明信用证规定的装货港为装货港,或者其载有"预期的"或类似的关于装货港的限定语,则需以已装船批注表明信用证规定的装货港、发运日期及实际船名。即使提单以事先印就的文字表明了货物已装载或装运于具名船只、本规定仍适用。

iv. 为唯一的正本提单,或如果以多份正本出具,为提单据表明的全套正本。

v. 载有承运条款和条件,或提示承运条款和条件参见另外(简式/背面空白的提单)。银行将不审核承运条款和条件的内容。

vi. 未表明受租船合同约束。

b. 就本条而言,转运系指在信用证规定的装货港到卸货港之间的运输过程中,将货物从船卸下并再装上另一船的行为。

c. i. 提单可以表明货物将要或可能被转运,只要全程运输由同一提单涵盖。

ii. 即使信用证禁止转运,注明将要或可能发生转运的提单仍可接受,只要其表明货物由集装箱、拖车或子船运输。

d. 提单中声明承运人保留转运权利的条款将被不予理会。

第二十一条 不可转让的海运单

a. 不可转让的海运单,无论名称如何,必须看似:

i. 表明承运人名称并由下列人员签署:

＊承运人或其具名代理人,或者

＊船长或其具名代理人。

承运人、船长或代理人的任何签字必须标明其承运人、船长或代理人的身份。

代理签字必须标明其系代表承运人还是船长签定。

ii. 通过以下方式表明货物已在信用证规定的装货上具名船只:

＊预先印就的文字、或者

＊已装船批注表明货物的装运日期。

不可转让海运单的出具日期将被视为发运日期,除非其上带有已装船批注注明发运日期,此明已装船批注注明的日期将被视为发运日期。

如果不可转让海运单载有"预期船只"或类似的关于船名的限定语,则需要以已装船批注表明发运日期和实际船只。

iii. 表明货物从信用证规定的装货港发运至卸货港。

如果不可转让海运单未以信用证规定的装货港为装货港,或者如果其载有"预期的"或类似的关于装货港的限定语,则需要以已装船批注表明信用证规定的装货港、发运日期和船只。即使不可转让海运单以预先印就的文字表明货物已由具名船只装载或装运,本规定也适用。

iv. 为唯一的正本不可转让海运单,或如果以多份正本出具,为海运单上注明的全套正本。

v. 载有承运条款的条件,或提示承运条款和条件参见别处(简式/背面空白的海运单)。银行将不审核承运条款和条件的内容。

vi. 未注明受租船合同约束。

b. 就本条而言,转运系指在信用证规定的装货港到卸货之间的运输过程中,将货物从船卸下并装上另一船的行为。

c. i. 不可转让海运单可以注明货物将要或可能被转运,只要全程运输由同一海运单涵盖。

ii. 即使信用证禁止转运,注明转运将要或可能发生的不可转让的海运单仍可接受,只要其表明货物装于集装箱,拖船或子船中运输。

d. 不可转让的海运单中声明承运人保留转运权利条款将被不予理会。

第二十二条 租船合同提单

a. 表明其受租船合同约束的提单(租船合同提单),无论名称如何,必须看似:

i. 由以下员签署:

＊船长或其具名代理人,或

＊船东或其具有名代理人,或

＊租船人或其具有名代理人。

船长、船东、租船人或代理人的任何签字必须标明其船长、船东、租船人或代理人的身份。

代理人签字必须表明其系代表船长,船东不是租船人签字。

代理人代表船东或租船人签字时必须注明船东或租船人的名称。

ii. 通过以下方式表明货物已在信用证规定的装货港装上具名船只:

* 预先印就的文字,或者

* 已装船批注注明货物的装运日期

租船合同提单的出具日期将被视为发运日期,除非租船合同提单载有已装船批注注明发运日期,此时已装船批注上注明的日期将被视为发运日期。

iii. 表明货物从信用证规定的装货港台发运至卸货港。卸货港也可显示为信用证规定的港口范围或地理区域。

iv. 为唯一的正本租船合同提单,或如以多份正本出具,为租船合同提单注明的全套正本。

b. 银行将不审核租船合同,即使信用证要求提交租船合同。

第二十三条 空运单据

a. 空运单据,无论名称如何,必须看似:

i. 表明承运人名称,并由以下人员签署;

* 承运人,或

* 承运人的具名代理人。

承运人或其代理人的任何签字必须标明其承运人或代理人的身份。

代理人或其代理人的任何签字必须标明其承运人或代理人的身份。

代理人签字必须表明其系代表承运人签字。

ii. 表明货物已被收妥待运。

iii. 表明出具日期。该日期将被视为发运日期,除非空运单据载有专门批注注明实际发运日期,此时批注中的日期将被视为发运日期。

空运单据中其他与航班号和航班日期相关的信息将不被用来确定发运日期。

iv. 表明信用证规定的起飞机场和目的地机场。

v. 为开给发货人或托运人正本,即使信用证规定提交全套正本。

vi. 载有承运条款和条件,或提示条款和条件参别处。银行将不审核承运条款和条件的内容。

b. 就本条而言,转运是指在信用证规定的起飞机场到目的地机场的运输过程中,将货物从一飞机卸下再装上另一收音机的行为。

c. i. 空运单据可以注明货物将要或可能转运,只要全程运输由同一空运单据涵盖。

ii. 即使信用证禁止转运,注明将要或可能发生转运的空运单据仍可接受。

第二十四条 公路、铁路或内陆水运单据

a. 公路、铁路或内陆水运单据、无论名称如何、必须看似:

i. 表明承运人名称;并且

* 由承运人或其具名代理人签署,或者

* 由承运人或其具名代理人以签字、印戳或批注表明货物收讫。

承运人或其具名代理人的收货签字、印戳或批注必须标明其承运人或代理人的身份。代理人的收货签字,印戳或批注必须标明代理人系代理承运人签字或行事。

如果铁路运输单据没有指明承运人,可以接受铁路运输公司的任何签字或印戳作为承运人签署单据的证据。

ii. 表明货物的信用规定地点的发运日期,或者收讫待运或待发送的日期。运输单据的出具日期将被视为发运日期,除非运输单据上盖有带日期的收货印戳,或注明了收货日期或发运日期。

iii. 表明信用证规定的发运地及目的地。

b. i. 公路运输单据必须看似为开给发货人或托运人的正本,或没有任何标记表明单据开给何人。

ii. 注明"第二联"的铁路运输单据将被作为正本接受。

iii. 无论是否注明正本字样,铁路或内陆水运单据都被作为正本接受。

c. 如运输单据上未注明出具的正本数量,提交的份数即视为全套正本。

d. 就本条而言,转运是指在信用证规定的发运、发送或运送的地点到目的地之间的运输过程中,在同一运输方式中从一运输工具卸下再装上另一运输工具的行为。

e. i. 只要全程运输由同一运输单据涵盖,公路、铁路或内陆水运单据可以注明货物将要或可能被转运。

ii. 即使信用证禁止转运,注明将要或可能发生转运的公路、铁路或内陆水运单据仍可接受。

第二十五条 快递收据、邮政收据或投邮证明

a. 证明货物收讫待运的快递收据,无论名称如何,必须看似:

i. 表明快递机构的名称,并在信用证规定的货物发运地点由该具名快递机构盖章或签字,并且

ii. 表明取件或收件的日期或类似词语,该日期将被视为发运日期。

b. 如果要求显示快递费用付讫或预付,快递机构出具的表明快递费由收货人以外的一方支付的运输单据可以满足该项要求。

c. 证明货物收讫待运的邮政收据或投邮证明,无论名称如何,必须看似在信用证规定的货物发运地点盖章或签署并注明日期。该日期将被视为发运日期。

第二十六条 "货装舱面""托运人装载和计数""内容据托运人报称"及运费之外的费用

b. 载有诸如"托运人装载和计数"或"内容据托运人报称"条款的运输单据可以接受。

c. 运输单据上可以以印戳或其他方法提及运费之外的费用。

第二十七条 清洁运输单据

银行只接受清洁运输单据,清洁运输单据指未载有明确宣称货物或包装有缺陷的条款或批注的运输单据。"清洁"一词并不需要在运输单据上出现,即使信用证要求运输单据为"清洁已装船"的。

第二十八条 保险单据及保险范围

a. 保险单据、例如,保险单或预约保险项下的保险证明书或者声明书,必须看似由保

险公司或承保人或其代理人或代表出具并签署。

  b. 如果保险单据表明其以多份正本出具,所有正本均须提交。

  c. 暂保单将不被接受。

  d. 可以接受保险单代预约保险项下的保险证明书或声明书。

  e. 保险单据日期不得晚于发运日期,除非保险单据表明保险责任不迟于发运日生效。

  f. i. 保险单据必须表明投保金额并以与信用证相同的货币表示。

  ii. 信用证对于投保金额为货物价值、发票金额或类似金额的某一比例的要求,将被视为对最低保额的要求。

  如果信用证对投保金额未做规定,投保金额或类似金额的某一比例的要求,将被视为对最低保额要求。

  如果信用证对投保金额未做规定,投保金额须至少为货物的 CIF 或 CIP 价格的 110%。

  如果从单据中不能确定 CIF 或者 CIP 价格,投保金额必须基于要求承付或议付的金额,或者基于发票上显示的货物总值来计算,两者之中取金额较高者。

  iii. 保险单据须表明承保的风险区间至少涵盖从信用证规定的货物接管地或发运地开始到卸货地或最终目的地为止。

  g. 信用证应规定所需投保的险别及附加险(如有的话)。如果信用证使用诸如"通常风险"或"惯常风险"等含义不确切的用语,则无论是否有漏保之风险,保险单据将被照样接受。

  h. 当信用证规定投保"一切险"时,如保险单据载有任何"一切险"批注或条款,无论是否有"一切险"标题,均将被接受,即使其声明任何风险除外。

  i. 保险单据可以援引任何除外条款。

  j. 保险单据可以注明受免赔率或免赔额(减除除额)约束。

  第二十九条 截止日或最迟交单日的顺延

  a. 如果信用证的截止日或最迟交单日适逢接受交单的银行非因第三十六条所述原因而歇业,则截止日或最迟交单日,视何者适用,将顺延至其重新开业的第一个银行工作日。

  b. 如果在顺延后的第一个银行工作日交单,指定银行必须在其致开证行或保兑行的面函中声明交单是在根据第二十九条 a 款顺延的期限内提交的。

  c. 最迟发运日不因第二十九条 a 款规定的原因而顺延。

  第三十条 信用证金额、数量与单价的伸缩度

  a. "约"或"大约"用于信用证金额或信用证规定的数量或单价时,应解释为允许有关金额或数量或单价有不超过 10% 的增减幅度。

  b. 在信用证未以包装单位件数或货物自身件数的方式规定货物数量时,货物数量允许有 5% 的增减幅度,只要总支取金额不超过信用证金额。

  c. 如果信用证规定了货物数量,而该数量已全部发运,及如果信用证规定了单价,而该单价又未降低,或当第三十条 b 款不适用时,则即使不允许部分装运,也允许支取的金额有5％的减幅。若信用证规定有特定的增减幅度或使用第三十条a款提到的用语限定数量,则该减幅不适用。

第三十一条　部分支款或部分发运

a. 允许部分支款或部分发运。

b. 表明使用同一运输工具并经由同次航程运输的数套运输单据在同一次提交时,只要显示相同目的地,将不视为部分发运,即使运输单据上表明的发运日期不同或装货港、接管地或发运地点不同。如果交单由数套运输单据构成,其中最晚的一个发运日将被视为发运日。

含有一套或数套运输单据的交单,如果表明在同一种运输方式下经由数件运输工具运输,即使运输工具在同一天出发运往同一目的地,仍将被视为部分发运。

c. 含有一份以上快递收据,邮政收据或投邮证明的交单,如果单据看似由同一快递或邮政机构在同一地点和日期加盖印戳或签字并且表明同一目的地,将不视为部分发运。

第三十二条　分期支款或分期发运

如信用证规定在指定的时间段内分期支款或分期发运,任何一期未按信用证规定期限支取或发运时,信用证对该期及以后各期均告失效。

第三十三条　交单时间

银行在其营业时间外无接受交单的义务。

第三十四条　关于单据有效性的免责

银行对任何单据的形式、充分性、准确性、内容真实性,虚假性或法律效力,或对单据中规定或添加的一般或特殊条件,概不负责;银行对任何单据所代表的货物,服务或其他履约行为的描述、数量、重量、品质、状况、包装、交付、价值或其存在与否,或对发货人、承运人、货运代理人、收货人、货物的保险人或其他任何人的诚信与否、作为或不作为,清偿能力、履约或资信状况,也概不负责。

第三十五条　关于信息传递和翻译的免责

当报文、信件或单据按照信用证的要求传输或发送时,或当信用证未证未作指示,银行自行选择传送服务时,银行对报文传输或信件或单据的递送过程中发生的延误、中途遗失、残缺或其他错误产生的后果,概不负责。

如果指定银行确定交单相符并将单据发往开证行或保兑行,无论指定银行是否已经承付或议付,开证行或保兑行必须承付或议付,或偿付指定银行,即使单据在指定银行送往开证行或保兑行的途中,或保兑行送往开证行的途中丢失。

银行对技术语的翻译或解释上的错误,不负责任,并可不加翻译地传送信用证条款。

第三十六条　不可抗力

银行对由于天灾、暴动、骚乱、叛乱、战争、恐怖主义行为或任何罢工、停工或其无法控制的任何其他原因导致的营业中断的后果,概不负责。

银行恢复营业时,对于在营业中断期间已逾期的信用证,不再进行承付或议付。

第三十七条　关于被指示方行为的免责

a. 为了执行申请人的指示,银行利用其他银行的服务,其费用和风险由申请人承担。

b. 即使银行自行选择了其他银行,如果发出的指示未被执行,开证行或通知行对此亦不负责。

c. 指示另一银行提供服务的银行有责任负担被指示方因执行指示而发生的任何佣金、手续费、成本或开支("费用")。

如果信用证规定费用由受益人负担,而该费用未能收取或从信用证款项中扣除,开证行依然承担支付此费用的责任。

信用证或其修改不应规定向受益人的通知以通知行或第二通知行收到其费用为条件。

d. 外国法律和惯例加之于银行的一切义务和责任,申请人应受其约束,并就此对银行负补偿之责。

第三十八条　可转让信用证

a. 银行无办理信用证转让的义务,除非其明确同意。

b. 就本条而言:

可转让信用证系指特别注明"可转让(transferable)"字样的信用证。可转让信用证可应受益人(第一受益人)的要求转为全部或部分由另一受益人(第二受益人)兑用。

转让行系指办理信用证转让的指定银行,或当信用证规定可在任何银行兑用时,指开证行特别如此授权并实际办理转让的银行。开证行也可担任转让行。

已转让信用证指已由转让行转为可由第二受益人兑用的信用证。

c. 除非转让时另有约定,有关转让的所有费用(诸如佣金、手续费,成本或开支)须由第一受益人支付。

d. 只要信用证允许部分支款或部分发运,信用证可以分部分转让给数名第二受益人。

已转让信用证不得应第二受益人的要求转让给任何其后受益人。第一受益人不视为其后受益人。

e. 任何转让要求须说明是否允许及在何条件下允许将修改通知第二受益人。已转让信用证须明确说明该项条件。

f. 如果信用证转让给数名第二受益人,其中一名或多名第二受益人对信用证修改并不影响其他第二受益人接受修改。对接受者而言该已转让信用证即被相应修改,而对拒绝改的第二受益人而言,该信用证未被修改。

g. 已转让信用证须准确转载原证条款,包括保兑(如果有的话),但下列项目除外:

——信用证金额
——规定的任何单价
——截止日
——交单期限,或
——最迟发运日或发运期间。

以上任何一项或全部均可减少或缩短。

必须投保的保险比例可以增加,以达到原人信用证或本惯例规定的保险金额。

可用第一受益人的名称替换原证中的开证申请人名称。

如果原证特别要求开证申请人名称应在除发票以外的任何单据出现时,已转让信用证必须反映该项要求。

第一受益人有权以自己的发票和汇票（如有的话）替换第二受益人的发票的汇票，其金额不得超过原信用证的金额。经过替换后，第一受益人可在原信用证项下支取自己发票与第二受益人发票间的差价（如有的话）。

如果第一受益人应提交其自己的发票和汇票（如有的话），但未能在第一次要求的照办，或第一受益人提交的发票导致了第二受益人的交单中本不存在的不符点，而其未能在第一次要求时修正，转让行有权将从第二受益人处收到的单据照交开证行，并不再对第一受益人承担责任。

在要求转让时，第一受益人可以要求在信用证转让后的兑用地点，在原信用证的截止日之前（包括截止日），对第二受益人承付或议付。该规定并不得损害第一受益人在第三十八条 h 款下的权利。

k. 第二受益人或代表第二受益人的交单必须交给转让行。

第三十九条 款项让渡

信用证未注明可转让，并不影响受益人根据所适用的法律规定，将该信用证项下其可能有权或可能将成为有权获得的款项让渡给他人的权利。本条只涉及款项的让渡，而不涉及在信用证项下进行履行行为的权利让渡。

参 考 文 献

1. 姚新超. 国际结算[M]. 北京:对外经济贸易大学出版社,2008.
2. 徐立平. 国际结算[M]. 杭州:浙江大学出版社,2011.
3. 邵新力. 国际结算[M]. 北京:机械工业出版社,2012.
4. 蔡慧娟. 国际结算[M]. 北京:清华大学出版社,2010.
5. 梁志坚. 国际结算[M]. 北京:科学出版社,2008.
6. 梁琦. 国际结算[M]. 北京:高等教育出版社,2005.
7. 贺瑛. 国际结算[M]. 上海:复旦大学出版社,2006.
8. 刘铁敏. 国际结算[M]. 北京:清华大学出版社,2010.
9. 李昭华. 国际结算[M]. 北京:对外经济贸易大学出版社,2011.
10. 赵明霄. 国际结算[M]. 北京:中国金融出版社,2010.
11. 吴国新. 国际结算[M]. 北京:清华大学出版社,2008.
12. 叶陈刚,叶陈云. 国际结算[M]. 上海:复旦大学出版社,2007.
13. 岳华,杨来科. 国际结算双语教程[M]. 上海:立信会计出版社,2007.
14. 吴萍,翁玮. 国际结算 双语[M]. 北京:高等教育出版社,2012.
15. 蒋琴儿. 国际结算 理论?实务?案例 双语教材[M]. 北京:清华大学出版社,2012.
16. 赵明霄. 国际结算习题与案例[M]. 北京:中国金融出版社,2010.
17. 许南,张雅. 国际结算(英文版)[M]. 北京:中国人民大学出版社,2013.
18. 赵薇. 国际结算与融资 双语版 汉、英[M]. 南京:东南大学出版社,2015.
19. 秦定,高蓉蓉. 国际结算(英文版)[M]. 北京:清华大学出版社,2010.
20. 傅泳. 进出口贸易结算(双语版)[M]. 成都:西南财经大学出版社,2013.
21. 朱文忠. 新编国际结算与案例(英文版)[M]. 北京:对外经济贸易大学出版社,2010.
22. 王慧敏. 国际贸易单证操作[M]. 北京:北京大学出版社,2014.
23. 吴国新,李元旭. 国际贸易单证实务 第2版[M]. 北京:清华大学出版社,2008.
24. 李一平,梁柏谦,张然翔. 跟单信用证项下出口审单实务[M]. 北京:中国商务出版社,2004.
25. [瑞士]阿克曼,等. 国际贸易安全结算指南 跟单信用证、跟单托收、银行担保[M]. 中国人民建设银行总行国际业务部,译. 北京:新华出版社,1990.
26. 国际商会中国国家委员会(ICC CHINA)组织翻译. 关于审核跟单信用证项下单据的国际标准银行实务 ISBP 中英文对照本[M]. 北京:中国民主法制出版社,2003.
27. [美]爱德华·G. 辛克尔曼(Edward G. Hinkelman). 国际支付 信用证、跟单托收和国际交易中的电子化支付[M]. 顾继红,周林,译. 北京:经济科学出版社,2002.
28. [美]爱德华·辛克尔曼. 国际结算(第四版)[M]. 北京:中国人民大学出版社,2012.
29. 陈立金. 银行保函产品培训[M]. 北京:中国经济出版社,2010.
30. 邹小燕,张璇. 银行保函[M]. 北京:机械工业出版社,2013.
31. 于强. URDG758与银行保函实务操作指南 3册[M]. 北京:中国海关出版社,2011.
32. 于立新. 现代国际保理通论[M]. 北京:中国物价出版社,2002.
33. 李华根. 国际结算与贸易融资实务[M]. 北京:中国海关出版社,2012.
34. Central Organization for a Durabl Hague. Problems of the International Settlement[M]. Hard Press Publishing,Jan. 2013.

35. Peter Briggs. Principles of International Trade and Payments [M]. Wiley-Blackwell, Jul. 1994.
36. U. S. Government Accountability Office. Auditing and Financial Management: Perspectives on Trade and International Payments[M]. Biblio Gov, May 2013.
37. U. S. Government Accountability Office. International Affairs: Perspectives on Trade and International Payments[M]. Biblio Gov, Jun. 2013.

教师服务

感谢您选用清华大学出版社的教材！为了更好地服务教学，我们为授课教师提供本书的教学辅助资源，以及本学科重点教材信息。请您扫码获取。

▶ 教辅获取

本书教辅资源，授课教师扫码获取

▶ 样书赠送

国际经济与贸易类重点教材，教师扫码获取样书

 清华大学出版社

E-mail: tupfuwu@163.com
电话: 010-83470332 / 83470142
地址: 北京市海淀区双清路学研大厦 B 座 509

网址: https://www.tup.com.cn/
传真: 8610-83470107
邮编: 100084